AF560119

THE CONCEPT OF HERO IN INDIAN CULTURE

SOUTH ASIA INSTITUTE
HEIDELBERG UNIVERSITY
SOUTH ASIAN STUDIES NO. XLIV

The Concept of Hero in Indian Culture

Edited by

Heidrun Brückner
Hugh van Skyhawk
Claus Peter Zoller

MANOHAR
2007

First published 2007

ISBN 81-7304-710-3

Published by
Ajay Kumar Jain for
Manohar Publishers & Distributors
4753/23 Ansari Road, Daryaganj,
New Delhi 110 002

Printed at
Lordson Publishers Pvt. Ltd.
Delhi 110 007

Contents

Editor's Note

In the summer term of the year 1990, Günther-Dietz Sontheimer, head of the department of Indian Philosophy and History of Religion within the larger department of Indology at the South Asia Institute of the University of Heidelberg, conducted an Interregional Seminar on The Concept of Hero(-ine) in Indian Culture. Participants came from India, Canada, various European countries including Poland and the former Soviet Union as well as from within the South Asia Institute. Since the contributions showed considerable potential for interest to a wider audience, Sontheimer decided to publish them as a book under the same title as the seminar. At the time of his sudden death in spring 1992 he had received manuscripts of about two thirds of the prospective contributions. The secretary of the department of Modern Indian Languages, Mrs. Christine Walter-Mendy, who died at a young age only a few months after Sontheimer, had helped with some of the typing.

When we went through Sontheimer's unfinished work after his death, Hugh van Skyhawk volunteered to continue with the editing of the "hero-volume" as we called it. Assisted by Sibylle Zerr he sent circulars to all contributors in 1993 and made sure they were still willing to have their papers published. Two participants were not able to submit their papers and we invited two additional contributions, from Ian Duncan and T.N. Shankaranarayana respectively. When Hugh van Skyhawk obtained an assignment to do research in Pakistan in the same year the work was handed on to Claus Peter Zoller, assisted by Susanne Späinghaus-Monschau. In 1996, Zoller, too, went to Pakistan for fieldwork and could not spare much time for the volume any more. In the same year, the computer programs employed so far in the centre were discontinued and all files had to be converted onto PC-programs. In the process, a number of minor and major catastrophes happened: diacritics in the many different Indian languages quoted in the contributions and some of the formatting were lost and had to be restituted on the basis of the original manuscripts. The file was affected by a computer virus and partly destroyed. Funds for editorial assistance were exhausted before the additional work could be completed. Finally, my Ph.D. candidate Matthias Ahlborn, a former student of Sontheimer, and I continued the work at Tübingen from August 1998 onwards. I submitted a fresh application to the publication committee of the South Asia Institute to include the book in the South Asian Studies series. The manuscript was evaluated and recommended for publication in 1999. The contributors consented one more time to have their papers published after so many years, feeling they had to fulfil their obligation entered vis-à-vis Sontheimer. Some of them revised their original papers or updated their bibliography. The editorial work at Tübingen including the preparation of the index, checking of references, proof-reading, etc., was continued with the assistance of Thorsten Fessel, Anton Kollmann and Anna Aurelia Esposito. Anne Feldhaus, Tempe, did some of the English language editing, W.B. Bollée, Bamberg helped with some proof-reading and indexing. When I left Tübingen in 2001 and joined the University of Würzburg, this, again, caused some delay. The manuscript was sent to the press in September 2002, editorial processes were completed in 2005. The main credit for technical assistance goes to Matthias Ahlborn without whose computer expertise the volume would not have seen the light of day. I thank all the above-named people involved in the preparation of the manuscript. I apologize to the contributors for the long delay and thank them for their endurance.

Würzburg,
September 2005

HEIDRUN BRÜCKNER

Introduction

Heidrun Brückner

The fourteen papers in the present volume deal with the hero and the concept of hero as found in different kinds of sources (such as written, oral, ethnographic), in different historical epochs and in different regions of India. In terms of regional distribution, Maharashtra, with contributions from Duncan, Jansen, Shelke, and Wagle, receives the maximal attention. There is one paper each on material from Karnataka (Shankaranarayana), Tamil Nadu (Eichinger Ferro-Luzzi), Garhwal Himalaya (Zoller), Karakoram (van Skyhawk) and the Hindi- (Gatzlaff) and Urdu-speaking (Oesterheld) areas of northern India and Pakistan. The disciplines and methodologies of the contributors comprise philologically oriented ancient Indian studies, i.e. the classical field of Indology, ancient and modern history, ancient, modern and oral literature, linguistics, anthropology, religion and folklore.

The contributors were brought together by Günther-Dietz Sontheimer in 1990 at Heidelberg at an Interregional Seminar entitled "The Concept of Hero(-ine) in Indian Culture". This concept, especially its expression in folk religion, had been a fascination for Günther Sontheimer at least since the early seventies when he started documenting Hero- and Satī-stones in Rajasthan, Maharashtra, the Deccan and other regions of India. One major outcome of this work was a book on "Memorial Stones" (which he co-edited with S. Settar) published in 1982. Besides his two contributions in that volume, he has also treated the topic in an article on Memorial Monuments in Western India (Sontheimer 1976).[1] He identified the worship of Heroes and Satis as an important element of folk religion and tried to understand the memorial stones in their historical, iconographic, epigraphic as well as socio-religious dimensions.

In his introductory lecture at the 1990 Heidelberg seminar,

Sontheimer discussed the terms used in Sanskrit and other Indian languages to denote a "hero", such as *vīra, marya, śūra/śūla*, and *malla* which can be considered to correspond to the ancient Greek term *heros*. Starting from Vedic references associated with Indra, the Vrātyas, etc., he tried to pin down the characteristics of the hero in those texts. They frequently describe the hero as a military leader, who excells in battle and often dies in combat. He is involved in cattle raids or in defending the herds. Hunting is another field for heroism where ancient and medieval textual and popular notions meet. There is often a close association between the village goddess as huntress and the hunters of a village – the villagers go to the forest to hunt boar, which is then first offered to the goddess. Heroic feats may also consist of self-mutilation, or even self-sacrifice for a deity or for the king. Heroes who are killed in battle as well as victims of other kinds of violence are often deified. This also applies to Satis. In Maharashtra and elsewhere, ancestors too may be referred to as *vīra*. Deified heroes have the power to heal and to bestow fertility. Folk deities like Khaṇḍobā are said to be surrounded by groups of heroes (vīra) who mix with demi-gods, demons and Yakṣas. Heroes are worshipped in order to acquire similar extra-ordinary powers. They are supplicated to bring rain. Their memorial stones are used to whet one's arrows and bards are asked to sing songs in their praise. The medieval Kannada poet Ranna refers to occasions necessitating the hero's interference, such as during raids of the herds, or of the village, to avert some danger to the family, to comply to an order of the king or to redress the complaints of women.

Sontheimer went on to contrast such a concept of hero to notions of the Dharmaśāstras that try to define the hero as protector of the Varṇāśramadharma and extend the use of the term to other areas. Thus, besides yuddhavīras (martial heroes) they also mention dānavīras (heroes of liberality). A similar list is found in the *Mahābhārata*. The Yogin, too, is considered a hero. Finally, in Bhakti religion, heroism is internalised. An ethicized concept of hero was probably first developed in Jaina and Buddhist contexts. In other realms, the power of the hero transgresses notions of morality, of good and evil. In classical drama, the terms *nāyaka* (and *nāyikā*) which literally mean "leader", came to designate the protagonist of a play. Whereas in classical literature the *nāyaka* often is a king and a *vīra* at the same time, the usage of *nāyaka as* merely referring to the main "protagonist" of a story is common in the literatures of almost all modern Indian languages.

The fourteen papers assembled in the present volume have been arranged in alphabetical order. W.B. Bollée's "Note on the Birth of the Hero" makes for a good beginning and provides reference material for a couple of other contributions. The heroes whose conception, gestation, birth and bodily marks Bollée studies include Vedic gods as well as the Jīna and the Buddha. Bollée's discussion of terms like *vīra* and *mahāvīra* elaborates some of Sontheimer's introductory remarks.

M. Christopher Byrski ("The Hero in Sanskrit Drama") takes us from the *vīra* to the *nāyaka* of Sanskrit drama. We learn what the dramatists themselves have to say about their heroes and how the theoreticians describe them. Byrski goes on to interpret theatre as a "visual sacrifice" with Vedic connotations – hero and heroine taking the place of Indra and Sarasvatī. His discussion confirms the close association of the notions of hero, king and protagonist.

Ian Duncan, dealing with "Hanumān Mahāvīrasvāmī" presents and analyses ethnographic data from central India, supplemented by data from other regions like Maharashtra, in order to throw light upon particular features of Hanumān's heroic nature. Hanumān emerges as a very popular folk deity in his own right whose picture is much more complex and comprehensive than his role in the Tulsi-*Rāmāyaṇa* would suggest.

Gabriella Eichinger Ferro-Luzzi's contribution on "Two Clever Heroes of Tamil Folk Narrative" is the only one in the book that refers to Tamil concepts of heroism. Having briefly sketched classical Tamil notions of the hero in the introductory part of her paper, she goes on to discuss the heroes of fairy tales and folk narratives. The two heroes she focuses on, the judge Mariyātai Rāman ("the honorable Rāma") and his counterpart, an unnamed master thief, belong to the realm of popular cultures, the printed sources being transitional between oral traditions and written literature. Besides ingenuity and "cleverness", it is certainly his notion of "honour" that makes the judge a hero. The master thief's exploits are set in 17th-century Madurai. Like many of his classical predecessors, this hero transgresses the moral notions of good and evil. But he ends up putting his skills in the service of justice and law represented by the king.

With Margot Gatzlaff's paper "Kālī – A Hero beween Tradition and Progress" we enter the field of modern society and social struggle as reflected in modern Hindi literature of the 20th century. The Chamar protagonist Kālī appears as a hero in the sense of a modern rebel who stands up against tradition and the village establishment, but ultimately fails to win for himself a better position in life. When Gatzlaff considers Kālī a "victim" of tradition, we are reminded of the heroes in folk literature and folk epics who have to pay with their lives for their attempts to enforce justice. Ultimately, it is their violent deaths that makes them heroes to be commemorated in oral texts and rituals for all time to come.

Roland Jansen deals with the 17th-century Marāṭhā leader Śivājī as "Hero and King". He focuses on a central episode in the course of the hero's rise to power as it is depicted and interpreted in the Bakhars – traditional accounts of Marāṭhā history in Marāṭhī language. Jansen also considers the role of Śivājī's Kulasvāminī, the goddess Bhavānī of Tuḷjāpur, in shaping his political career.

Christina Oesterheld, in her paper "The Frustrated Hero: The Image of the Hero in Contemporary Urdu Stories" uses the term "hero" in the general sense of protagonist common in modern literature, but focuses especially on the concept of the "anti-hero", often depicted as a victimised hero. In her paper, Oesterheld also gives an overview of the history of modern Urdu literature and a typology of its heroes and heroines, noting that women are reduced to the role of victims more frequently than men are.

Peter D. Sakharov's paper "From Sacrificer to Hero" takes the Puranic story of king Hariścandra as a starting point, a true "hero of liberality" who sacrifices all his belongings and even his wife, son and his own person in order to satisfy the demands of the angered sage Viśvāmitra. Sakharov tries to trace the origin of the myth in earlier literature, such as the story of Śunaḥśepa in the Aitareya Brāhmaṇa, assuming a common source for the Hariścandra- and the Śunaḥśepa stories. Some structural elements are linked to the Triśaṅku myth and other Vedic, epic and Puranic texts. Sakharov suggests a pattern of interpretation and historical development leading from a ritual / sacrificial structure to a narrative one, from sacrificer (king) to hero (protagonist), thus explaining "one possible way of herogenesis in ancient Indian literature".

T.N. Shankaranarayana treats "The Hero in the Junjappa Epic". Junjappa is a popular pastoral deity and a cultural hero of the Kannaḍa speaking Kāḍugolla community in south-central Karnataka which is in transition from pastoralism to agriculture. The oral epic of Junjappa, called "Junjappa's Song" (pada, hāḍu) or "Junjappa's Story" (kathe) in Kannaḍa, is concerned with intratribal conflicts between two clans of Kaḍugollas and between the latter and a community of hunters (Myāsabeḍa). It covers a time-span of three generations. Supernatural elements point to the heroic qualities of the child Junjappa, who is born out of his mother's backbone and performs miracles before and after his birth, as well as after his premature death. His maternal uncles, jealous of Junjappa's success in breeding cattle, are responsible for the death of the sixteen-year-old boy. Usually, only some episodes of the story are performed at certain occasions such as the annual fair (*jātre*) held in honour of the deified hero. The fair also comprises a ritual performance. Nowadays, Junjappa is generally identified with Vīrabhadra.

Christopher Shelke's contribution on "Leadership in Maharashtra during the British Raj" addresses the political dimension of heroism. Shelke attempts to outline and discuss the rise of two very different Maharashtrian leaders, Mahadev Govind Ranade and Gangadhar Tilak, and their impact on the social and political spheres of Maharashtra and of India as a whole.

Hugh van Skyhawk opens his paper "On Heroes in the Karakoram" with an account of oral traditions in the Karakoram and goes on to discuss the oral epic of Kisar in more detail. He points out various sources for individual sections and episodes ranging from the *Šāh-nāma* to the Ladakh and Balti-Stak versions of the Gesar-Kesar epic and possibly even to the *Mahābhārata*. In a concluding section on "cultural geography" van Skyhawk suggests a spread of the epic's cultural area from central Asia through the Himalayas and the Karakoram to the Kulu Valley and Lahūl. He also refers to the impact of Islam, Hinduism, Buddhism, autochthonous spirit cults, and Iranian notions of the ideal king on the character of Kesar, "the folk hero *par excellence* of the Karakoram."

Romila Thapar's discussion "Of Kings as Heroes" focuses on the medieval carita literature, biographies mainly of kings. From Bāṇa's 7th-century *Harṣacarita*, the precursor of the genre, she moves on to Bilhaṇa's *Vikramāṅkadevacarita*, a biography of the

Cālukya king Vikramāditya VI written in the late 11th century, relating it to inscriptural sources and later literary works in the context of the growing significance of literacy. Thapar views the *carita* as a new genre in terms of historical change in the post-Gupta period. The changing concept of the hero required a new literary form to portray him. The *caritas* projected the king as the new hero. In contradistinction to the elaborate time cycles of the Purāṇas, their time frame is brief and linear, cyclical time is not emphasized. Unlike the attitude of the Puranic bards, the court poets also included biographical information about themselves as authors, probably a means to legitimise the subject as well. Thapar stresses the interlocking of dynasty, court and chronicler. The role of the king is also contrasted to that of the epic hero and to the legends of the Purāṇas.

N.K. Wagle's contribution "Heroes in the Caritra-Bakhar, Povāḍā and Ākhyāna of Seventeenth and Eighteenth Century Mahārāṣṭra" deals with the concept of heroes in Marāṭhī historical biographies. Among the historical personalities treated are Śivājī, the founder of the Marāṭhā kingdom, warrior heroes such as Tānajī Mālusare as well as aristocrats and generals who fought and were killed in battle. Whereas the Caritra-Bakhar is based on Puranic traditions, the Povāḍās are popular and more localised ballad-like compositions by bards. Thus Śivājī commissioned a bard from Puṇe to compose a Povāḍā of Tānājī Mālusare, Śivājī's brave warrior who had died in his service. Other Povāḍās also include heroic feats by people of low castes and by women. Ākhyāna is an essentially biographical genre dealing with a single issue, such as the exploits of Mālojī, the martyred warrior.

Claus Peter Zoller ("Himalayan Heroes") studies the heroic traditions of the Garhwal region in the Indian Himalayas. His focus is on material from the peripheral area of Bangan where the heroic tradition is still very much alive in the minds of the people. Zoller analyses Bangani notions regarding body, soul and the psycho-physical processes associated with fighting in order to reach a deeper understanding of heroism in Bangan. At the same time, he investigates notions regarding the village sanctuaries associated with heroic fighting as well as with lineages, clans, chieftainships and similar concepts. In this context, the Bangan heroes emerge as media and catalysts. Through singing and recitation of ballads recounting their past feats a link between bygone action and contemporary practice is created.

It is hoped that these articles will not only provide a comprehensive discussion of the hero in Indian culture, but also stimulate further investigation of this important concept.

NOTES

1 Reprinted in: Günther-Dietz Sontheimer, *Essays on Religion, Literature and Law,* ed. H. Brückner, A. Feldhaus and A. Malik, Delhi 2004, pp. 123-55. The volume contains 14 articles some of which had appeared in publications difficult to access. It also provides an index to the articles and a complete list of Sontheimer's publications and other materials.

A Note on the Birth of the Hero in Ancient India

in memoriam Otto Rank

W.B. Bollée

The present paper is somehow based on a system of coordinates the vertical line of which features the heroes, viz., Indra, Vrātya, Prajāpati, Nārāyaṇa, the Jina, and the Buddha, while the horizontal line is divided into conception, gestation, birth, and certain bodily marks. As is well-known, there are two words for the concept "hero" as early as the *Ṛgveda*, viz., *vīra* and *śūra*, which apparently differ very little in meaning. Though we only find compounds with *śūra*, like *dāna-śūra* when we consider the scholastic list of hero types in the *Mahābhārata* (cr. ed. 13, 74, 22 sqq.), *dāna-vīra* has also been noted by Monier-Williams (*MW*: 474).

Further, since Indians do not seem to distinguish their heroes anything more by formal designation than by class of beings, neither shall we separate divine and human heroes in the following discussion. The heroic ideal of the Vedic Āryans is particularly represented by the god Indra as a fighter against human as well as demon-enemies, alone (*ṚV* 3, 30, 4) or as a leader (*ṚV* 8, 46, 13). He is born for battle (*ṚV* 7, 20, 5) and victory (*ṚV* 4, 20, 6); the complete conqueror (*ṚV* 3, 51, 3), who brings about peace (*ṚV* 10, 30, 7) and escapes the goddesses of death (*ṚV* 8, 24, 24). It is this ideal which, modified in the times of the *Brāhmaṇas*, and in a largely sedentary society, is transferred to the old creator deity Prajāpati, who is then put on a par with Indra (*TB* 1, 2, 2, 5) and the sacrifice (*ŚB* 1, 7, 4, 4). Later, between the 7th and the 5th century B.C., the notion of a single-handed religious fighter comes up among the descendants of the non-Vedic Āryans in Magadha possibly beside the long-haired, perhaps Śivaitic *muni* who overcomes attachment to this world. For this reason, Jains and Buddhists confer on him the title *mahāvīra* or *vīra.* To use Hertha Krick's (1982: 5) definition, a *vīra* originally is a traditionally educated young Āryan who is entitled to the status of a priest and a warrior, has been admitted into the society of the *āhitâgnis*, is allowed to partake of the *soma* drink, is married and has a son. In the following I should like to deal especially with Jaina conceptions, compare them with and supplement them by the approximately synchronous data provided by Pāli literature, and outline their possible historical development. First some remarks about the name *mahāvīra.*

According to Viśvabandhu's *A Vedic Word-Concordance*, *vīra* and *śūra* are mainly epithets of Indra, much less frequently of Agni and Soma. Furthermore, *vīra* is used with regard to groups of deities (sons of Aditi, the Aṅgiras and the Maruts); sometimes it also designates demons. Once Rudra is called a *vīra.* The *karmadhāraya* compound *mahāvīra* is in Vedic literature first used with regard to Indra: (*Vṛtró*) *ā́ hí juhvé mahā-vīrám* (*Índram*),[1] in the late *Śarabhôpaniṣad*[2] regarding Rudra and, in *YV* texts like *VS* 19, 14 and *KāṭhS* 21, 2, 3, as well as in the *Brāhmaṇas*, in connection with the *pravargya.* I shall summarize these references here after van Buitenen's (van Buitenen 1968) study.

According to tradition, the *pravargya* arose out of the deity Rudra's crushed head. This recalls popular beliefs and practices described in various oral traditions up to the present day, that heroes who lose their heads in combat or by ritual self-decapitation maybe deified and worshipped as sources of new life. Günther Sontheimer referred to this phenomenon in his introduction to this seminar, and Heidrun Brückner pointed out similar practices in Tuḷunāḍu.[3] The *pravargya* designates a Vedic ritual which can precede certain *soma* sacrifices. At this ritual, originally in the early morning, later on also in the evening, the Aśvins were offered freshly milked warm cow's milk. In *ṚV* times, for this purpose the milk was heated in a pot (*gharma*) made of non-precious metal (*ayas*, *ṚV* 5, 30, 15) and smeared all around with butter (van Buitenen 1968: 24, 26, 30).

In the post-*saṃhitā* period this simple sacrifice underwent a substantial change by being connected with a perhaps non-Vedic or non-brahmanical rite implying the manufacture, heating, worship, and removal of an earthen vessel called *mahāvīra.* This change also implied that the secret knowledge referring to this should be passed on outside the village in the *araṇya* (van Buitenen 1968: 38, 137 and 140), and that the execution, which is forbidden at a *yajamāna*'s first *soma* sacrifice, must be screened off against *śūdras* and women,[4] particularly, the *yajamāna*'s wife. The said vessel, which is addressed as *deva puraś-cara* "deity who goes in front" (*TA* 4, 3, 3[10]) and for which a *saṃrāḍ-āsandī* "emperor's throne" (*ĀpŚS* 15, 5, 7) is prepared (this reminds us of the *cakravartin*), consists of three clay balls one on top of the other. The one at the top has been hollowed out and provided with an opening; the middle one is solid, and the broader lower one, which is flat at the bottom, serves as the basis (van Buitenen 1968: 10). A thin channel, van Buitenen supposes, runs from the top down to the base of the lower clay ball (id., 34, 59). The *mahāvīra* vessel, with its height of about twenty centimetres, reminds van Buitenen of a man sitting tailor-fashion (id., 11, 23 sqq., 59), also, because in *ŚB* 14, 1, 4, 16 the vessel is expressly defined as a male: (id., 11, 22, 31) *Vṛṣā vai Pravargyo, yoṣā patnī; mithunam evâitat prajananaṃ kriyate* "The Pravarga is a male, and the wife is a female: a productive pair is thus produced" (Eggeling). This symbolism is no longer clear from the vessel's present form (id., 9; plate 3: 1). The meaning of the *parigrīvam* 'ring around the neck' or of the *rāsnā* 'belt' surrounding the figure three or four fingers from the top remains obscure (id., 11, 59). The manufacture of the *mahāvīra*, according to van Buitenen, takes place before the rains begin (id., 31), and is done for the invigoration of the sun, which the vessel represents (id., 27 sq., 31). It is made out of various kinds of earth, animal hair, and goat's milk (id., 57 sq.). Goat's milk is used instead of cold water, against which the *pravargya* must be protected (id., 30 sq. and 58). Then *ghī* is poured over it, set on fire, made red-hot, and then worshipped (id., 26).

In 1975, van Buitenen's *mahāvīra* vessel theory, particularly its anthropomorphism (id., 11 sq.) and the idea of the invigoration of the sun,[5] were rejected by Kashikar (1975: 137 sqq. and 141 sq.), who recurs to Lüders' position. The latter scholar based his interpretation on Baudhāyana as the oldest source. There, mention is made only of three clay balls from which the parts of the *mahāvīra* are shaped and then placed one on top of the other. It was also Lüders who had argued (1951: 359 sqq.) that not the sun, but the milkstream of the sky from which the rain falls has to be invigorated before the monsoon starts, as the milk sacrifice is then discontinued. The three parts of the vessel correspond to the tripartite sky and, consequently, to the trebling of the skystream, which, in the shape of the heated milk, contributes to the heat of the sun. Later,[6] the vessel is put on a par with the life-giving sun and the year, i.e. time – the latter being, since the family books of the *ṚV*, intimately related to Indra[7] and afterwards to Prajāpati, his successor in the *Brāhmaṇa* period.[8]

Critical of van Buitenen's ideas is also Rau[9] who describes the *mahāvīra* as a cooking vessel made of the three strips (*piṇḍa*) of clay, flat-bottomed, 24–60 cm in diameter, hourglass shaped, with a belt, (or?) a collar and a noselike snout about 6 cm long at the top.[10]

Up to now, scholars have paid little attention to the relation of the name "*mahāvīra*" to the object, the vessel. van Buitenen rendered *mahāvīra* by 'Large Man' (1968: 9), Oldenberg by '*der große Held*',[11] Renou by '*grand homme*' (Renou/Filliozat 1949: § 721) and '*souverain*',[12] whereas Caland (1924: 423, 427) and Hillebrandt (1897: 135) did not translate the word.

Now there is a tradition (*TA*, etc.) that at the end of the milk sacrifice the utensils are laid together near the *mahāvīra* vessel in the shape of a man. These are then sprinkled with the flour left over from the sacrificial cake by way of marrow and with a mixture of sour milk and honey representing blood (Hillebrandt, ibid.). On the one hand, all this reminds us of the common group of myths in which a primeval giant or cosmic man like the *ṛg-* and *atharvavedic Puruṣa* is sacrificed so that the world can be created from him. On the other hand, we have Mahādeva, the Vrātya, who emerges from a piece of gold (*suvarṇa*) that Prajāpati, the *ṛgvedic* creator god, sees in himself (*AV* 15, 1, 2), a golden germ (*hiraṇya-garbha*), as it were. Similarly, Queen Māyā beholds the Bodhisatta in her womb. In addition, the Vrātya appears as a manifestation of the god Rudra,[13] who is later euphemistically called Śiva and is given the epithet Mahādeva as well. Moreover, the Vrātya has close relations with the *pravargya* in other respects.[14]

As is well-known, the Mahādeva worshippers belonged to an older Āryan wave of invaders who had penetrated into eastern India before the Vedic brahmins. We first hear of them in *AV* 15, but after that only sporadically in literature up to the *Mbh.* Then they disappear from literary, i.e. brahmanical, tradition. But first they leave clear traces in two religions appearing in Magadha centuries later: Jainism and Buddhism, which borrowed from the *vrātyas*, e.g. the title *arhant* for the person liberated (Hauer 1927: 202) and the designation *gaṇa* for a group of monks (see Bollée 1981: 184). For the fact that the Vedic Āryans evidently could communicate with them shows already that the *vrātyas* were Āryans – a point which was formerly often denied. Otherwise, the latter would have called the former *mlecchas*, the special importance of the language in accepting strangers in India having been shown by Romila Thapar in a lecture in Heidelberg in 1990 (Thapar 1990).

Vagrant life as almsmen at times other than the rainy season may also belong to the above traces (cf. Hopkins 1909: 32), gifts of food, etc. to monks, which are rather a kind of *dakṣiṇā* (i.e. passing on or redeeming the guilt the *yajamāna* had incurred by the killing of the sacrificial victim) than alms. Besides, this notion still lives on in the minds of the Siamese, for, at the Loi Krathong, a festival celebrated especially in Chieng Mai in November, play-boats (*krathong*) made of banana leaves and holding a light, flowers and money are made to flow downstream.[15] At some distance poor people are allowed to land them and take the money, yet with that also the sender's/donor's evil (*pāpman*), represented by the money. Further, just as one is a *vrātya* at a particular period of one's life and sets out on a predatory expedition, Buddhist boys, especially in Siam, go and live for some time in a monastery, following regular monastic practice during the rains.

Until Günther Sontheimer's discovery, the survival of the *vrātyas* with their typically shamanistic costume in Lord Khaṇḍobā's Vāghyās in Mahārāṣṭra was unknown.[16] Did they emigrate from Magadha to the west and south at some time at some point, as did the Jains and the Buddhists? Now, as we have seen, the *vrātyas* on the one hand influenced the two religions mentioned. They represent, therefore, not only a reaction to the post-Vedic sacrificial speculations of the brahmin priests, which were unintelligible for the ordinary warrior, peasant, or herdsman, but also carry on pre-Vedic traditions. On the other hand, popular Buddhism took over features of Indra, the *Ṛgveda*'s central hero, and of Prajāpati. In what follows we shall have a closer look at some characteristics of these deities in order to show how, already in pre-Christian times, they were applied to the *mahāpuruṣas*, as the Great Men of the Indian religions are called. To that end, we shall begin with their conception, because, as is well-known, exceptional beings do not come into existence in the normal fashion, neither in India nor elsewhere (see, e.g. Jones 1970: 37 sqq.). Among the unusual ways of conception we have that of a woman's navel being touched by a god or an ascetic.[17] This type of birth occurs in Buddhist legends, too, but not in Jaina hagiography. However, both Vaddhamāṇa Mahāvīra and Gotama Siddhattha drop from heaven, where, in a previous existence, they had divine status, into their mother's womb.

The Jaina canon does not yet know of a reminiscence of previous existences which, still present in the womb, disappears at birth through claustrophobia or pains, as is described, e.g. in the *Garbhôpaniṣad*.[18] This reminiscence does not recur before the Jina reaches transcendental knowledge (*avadhi-jñāna*).[19] The future Jina, however, knows that he has to descend into a new existence; he is conscious of having accomplished the descent. All that he does not know is the exact moment (*Āyār* 2, 15, 3 = *Kappa* § 3). In post-canonical Buddhist literature we shall meet with similar phenomena.

Given the importance placed on ritual purity already by the *vrātyas*, we may add here that the canonical texts of both new religions mention explicitly the purity of descent of Mahāvīra's and Gotama's princely parents on the maternal as well as the paternal side (in this order!).[20] In the case of the former, both his mothers (on whom more below) see already in the *Siddhânta* (*Kappa Jinac* § 4) fourteen dreams with auspicious images, such as are typical of the Jaina religion, viz., static ones. Besides, the wealth of the royal family increased (*Kappa* § 91), even by the discovery of money-pots that had been hidden in former days and then forgotten (*Kappa* § 89). This too, I think, may be characteristic of Jains as well as Buddhists,[21] the laity of both mainly belonging to the third, or merchant (*vaiśya*) class. Unlike Buddhist literature, however, Jaina texts mention that Queen Tisalā did have *dohadas*,[22] but omit the details usual in narrative texts.

We now come to the Bodhisatta's mother, whom we only know as such, i.e. as Māyā,[23] just as his wife is called Rāhulamātā.[24] At the descent of her child, the *Tipiṭaka* tells us only that she did not think of men, not even of her husband,[25] yet otherwise indulged in the pleasures of the five senses.[26] In the likewise pre-Christian *Mahāvastu*, Brahmā prophesies to Māyā the birth of an elephant among men, and she welcomes this message since she has conceived from her husband. In the *Mahāvastu* and the *Lalitavistara*, but not in the *Nidānakathā* and in Aśvaghoṣa, this elephant comes to have six tusks (see Lüders 1941: 52) – probably an intended one-upmanship of its fellow Airāvata, *devarājā* Indra's mount, who possesses only four tusks. In her dream it touches her right side[27] and seems to enter her womb. On that occasion, Māyā's husband is not mentioned, in other words, he is excluded (ibid., 95). This pregnancy dream motif is apparently a variation of the ascetic's touching a woman's navel (see above). So much for the hero's conception. We now pass on to his gestation.

The first case of this kind is found already in the 2nd millennium B.C., viz., in the old nucleus, the 'family books', of the *ṚV*. Here it is Indra's mother, again not mentioned by name, who, at *ṚV* 4, 18, 4 is said to carry her son for a thousand months[28] and many autumns beyond full term apparently, like Agni's mother (*ṚV* 5, 2, 1 sq.), in order to protect him against his jealous father (whose name is not mentioned).[29] Or, does she carry Indra so long because she does not want him to be born?[30] She knows that he would kill her, as is said in the first stanza in which Indra refuses to go the usual way of the gods, viz., "down the drain", for they did not become heroes.[31] Thus the hymn commences amidst an obscure dialogue with words spoken either by the mother or by the gods: "Dies ist der erprobte alte Weg, auf dem alle Götter geboren wurden. Auf diesem soll auch er ausgereift geboren werden. Nicht soll er seine Mutter derartig zugrunde gehen lassen" (Geldner). Even as early as Oldenberg it was remarked that birth in a way other than the natural way is found in the most different peoples' ideas with regard to their most powerful gods and heroes (Oldenberg 1917: 132 n. 3).

The text does not tell us which side,[32] nor the bearing stance. Not before Gotama the Bodhisatta do we hear of these details. Yet the origin of the lateral birth idea, just as that of the lateral conception in Gotama's case, has not yet been explained, as far as I know. Perhaps the idea originated in the custom of carrying children on the hip, but Indra's lateral birth must be connected with his splitting heaven and earth,[33] this being a horizontal movement in the middle of the cosmic egg,[34] and also of his mother's waist, which is the middle of her body. Cf. also passages like *ŚB* 6, 1, 1, 2 *sa yo 'yaṃ madhye prāṇaḥ, eṣa evêndraḥ* "This same vital air in the midst doubtless is Indra" (Eggeling) and perhaps *MN* III 231, 13 where the Buddha explains his *majjhimā paṭipadā* 'middle way' between *kāma* (Indra) and *tapas* (Prajāpati).

Besides, it may be noticed that in the *ṚV* we meet with the first, though mythical, case of intra-uterine communication between mother and child. Popular belief, especially in India.[35] was acquainted with this long before Western prenatal psychology began taking note of it in this century.[36]

Of Mahāvīra, tradition tells us that for the first 82 days[37] he stayed in the womb of Devânandā, a brahmin lady, and was then transplanted by Indra (*Āyār* 2, 15, 4), or, at his command, by his army commander Hariṇegamesī (*Kappa Jinac* § 30) into the *kṣatriya* Queen Tisalā's womb, for the idea had come to Indra's mind that Jinas are never reborn into lower class, poor, or brahmin families (*Kappa Jinac* § 17). Later, when Devânandā and Usabhadatta, her husband, happen to call on Mahāvīra in a temple in order to pay their respects to him, the latter designates her as his mother.[38] The *Āyāraṅga*, the oldest Jaina *Āgama*, complicates things in that it gives brahmin *nomina gentilicia* to Usabhadatta as well as to Siddhattha, Tisalā's consort, i.e. Koḍāla (Sa. Kauṭalya)[39] resp. Kāsava (Sa. Kāśyapa) (*Āyār* 2, 15, 4). Both Jainism and Buddhism, however, are *kṣatriya* religions and therefore Mahāvīra could not be a brahmin. This was a "misconception", which the later church leaders did away with by means of the miraculous foetus exchange by the goat-headed god Hariṇegamesī.

The Jains, as is well-known, adopted and adapted this *vaiṣṇava* mythologeme in which Nidrā, the goddess of sleep, exchanges the foetus of Baladeva from the womb of his mother Devakī into that of her sister Rohiṇī, in order to save him from the mortal grip of his Herodes-like father Kaṃsa.[40] Here, the point of departure for the Jains was the name Devakī, for, in the *Antagaḍadasāo* 3, 8 § 41 sqq. Devaī, consort of Vasudeva, the king of Bāravaī (Dvāravatī), bore him six sons. Hariṇegamesī, however, seized them in order to transfer them to the rich lady Sulasā's womb. Because she gave birth only to still-born babies, she had an image of the deity made and worshipped it daily, intending to induce him to perform the said operation – everything conditioned by *karman*, of course.

With the inclusivism typical of the Indian way of thinking, Hariṇegamesī here unites the positive qualities of a bringer of children, as was expressed as early as the *ṚV Khilāni* ad 10, 84[41] with negative ones of a demon who seizes children, as he is known to Suśruta.[42] In Vedic texts the deity is called Nejameṣa, but in the *Mbh* Naigameya and Naigameṣa, whereas Suśruta only knows of the latter form. Finally, a Mathurā inscription has Nemesa; this means that the form ending in -*eya* may be due to a scribal error.

The name itself is nowhere explained, nor is the he-goat's (*chāga-vaktra*; Suśruta, *Uttarasthāna* 36, 2 *ajânana*) or ram's face (id. 37, 2 *meṣânana* [cty. *eḍaka-mukha*]) the latter, adopted by *PWB*, probably being a later contamination, as the ram belongs to Varuṇa.[43] The he-goat, however, especially belongs to Agni[44] whose son is called Skanda or (Sanat)kumāra and his grandson Naigameṣa.[45] Skanda, said to be Śiva's son,[46] is appointed general of the gods by Indra.[47] Perhaps in Mathurā this already complex figure, which was adopted by the Jains and under the influence of Viṣṇuism, obtained the name Hariṇegamesī, i.e. 'Naigameṣa merged with Hari'.[48] Thus it can be explained that Indra, who in Jainism and Buddhism became a devoted servant of the respective Jina, orders his commander – both a seizer and a bestower of children – to perform such a fitting operation as was the foetus exchange for him.

As to the etymology of the name and its consequences for the presentation in pictorial form of Hariṇegamesī, whose fiery character, which is not only destructive, as we have seen, but also positive (erotic and promoting fertility), reach back to Agni, the following observations become relevant. The ancient Jaina theologians of course did not place great value on preserving the memory of the fact of their having come under *vaiṣṇava* influence,[49] and thus the two parts of the name, Hari and Negamesin (as the Middle Indo-Āryan form must be) were joined into one compound. Thereupon, commentators (intentionally?) analysed it in the wrong way, viz. in *hariṇa* 'deer' and, apparently, **egamesin*, whatever that in their opinion may have meant. Here I must rely on a footnote in Hermann Jacobi's *Kalpasūtra* translation (Jacobi 1884: 227), as the *Pañjikā*[50] is not at my disposal. Thus, in Jaina art Nejameṣa's he-goat face turned into Hariṇegamesī's deer head. Hariṇegamesī's Hindu counterpart is Parivartaka (*MārkPur* 51, 14).[51]

There remains the question concerning the background of the whole motif in Jaina mythology. It is completely different from the Herodes motif in the *Mahābhārata* story. Connected with this I believe is also the idea that future Jinas and Buddhas must be reborn in *kṣatriya* families only – though this apparently was not always the case, as becomes evident in the Jaina legend, and as the *Nidānakathā* explicitly teaches us.[52] Among the five main considerations (*mahā-vilokana*) before being reborn, the Bodhisatta Gotama also thinks of his future family as follows: Buddhas are reborn neither in a *vaiśya* family nor in one of *śūdras*, but in these two families only, viz., either in a respected *kṣatriya* or in such a brahmin family. Nowadays a *kṣatriya* family is respected. Into that I shall be reborn (cf. Jaini 1985: 84). The apparent irrelevance *of karman* – also as regards the choice of the aim in life: whether to become a Buddha or a *cakravartin* – could point to a certain antiquity of this conception. Can it be a reminiscence of pre-Vedic times in Magadha, of fluid dividing lines, exchange, and rivalry between *brāhmaṇa-* and *kṣatriya-vrātyas*?

A characteristic of Jainism is its static nature, which manifests itself, e.g. in the above dream visions and in the staring statues of saints. It is found already in the womb, where Mahāvīra, who is conscious of his descent from heaven, of his embryonic status and of his transfer,[53] does not move out of pity for his mother until she thinks he is dead. Then he moves a little and, unlike the Bodhisatta, resolves not to go forth in his parents' lifetime (*Kappa* § 94). The latter detail, which is not found in the *Āyāranga*, seems odd in this context. However, a person destined to become a hero can only fulfil his mission after the death of his mother.[54] The case of the Bodhisatta did not require such a vow, as his mother was destined to die much earlier in any case.

Eventually, after nine months and seven and a half days[55] Mahāvīra is born in an apparently normal way under an auspicious constellation and a great lustre of descending and ascending deities (*Āyār* 2, 15, 7),[56] at night in the beginning of summer. Then *devas* (*Āyār* 2, 15, 8) and demons in animal form from Vessamaṇa's/Kubera's realm (*Kappa Jinac* § 98), the auspicious north, that is, produce a downpour of money, jewelry, fruits, etc. The *Āgama* does not elaborate on the bearing posture but – e.g. on a fresco in the Vardhamāna temple in Tirupparuttikunram near Kāñcipur in the Vijayanagara region, where, as a rule, at least nowadays women stand upright when giving birth[57] – the birth of the first and of the last Jina takes place in a crouching position behind a curtain covering the lower part of his mother's body.[58] On the occasion of the birth, not only the usual amnesty of the sympathetic-magical kind (*Kappa* § 100), and a grand popular festival take place (*Kappa* § 102), but there is also – after ten days of childbed impurity, the purification ritual on the 11th day (cf. Jolly 1901: § 43), and the naming festival – a family banquet and an exchange of gifts, possibly of potlatching nature.[59]

Returning now to Buddhism, we hear of the Bodhisatta descending from heaven into the womb of his 40–50 year old mother accompanied by a radiant brightness in the universe.[60] As to the descent, Buddhaghosa says, "Though knowing 'I shall fall from the world of the gods' yet he was not conscious of the process itself. He was aware of having been reborn, but could not remember entering a new body." Other monks, however, did not share this opinion, which also involves the moment of death – as is the case with the Jains.[61] Relevant *Theravāda* and Jain data when collected systematically may be taken into account in our thanatology, along with the discussion on possession going on in Heidelberg in 1991, in which only East Asian material, especially from Amida Buddhism, and case studies from India have been evaluated so far.[62]

The Pāli canon does not elaborate on the manner of descent, but since Buddhaghosa there is in Tusita a pleasure grove (*nanda/navana*) where the being to be reincarnated is seen off by the gods with the words: "Have a good course!"[63] In this context it may be remembered that at the end of their active life humans, too, retire to the forest, and the forth *āśrama*, that of the *saṃnyāsin*, might be compared to the roaming in the *saṃsāra*. The text emphasizes, that all the worlds of the gods have such a grove, but it does not deal with its significance.[64] Gods "die" in that they shrink and become sad only to dematerialize eventually. Does the reincarnand retire into this wood in order to save the other gods an unpleasant sight? Why, then, is it called *Nanda-vana*? Or can it be a state of preparation, perhaps like the Anūpiya mango grove, where the Bodhisatta spent a week enjoying the happiness of his *pabbajjā* before entering Rājagaha? It can, however, just as well be a mechanical adoption from Hinduism of a divine, esp. Indra's, garden (*PWB*).

Māyā sees her son sitting[65] or even standing,[66] then gives birth to him after a full ten months, not after 9 or 10, as is the case with other children. The canonical Pāli texts explicitly stress this.[67] Besides, she does so in an upright position after plucking a flower from a tree.[68]

Queen Māyā's erect posture is emphasized already in the canon as something special, something not done by common women.[69] This is interesting in connection with the fact that in modern gynaecology the delivering posture in general and the standing posture in particular have been much discussed of late. Its outcome was the insight that the specific surroundings and cultural development of primitive tribes also essentially shape childbirth circumstances. The way of living of these tribes and the specific bearing postures they practice are not natural as in the case of animals – quasi instinctive – but they are acquired by their whole mode of life; they represent an expression of a traditional social system that seems to be frozen, as it were, in its development (see Hauffe/Köster-Schlutz 1987: 395). Though tradition does not allow us to make a relevant statement as to the Śākya Queen, her standing posture may, nevertheless, not be self-determined. *DN* II 14, however, tells us that the lords of the quarters receive the child first, before the humans. Women of the Benín (Africa), as Richard Burghart has informed me, consider a birth in a standing position to be particularly heroic.[70] Did the Śākya women share this view? So much for the old tradition in Pāli.

Yet in the *Mahāvastu* the Bodhisatta suddenly comes into being, in a non-physical way, out of Māyā's right side,[71] without splitting it open, which may emphasize the miraculous character of the birth of the Bodhisatta. From the point of view of psychology of religion, a birth through the (right) side is, on the one hand, a shift from below, i.e. from the impure, upward, just as the birth of a hero takes place in a clean way, as is stressed in the texts.[72] On the other hand, it can be considered a degradation of the status of the mother, as higher beings are marked by an out-of-the-way coming into existence. Such an exceptional birth is known, apart from the case of Indra's mother, e.g. in the *MatsyaPur* 157, 39 sq., when Umā, Śiva's consort, gives birth to the six Kārttikeyas, of Sūravantī bearing Birobā (see Sontheimer 1989a: 104), and in the *VarāhaPur* 144, 67–143 even of the sage Sālaṅkāyana giving birth to his son Nandī from his right side. A still higher upward shift is shown by a Nepalese statuette of the 18th century that features the Bodhisatta jumping from his mother's armpit like Kakṣīvat in the *Buddhacarita* 1.10[73] (cf. already the seasons, *ghī*, etc., produced from Prajāpati's armpits).[74]

As soon as the gods have placed the Bodhisatta on the earth he takes seven strides to the north, reminding us, on the one hand, of a king's three strides at his *rājasūya* (*TS* 1, 8, 10g), thus imitating Viṣṇu's three strides in the *ṚV*, for, this god clears the way for somaholic Indra's battle against Vṛtra, the primaeval Ouroboros, and, in this way, favours the cosmic order that Indra is about to establish. On the other hand, Gotama was after all a prince who could also have become a ruler.

Buddhism adopts this battle, adapting it as the Bodhisatta's battle with Māra; the former by virtue of his final emancipation emerges victorious (see Bollée 1977: 371–81).

At the same time, one cannot help but think of the marriage ritual, though it seems difficult to connect it with the Bodhisatta's strides. The commentators and later Buddhist literature explain them allegorically for which see esp. Mus (1933: 887 sqq.) According to the French scholar, the seven strides signify a spacial transcendence through the seven cosmic stories corresponding to the planetary skies, and Eliade (1957: 139ff., esp. 142) points to the parallel of the Vedic sacrificer climbing the sacrificial post exclaiming "I have reached heaven, the gods. I have become immortal" (*TS* 1, 7, 9). This post is a replica of the *axis mundi*. Being at its top, outside space (and time) means being at a point before the world came into being – *nirvāṇa*. The Bodhisatta's seven steps may also be taken as a step up of Viṣṇu's strides,[75] rather than of those of Alexander the Great in a Caucasian folk tale.[76] Keith (1920: 503) compared the seven steps of the young Gotama to those of the mother-to-be of Christ and holds them to be ethnic.

At the seventh stride the Bodhisatta utters the (metrical) words of an "eminent person" (as nowadays Windisch's rendering by "*indem er die stiergleiche Rede von sich gehen ließ*" is translated) (Windisch 1908: 131), viz., *aggo 'ham asmi lokassa* 'I stand at the top of the world' (*DN* II 15 etc.). The expression *āsabha* 'eminent person' (*CPD*) does not only remind us of a melody used at magic rites in order to acquire power and sung to the words of a *ṛgvedic*

Indra-hymn,[77] but also of the sound of a bull-skin kettledrum in use at the *mahāvrata* ritual, where it is said: 'The bull is the highest sound.'[78] In post-canonical times this becomes, "He sang the song of victory."[79] As can be seen, e.g. from *Ja* V 360, 28, where *sīha-nāda* is said of a bird, it should not be rendered by 'lion's roar' and even less, of course, by 'halleluia' (*PED*), but as given in *PWB*: *'ein Wort, das ich mit Selbstvertrauen aussprechе und auf das man sich verlassen kann'*.

The *Tipiṭaka* uses *sīha-nāda* with regard to the Buddha,[80] just as he is also called *sakya-sīha* 'Lion among the Śākyas', his tribe. Yet it is interesting here, that in late Vedic *siṃha-nāda-nadin* is the epithet of a form of Rudra-Śiva (*AVPar* 36, 1, 15), whereas in the Jaina *Siddhânta* it is the *asura* Camara who expresses himself in this way before his attack on Indra (*Viy* 3, 2, p. 147 l. 24). More than once, as will be seen below, non-orthodox religions reflect first *śaiva* and later *vaiṣṇava* influences.

According to tradition, Māyā – as in Christian mythology the mother of St. George the dragon slayer – died after seven days – thus apparently in childbed. This possibly historical fact must have been too ominous to be accepted by the faithful. In the Pāli canon no explanation for it is given, and it seems to contradict a passage stating the resistance on the part of prince Gotama's mother (!) and father though they knew of his glorious future: *Gotamo a-kāmakānaṃ mātā-pitunnaṃ assu-mukhānaṃ rudantānaṃ* (...) *pabbajjito* (*DN* I 115, 18 sqq.) "Gotama, though his father and mother (!) were unwilling, and wept (...) went out from the houshold life into the homeless state" (Rhys Davids 1880). But this may be an oversight on the part of the redactor of the text. In *Ja* I 52, 2 and *Mvu* II 3, 9 sq. the reason is that, after giving birth to a Bodhisatta, sexual intercourse does not befit his mother any longer, whereas the *Lalitavistara* (98, 3) states that her death in childbed was not the child's fault, but was due to the shortness of her life span. For otherwise, her heart would have been broken at the departure of the adult Bodhisatta in search of a teacher.

Little Gotama was taken care of by his mother's sister Mahāpajāpatī, as, for different reasons, Tisalā took care of Vaddhamāṇa. Thus, in a way, both the Jina and the Buddha had two mothers, something, which, according to Jung (1976: § 494 sqq.) and Neumann (1962: 132 sqq.) is an essential item of heroic myth.

Ānanda's story in the *MārkaṇḍeyaPurāṇa* ch. 76 is a similar case of *dvi-mātṛtva* ('fact of having two mothers').

Now Nyberg (1938: 7) and Widengren (1965: 102) assume that the Buddha-*vita* for its part influenced the Eastern Zaraθuštra legend. Comparing the relevant Persian tradition to the Buddhist *Jātakas*, as Widengren demands, will not get us much further. Besides, he may mean the birth and life of Gotama Siddhattha in certain Indian texts other than the *Jātakas*. Moreover, one wonders that he does not mention Windisch's book *Buddha's Geburt*. Furthermore, details such as the statement in the late *Dēnkart* (7, 1, 56 sqq.), that Zaraθuštra's native village was quite bright three days before his birth, and the old legend in *Yašt* 17, 18 sq. that Zaraθuštra was the only child who laughed when he was born, at any rate only occurs of the Bodhisatta in the *Mahāvastu*.[81] On the other hand, a similar phenomenon to the bodily marks of the Indian *mahāpuruṣa* (*vide infra*) is not found in the culture of ancient Irān. This is all the more striking as they were known of in Sakian-Khotanese[82] and Tokharian (see Couvreur 1946: 577–610).

Though we meet with Vaddhamāṇa Mahāvīra and Gotama Siddhattha, notwithstanding the peculiar circumstances of their births, as human beings in the respective canonical traditions, they were deified very early. This, too, was a result of the belief that before their present existences they stayed in a heaven, and that their descents were accompanied by special phenomena in the sky,[83] and that the gods took an active interest in their passing away – in the case of the Buddha they stood packed together around his deathbed.[84] The Jains, for their part, began to perform *pūjā* in front of statues for the Jinas as if they were Hindu gods and later to speak of Mahāvīra as *gurudeva*.

Something similar developed, as is well-known, in the Buddhist *Mahā-sāṅghika* school as a precursor of *Mahāyāna* (Glasenapp, von 1936: 57 *and passim*).

Typical of the deification process may also be the male proper name Buddhadeva (*MW*) and the fact that in the lists of the 32 bodily marks (*lakṣaṇas*) of a *mahāpuruṣa*, which we shall now discuss, the feet are dealt with first, gods as well as great men (like kings) being looked up to from below, for, the viewer is lying at their feet. This begins already in *AV* 10, 2. Ordinary humans, however, are looked at the other way around. Further, in Śrī Laṅkā the Buddha is looked upon as a deity of sorts in popular Buddhism (Obeyesekere 1990: 111, 125).

One remark may yet be made in this context. Indian scholastics know of four postures, viz., walking, standing, sitting and reclining.[85] The latter posture is unheroic, because it is the posture of the dead and of sleeping people, though after his transition into *parinirvāṇa* the Buddha is depicted and worshipped in the reclining position.[86] Indra, however, in his fight against Vṛtra, is moving[87] in an upright position – the erect divine hero against the horizontal animal (*tiryak*),[88] for Vṛtra is lying in 99 coils around the cosmic mountain (*ṚV* 5, 29, 6).

In *ṚV* 10, 90, Puruṣa, the thousand-footed cosmic man whom the gods sacrifice, in my opinion stands ten fingers over the earth without touching it. His mouth becomes the brahmin (10, 90, 12), yet out of his mouth emerges Indra (10, 90, 13). This creation hymn, which stresses sacrifice, brahmin primacy, and the secondary rank of Indra, and thereby of the warrior class, already shows clear evidence of a transition toward the *Brāhmaṇa* literature. Furthermore, the cosmic giant reminds one of course of the Jainist concept of the universe as an erect human – woman or man – as well as of erect Jain ascetics like Bahubali in Śravaṇabeḷgoḷa.

Indra's successor, Prajāpati, is standing when *brahman* strikes the evil off him which is perhaps represented by the hair on his head.[89] This, then, would be a Vedic justification for the tonsure of the Buddhist monks and for the Jaina monks' even pulling out their hair. The hair is also a substitute for the head, which the hero has to sacrifice before he can be reborn in a higher state (Neumann 1962: 159, 59 sq.).

The Bodhisatta defends himself in an upright position in meditation against Māra, who wishes to prevent him from reaching final emancipation (cf. Bollée 1977: 377). This yogic posture, which is visible already on seal No. 420 in Mackay's list (Mackay 1937–38) and was formerly ascribed to "Proto-Śiva", is taken by Hiltebeitel to belong to "Proto-Mahiṣa".[90] But, perhaps, it is safer to designate it as proto-Indian as does Sontheimer (1987b: 124). The same *padmâsana* also marks the statues of Jinas, whereas standing Buddhas may be adaptations of *yakṣas* – an association aided by the well-known fact that the Buddha as well as the Mahāvīra often stayed in or near *yakṣa* shrines. Besides, the Buddha (see

Bollée 1977: 377), as also Indra (*Ja* IV 4, 11*), is called *Yakṣa* himself, and the *pipal* tree under which the Buddha reached his *bodhi* is also found on seal No. 335 in Mohenjo Daro.

The marks of the body are a product of brahmanic speculation on the physical externals of the ideal man and were adopted by Jains and Buddhists alike. Initially, they may go back to Nārāyaṇa and Indra, perhaps even to certain pre-Vedic concepts. In the course of the Vedic period prognostic teachings must have developed – probably first in a magical context, in order to enable brahmins to ward off evil from the ritual and recitation. Teachings of this kind may have begun in the fourth Veda, as is shown by the *Atharvaveda-pariśiṣṭa*.

As to the number 32, this, perhaps, has to do with a tradition of 32 *ākāras*, i.e. parts of the body as found, e.g. in the Pāli *Tipiṭaka*.[91] The references made by Weber (1878: 334 n. 5) are of little help, whereas Jolly does not deal with the topic at all in his *Medicin* (Jolly 1901). Besides, the portents at the Bodhisatta's birth are also 32 in number.[92] In the *Mahābhārata*, however, there is a list of 16 marks of Nara and Nārāyaṇa, seers in the sphere of Viṣṇu.[93] Since Burnouf dealt with the *lakṣaṇas* of the *mahāpuruṣa* – he was probably the first to do so in the West – in the 8th appendix to his translation of the *Saddharmapuṇḍarīka-sūtra*, they have undergone several treatments – complete and partial ones – which, however, with one exception, deal with the Buddha. For, only Weber[94] compared the person of the Mahāvīra with the Buddhist *lakṣaṇas* described by Burnouf. In doing so he could not but rely on Malayagiri's Sanskrit commentary on the *Sūrapannatti* – a representation of the activity of the sun and the moon in the Jaina *Siddhânta* – for, Leumann was the first scholar to edit the text containing the canonical list of the Jaina *lakṣaṇas* in his *Aupapātika-sūtra* (1883). This list does not correspond either in its wording or in its order to Malayagiri's list, which is more than a thousand years later.

Comparing the Jaina with the Buddhist *lakṣaṇas*, we first notice that – after some general features such as physical constitution, beautiful shape, condition of the flesh, purity and shine of the bodily appendages – the Jains treat the particulars of the body from top to bottom. There also occur some duplications and variants. Further, the *lakṣaṇas* are not always identical with those of the Buddha, and their description most often does not contain simple compounds like *dīghânguli* 'having long fingers resp. toes' or *eṇi-jaṅgho* 'with antelope-like legs', but *varṇakas*, i.e. in principle endless units of metrical prose. Thus, the depiction of the hair on Mahāvīra's head is a compound three and a half lines long in Latin transliteration. Strikingly, the compiler of this tradition and the redactor of the *Aupapātika* were not worried by the fact that, according to tradition, Mahāvīra at his *pabbajjā* pulled out his hair in five tufts – a praxis that may still take place when a novice enters the order, but otherwise seems to have fallen into disuse nowadays.

The removal of one's own hair means the renunciation of sexuality, just as baldness or cutting off someone else's hair means castration as a punishment for adultery. Thus, e.g. Indra branded his son and charioteer bald after the latter's intimacy with Indra's wife Śacī.[95] The foregoing is also founded on a concept that the late London Latinist Onians proved, inter alia, in Greek culture in his highly erudite study *The Origins of European Thought* – sperm was for the ancients a fluid which, like the soul, originated in the head. Its abundance – says Aristotle in his *Problemata* 867a 23 sqq. – causes the growth of hair. This would explain that a person about to join a religious order and thus to give up a layman's sexual activity, cuts off his hair. In this way, and by abstinence, the sperm accumulates, producing a kind of *hydrocephalus* – a protuberance more or less visible on pictures and statues of the Buddha and the Jina: the *uṣṇīṣa*. Further, as Hertha Krick (1982: 88 sq.) points out, the ritual haircut connects dedication to the deity by sacrificing the Self and returning vital power with separation from the past in order to be prepared for a new life period. Similarly, Siegel (1987: 222) opines that tonsure is a ritualized gesture of egolessness, purification and, presumably, desexualization.

The fact that, in spite of cutting off or pulling out their hair, both are nevertheless depicted with hair may be taken with Wendy O'Flaherty (1980: 45)[96] to mean that "the rich supply of semen stored in the yogi's head is symbolised by his high-piled hair; his powers, like those of the seduced Samson or the macho Sikh with his topknot, reside at the top of his head, in the 'snakelocks', that characterize the Sādhu". Ṛṣyaśṛṅga, too, belongs to this category (cf. O'Flaherty 1973: 50).

The point of departure of the above two scholars is *BĀU* 6,

4, 4 sq., which reads that the man who spills his seed puts it either in the middle of his chest or between his eyes. Later, in Kuṇḍalinī-yoga, these places are the *anāhata cakra*[97] – two interlocking triangles near the heart – where Viṣṇu[98] and the Jinas have a *śrīvatsa* (possibly a fertility symbol: frog or woman giving birth),[99] statues of the Buddha sometimes have a *svastika*[100] – and the *ājñā cakra* which appears among Buddhist *lakṣaṇas* as *ūrṇā*, a circle of hair between the eyebrows. From the latter the seed rises up to the highest *cakra* at the crown of the head,[101] the very spot of the cosmic man's (or woman's) head, where the Jains believe the liberated souls abide. Related to this topic can, but must not be such otherwise inexplicable words as *ūrdhva-reta(s)*,[102] *ūrdhva-manthin*,[103] and *ūrdhva-liṅga*[104] all of which mean 'sexually abstinent', though etymologically the sense should in fact be 'ithyphallic'.[105] However, "the phallus that draws up its seed is symbolic of the perfect man".[106]

Before concluding with these brief remarks on two of the *lakṣaṇas* on the *mahāpuruṣa*'s upper body – elsewhere[107] I have dealt with some marks on his feet that go back to Indra and Prajāpati – this note on the birth of the hero in ancient India, I shall return briefly to the name Mahāvīra. The Jina may have obtained this title for being considered a perfect man (*siddha*, cf. Duncan's paper in this volume, infra, p. 57) rather than as an "attribute inspired by profound reverence and traced back to the god's" (Schubring 1935: § 17). Because of their association with the Jina the Jains bow down also before Hanumān, for in a Hindu context nowadays *mahāvīra* usually stands for Hanumān e.g. *āṅgan ke dacchin-pūrab kone meṃ tulsī kā cabūtrā thā, vahiṃ Hanumān jī kī dhujā gaḍī huī thī.*[108] The earlier occurrences of this use of the word seem to be in the *SkandaPurāṇa*, e.g. 3, 36, 189; 37, 5 *namo 'stu te, Mahāvīra,* (...) *Vāyu-putrāya, te namaḥ*; 46, 23; in the *Lāṅgulôpaniṣad* (*Upaniṣatsaṃgraha* II 214, 21) *namo Bhagavate caṇḍa-pratāpa-Hanumate mahā-vīrāya* "homage to the divine Hanumān of fierce strength, the great hero"; and in Bhavabhūti's (8th cent.) *Mahāvīracarita* 5. Later, in Hindī literature, we find the word in the *Rāmcaritmānas* of Tulsīdās (1, 33, 5 and 9). The authors may have conferred this title on Rāma's devotee on the strength of enumerations of Hanumān's good qualities in Vālmīki's *Rāmāyaṇa* 7, 36, 43 sqq., where *sauvīrya* is ascribed to him, and a passage such as *Rām* 6, 128, 32 *vānarāḥ mānuṣaṃ vigrahaṃ kṛtvā* (said of Sugrīva's elephant corps mounted by monkeys in human shape proceeding to Laṅkā). Mrs Narula (1991: 21) points to Hanumān's resemblance to the *yakṣas* who are also called *vīra*, but further states that in Mahārāṣṭra and Uttar Pradesh there are Mahāvīra and Vīra cults not specifically affiliated with Hanumān worship. Hanumān is also called Langūr Vīr (Hiltebeitel 1989: 244 sqq.). According to Gupta (1979: 135), Pañcamukhī Hanumān, who is also called Vīra Hanumān, is a *śākta* god and is to be separated from Dāsa Hanumān, the *vaiṣṇava* deity. Hanumān is a son of Vāyu, the wind god, and to my knowledge there are no particulars as to his birth. Mahāvīra is further found as the name of a son of Bṛhadratha (*Rām* 1, 71, 7), and, in the last century, as that of the man who revived Buddhism.

Conclusion

In Old-Indian as well as in Latin writing a text can be compared to weaving. When this simile is adopted for the present article the loom thereof shows for its warp various beings designated as heroes: gods like Indra and Prajāpati, perhaps the sun, too, represented by an earthen vessel at the *pravargya* ritual – and humans like Vaddhamāṇa Jina and Gotama Buddha.

Special beings are conceived, gestated and born with remarkable bodily signs in a miraculous way (these features form the paper's woof), esp. Indra and the Buddha whose mythology shows various parallels. They are called heroes because of their victory over the main obstacle in their existence, viz, the demonized cosmic inertia, the Evil of clinging to this world in ignorance, and of its consequence: rebirth, and darkness. Indra was born to kill Vṛtra and thus enable, inter alia, the sun to shine. The Jinas were born to enlighten the world.

NOTES

U.P. Shah's long article on Hariṇegamesi came too late to my knowledge for use and Ralph Strohl's thesis is not available in any public library in Germany.

1 *ṚV* 1, 32, 6 and *AVPaipp* 13, 6, 6.

2 *Upaniṣatsaṃgraha* I 355: 8f. *kṛpayā Bhagavān Viṣṇuṃ vidadāra nakhaiḥ kharaiḥ | carmâmbaro mahā-vīro vīra-bhadro babhūva ha ||*

"Out of pity the divine One tore up Viṣṇu with his sharp nails. Vīrabhadra (Rudra), clad in skin, was a great hero."

3 Brückner 1995: 178 and 217; see also Roghair 1982: 297 (I am obliged to Heidrun Brückner for this reference); Krick 1982: 499 *and passim* and Filliozat 1967: 74 sqq.

4 Van Buitenen 1968: 40; 58. On a possible reason for this see Neumann 1962: 143.

5 Van Buitenen 1968: 37 (the latter goes back to Oldenberg 1917: 447).

6 E.g., in the *AitĀr* 3, 2, 3. *KauṣB* 8, 3, 7 the sun is called *mahāvīra*.

7 Indra is the sun: *ṚV* 3, 44, 4; *ŚB* 1, 6, 4, 18; Indra regulates time: *ṚV* 3, 30, 12 sq.

8 Prajāpati is identified with the sun at *TB* 1, 6, 4, 1; *ŚB* 12, 3, 5, 1 etc.; with the year: *AitB* 1, 1; 4, 25 etc.

9 Rau 1972: 72.

10 Rau 1972: 21 "*aus drei Tonstreifen aufgebauter Kochtopf mit flachem Boden, 0.24 m bis 0.60 m Durchmesser, in der Mitte ähnlich einem Stundenglas zusammengezogen, mit einem Gürtel, (oder?) einem Halsband und oben einer etwa 0.06 m langen, nasenförmigen Tülle.*"

11 Oldenberg 1917: 86; cf. Macdonell/Keith 1912: II 142 'great hero'.

12 Renou 1954: 124. Thus also Minard 1956: § 116 a.

13 See, e.g. Srinivasan 1983: 543–56.

14 The *mahāvīra* vessel is covered with a gold plate and stands on a silver plate, between heaven and earth, as it were. The *vrātya* wears a couple of such plates as a necklace (see Hauer 1927: 129). Van Buitenen apparently was not acquainted with Hauer's remarks.

15 See also Meyer 1937 II 238f. and 1939: 104.

16 Sontheimer 1987a: 8 sq.; id. 1989b: 302; id. 1997: 95.

17 E.g. in the case of Kuntī (*Mbh* cr. ed. 3, 291, 23) and Dīrghatamas (*Mbh* 1, 98, 31), cf. also Windisch 1908: 20–9. The navel is a place of origin: Brahmā on a lotus arises from Viṣṇu's navel, etc. Cf., e.g. Fodor 1949: 143 sqq.

18 *Upaniṣatsaṃgraha* 1970: 150 § 4 *in fine: atha jantuḥ strī-yoni-śataṃ yoni-dvāri saṃprāpto yantreṇâpīḍyamāno mahatā duḥkhena jāta-mātras tu vaiṣṇavena vāyunā saṃspṛśya tadā na smarati janma-maraṇaṃ na ca karma śubhâśubham* "in hundreds of cases (lit.: of wombs of women) when the child has reached the orifice of the womb it is squeezed with a forceps, but as soon as it is born with great pain and has made contact with Viṣṇu's wind (i.e. fresh air), then it does not remember anymore birth and death nor good and bad deeds (of his previous birth?)." On suffering in the womb (*gabbha-vāsa-dukkha*) see Vasudevahiṇḍī 9, 5ff. (Jain 1977: 561ff.).

19 Implicit at *Āyār* 2, 15, 26 corresponding to *Kappa Jinac* § 121.

20 *Kappa* § 18, cf. *DīghaN* I 115, 5.

21 Cf. *Ja* I 54, 7 where among the Bodhisatta's co-natals four *nidhi-kumbhas* 'treasure-pots, hidden treasures' are mentioned.

22 *Kappa* § 95. According to the Jains, *dohadas* 'pregnancy whims' appear in the third month (Caillat 1974: 51), yet they are not mentioned of Devânandā.

23 Oldenberg 1881/1959: 105 and Glasenapp, von 1936: 21 take *Māyā* to be a proper name meaning '*Wundermacht*' and are not bothered

by the oddity of such a name. With it, Senart (1881: xxvi) associated "*des attaches supra-terrestres*" (cf. p. 275). In the *Tipiṭaka*, *Māyā* only occurs as a nominative: *Bhagavato Suddhodano rājā pitā Māyā devī mātā*, *DN* II 52, 10; *Th* 534 etc.

24 See Windisch, 1908: 140 and, e.g. Thomas n.d.: 81. The tendency to designate female "*Respektspersonen*" in a religious context as 'mother', whose devotees then are her children, is found up to the present day, e.g. regarding Śrī Aurobindo's wife, Jillellamudi Amma in Bapatla (Guntur), Yoginī Ammajī near Trichur (Kerala), Ānandamayī Mā in Bhadaini (Benares), etc. See also Gupta 1979: 116 sqq.

25 For this detail see Jolly 1901: § 40 and, e.g. Neumann 1962: 52.

26 *DN* II 12 sq.; *MN* III 122 sq.

27 Printz 1925: 125 stresses the fact that the indication "right" only appears at *Ja* I 50, 22 (Māyā's dream). See also Lüders 1941: 45 sqq.

28 I.e., 100 times the usual period. The full term of the gods takes millennia, e.g. twenty in Kārttikeya's case – with several foetus transfers (see Mani 1975: 747).

29 See Rank 1909: 74 and Neumann 1962: 132 sq.

30 In *MS* 2, 1, 12 Aditi as Indra's mother even binds her son in her womb with an iron fetter and in this state he was born. Cf. Neumann 1962: 300.

31 Cf. Neumann 1962: 154; 164, but already indicated by Jung, e.g. 1976, ch. VI, esp. § 456 sq. and in other works.

32 Geldner (1951), in his introduction to the hymn, even speaks of *Seiten*, i.e. plural.

33 *ṚV* 7, 23, 3 cd: *ví bādhiṣṭa syá ródasī mahitvéndro vṛtrā́ṇy a-pratí́ jaghan vā́n* "*Indra drängte beide Welthälften durch seine Größe auseinander, als er die Dämonen erschlagen hatte, denen keiner gewachsen war*" (Geldner, id.). *Vṛtrāṇi*, however, should here be translated by "obstacles", I think.

34 At *ṚV* 3, 49, 1 and 8, 61, 2 both worlds, which originally were united (*ṚV* 3, 38, 3 with Geldner's note), are said to have created Indra and at *ṚV* 4, 17, 2 heaven and earth tremble at his birth.

35 Also, e.g. *ṚV* 4, 27, 1 (Soma); *Mbh* cr. ed. 1, 98, 13 and 12, 328, 46 (Dīrghatamas); Dange 1986: 386. For parallels in non-Indian literatures see Glasenapp, von 1954: 91 and for modern examples see, e.g. Gupta 1979: 121; Oman 1908: 69; Thompson and Balys 1958: T 575.1.

36 See, e.g. Janus 1990: esp. 76 sqq.

37 I cannot offer an explanation of, nor parallels for this number.

38 See Glasenapp, von 1925: 297; Schubring 1935: 26 (§ 17), and Jaini 1980: 232.

39 As against Koḍillaya, Jain 1984: 226 did not mention Koḍāla. Perhaps the Jain interest in Cāṇakya (for whom see Chandra and Mehta 1970 s.v. Cāṇakka) is connected to Koḍāla, Mahāvīra's brahmin father.

40 *Harivaṃśa* cr. ed. 47–48; *BhāgPur* 10, 2, 8. See also, e.g. O'Flaherty 1975: 206–13 and Spratt 1966: 302 (according to whom "the psychoanalytic view [of the foetus transfer] is that it is intended to diminish the hostility between father and son"). Further, Printz 1925: 124 expresses

doubt as to a direct borrowing from the Kṛṣṇa legend. According to Dundas 1992: 23 this event can be interpreted either as "an attempt to devalorise the authority of the brahman caste" or "might suggest a desire to present Mahavira (...) as both human and at the same time transcending the normal mortal state".

41 See Scheftelowitz 1906: 130. Here a woman says: *Néjamesa, párā pata sú-putraḥ púnar ắ pata / asyaí me putrá-kāmāyai gárbham ắ dhehi yáḥ púmān //* "Nejameṣa, fly away and quickly return with an excellent son. Get me with child (...)!". – As the exposure motif as a symbol of the procedure of birth is known also to Indian stories (see, e.g. Bollée 1967: 138; 140), one can ask if Nejameṣa is considered here a bird, like the stork with us. See, e.g. Rank 1909: 88 sq., Fodor 1949: 144, and Neumann 1962: 22.

42 *Śarīrasthāna* 10, 52. At *Uttarasthāna* 37, 2 Suśruta mentions scholars who assume two Naigameṣas since a divine being generated by Agni and Rudra would not cause a dangerous disease. He himself, however, thinks that Naigameṣa only shows his ugly side if the child's family is derelict in its religious duties. See also Winternitz 1895: 149 sqq.

43 *Mbh* cr. ed. 12, 79, 6 *ajo 'gnir, Varuṇo meṣaḥ.*

44 *ŚB* 6, 4, 4, 15; *SkandaPur* 6, 4 *Agneyaṃ Kṛttikā-putram Aindram kecid adhīyate, / kecit Paśupataṃ Rudraṃ; yo 'si so 'si: namo 'stu te.*

45 *Mbh* (Poona, 1929) 1, 66, 24 = *ViṣṇuPur* 1, 15, 116. Cf. *Mbh* cr. ed. 3, 215, 23 *Agnir bhūtvā Naigameyaś chāga-vaktro bahu-prajaḥ / ramayāmāsa śaila-stham bālaṃ (Skandaṃ) krīḍanakair iva* "Agni as Naigameya with the muzzle of a he-goat and numerous progeny gladdened his child (Skanda) on the mountain (Udaya) to amuse himself a little with" and 3, 217, 1 *Skandasya pārṣadān ghorān śṛṇuṣvâdbhuta-darśanān / vajra-prahārāt Skandasya jajñus tatra kumārakāḥ / ye haranti śiśūn jātān garbha-sthāṃś câiva dāruṇāḥ* "Hear of the frightful and strange looking followers of Skanda. As Skanda was struck by a thunderbolt boys were born, terrible ones who take away children, born ones and such as are still in the womb."

46 See Banerjea 1956: 363; 367 and 562; Mani 1975: 748; Sontheimer 1987b: 124. On the multiple transfer of Śiva's semen see Mani 1975: 747 and O'Flaherty 1980: 171.

47 *Mbh* cr. ed. 7, 5, 37.

48 Liebert 1976: 102 takes the name to mean 'Hari, i.e. Indra, as Ṇegamesi.'

49 Another example hereof is the name Jamāli, Sa. Yamâri.

50 Of Jinaprabha 1913 (Jacobi 1879: 25).

51 Apparently, demons exchanging foetuses are often male, and those who take away new-born children (and occasionally devour them) are female, e.g. Jāta-hāriṇī in *MārkPur* 51, 106 sq. and 76, 9. A Sāñci inscription mentions Naigameśa as the tutelary Yakṣa of Pañcālī (Coomaraswamy 1971: I 12). See also Meyer 1937: I 136; 140 sq.

52 *Ja* I 49, 22 sq. – For a further development of this idea in medieval Jainism see Merutunga's *Prabandhacintāmaṇi* p. 83, 9 with regard to young Cāṅgadeva, who later became famous by his monastic name Hemacandra: (*Śrī Devacandrâcāryas*) *tad-aṅga-pratyaṅgānāṃ jagad-*

vilakṣaṇāni lakṣaṇāni prekṣya "ayaṃ yadi kṣatriya-kule jātas, tadā sārva-bhauma-cakravartī; yadi vaṇig-vipra-kule jātas, tadā mahâmātyaḥ; ced darśanaṃ pratipadyate, tadā yuga-pradhāna iva Kali-kāle 'pi Kṛta-yugam avatārayati sa ācārya" iti vicārya (...) "When Devacandra saw the world-surpassing marks on the greater and lesser limbs of the boy, he came to the conclusion that, if he were born in the Kṣatriya race, he would be a universal emperor, if he were born in a family of merchants or Brahmans, he would be a great minister, but if he adopted the true faith, he would, like the chief saint of a Yuga, bring back the Kṛta age even in the Kali age" (Tawney 1901: 127).

53 *Āyār* 2, 15, 5 and *Kappa* § 3 refer to his knowing to descend, *Āyār* 2, 15, 5 and *Kappa* § 29 to his transfer. As to the time of the exchange there is a marked difference between the two canonical texts in that according to *Āyār* Mahāvīra knows of the moment, whereas according to *Kappa* he does not.

54 Freud 1960: ch. 8 and Neumann 1962: 154 where it is stressed that not the hero's real mother as such, but his mother as the representative of the Great Mother is meant.

55 This is the average with the Jains, see Schubring 1935: § 95.

56 See on this light the critical remarks of Eliade 1976: 96.

57 Cf. Engelmann 1884: 73 (for which reference I thank Eva Tornow); Kuntner 1985: 34 (Switzerland, 19th cent.), 91 (Iroquois), 96f. (south India); the 18th cent. wooden sculptures in Rawson 1973: 99, plate 10 (image of a birth, analogous to the creative function of the goddess; south India) and Mookerjee and Khanna 1977: 171.

58 I owe this information to the kindness of Anna L. Dallapiccola, who here refers to an incorrect observation made by Thomas in his unpublished thesis (1979: 335, panel 17 [1: 17]). Here, he discusses Ramachandran 1943: 82 and plate XI (Ṛṣabhadeva) and XII (Vardhamāna).

59 *Āyār* 2, 15, 11 and, in greater detail, in *Kappa* § 103–05. Similarly in *Divy* 282 (see Schlingloff 1962: 20).

60 Windisch 1908: 111; Eliade 1965: 33.

61 *Sumangala-vilāsinī* 430, 15 sqq. (not *Ja* I 50) and cf. *Vism* 548.

62 Schröter-Kunhardt 1990: 1017; id., *Nachtodeserlebnisse – eine wissenschaftliche Untersuchung* (working title).

63 *Sv* 430, 12 *su-gatiṃ gaccha!*

64 Cf. Kirfel 1920: 230 sq.

65 *Ps* IV 181, 21 sqq. *(Mātā) nisinnaṃ Bodhisattaṃ kucchi-gataṃ taco paṭicchādetuṃ na sakkoti. Olokentiyā ca bahi ṭhito viya paññāyati* (30ff.) *Bodhisatto pana anto-kucchi-gato mātaraṃ na passati, na hi anto-kucchiyaṃ cakkhu-viññāṇaṃ uppajjati* = *Sv* 436, 18 sqq. "(His mother) could not make the skin of her abdomen cover the Bodhisatta as he sat in her womb. In her view he appeared as if being outside her, whereas the Bodhisatta being in her womb did not see his mother for there is no intrauterine visual cognition." In art, this has never been represented, as far as I know, e.g. in the way Marx Reichlich depicted the Christ child in his mother's womb (1502; see, e.g. Lechner 1981: plates 231–34) to which Johann-Michael Fritz (Heidelberg) kindly drew my attention. Foetal animals, however, are known in Indian art

from prehistoric and historical rock shelters in Bhimbetka, Satkunda and Ramchaja south and east of Bhopal (see, e.g. Neumayer 1983: 75d and 77h [bovid with foetus inside body], 77a and 77g [antelope with foetus]).

66 *Mvu* I 144, 3 sqq.

67 *DN* II 14; *MN* III 122. Cf. the discussion in Printz 1925: 119 sqq.

68 Usually, trees like the *aśoka* here (thus Lüders 1941: 62 against *Ja* I 52, 24 sq., where it is a *śāla* tree. See also Printz 1925: 126) flower when touched by a lady's foot. Here we have the case of a woman delivering after touching a tree with her hand. According to Lüders in his argument with Barua, who thinks it is a *śāla* tree, Māyā is plucking *aśoka* flowers. On the miraculous character of the *śāla* tree see Viennot 1954: 236 and Gupta 1991: 89. The latter states that "the tree in blossom is worshipped by those desiring offspring[s]. In Bengal certain tribes use the branches of the Sala tree for marriage ceremonies." In Māyā's situation a *śāla* tree seems therefore to make more sense, but what she in fact needed was not so much flowers as rather a branch to take hold of as a support if she was to get her child in a standing position. Perhaps also custom required Māyā to seek refuge from the (hostile) sun under a tree while giving birth (cf. Abbott 1932: 476). For birth under a tree see also Ruben 1941: 290.

69 *DN* II 14; *MN* III 122.

70 Giving birth in a standing position quickens the first phase of labour and eases it (Kuntner 1985: 159). This position, customary e.g. in France in the country up to 1914, can, however, be dangerous to mother and child, if there is no one near, like the deities in the case of the Buddha's mother, to catch the child (Gélis 1992: 195ff.). Perhaps the way the Bodhisatta leaves his mother's body can also be seen to symbolize his descent from the Tuṣita heaven he stayed in (Windisch 1908: 108f.).

71 *Mvu* II 20, 14 > Windisch 1908: 121. Hieronymus, the Christian Father of the Church (4th cent.), already mentions this, adding that the mother is a virgin. See also, e.g. Neumann 1962: 133.

72 *DN* II 14; Windisch 1908: 127 and 138.

73 See Bollée 1983: 265 and cf., e.g. Franz, von 1982: 75.

74 *TB* 2, 2, 9, 7; see Minard 1956 § 874; 918. For the armpit as a pubic region see e.g. Hāla, *Sattasaī* 597; 599.

75 Kirfel 1920: 23* "Auf die Idee der Dreizahl folgte die der Siebenzahl." In direct imitation of Indra the Buddha in three strides reaches the *Tāvatiṃsa* heaven in order to preach the *Abhidhamma-piṭaka* to his mother (*Dhp-a* III 216, 20 *tayo va pāda-vārā ahesuṃ*).

76 As Ruben 1944: 70 thinks referring to Dirr 1920, No. 259. Eva Tornow has reminded me of *Śakuntala* 7, 33, where Mārīca prophesies that his grandson will be a *cakravartin* and *rathenânuddhāta-stimita-gatinā tīrṇa-jaladhiḥ / purā sapta-dvīpāṃ jayati vasudhām a-pratirathaḥ //* "First, a matchless warrior, he will cross the ocean in a chariot whose motion would be steady and free from jolts and conquer the earth consisting of her seven islands" (Devadhar/Suru). That would be an interesting counterpart to the Bodhisatta here, also because of *tīrṇa-jaladhiḥ*. Pāli literature, however, to my knowledge, does not know

of an earth consisting of seven islands, the idea apparently being brahminical (see Kirfel 1920: 57; Kloetzli 1983: 25, 28, 58).

77 *PVB* 9, 2, 15 = *JB* 1, 222 "*abhí tvā vṛṣabhā (suté) sutám*"; (*ṚV* 8, 45, 22) *ity ārṣabhaṃ kṣatra-sāma kṣatram evâitena bhavati* "On (the verses beginning): 'Unto the soma thee, o Bull' [they chant] the bull-chant (ārṣabha). It is a might-chant; by it he becomes mighty" (Caland 1919: 201).

78 *Paramā vā ṛṣabho vāk*, *JB* 2, 404 (Caland 1919: § 165 = p. 215 "*Der Stier ist der höchste Klang*").

79 Rhys Davids' (1880: 156) translation of *Ja* I 53, 19 *āsabhiṃ vācaṃ nicchārento sīha-nādaṃ nadi.*

80 Hiltebeitel 1978: 775 note 27 connects the *sīha-nāda* with the Bodhisatta's numerous animal *lakṣaṇas*, which remind him of the numerous postures in classical *yoga* that are named after animals and thus suggesting an affinity between *yoga* and the assimilation of powers of those animals.

81 Widengren 1965: 101; Printz 1925: 127 sq.

82 See Leumann 1920: 116–22; Bailey 1963: 91 sq.

83 For extraordinary phenomena of nature at the birth of royalty see e.g. Thompson/Balys 1958: 148 sq.

84 Bollée 1984: 177 note 27 (which should read: *Kalpasūtra* § 125f.).

85 E.g. *AitB* 7, 15, 3. See also Bollée 1983a: 112 sqq. and cf. *AV* 4, 16, 2 and *RE* 1912: col. 1142 l. 10 sq.

86 Cf. Hiltebeitel 1978: 775 n. 27; 783 n. 47, and 787 n. 64. Filliozat 1967: 75 stresses the meaning of the direction of the head toward the north.

87 Indra also "sides with the wanderer"(*Indra ic carataḥ sakhā, AitB* 7, 15) etc.

88 The *Ṛgveda* uses the word *mṛgá* only.

89 *JB* 2, 369 (Caland 1919 § 160). In *BaudhŚS* 17, 40 hair is equated to Evil. See also Onians 1954: 108.

90 1978: 767–97, esp. 775 sq.

91 *DN* II 293 sqq. etc. (see *CPD* s.v. *ākāra* 7).

92 *Ja* I 51, 3–28 (cf. *Lalit* [L.] 85, 11–86, 17).

93 Cr. ed. 12, 331, 24 sqq.

94 1867: 306 sqq. Later (1883: 377 sqq.) he refers to Leumann, yet in his description of the contents of the *Aupapātika* he does not mention the physical description of the *tīrthaṃkara* at all.

95 *JB* 3, 199. See also Obeyesekere 1990: 78.

96 She apparently refers to articles by E.R. Leach and G. Obeyesekere, the former of which is missing in the bibliography (p. 356), whereas the latter is not available to me.

97 See, e.g. Mookerjee 1982: 49 *and passim.*

98 *Mbh* cr. ed. 12, 329, 42, 2.

99 See Bolon: 1983, to which Anna L. Dallapiccola kindly drew my attention, and id., 1992: 57ff. Cf. perhaps the 11th cent. C.E. sculpture of Ādyā-Śakti in the Alampur Museum, Hyderabad (Rawson 1973: 100 plate 15; Mookerjee and Khanna 1977: 181) and perhaps in Europe, the "Frauenkröte von Maissau", a fragmentary 3000 year-old statuette found by A. Gulder in Lower Austria (see Hirschberg 1988: 77 sq.). See also Ḍhere 1978: 2 sqq.

100 As, e.g. in the Kek Lok Si temple near the village of Ayer Itam on Pulau Pinang. It has been under construction for about a century now in a syncretistic or pan-Buddhist style and is the largest pagoda complex in Malaysia.

101 The concept of semen as residing in the head is widespread (Das 1992: 391 n. 18).

102 *TaittĀr* 10, 12, 1; *MaitrīUp* 2, 3; *Mbh* cr. ed. 1, 13, 10; 13, 17, 45 (Nīlakaṇṭha: *a-vipluta-brahmacaryaḥ*); 13, 74, 35.

103 *TaittĀr* 2, 7, 4.

104 *Mbh* 13, 17, 45 (Nīlakaṇṭha: *adho-liṅgo hi retaḥ siñcati, na tûrdhva-liṅgaḥ*).

105 One can, however, also think of avoidance of ejaculation in a state of high sexual excitement (Das in a private communication).

106 O'Flaherty 1973: 44. Cf. Kakar 1989: 119; Das 1992: 391.

107 Bollée 1977: 372 *and passim*.

108 *Nāgârjun* 1978: 20. For this reference I am indebted to Lothar Lutze, cf. Narula 1991: 22f. The Jain form of Hanumān is called Ghaṇṭākarṇa Mahāvīra (Cort 1989: 428). See also Ian Duncan's paper in this volume, infra, p. 41.

REFERENCES

Abbreviations of Sanskrit and Pāli texts follow the system adopted by Monier Williams' and the *Critical Pāli Dictionary*.

Abbott, J. 1932. *The Keys of Power*. London.

Antagaḍadasāo 1974. Nathmal, Muni (ed.). Lāḍnūn: Jain Viśwa Bhāratī.

Bailey, H.W. 1963. *Kothanese Texts* 5. Cambridge.

Banerjea, J.N. 1956. *The Development of Hindu Iconography*. Calcutta.

Bollée, W.B. 1967. *Kuṇālajātaka*. London.

———. 1977. A Note on Evil and its Conquest from Indra to Buddha. In: *The Prajñāpāramitā and Related Systems*, edited by L. Lancaster. Berkeley, 371–81.

———. 1981. The Indo-European Sodalities in ancient India. *ZDMG* 131, 1: 172–91.

———. 1983a Notes on Middle Indo-Aryan Vocabulary II. *JOIB* 33, 1.2: 108–22.

———. 1983b Traditionell-indische Vorstellungen über die Füße in Literatur und Kunst. *BAVA* 5: 227–81.

———. 1984. Zur Typologie der Träume und ihrer Deutung in der älteren indischen Literatur. *StII* 10: 169–86.

Bolon, C.R. 1983. Problems of the Origin and Identity of a Frog-goddess Figure in the Victoria and Albert Museum. Paper read at the International Conference on "Influences and Interaction in Ancient Indian Art". Lucknow.

———. 1992. *Forms of the Goddess Lajjā Gaurī in Indian Art*. Delhi.

Brückner, H. 1995. *Fürstliche Feste. Mythologie und Rituale eines Volkskultes an der Westküste Südindiens*. Stuttgart.

Buddhacarita. 1935. of Aśvaghoṣa. Edited by E.H. Johnston. Calcutta.

Buitenen, J.A.B. van 1968. *The Pravargya*. Poona.

Caillat, Colette 1974. Sur les doctrines médicales dans le Tandulaveyāliya. *Indologica Taurinensia* 2: 45–55.
Caland, W. 1919. *Das Jaiminīya Brāhmaṇa in Auswahl.* Amsterdam.
———. 1924. *Das Śrautasūtra des Āpastamba II.* Amsterdam.
Carman, J.B and F. Apffel Marglin 1985. *Purity and Auspiciousness in Indian Society.* Leiden.
Chandra, K.R. and M. Mehta (eds.) 1970. *Prakrit Proper Names I.* Ahmedabad.
Coomaraswamy, A.K. 1971. *Yakṣas I-II.* New Delhi.
Cort, J.E. 1989. *Liberation and Wellbeing: A Study of the Śvetāmbar Mūrtipūjak Jains of North Gujarat.* Cambridge (Mass.).
Couvreur, W. 1946. Le caractère Sarvâstivādin – Vaibhāṣika des fragments tochariens. A d'après les marques et épithètes du Bouddha. *Muséon* 59.
Dange, S.A. 1986–1990. *Encyclopaedia of Purānic Beliefs and Practices.* Delhi.
Das, R.P. 1992. Sexual Rituals of the Bauls of Bengal. *JAOS* 112.3: 388–432.
Dundas, P. 1992. *The Jains.* London.
Ḍhere, R.C. 1978. *Lajjā Gaurī.* Puṇe.
Dirr, A. 1920. *Kaukasische Märchen.* Jena.
Eliade, M. 1957. *Mythes, rêves et mystères.* Paris; repr. 1981.
———. 1965. *The Two and the One.* London.
———. 1976. *Occultism, Witchcraft and Cultural Fashion.* Chicago.
Engelmann, G.J. 1884. *Die Geburt bei den Urvölkern.* Wien.
Fedor Freybergh, P.G. (ed.). 1987. *Pränatale und perinatale Psychologie und Medizin.* Alvsjö.
Feher, M. 1989. *Fragments for a theory of the Human Body.* Cambridge (Mass.)
Filliozat, J. 1967. L'Abandon de la Vie par le sage et les suicides du criminel et du héros dans la tradition indienne. *Arts Asiatiques* XV: 65–88.
Fodor, N. 1949. *The Search for the Beloved.* New Hyde Park.
Franz, M.-L. von 1982. *Les Mythes de Création.* Paris.
Freud, S. 1960. *Standard edition*, vol. 6 (containing *the Psychopathology of Everyday Life*). London.
Geldner, K.F. 1951. *Der Rig-Veda.* Cambridge (Mass.): H.O.S. 33–35.
Gélis, J. 1992. *Das Geheimnis der Geburt.* Freiburg.
Glasenapp, H. von 1936. *Der Buddhismus.* Berlin.
———. 1925. *Der Jainismus.* Berlin.
———. 1954. Buddhismus und Gottesidee. *ADWLMainz* No. 8.
Gupta, Beni 1979. *Magical Beliefs and Superstitions.* Delhi.
Gupta, Sh.M. 1991. *Plant Myths and Traditions in India.* Delhi.
Hauer, H.W. 1927. *Der Vrātya.* Stuttgart.
Hauffe, U. and M. Köster-Schlutz 1987. Gibt es natürliche Gebärhaltungen und welche Bedeutung haben sie für das Geburtserleben. In: *Pränatale und perinatale Psychologie und Medizin.* Edited by P.G. Fedor Freybergh. Alvsjö, 393–99.
Hillebrandt, A. 1897. *Ritual-Litteratur.* Straßburg.
Hiltebeitel, A. 1978. The Indus Valley 'proto Śiva'. Reexamined through Reflexions on the Goddess, the Buffalo, and the Symbolism of *vāhanās*. *Anthropos* 73: 767–97.

———. (ed.). 1989. *Criminal Gods and Demon Devotees.* Albany.
Hopkins, E.W. 1909. Gods and Saints of the Great Brāhmaṇa. *Transactions of the Connecticut Academy of Arts and Sciences* 15: 1–69
Israel, M. and N.K. Wagle (eds.) 1987. *Religion and Society in Mahārāṣṭra.* Toronto.
Jacobi, H. 1879. *The Kalpasūtra of Bhadrabāhu.* Leipzig.
———. 1884. *Jaina Sutras.* SBE XXII. London.
Jain, J.C. 1977. *The Vasudevahindī.* Ahmedabad.
Jaini, P.S. 1980. Karma and the Problem of Rebirth in Jainism. In: *Karma and Rebirth in Classical Indian Traditions.* Edited by W.D. O'Flaherty. Chicago, 217–38.
———. 1985. The Pure and the Auspicious in the Jaina Tradition. In: *Purity and Auspiciousness in Indian Society.* Edited by J.B. Carman and F. Apffel Marglin. Leiden, 84–93.
Janus, L. 1990. *Die Psychoanalyse der vorgeburtlichen Lebenszeit und der Geburt.* 2nd edn. Pfaffenweiler.
Jolly, J. 1901. *Indische Medicin.* Straßburg.
———. 1977. *Indian Medicine.* Delhi.
Jung, C.G. 1976. *Symbols of Tranformation.* Collected Works 5. New York.
Kakar, S. 1989. *Intimate Relations.* Delhi.
Kashikar, C.G. 1975. A propos of the Pravargya. *AIOC* 26: 137–47.
Keith, A.B. 1920. *A History of Sanskrit Literature.* London.
Kirfel, W. 1920. *Die Kosmographie der Inder.* Bonn.
Krick, Hertha. 1982. *Das Ritual der Feuergründung.* Wien.
Kloetzli, W.R. 1983. *Buddhist Cosmology.* Delhi.
Kuntner, L. 1985 (4th edn. 1994). *Die Gebärhaltung der Frau:* Schwangerschaft und Geburt aus geschichtlicher, völkerkundlicher und medizinischer Sicht. München.
Lancaster, L. (ed.). 1977. *The Prajñāpāramitā and Related Systems: Studies in Honor of Edward Conze.* Berkeley.
Lalitavistara 1902. Edited by S. Lefmann. Halle.
Lāṅgulôpaniṣad see *Upaniṣat-saṃgraha.*
Lechner, G.M. 1981. *Maria Gravida.* München.
Leumann, E. 1920. Buddhistische Literatur nord-arisch und deutsch 1: *AKM* 15, 2. Leipzig.
Liebert, G. 1976. *Iconographic Dictionary of the Indian Religions.* Leiden.
Lüders, H. 1941. Bhārhut und die buddhistische Literatur. *AKM* 26, 3. Leipzig.
———. 1951. *Varuṇa.* Göttingen.
Macdonnell, A. and A.B. Keith 1912. *Vedic Index of Names and Subjects.* London.
Mani, Vettam. 1975. *Purāṇic Encyclopaedia.* Delhi.
Meyer, J.J. 1937. *Trilogie altindischer Mächte und Feste der Vegetation.* I-III. Zürich.
———. 1939. Zusätze zur "Trilogie altindischer Mächte und Feste der Vegetation." *WZKM* 46: 104.
Minard, A. 1956. *Trois énigmes sur les cent chemins.* II. Paris.
Mookerjee, A. 1982. *Kuṇḍalinī.* London.
Mookerjee, A and M. Khanna 1977. *The Tantric Way.* London.
Mus, P. 1933. Barabudur. *BEFEO* 33. Hanoi (repr. N.Y., 1978).

Neumann, E. 1962. *Origins and History of Consciousness.* New York. (Zürich 1949; New York, 1954).
Narula, J. 1991. *Hanuman God and Epic Hero.* Delhi.
Nidenmayer, E. 1983. *Prehistoric Indian Rock Paintings.* Delhi.
Nyberg, H.S. 1938. *Die Religionen des alten Iran.* Leipzig.
Obeyesekere, G. 1990. *The Work of Culture.* Chicago.
O'Flaherty, W.D. 1973. *Asceticism and Eroticism in the Mythology of Śiva.* Chicago.
———. 1975. *Hindu Myths.* Harmondsworth.
———. 1980. *Women, Androgynes and Other Mythical Beasts.* Chicago.
———. (ed.). 1980. *Karma and Rebirth in Classical Indian Traditions.* Chicago.
Oldenberg, H. 1959. *Buddha.* Stuttgart 13th edn. (1881).
———. 1917. *Die Religion des Veda.* Stuttgart.
Oman, J.C. 1908. *Cults, Customs and Superstitions of India.* London.
Onians, R.B. 1954. *The Origins of European Thought.* Cambridge, 2nd edn.
Printz, W. 1925. Buddha's Geburt. *ZDMG* 79: 119–32.
Rāmcaritmānas 1922. of Tulsīdās. Allahabad.
Rāmāyaṇa. 1930. of Vālmīki. Bombay.
Rank, O. 1909. *Der Mythus von der Geburt des Helden.* Leipzig and Wien.
Rau, W. 1972. Töpferei und Tongeschirr im vedischen Indien. *AdWL* Mainz Geistes- und sozialwissenschaftliche Kl. 10.
Rawson, Ph. 1973. *Tantra.* London.
RE 1912. *Realencyclopädie der klassischen Alterthumswissenschaft.* VIII, 1. Pauly, A. and Wissowa, G. Stuttgart.
Renou, L. and J. Filliozat 1949. *L'Inde classique I.* Paris.
Renou, L. 1954. *Vocabulaire du rituel védique.* Paris.
Rhys Davids, T.W. 1880. *Buddhist Birth Stories.* London. 2nd rev. edn. by C.A.F. Rhys Davids. Lodon, n.d. (c. 1925).
Roghair, G.H. 1982. *The Epic of Palnāḍu.* Oxford.
Ruben, W. 1944. *Kṛṣṇa.* Istanbul.
Scheftelowitz, I. 1906. *Die Apokryphen des Ṛgveda.* Breslau.
Schlingloff, D. 1962. *Die Religion des Buddhismus I.* Berlin.
Schröter-Kunhardt, M. 1990. Erfahrungen Sterbender während des klinischen Todes. *Zeitschrift für Allgemeinmedizin* 66.
Schubring, W. 1935. *Die Lehre der Jainas.* Leipzig.
Sha, U.P. 1953. Harinegameṣin. *JISOA* XIX: 19–41.
Shrinivas, Doris. 1983. Vedic Rudra-Śiva. *JAOS* 103.3: 543–56.
Siegel, Lee 1987. *Laughing Matters.* Chicago.
Skandapurāṇa 1961. Calcutta.
Sontheimer, G.-D. 1987a. Rudra and Khaṇḍobā: Continuity in Folk Religion. In: *Religion and Society in Mahārāṣṭra.* Edited by M. Israel and N.K. Wagle. Toronto, 1–31.
———. 1987b. The Vana and the Kṣetra. In: *Eschmann Memorial Lectures I.* Edited by G.C. Tripathi and H. Kulke. Bhubaneswar, 117–64.
———. 1989a. *Pastoral Deities in Western India.* New York.
———. 1989b. Between Ghost and God: A Folk Deity of the Deccan. In: *Criminal Gods and Demon Devotees.* Edited by A. Hiltebeitel. Albany, 299–337.

———. 1997. *King of Hunters, Warriors, and Shepherds*. Edited by A. Feldhaus et al. New Delhi.

Spratt, P. 1966. *Hindu Culture and Personality*. Bombay.

Strohl, R. 1984. *The Image of Hero in Jainism*. Chicago University (*non vidi*).

Thapar, Romila 1990. Indian Views of Europe: Representations of the "Other" in History? Ajñeya Commemoration Lecture. Heidelberg.

Thomas, I.J. 1979. Painting in Tamil Nadu A.D. 1350–1650. Ann Arbor (Mich.). Unpublished thesis.

Thomas, W. (n.d., c. 1930). *Hindu Religion. Customs and Manners*. Bombay.

Thompson, St. and J. Balys 1958. *The Oral Tales of India*. Bloomington.

Tripathi, G.C. and H. Kulke (eds.) 1987. *Eschmann Memorial Lectures I*. Bhubaneswar.

Upaniṣatsaṃgraha. 1970. I-II. Delhi (Bombay, 1913).

Vasudevahiṇḍī 1930. Edited by Caturvijaya and Puṇyavijaya. Bhāvanagara.

Viennot, O. 1954. *Le culte de l'arbre dans l'Inde ancienne*. Paris

Viśvabandhu. 1935–45; 1955–61. *A Vedic Word-concordance*. Lahore; Hoshiarpur.

Viyāhapannatti 1974. Edited by B.J. Doshi. Bombay: Mahāvīra Jain Vidyālaya.

Weber, A. 1866. Über ein Fragment der Bhagavatī I. *AdW* Berlin, 367–444.

———. 1867. Id., II. *AdW* Berlin, 155–352.

———. 1878. Über die Siṃhâsanadvātriṃśikā. *Indische Schriften*. 15, 185–455.

———. 1883. Über die heiligen Schriften der Jaina. *Indische Studien*. 16, 211–480.

Widengren, G. 1965. *Die Religionen Irans*. Stuttgart.

Windisch, E. 1908. *Buddha's Geburt und die Lehre von der Seelenwanderung*. Leipzig.

Winternitz, M. 1895. Nejamesha, Naigamesha, Nemeso. *JRAS*: 149–55.

The Hero in Sanskrit Drama[1]

M. CHRISTOPHER BYRSKI

THE root "*nī*" in Sanskrit means to lead, guide, conduct, direct, govern. Its *nomen agentis* "*netṛ*" as also "*nāyaka*" are commonly used to denote a hero in Sanskrit drama. The question that should be asked now is whether this term applies exclusively to the theatre, and means simply the leading role in a performance, or whether it should be associated with the broader cultural context that moulded theatre and determined its intellectual framework.

For, whenever we think about a hero we invariably ask: A hero of what? Naturally, our attitude depends on whether we deal with a hero in soccer, in war, or a hero with regard to renunciation and altruism. Thus, in the course of the present study we shall have to try to answer not only questions that directly concern his looks and behaviour, but also those that pertain to the nature of the involvement that creates a hero. In order to do justice to the needs outlined above we shall first turn our attention to what the dramatists themselves have to say about their heroes. After that, we shall review briefly the opinions of theoreticians and, finally, we shall try to answer the seemingly simple question: What is Sanskrit drama? Or, more precisely, what is the nature of performance in classical Indian theatre, and in what way does it determine the character of the hero? There can be little doubt about the idealistic treatment of the hero by Sanskrit dramatists. He has to be both an ideal lover and an ideal warrior; he must be both tender to his lady-love and tough with his enemies. Generally speaking, he must be the embodiment of all virtues, and a perfect example of manliness and valour. In addition, he must be exceedingly handsome and strong, yet delicate, gifted both for the fine arts and for warfare.

Bhavabhūti makes Sītā in his "Rāma's later history" exclaim when she sees Rāma's picture:

> Lo! Like a newly expanding lotus, dark and soft, tender and fully developed in the charms of his person – (my) father gazing in rapt amazement on his mild and lovely form – the bow of (god) Śaṅkar broken (in twain) with careless ease – the (waving) tufts of hair gracefully adorning (his face) – thus is my noble Lord painted here! (Belvalkar 1915: vol 4, 19f.)

Kālidāsa in turn makes the general in Śakuntalā describe in the following words Duṣyanta naturally underlining his martial features:

> *anavaratadhanurjyāsphālanakrūrapūrvaṁ*
> *ravikiranasahiṣṇu kleśaleśair abhinnam* |
> *apacitam api gātraṃ vyāyatatvād alakṣyam*
> *giricara iva nāgaḥ prāṇasāram bibharti* ||

> Like a mountain-roving elephant, (he) possesses a body the fore part of which is hardened by the incessant friction of the bow-string, which can stand the rays of the sun and is not affected by the slightest fatigue, which, though reduced in bulk, is not noticeable (as such) owing to its muscular development and which is the very essence of strength.
>
> (Gajendragadkar 1920: 36, verse II.4)

Further on it is said that in the eyes of hermit youths he is resplendant (*dīptimat*) and his arms are long like the city gates (literally: the bars of the city gates, *nagaraparigha prāmśubāhuḥ*) (Gajendragadkar 1920: 44f.), and one of the pupils in Kaṇva's hermitage says that there is no need to talk of Duṣyanta aiming his arrows. It is by the mere twang of his bow from afar, as if by the roar of the bow, that he dispels obstacles:

> *kā kathā bāṇasamdhāne jyāśabdenaiva dūrataḥ* |
> *huṃkāreṇaiva dhanuṣaḥ sa hi vighnān apohati* ||
> (Gajendragadkar 1920: 50, verse III.1)

Similarly, Śārṅgarava calls him the foremost of the worthy (*arhatāṃ prāgrasaraḥ*) (Gajendragadkar 1920: 111, verse VI.15). Bhāsa, too, does not stint with regard to superlatives for his hero. For instance, in the *Avimāraka* he puts the following words concerning the prince Avimāraka in the mouth of one of his ministers: "He was a handsome youth, but not conceited; young but modest, brave but courteous, delicate but strong" (Woolner 1930: 66). Still another minister adds: "This form divine, his speech saintly with the brilliance of a warrior, with tenderness and strength."

Speaking about the hero's father, a hero himself, the minister says:

> *vyāyāmasthiravipulocchritāyatāṁso*
> *jyāghātapracitakiṇolbaṇaprakoṣṭhaḥ* |
> *pracchanno 'py anukṛtilakṣyarājabhāvo*
> *meghāntargataravivat prabhānumeyaḥ* ||

> I saw the gentleman, a worthy father of a virtuous son. His shoulders were broad and lofty, huge and firm with exercise; his powerful wrist bears the familiar mark of rubbing on a bowstring. Though in concealment, his appearance proclaims his royal birth. He is like the sun – hidden behind a cloud, but revealed by its radiance.
>
> (Woolner 1930: 68, I.8)

If we add that the beauty of Avimāraka is considered by Vidyādhara to be equal to his own (Woolner 1930: 89), then the picture of the hero as painted by Sanskrit dramatists will almost be complete, though, of course, one can endlessly add epithets, similies, and eulogies. Now, there is one absolutely obvious feature of the description of the hero in Sanskrit drama which must be discussed: departicularisation, or, if one prefers, generalisation. It would be singularly unproductive to search for elements of the hero's picture that would allow the creation of a truly individualised image of the hero. At best, what would emerge from such an attempt would be a sort of 'Bombay oil-print'. There is nothing surprising or unusual about this if we remember that the principle of such generalisation was worked out theoretically by the ancient Indian aestheticians and, later, most pointedly expressed by Abhinavagupta (10th–11th century A.D.). The lack of individual characteristics of the hero is a direct consequence of the fact that whatever happens on the stage must happen in general. Thus, the hero of a given event must represent in himself the pure, refined, not to say distilled essence of valour and charm, which in the course of its dramatic development sheds all characteristics that would link it to a particular person, time, or place. The characterisation of the hero of a Sanskrit drama clearly reflects the musical quality of ancient Indian theatre. The aesthetic impulses, *vibhāva*-s, *anubhāva*-s, and *vyabhicāribhāva*-s, that come from the stage must evoke in the audience a purely emotional response that differs from an emotional response in everyday life by virtue of its being shorn of any particular associations, or any direct connection to the experiences of everyday life. Such an experience is called the essence or *rasa*. Thus, every dramatic role and situation on the stage has an obvious pattern of musical notes and chords that evoke emotional responses, though we can hardly associate them with anything that we know from our everyday audial experiences.

Whatever can be found on the hero in ancient theoretical treatises clearly supports this contention. The earliest among these texts, the *Nāṭya-śāstra*, deals with the topic in chapter XXXIV, verses 17–21 and 23f. (see Ghosh 1956). To a certain extent, the remarks concerning the king (84–88) and the leader of the army (89f.) also apply to the hero; so also the instructions about the distributions of roles that can be found in chapter XXXV, verses 5f., the role of the gods (9ff.), the role of kings (12f.), and the role of army leaders and secretaries. Thus, the *Nāṭya-śāstra* introduces a double category according to which it classifies the hero. Consequently, it discusses four classes: the self-controlled but vehement (*dhīroddhata*), the self-controlled but lighthearted (*dhīralalita*), the self-controlled and exalted (*dhīrodātta*), and the self-controlled and calm (*dhīrapraśānta*). These four classes may be either superior (*uttama*) or middling (*madhyama*). Gods belong to the first class, kings to the second, ministers to the third, and brahmins and merchants to the last. Here too, the *Nāṭya-śāstra* gives a definition of the hero:

> *vyasanī prāptaduḥkho vā yujyate 'bhyudayena yaḥ |*
> *tathā puruṣabāhulye pradhāno nāyakaḥ smṛtaḥ ||*
> *yatrānekasya bhavato vyasanābhyudayau punaḥ |*
> *prakṛṣṭau yasya tau syātāṁ sa bhavet tatra nāyakaḥ ||*
> (XXXV.23,24)

> If there are several male characters in a play, then the one who, though in distress, ultimately attains elevation, is considered the hero. And if there are more than one who (fit such a description), then the one whose misfortune and (subsequent) elevation are prominent should be (deemed) the hero. (Cp. Ghosh 1961: 203)

The hero is clearly classified from the point of view of his role in generating emotional responses. Though different categories of this principal character of the play are defined, no scope is given to any further individualisation of the hero. Applying a musical analogy, it can be said that this definition determines the key in which the dramatic role should be played or acted. It simply connects the state of being a hero to the specific predicament that most obviously creates a hero. A more detailed definition of one of the four classes, i.e. the *dhīralalita* one, does not adduce anything that would cause us to modify essentially the opinion we have formed so far. Here is what the *Nāṭya-śāstra* has to say on the subject:

> The king should be: intelligent, truthful, master of his senses, clever, and of good character, he should possess a good memory, be powerful, high-minded, and pure, be farsighted, possess people, be an expert in the methods of various works, he should be alert, without carelessness, he should associate with old people, be well versed in the *Artha-śāstra* and in the practice of policies, he should be a promoter of the various arts and crafts, be an expert in the science of polity, and should have a liking for (all) this. (In addition), he should know his real situation, prosperity and decline, the weaknesses of his enemies, the principles of *dharma*, and he should be free of evil habits. (NS 34, 84–88; cp. Ghosh 1961: 211)

Similar descriptions can be found in the *Artha-śāstra* and the *Manu-smṛti*. An exhaustive review of what other ancient theoreticians have to say on the subject has been undertaken by S.N. Shastri (1961: 203–210).

Following the *Daśarūpaka* of Dhanañjaya (10th century A.D.), Shastri adds three classes of the *dhīralalita*-hero (1961: 207): gallant (*dakṣiṇa*), deceitful (*śaṭha*), and bold (*dhṛṣṭa*). Following Dhanañjaya as well as some other authorities, Shastri lists the eight personal merits of the hero (1961: 209): beauty of character (*śobha*), vivacity of character (*vilāsa*), sweetness (*mādhurya*), mental equilibrium (*gāmbhīrya*), steadfastness (*dhairya* or *sthairya*), brilliance (*tejas*), affability (*lālitya*), and magnanimity (*audārya*). This appears to exhaust all that the theoreticians have to say about their hero. When we add that the roles of heroes should be played by "actors of the best kind who have beautiful eyes, eyebrows, forehead, nose, lips, cheeks, face, neck, and other beautiful limbs, who are tall, possessed of pleasant appearance, dignified gait, and are neither fat nor lean, are well-behaved, wise, and steady by nature ..." (*NŚ* 35, 9–1; cp. Ghosh 1956: 215) the picture becomes almost complete. We must say almost, because in actual theatrical practice – known to us from the surviving classical theatre of Kerala, the Kūṭiyaṭṭam – the costume and make-up of a hero is strictly conventionalized and unchangeable. Thus, it would have obliterated all individualistic traits that may have persisted, making the analogy to a musical score fully pertinent.

At this point we may ask ourselves if the description of the hero in Sanskrit drama that has been offered above, and which boils down to underlining his basic function as an appropriate impulse to evoke a suitable emotional response called the essence (*rasa*) is all that can be said about him. Technically speaking this may be so. But, on the other hand, it would leave outside the purview of our investigation the nature of theatre and its interpretation according to the basic notions of the traditional Indian *Weltanschauung*. Since the hero in Sanskrit drama is our main consideration here we shall limit ourselves to a very brief presentation of conclusions that have been worked out in detail elsewhere.

"Theatre is the nature of the world with its happiness and despair, endowed with the actor's fourfold means of expression" (*NŚ* I.121). This nature of the world is nothing more and nothing less than the sacrifice (*yajña*). What is *yajña?* The one-without-second (*ekam eva advitīyam*) becomes many for the sake of creation and, in turn, the many of creation strive for merger into the one, i.e. for liberation (*mokṣa*). One of the innumerable participants in this eternal sacrifice is the desiring subject and the desired object – the hero and the object of his desire, i.e. the heroine. And as the *yajña* of yore was accomplished in the teeth of opposition from the *asura-rākṣasa*-s with whom the gods waged incessant war (*daivāsuram*), so this *nāṭyavedamahāsattra* – as Abhinavagupta would have it, or this *kāntaḥ kratuḥ cakṣuṣām* of Kālidāsa is also carried to its fruition in the contest and strife inherent in the predicament that creates a hero. Before we carry the argument further let us return for a moment to the dramatist and hear how Kālidāsa makes the heroine and her companion speak about King Purūravas, the hero of the *Vikramorvaśīyam*. When she regains her senses and opens her eyes she says: "Was it great Indra who saved me having seen the supernatural power?" Her friend Citralekhā answers: "Not great Indra but the royal sage Purūravas, who is like Indra in his prowess." Later on Citraratha will say to Purūravas about Urvaśī that she was previously created by Nārāyaṇa for Indra and that now she has been rescued from the hands of the demon by you (Purūravas), his friend:

> *purā Nārāyaṇeneyam atiṣṛṭā Marutvate* |
> *daityahastād apācchidya suhṛdā samprati tvayā* ||
> (Kālidāsa, *Vikramorvaśīya*, I.14)

We have quoted this passage because it seems to paint unmistakeably the *daivāsuram* conflict as the prime source of inspiration. And justifiably so, because chapter I of the *Nāṭya-śāstra* mentions *daivāsuram* as the subject of the first, or 'première' performance (*yathā daitya suraiḥ jitāḥ*) and makes Indra the patron deity of the hero and Sarasvatī of the heroine. Indra is indeed the uncontestable hero of the *daivāsuram* conflict. Nothing, therefore, prevents us from believing that Indra was also the chief hero of the first performance, which, as we remember, was a representation of the victory of the gods over the *asura*-s. Thus, the association of Indra and *nāyaka* in each subsequent performance, which, in a way, is always a representation of some or other manifestation of the universal conflict between the gods and the *asura*-s, needs no further comment for the time being. It is Sarasvatī, who in this particular association seems to be something of a mystery. Yet, the moment we consider her presence in the *Nāṭya* in the light of her brahmanical association with Indra, the mystery becomes apparent.

If the dating of the antiquity of the kernel of the first *adhyāya* of the *Nāṭya-śāstra* is accepted as the middle of the first millennium B.C., then there can be little doubt about the identity of the Sarasvatī of the *Nāṭya-śāstra* with the brahmanical goddess of the same name.[2] The association of our Sarasvatī with Indra makes the possibility of her being directly identical with the river Sarasvatī remote, since it is difficult to detect any meaningful relationship between Indra and this river goddess. This fact makes the idea of the existence of any *Ṛgved*-ic source of this association also very improbable since, as Macdonell puts it "there is nothing to show distinctly that Sarasvatī is ever anything more in the *Ṛg-veda* than a river goddess, and even then her only association comes through vāc" (Macdonell 1897: 87). The post-*Brāhmaṇa* association of Indra and Sarasvatī is also negligible and overshadowed by the unusual relationship of that goddess with her father, Brahmā (see Hopkins 1915: 53). Thus, the goddess Sarasvatī of the *Brāhmaṇa*-s, who is usually identified with Vāc[3] appears to be identical with the goddess Sarasvatī of the *Nāṭya-śāstra*.

The *Śatapatha-brāhmaṇa* has the following passages:

> Now the gods and the Asuras, both of them sprung from Prajāpati, entered upon their father Prajāpati's inheritence: the gods came in for Mind and the Asuras for Speech. Thereby, the gods came in for the sacrifice and the Asuras for Speech; the gods for yonder (heaven) and the Asuras for this (earth). The gods said to the *Yajña* (m. the sacrifice): "That *Vāk* (f. speech) is a woman; beckon her, and she will certainly call thee to her ... Say to her: 'Come hither to me where I stand' and report to us her having come saying: 'She has indeed come'." The gods then cut her off from the Asuras; and having gained possession of her and enveloped her completely in fire, they offered her up as a holocaust, it being an offering of the gods. And in that they offered her with an *anuṣṭubh* verse, thereby they made her their own; and the Asuras being deprived of Speech were undone crying "*He lavaḥ, he lavaḥ!*"
>
> (*ŚB*, 3.2.1.18–23)

"They (*Āditya*-s?) brought Vāc (speech) to them (*Aṅgirasas*) for their sacrificial fee. They accepted her

> not, saying: 'We shall be losers if we accept her' ... Now Vāc was angry with them: 'In what respect, forsooth, is that one (*Sūrya*) better than I? Wherefore is it that they should have accepted him and not me?' So, she went away from them. Having become a lioness she went on seizing upon (everything) between those two contending parties, the gods and the Asuras ... Being willing to go over to the side of the gods, she said: 'What would be mine if I were to come over to you?' 'The offering will reach thee even before (it reaches) *Agni*.' She then said to the gods: 'Whatsover blessing you will invoke through me, shall be accomplished unto you.' So, she went over to the gods".
>
> (*ŚB*, 3.5.1.18–22)

Probably, on the strength of these and similar passages, Keith concluded that speech forms a ground of contest between the gods and the *asura*-s. But the gods finally win her (Keith 1925). Thus, the *daivāsuram* wars are fought among others also for the possession of Speech. The question now arises: What has made Speech so important that the gods deemed it worthwhile to fight the *asura*-s for her sake?

The *Śatapatha-brāhmaṇa* quotes the following *mantra* of the *Vājasaneyī* (V.14) and *Ṛg-veda* (V.18.1) *saṃhitā*-s: "They harness the mind and they harness the thought." The *Śatapatha-brāhmaṇa* offers the following gloss on this passage:

> "With the mind and with speech they truly perform the sacrifice. When he says 'They harness the mind', he harnesses the mind; and when he says 'and they harness the thoughts', *dhī*, either by reciting the Veda, or by readiness of speech, or by songs, – with those two thus harnessed – they perform the sacrifice".
>
> (*ŚB*, 3.5.3.11)

Still elsewhere the *Śatapatha-brāhmaṇa* will say:

> "That same fire, then, they have kindled (thinking): 'In it, when kindled we will sacrifice to the gods'. In it, indeed, he makes these first two oblations 'to Mind and Speech (or Voice)'. For, Mind and Speech when

> yoked together convey the sacrifice to the gods. Now what is performed (with formulas pronounced) in a low voice, by that the mind conveys the sacrifice to the gods; and what is performed (with formulas) distinctly uttered by speech, by that the speech conveys the sacrifice to the gods. And thus takes place here a twofold performance whereby he gratifies these two thinking: 'gratified and pleased these two shall convey the sacrifice to the gods'."
>
> (*ŚB*, 1.4.4.1–2)

But finally, who are these two and what is their connection with our subject? As an answer to this query we shall once more quote a passage from the *Śatapatha-brāhmaṇa*: "Indra, assuredly, is the mind, and Sarasvatī is speech ..." (*ŚB*, 13.9.1.13). Thus, the sacrifice cannot be accomplished without Indra and Sarasvatī. Because as Mind and Speech they are interdependent, for with Mind one sets Speech in motion, with Speech set in motion by Mind he provides the oblation for the gods (Keith 1920: 138). The communion between Indra (Mind) and Sarasvatī (Speech) is so close that the *Kauṣītaki-brāhmana* actually identifies Indra with Speech (Keith 1920: 354).

The meaning of the association of Indra and Sarasvatī with the hero and heroine of *Nāṭya* now becomes abundantly clear. Every performance is a *daivāsuram* conflict in its course and a sacrifice in its meaning. In every performance, therefore, the union of a *nāyaka* with a *nayikā* is as substantial as the union of Indra with *Vāc-Sarasvatī*, which, being brought about through the victory over the demons in the *daivāsuram* struggle, is an integral part of every sacrifice.[4]

Nāṭya was created in the likeness of the sacrifice, its heroes and heroines in the likeness of Indra and Sarasvatī. What it has to convey to men is the truth, the entire and exact truth, about the nature of the world.

We may, therefore, conclude now and try to answer the questions that have been formulated at the outset of this enquiry. A hero of Sanskrit drama is actually called a leader because, on the one hand, he is a sort of leading 'tone' of an audio-visual composition (*dṛśyam, śravyam*) that every *nāṭyaprayoga* is. In his other incarnation as the Mind-Indra yoked together with Speech-Sarasvatī he conducts this delightful sacrifice for the eyes through its course of the five *sandhi*-s to its fulfilment when the desiring subject and the desired object become one-without-the-second, bestowing upon the *sahṛdaya* the essence of wonder (*adbhuta rasa*).

NOTES

1 The present paper is a slightly re-edited version of my original paper, which has been published as ch. IX of Byrski, Ch., *Methodology of the Analysis of Sanskrit Drama*, Delhi etc. 1997.

2 This and the following remarks were made by me for the first time in Byrski 1974.

3 *Śatapatha-brāhmaṇa* (hereafter *ŚB*), 4.5.8.10, 5.2.2.13f., 5.3.4.25, 5.3.8., 7.5.1.31, 11.2.4.9, 2.6.3, 13.1.8.5, 14.2.1.15; see also Keith 1920: XLV, 153, 264, 371, 405, 417, 426.

4 The intimate relationship between Indra and *Vāc-Sarasvatī* allows us to take her as being identical with *Indrāṇī*. Both *Sarasvatī* and *Indrāṇī* are identified with Vāc (Macdonell 1904: 51ff. [II.72ff.]). Both are associated with the Maruts (Macdonell 1904: 78). Besides, Indrāṇī seems to have had a rather meagre independent existence. Her name appears to be a simple epithet of the wife of Indra (ibid.). If we admit such a possibility in spite of the lack of any specific identification of the two, then a *Ṛgved*-ic hymn about Indra, Indrāṇī, and Vṛṣākapi (*RV* 10.72, Macdonell 1897: 153ff.) can acquire some meaning for *Nāṭya*. Consequently, it may not be altogether unjustified to suppose that there is some kind of relationship between Vṛṣākapi and Vidūṣaka. Both are the hero's (or Indra's) beloved friends. Both incur the anger of the hero's partner (Indrāṇī, the heroine). Finally, both are compared to the monkey. This would give a new strength to the hypothesis made almost half a century ago by Gawronski (1946: 30ff.) that Vṛṣākapi is a prototype of the Vidūsaka.

REFERENCES

Belvalkar, S.K. (tr.). 1915. *Rāma's Later History, or Uttara-rāma-caritam.* Harvard University Press.

Byrski, M. Christopher. 1974. *Concept of Ancient Indian Theatre.* Delhi: Munshiram Manoharlal.

Devadhar, C.R. (ed., tr.). 1966. *Vikramorvaśīyam* of Kālidāsa. Crit. edn. with Intr., Notes, Transl. & Appendices. 2nd rev. ed. Delhi: Motilal Banarsidass.

Gajendragadkar, S.D. (ed., tr.). 1920. *The Abhijñāna-śākuntala of Kālidāsa.* Bombay.

Gawronski A. 1946 *Poczatki Dramatu Indyjskiego a Sprawa Wpĩywów Greckich.* Krakow.

Ghosh, Manomohan (ed.). 1956. *Nāṭya-śāstra.* Calcutta.

———. (tr.). 1961. *The Nāṭya-śāstra.* Calcutta.

Hopkins, Edward Washburn. 1915. *Epic Mythology.* Straßburg. (new edition: Delhi 1974).

Keith, Arthur Berriedale (tr.). 1920. *The Ṛg-veda-brāhmaṇas: The Aitareya- and Kauṣītaki-brāhmaṇas of the Rigveda.* Harvard Oriental Series, 25. Cambridge, Mass.

———. 1925. *The Religion and Philosophy of the Vedas and the Upanishads.* Harvard Oriental Series, 31–32. Cambridge, Mass.

Macdonell, Arthur Anthony. 1897. *Vedic Mythology.* (Grundriß der Indo-Arischen Philologie und Altertumskunde). Straßburg.

———. (ed., tr.). 1904. *Bṛhad-devatā Attributed to Śaunaka.* Vols. V, VI. Harvard Oriental Series. Cambridge Mass.

Shastri, S.N. 1961. *The Laws and Practice of Sanskrit Drama.* Varanasi.

Woolner, A.C. and L. Sarup 1930. *Thirteen Plays of Bhāsa.* Punjab University Oriental Publications. (rpt.: New Delhi 1985).

Hanumān Mahāvīrasvāmī

The Mountain Hero in a Plains Village

Ian Duncan

It might be proposed as a methodological principle that any deity of either totally animal or mixed human-animal characteristics is likely to have very archaic roots. Arguably, the two best known and most widely worshipped deities of this type in India are the elephant-headed Gaṇeśa and the divinised monkey Hanumān. The antiquity of Gaṇeśa has been thoroughly discussed by Courtright (1985). It was in the process of coming to understand the cult of Hanumān in a peasant village in central India, of unfolding the layers of practice, and of the popular, literary and cultic conceptions about the deity, that some of the marvellously complex and archaic features of this figure came to be revealed.

The intensive study of the development of the cult of a Hindu deity, of the practice of its worship and the varied conceptions held by the believers, is one way of acquiring some grasp on the elusive and seemingly ungraspable phenomenon of Hinduism. What follows is not an exhaustive study of Hanumān, but the presentation and analysis of ethnographic data from central India, supplemented by comparative data from other regions, in order to throw some light upon the particular features of Hanumān's heroic nature.[1]

Hanumān is of course most widely known in contemporary India for his exploits in helping Rāma rescue Sītā from the captivity of Rāvaṇa, for his miraculous feats of bridge-building, mountain-carrying, reviving the stricken Lakṣmaṇa and so on, and thus for his rôle as an exemplar of the *dāsya-bhāva* mode of *bhakti*. Indeed, it is mainly for this example and these deeds that he is explicitly remembered and glorified in the evening hymn-singing sessions and recitations from the *Rāmcaritmānas* of Tulsīdās, so popular with the villagers of central India. As Allchin points out, Hanumān was Rāma's messenger (and hence his suitability for carrying Tulsīdās' message to Rāma in the *Viṇayapatrikā*); he was also a bold warrior, worthy of the poet's admiration, and he was "the pattern of the ideal servant of the ideal Master" (Tulsīdās 1966: 50).

However, if we turn from such devotional conceptions to the data of ethnography, a very different, and older, Hanumān emerges, as Jacobi (1913: 661) suggested. Thus, throughout his works William Crooke (e.g. 1909, 1912, 1926) described him as the ape godling, a mighty warrior, a magician, a grammarian, a herbalist, a creator of hills, a giver of offspring, a wrestler, a curer of snake bites, a controller of weather, a protector of villages, a caster-out of evil spirits, a doorkeeper, the consort of the Earth Mother, and the ancestor of some Rājpūt clans and some tribal peoples – and we can add other qualities from other sources: a curer of smallpox and cattle disease, the god of strength and swiftness, the faithful servant of Rāma, the immortally young celibate, the destroyer of Rāvaṇa's capital, and the guardian of mountain passes.

Clearly, Hanumān is an extremely complex figure, in both conception and practice. Wolcott has draw our attention to the cult of Hanumān in the Bhojpurī-speaking regions of eastern Uttar Pradesh and western Bihar, and, after surveying Hanumān's rôle as Rāma-*bhakta*, comments that

> it appears that Hanumān is a popular figure because of his place in the *Rāmāyaṇa*, and that his significance derives from the fact that he is a *bhakta* (a religious server) of Rāma. But these conclusions do not square with folk religion and stories, or with popular use of the epic poem. For example, in the *Rāmāyaṇa*, Hanumān's *bhakti* is expressed in passionate and thrilling terms; however, it is referred to only a third as many times as is that of Bharat (a half-brother to Rāma) and Sītā (Rāma's wife), and much less frequently than that of the devoted half-brother Lakṣmaṇ. These three are the leading exemplars of *bhakti* to Rāma, according to Tulsīdās. Nevertheless, they are not quoted or sung about among the masses

> who recite the *Rāmāyaṇa*; only Hanumān receives such attention. Unlike them, Hanumān has a firmly fixed folkloric position, even apart from his rôle in the *Rāmāyaṇa*. (Wolcott 1978: 655)

Furthermore, in this region not only are there more shrines and temples to Hanumān than to Rāma and Sītā, Hanumān often appears in Śiva shrines, not, like Gaṇeśa, as a doorway figure, but standing to the right of the Śiva-*liṅga*, balancing the image of Kālī on the left of the *liṅga* (ibid.: 656). Worshippers will rub his image with oil and vermilion or red ochre, which are said to be pleasing to him. "The color of his strong body is likened to vermilion-colored stones which are considered effective for crushing giants" (ibid.). Hanumān is regarded as a protector. The *Hanumān-Cālīsā* "Forty Verses of Hanumān" is recited as a protective or talismanic prayer, mantras "invoking the name of Hanumān, the red-bodied hero, are used to exorcise demons or to gain power over enemies" (ibid.). Popularly named Mahāvīr-jī "Great Hero", stories are told of his conception and birth, of his leaps in the sky, his mighty feats and enormous size, and his ability to change shape. Most popular with these Bhojpurī hero-worshippers are the stories in the *Rāmcaritmānas* about his acts of leadership, his ability to change form, his great strength, his leap across the ocean, his defeat of a female ocean demon, and so on. He is worshipped for bodily strength and virility, to ward off ghosts, spirits of the dead and other diabolic influences. Wolcott emphasises that he is not relevant to any desire for *mokṣa* or liberation, he is no model for a subservient people, nor for religious fidelity. He is not worshipped by women for barrenness (a feature noted by Crooke (1926: 175) in regions further west).[2] He is a man's god. And finally Wolcott notes his association with Śiva. Bhojpurī folk tales even imply that Hanumān is the son of Śiva,[3] allowing Marut, the wind god, who is conventionally taken as Hanumān's father, more of a foster-father kind of a rôle.

I wish now to describe those aspects of his cult that I was able to record in Jamnā Kheṛā (a pseudonym), a village in Bundelkhaṇḍ, a region southwest of Bhojpur and just to the north of Maharashtra.[4]

Most popularly known in the region as Mahāvīr, Mahāsvāmī, Bajrangbalī or Hanumān Bābā, he possesses two shrines in Jamnā

Kheṛā. The first is relatively new and unimportant. It is found on the stream at the border of the village with Candrapur, a larger village with a bus-stop on the main road, and consists of a large rocky platform, the deity being represented by a large red-painted stone. It was gradually built up by passing children, on their way to and from school in Candrapur, and has become fully operational. Wedding parties passing may offer coconuts at the same time as offering them to Kṣetrapati, "Master of the Fields", the deity of the village boundaries located nearby. Because of the association by name with Mahāvīr, the founder of Jainism, Jain as well as Hindu schoolboys, bow down before it to show their respect. However, at this shrine, there is no cult as extensive as that at the other shrine, which is located within the village. This main shrine stands about fifteen feet high from the ground to the top of the dome and is surrounded by a paved platform. Inside is a wooden image of Hanumān about nine inches high, the deity being represented in relief in the usual rampant position, a mace in his hand and his tail over his head. This rests against a large stone, and both are red from constant applications of vermilion.

He is worshipped regularly by many villagers, many of whom fast in his name on Tuesdays and Saturdays. At their midday meal they eat only *phalāhār*, which includes such fruit and vegetables with red flesh as tomato, pomegranate, papaya, carrot, oranges, etc. plus sago and sweets made of boiled milk. The fast ends in the evening after worshipping the deity. However, as Hanumān is a *brahmacārī* or a celibate, people refrain from sexual relations during these two nights. Those who observe this fast regularly, usually observe Hanumān Jayanti on Cait Bright 13 (April), a festival otherwise not widely observed in this region. Some people may offer Hanumān water after their daily bath, some may recite Tulsīdās' *Rāmcaritmānas* on Tuesdays, and for some time there was a regular hymn session or *rāmdhun* "Rām chant" as it was called on Tuesday evenings in the Grām Pañcāyat office, in which many villagers participated, until, for factional reasons, it ceased. Some may worship Hanumān for astrological reasons, primarily to counteract the inauspicious influence of Saturn. Sometimes the worship of Hanumān on Tuesdays may be more elaborate if this coincides with any other important event. Thus a public reading of the *Bhāgavat Purāṇa*, lasting several days, sponsored by one of the villagers, came to an end on a Tuesday; after a large sacrifice or *havan* at the village temple where the reading had taken place, the whole crowd moved in procession singing *bhajans* (hymns), and accompanied by drums, to Hanumān's shrine for another, though smaller, *havan*. *Pūjā* was performed by a village Brāhmaṇ and a wandering Rāmānandī devotee of Hanumān who happened to be in the village at the time.

This concludes the description of the regular worship of Hanumān and so we now turn to other aspects of his cult. Firstly, then, Hanumān is a controller of weather. Crooke gives a very interesting description of this:

> the Gārpagārī, or 'white hail scarer', in the Central Provinces, when a storm is threatened implores Mahābīr-Hanumān, the ape godling, to disperse the clouds. If this appeal fails, he proceeds to threats, declaring that he will kill himself, and throws off his clothes. If her husband happens to be absent at this critical time, his wife goes to the shrine of Hanumān and stands naked before his image, Hanumān being one of the chief village guardians and the giver of fertility. In former times the Gārpagārī used to slash and cut himself before the shrine, but now the utmost he does is to draw blood from his finger. (1926: 75)

This is a good example of the use of "shock tactics" in worship, to compel the deity to do one's bidding. Being a celibate, Hanumān's reaction to a naked woman would certainly be quite strong, and presumably he would do her will immediately to get her out of his sight. The following is a Bundelkhaṇḍī folk-song to Hanumān for stilling a storm (collected by Dr B.P. Tiwari of the University of Saugar):

> *pavana ke Hanumata he rakhavāre*
> *āndhī behaṭa ko bandha karata hai*
> *dīlana kāja savāre*
> *pavana ke Hanumata he rakhavāre*
> *hamāre Hanumata Bābā aise garajata hai*
> *jaise Indara akhāḍe*
> *pavana ke Hanumata hai rakhavāre*

which may be translated as: "Hanumān is the guardian of the winds, he stops heavy dust storms, and fulfils all our undertakings.

Our Hanumān Bābā roars like Indra's court. Hanumān is the guardian of the winds". Crooke also records rituals of compulsion for the sake of fertility: "those who are barren go to the shrine at dawn, strip themselves naked and embrace him" (op. cit.: 175).

Secondly, Hanumān may be worshipped in connection with curing diseases in both men and animals. One instance is recorded from a neighbouring village where smallpox had attacked several people. The villagers gathered at Hanumān's shrine at night to sing hymns to the goddess. The usual term for smallpox is *Mātā* or *Mātābāī*, meaning "mother", a name for Devī, and so it is she to whom one would expect the prayers to be addressed, but the association of Hanumān with the goddess is something we shall meet again. During the course of the disease the village women would offer water to a stone under a *peepal* tree at a nearby river, and in Hanumān's shrine, after their daily bath. In the same village a man of the Kāchī (Market gardener) caste specialised in curing *baikharā*, a cattle disease. The owner of a sick beast would provide sweets, a coconut and ghee, and the Market gardener would arrange a *baiṭhak* or gathering for hymn-singing at Hanumān's shrine to exorcise the illness. (I am grateful to Shri C.S. Rajput of the Department of Anthropology, University of Saugar, for these data.)

Thirdly, Hanumān is worshipped during the Navarātri ceremonies associated with the worship of the goddess Durgā, and this aspect of his cult draws attention to his association with monkeys, and hence trees. On the first of these nine nights, wheat is sown in small earthenware pots; it is then tended throughout the observations. When the latter come to an end the sprouted seeds are examined to see how the crops will do. In the Sagar District Gazetteer we read: "the wheat which is sown in Kuā̃r (the autumn month of Āśvina or September-October) gives a forecast of the spring crops. A plant is pulled out, and the return crop will be the same number of times the seed as its roots" (Russell 1906a: 45). At the time the pots of seedlings are prepared the person looking after them puts aside a separate portion known as the *langare-kī gẽd* (literally "the monkey's ball"). The usual mixture of earth and manure is poured onto a cloth and the wheat seeds are sown there. This may be gathered up and hung on a wall near the pots or placed on a small slabstone known as a *bajarsil*. A *sil* is the stone on which spices are ground with a stone muller, *bajar* is derived from the Sanskrit *vajra* "diamond", so the *bajarsil* is a stone as hard as a diamond. Further, one of Hanumān's names is Bajrang, meaning "he with a body as hard as diamond". The "monkey's ball" is offered to Hanumān when the seedlings are taken out, but not at his own shrine. Instead, it is tied to a *peepal* tree above the shrine of Kher Buḍhī, the village goddess (literally "Village Old Woman"). Thus it may be interpreted as an offering to Hanumān to prevent either his arboreal kinsmen or hail from damaging the crop. Both interpretations may be drawn from the possible meanings of *bajarsil*, though the first seems more likely. (See Mayer 1960: 99–103 for a description of similar observations with seedlings.)

Hanumān's rôle as a guardian of the village emerges in the above material. Russell has called him an "averter of calamities" (1960: 50). Writing about Malwa, Mathur (1964: 86) says, "He is one of those deities whose worship is very popular with villagers of all castes. He is worshipped by the offering of a coconut on most festival days and in times of distress and trouble". Crooke calls him a village guardian, and says that his image is found guarding the entrances of towns and villages (1926: 175) (note that the schoolchildren's shrine is at the village boundary). And G.S. Ghurye records that in rural Deccan the fourteenth-century poet-saint Namdev "says that the Hanumanta of a deserted village is incompetent and useless. He implies (1) that in the Deccan villages of his time Hanumān was a deity put up in almost every village as its protector; (2) that He could be a potent force in a village which was in a flourishing condition" (Ghurye 1962: 231–32). Babb (1970: 146–48) makes a passing though valuable reference to Hanumān in the context of a discussion of sexual complementarity among deities in Chhattīsgaṛh. He argues that a local male protective figure, Ṭhākur Deo, is subordinate to the village goddess, who is considered to be a dangerous figure. Similarly to Ghurye (op. cit.: 238–63), he argues that the goddess fills a rôle on both Sanskritic and non-Sanskritic levels, and that Hanumān also does so, inasmuch as there are signs that he is becoming more popular than Ṭhākur Deo as a protective god in that region. Chhattīsgaṛh is not Bundelkhaṇḍ, but there is enough similarity in the religious life of the two regions, as shown by Babb, for us to appreciate this change, and note particularly the implied association with the goddess. Other examples of this association with the goddess will be given below.

In Jamnā Kheṛā Hanumān is most specifically worshipped for peace in, and the protection of, the village, on the day of Nāg Pañcamī in July-August. It is this association of Hanumān with the snake, *nāg*, that forms one of the most significant aspects of his cult met hitherto. The observance takes place in the morning, when the villagers individually worship Nāg Dev, "Snake God", either at their houses or at a snake-hole in the fields. All work involving the soil ceases for the day. In the afternoon a large crowd assembles on the verandah of a house belonging to a Market gardener. After a few hymns have been sung, the wooden image of Hanumān is brought from the village shrine. It is placed on a low wooden seat, a ghee lamp is set in front of it, and it is worshipped by the temple priest. Many offerings are presented: small *purīs* or deep-fried bread rounds, ghee, camphor, scent, incense, a folded betel leaf with five cloves in it, cardamom, crystallised sugar, *peṛā* (sweets made from condensed milk), coconut, vermilion and flowers. After this, many other villagers worship the god. The expressed purpose of the worship was that peace should remain within the village, but all those who worshipped Hanumān and chanted were those who knew his *mantra*, and on this occasion they were recharging or awakening it. Now this *mantra* is mainly used to cure snake bites. It was described by the temple priest as a *jantā mantra* ("popular" *mantra*), and is known by many people, including Brāhmaṇs. In this it contrasts with those *mantras* known by *guniyās*,[5] who are usually not Brāhmaṇs. Apart from curing snake bites, it may be used for medical treatment – the various septic swellings that people get are often relieved by them. The practitioner usually works by placing cow dung ash in his hand, saying the *mantra* over it, moving his finger in the ash in various patterns, and then applying it to the afflicted spot.

Curing snake bites, however, is considerably more elaborate. According to the temple priest, Hanumān is a hero among heroes, so that one who possesses his *mantra* has great power. Now, when a snake bites someone, he said, he does not really die, rather his *prāṇa*, his vital energy or life force, goes to a psychic centre, the *brahmāṇḍ* (this was the word used by the informant, though presumably he meant *brahmarandhra*[6]), at the top of his head, and he simply appears dead. Thus a man who "dies" of a snake bite should not be cremated but buried. After the snake has bitten someone, the practitioner, by the great power of his *mantra*, will call the actual snake back, and ask him why he bit his victim. When the snake tells him the reason, the practitioner will ask him to excuse that person and let him "live", whereupon the snake may demand some compensation, some offerings in worship. If the snake accepts the man's guarantee, he will put his fangs back in the wound and drawn the poison out of the victim. The practitioner may then stipulate some sort of ceremony in honour of Hanumān – for instance, the person may be instructed to hold a *baiṭhak* with offerings worth, say, five to ten rupees. The practitioner himself cannot eat any of these offerings, otherwise his *mantra* would become worthless. When he has cured someone, the practitioner will prescribe certain rules. He ties a band of grass around the person's neck with a number of knots in it representing the days within which the "patient" must hold the *baiṭhak* and distribute the food offerings. The person may not leave the village until he has completed this, otherwise his *prāṇa* will go back to his "*brahmāṇḍ*", and he will "die".

Thus the following aspects of Hanumān are prominent locally: the counteracter of bad astrological influences, the protector of crops from bad weather and stiller of storms, the healer of sickness in man and cattle, the protector of crops from monkeys, the guardian of the village and its entrance and the curer of snake bites. There is also the aspect of Hanumān as the devoted servant of Rām, which is recalled at the weekly feasts and Hanumān Jayantī, where chanting and hymn-singing and the reading of the *Rāmcaritmānas* take place. In tracing out the different associations of Hanumān, we are able to see how several elements have blended into this one composite figure.

Firstly, there is his association with hail and with the Navarātri observations. Hanumān is the son of the wind, Marut, whence his name Mārutī, and he is the half-brother of Bhīmsen by the same father. Ghurye says that "the two great services for which Hanumān has always been liked, respected and also venerated are first, his flight to Lanka and bringing full information about Sita and Rama and His helpers; second, his lifting up a portion of a distant mountain on which alone was to be found a particularly efficacious herb and bringing it to the battlefield in Lanka where Lakshmana was lying unconscious" (1962: 227). Here then we have three important aspects – Hanumān's ability to fly, his ability to lift mountains, and his knowledge of curative herbs. We have already described his connection, albeit not entirely direct, with healing the diseases of man and beast, and we shall return to this later. Meanwhile it is Hanumān's flight which concerns us. It is reasonable to assume that being the son of a deity connected with the air he would possess this ability. He is not a terrestrial figure, and of course the fact that monkeys, like birds, spend a great deal of their life above the ground, leaping from one tree to another, is of special relevance here. Thus an aërial deity may easily be considered to have powers over aërial conditions, namely the weather, and hence be asked to control it. It may be noted, however, that his specific relationship with the weather is that of controlling hail and storms, and not that of bringing rain (he was not invoked in village ceremonies to ask for rain)[7]: there is nothing "watery" about him, and this will be seen to be related to other aspects of him. In describing the *langare-kī gẽd* we concluded that it was an offering to Hanumān, as monkey god, to prevent his clan's depredations of the village crops.

Bhīmsen is also present in Jamnā Kheṛā. He is located in a small shrine, consisting of a platform under a peepul tree in a vegetable garden belonging to a man of the Market gardener caste. On the platform are representations of three deities: a large stone on the right represents Bhīmsen, who is more popularly known as Siddha Bābā in the village, a smaller stone in the centre represents Janglī Guru ("jungly teacher"), and a small trident, a pair of tongs[8] and a stone covered with vermilion represent Juvālā.

The shrine was built by the informant. He related that the idea had come to him in his sleep – he got up and came to the tree where he woke up, having had some sort of revelation that he should build the shrine. He said that for some time his mind had been bad but that after the revelation in his sleep he had become normal. He now acts as the priest of the shrine.

Historically Bhīmsen is ubiquitous. Verrier Elwin writes:

> The cultus of Bhimsen is strange and interesting. Originally one of the five Pandava brothers, he has been selected out of the entire body of Hindu legend for special honour by the aboriginal tribes. To the Baigas, he is the god of rain. To the Goṇḍs, he is

> the embodiment of manly strength. He is associated mainly with rocks, mountains and rivers. Not far from Karanjia are two hills on each side of the valley. The story is that Bhimsen, carrying a *cowar* (a pole laid across the shoulders, from either end of which hangs a basket for carrying loads) like any Goṇḍ, was walking up the valley, grew tired and dumped his two great loads on either side, whereupon they turned into the two hills, Dhuti and Lingo. (Elwin 1958: 183)

The rest of the entry records Bhīmsen's exploits in altering rivers, creating hills etc., and a rôle in the Bhīmā (a sub-tribe of Goṇḍs) creation story not unlike that of Atlas. Crooke says he has become "the chief rain-god in the Central Provinces" (1926: 70). The Gonds celebrate a festival in his name, the Parjās worship him by pouring water on his image for rain. The Gonds offer he-goats and chickens to him on Tuesdays and Saturdays (ibid.: 176) (note that these two days are widely observed as dedicated to Hanumān). Elsewhere Crooke gives a rather ethnocentric description of Bhīmsen's image: "He is generally adored under the forms of an unshapely stone covered with vermilion or of two pieces of wood standing from three to four feet out of the ground, which are probably connected with the phallic idea towards which so many of these deities often diverge [*sic*]" (1896: 90). He indicates that Bhīmsen is connected with Gorakhnāth, the "patron saint" of yogis and *siddhas*, in legends about the Himālayas, and points out that he is a brother, in fact a half-brother, of Hanumān. Both deities are sons of the wind, *vāyu-putra*, so that much of what is said about Bhīmsen here could be said about Hanumān.

Of the two other deities at Bhīmsen's shrine, Janglī Guru, according to the informant, is the guru of the Pāṇḍavas, and Juvālā their Bhuvānī or goddess. Janglī Guru is said to be the master of eighty-four *vidyās*. The informant was not able to explain this traditional idea. When describing the cult he used the expression *vīr vidyā*, literally "hero knowledge", by which he meant the control of *bhūts* or ghosts, exorcising them and getting them to attack people. However he said that he did not know these practices, with the exception of exorcism.

The three deities are regularly worshipped on Saturdays, New and Full Moons, at Durgāṣṭamī in Cait and Kuār and at Daśahrā,

Divālī, and Baisākh (when the wheat seedlings are grown). They are offered a coconut, camphor, incense, vermilion, lemon, red *hom* (ghee mixed with vermilion), milk, fruit and flowers. They are never offered meat, though the lemon may be considered a substitute for this, as it is elsewhere. If anyone's mind is bad he may be cured by Bhīmsen. He brings children to the childless, and protects the village, especially with regard to rain. He is worshipped that one's activities may be fruitful, hence his more common name, Siddha Bābā. He does not possess his priest, though the man said that the deity "comes on his head or his shoulder" and then he can see if a *bhūt* has attacked someone. When a *bhūt*-stricken man is brought to the shrine he starts to tremble violently, such is the power of Bhīmsen. The informant used the word *vas,* meaning "power, desire or authority", in the sense that when Bhīmsen comes under his *vas* he can exorcise *bhūts.*

It is not surprising therefore to find that the two deities have much in common. Dowson says: "As 'son of the wind', Bhima was brother of Hanumān, and was able to fly with great speed. By this power of flight, and with the help of Hanumān, he made his way to Kuvera's heaven, high up in the Himalayas" (1950: 50). Furthermore, both possess great strength, carry the same weapon, the mace or club (*gadā*), and both are able to lift mountains. Hanumān's feat has already been mentioned, and in central India, particularly among tribal people, we find Bhīmsen lifting mountains, diverting rivers, *etc.* (Elwin 1958: 183). (The other deity who lifts mountains is Kṛṣṇa, who lifted Mt Govardhan in Vṛndāvan to protect the cowherds from Indra's anger, again a feat connected with weather.) Now, as the cult of Bhīmsen in Jamnā Kheṛā is related to exorcism, to making one's work successful, and to *vīr vidyā*, and in view of the common features of the two half-brothers, we should expect to find some connection between Hanumān and such cults, and here Ghurye's remarks are most pertinent:

> The complex of beliefs which ... appears to have aided the process of upgrading Hanumān from a mere dutiful attendant, ... to that of a powerful deity, ... was that about dead heroes. In other words the current beliefs about 'Viras' as they are called, which has been known

> to prevail not only in U.P. but also in the Panjab. In the latter region Bir is equivalent to Sidh, which is dialectical and popular for the Samskrit 'Siddha', meaning 'perfect'. It must be borne in mind that the belief about perfect individuals or Siddhas whose powers are unlimited owing to their mastery of Yoga is old and even their standard number of eighty-four was fixed long ago. (op. cit.: 228)

Furthermore, Motichandra has pointed out similarities between the cult of the *yakṣas* in ancient India and the contemporary cult of *bīrs*, and between the cult of Hanumān and that of *bīrs* and *yakṣas*. With reference to Hanumān, Motichandra writes:

> In his enquiry of Bira and Brahma cult at Benares, Dr. Agrawala made certain interesting discoveries. For instance, in Hanumat as Mahavira, worshipped at Benares, the Deccan and Central and Northern India, he sees the survival of Bira cult. Hanumat, as is well known, was an ally of Rama against his war with Ravana. He was held to be the son of Pavan or Maruta, and is said to have assumed any form at will, wielded rocks, removed mountains, mounted air, seized the clouds, and rivalled Garuda in swiftness of flight. ...In the attributes of Hanumat, therefore, Yaksha characteristics such as flying through the air, assuming any shape at will etc. are apparent. ...His preference for red lead with which his images are coated, and his love for flowers and perfumes are also Yaksha characteristics. (Motichandra n.d.: 263)

Thus Hanumān is connected with the same type of cult as Bhīmsen, he is a *vidyādhara*, a possessor of magical knowledge, but he is not connected with water in quite the same way as *yakṣas*, who live in trees overlooking the water.

It is Hanumān's ability to cure snake bites that is the most interesting problem. A psychological explanation immediately occurs to us if we recall the identification of the snake as a phallic symbol (Jones 1948: 101, 127–28). The effectiveness of the *mantra* of a celibate over a sexually potent image could be considered to represent an ideal of celibacy[9] in Hindu religious life. We feel, however, that in this case there are enough data in the associations of Hanumān, Bhīmsen and the snake to dispense with recourse to such explanations. We have pointed out that Hanumān and Bhīmsen are aërial figures, they can fly – Hanumān as a monkey lives in trees, and they are both associated with mountains, which are more aërial, so to speak, than plains or valleys. Now the most common antagonist of the snake in Hindu mythology is the eagle, Garuḍa. Zimmer has written: "At Puri, in the Indian province of Orissa, persons suffering from snakebite are taken to the main hall of the Great Temple, where they embrace a Garuda pillar filled with the magic of the celestial bird" (Zimmer 1962: 75). (Cf. Hopkins [1968: 22]: "He [Garuḍa] shares with Hanumat the glory of sitting on a flag-staff of Kṛṣṇa [*Rāmāyaṇa* 2, 24, 23]".)

What does the mythology say about Hanumān and Bhīmsen? Vogel records that snake poison has no effect on Bhīmsen: his great strength had excited the envy of his cousin Duryodhana who poisoned him with a vegetable compound and threw him into the Ganges.

> Being insensible the son of Pāṇḍu sank to the bottom of the water, where he came down heavily in the abode of the Nāgas, threatening to crush the little Nāga children. Then a number of very venomous Nāgas gathered and bit Bhīma violently with their large poison-clotted fangs. But when he was bitten by them the *kālakūṭa*-poison (administered by Duryodhana) being vegetable, was killed by the serpents' poison, being animal . . . The fangs of those snakes even where they bit the vital parts, did not pierce his skin, so massive was that broad-chested youth. Then the son of Kuntī woke up, tore his fetters asunder, and smote the snakes so that several were killed. (Vogel 1926: 72–73)

Bhīmsen was eventually restored to vigour through drinking nine cups of an elixir containing the strength of a thousand Nāgas, and returned to the world of humans, after which any further attempts at poisoning him with *kālakūṭa* poison were of no avail. Vogel gives only one instance of Hanumān's encountering a snake:

> In the fifteenth canto of the *Rāmāyaṇa* (*Sundarakhaṇḍa*, i, 137–60), which is devoted to the account

> of the exploits of Hanumān, the Nāga-mother, Surasā, appears in the shape of a Rākshasi in order to prove the strength of the monkey hero during his flight to Lankā. She suddenly rises from the ocean and threatens to devour Hanumant, who, through his cunning, escapes from her jaws. (op.cit.: 20)

Vogel has a small problem with Surasā, who is supposed to be an earth goddess yet here rises from the sea, and a similar problem arises in Jamnā Kheṛā. The snake is associated with both water and the earth. Snakes abound in the rainy season, and Nāg Pañcamī is celebrated at that time, yet a prohibition on working the land and eating *capātīs* or bread on that day, a ceremony at snake holes in the fields, the association of snakes with Kher Buḍhī (through cooking roasted wheat cakes at her shrine) and with Kher Mātā (the "village mother" of a former settlement of the village – there is a ban on killing snakes in her vicinity) – all these practices point to an association with earth rather than with water. This problem is resolved insofar as it is seen in relation to Hanumān. It has been shown that his only connection with water, or rain, is in his capacity to still storms, and thus he stands in opposition to weather and earth, as a controller of the former and as an aërial figure vis-à-vis the latter. In fact all three aërial figures, Hanumān, Bhīmsen and Garuḍa, stand in opposition to snakes.

Another victory of Hanumān over a snake occurs in the slaying of Ahirāvaṇ. This story is given by Citrāv (1964: 54). Briefly, Ahirāvaṇ and Mahirāvaṇ (*ahi* = "snake", *mahi* = 'earth') were two demons who lived in Pātāl, the navel of the Nāgaloka or world of snakes (Hopkins 1968: 26) and were friends of Rāvaṇ. They were asked by him to destroy Rām, so they entered his camp and carried off Rām and Lakṣmaṇ while they were asleep. Hanumān pursued them, and was advised by Makardhvaj, his hitherto unknown son, to go to a certain temple of Kāmākṣī ("the goddess with eyes of desire"). The demons arrived there to sacrifice Rām and Lakṣmaṇ to the goddess, but by a stratagem involving imitating the goddess' voice, Hanumān was reunited with Rām and Lakṣmaṇ, and the three of them, with the cooperation of Ahirāvaṇ's wife, a daughter of the Nāgas, killed the demons. Citrāv takes this from a fifteenth-century version of the story of Rām, the *Ānanda Rāmāyaṇa*, canto 11, but the episode also appears in Tulsīdās' *Rāmcaritmānas* (Bulcke 1950: 166, 225), which accounts for the presence of posters in some of the houses of Jamnā Kheṛā, showing Hanumān killing the serpent-bodied Ahirāvaṇ.

There is, however, another factor, the presence of the goddess. In Jamnā Kheṛā, according to the temple priest, only Hanumān and the goddess may be offered vermilion. What then is the relationship between these two deities? The most significant goddess temple in the region was that dedicated to Harsiddhī in a small village called Rāngir.[10] The image of Harsiddhī stands just over a metre tall, is coated with red lead and vermilion, and is crudely female in form, with two large black and white enamel eyes. It is a peculiarity of the image that its appearance seems to change during the day, so that in the morning it looks like a young girl, by midday it appears to be a mature woman and in the evening it looks like an old woman. To her left, standing under the shelter of her left arm, is an image about half a metre high of her brother, Langure Bhāī. To the left of this pair is a long piece of broken statuary which represents the sixty-four *yoginīs*. The temple priest assumed from the name that he was the brother of the goddess, but as it appears to be extremely rare for a goddess to have a brother it is equally likely that the appellation *bhāī*, though literally meaning "brother", may here simply be a familiar term of the same type as *māī* "mother", and *bābā* "old man", "respected man". This is the figure to whom the *langure-ki gẽd* is offered at Kher Buḍhī's shrine at Navdurgā. Is he a monkey? Langar, or langur, is the black-faced, gray-coated, long-tailed langur (*Presbytis entellus*) common in northern and central India. It is this species that has been identified with Hanumān (Jay 1965: 197).

It is perhaps not without significance that the site of Harsiddhī's temple is like a mountain (as may be inferred from the name of the village where she is found), to a certain degree aërial, as it is built on the top of a cliff overlooking a river. However, there is better evidence in a local folk song sung during Navarātri.[11] Called a *maiyā-kī gīt* ("Mother's song"), it contains two motifs attached to the familiar story of an encounter between a docile animal such as a cow or a deer and a dangerous one such as a tiger or a huntsman. The first motif is that of the mother's brother-sister's son relationship, the second that of a relationship between Devī and Hanumān. The story tells of how a cow called Surhan was grazing in the jungle when a tiger came up and threatened to eat her. Surhan pleaded that she had a calf at home who had to be fed, and that should the tiger let her go and feed it she would return and give herself up. The tiger asked her how he could believe that, so Surhan named the sun, the moon and *vanaspati* (vegetation) as witnesses to her fidelity to her word. However, the tiger would not accept this as the sun and moon, because they rise and set and wax and wane, are not stable, and *vanaspati* may be broken, so Surhan named the earth and Hanumān, and the tiger accepted this. Surhan went home and told her calf to drink its fill as she had pledged her word and would never return again. The calf then refused to drink and said it would go back with his mother. When the tiger saw them he was very impressed with Surhan's fidelity, for one had gone but two had come back. Then the calf spoke up, saying, "O *mamaiyā*, eat me first, and then eat my mother" (*mamaiyā* = *māmā* "mother's brother"). Having been addressed thus, the tiger was unable to eat his nephew, nor his sister, so he asked the calf who had taught him the stratagem. The calf said,

> *Hinglājan-ne sudha-budha dīnī,*
> *Langure lage more kāna ho māy.*

That is, "Hinglāj Mātā reminded me, Langure told me, *ho māy* (a refrain, literally meaning 'O Mother')". So the tiger was very pleased and said that they should go freely in the forest, and that Surhan's fame would be sung and people come to touch her lotus feet.

The first motif expresses the respect shown by a mother's brother to a sister's son which is significant in the north Indian kinship system. The second points to a clear relationship between the goddess and Hanumān. Hinglāj Mātā is the very famous goddess at a *śākta-pīṭha* in Baluchistan, where the *brahmarandhra* of Sati fell (Sircar 1948), and according to Briggs, she has a brother called Gaibi Pir by Muslims and Mahādev by Hindus, though this figure is connected with an unlocated village called Khajuri, where he sank into the ground in flight from Gabars and Zoroastrians and caused a spring to flow (Briggs 1938: 108). His association with earth and water may be significant, in view of the fact that Harsiddhī has a watery origin – although data from a place so far from Jamnā Kheṛā may not be reliably utilised here. However, the other pairing of Hanumān and the earth, named Pṛthvī in the song, followed by the pairing of Langure and Hinglāj Mātā, confirms the identification of Hanumān with Langure Bhāī.

The clear import of these ethnographic and textual data is that the figure of Hanumān is of very archaic origin. His primary association would seem to have been aërial; in other words, that he is above the ground in several ways, initially in trees, leaping (flying) among the branches. It is beyond the limits of this article to investigate this association with mountains or some other feature. However, it is clearly present, as it is with Bhīmsen (and possibly Kṛṣṇa Giridhar). Those familiar with Maharashtra will readily recall the number of shrines to Hanumān on the roads over the Ghats, a fact that Ghurye (1962: 226–37) inexplicably fails to mention. Hanumān's aërial domain also associates him with metereological matters.[12]

Hanumān's association with the goddess is well-enough documented, but not so easy to explain. While exploring the character of this association, one is forced to the conclusion that despite his aërial nature, Hanumān is nevertheless closely associated with the physical dimensions of villages. In some regions he is a boundary deity, as Ghurye noted. In some he is a guardian, in some the aboriginal settler. Two quotations from the treasure troves of ethnographic and folkloric data to be found in Crooke:

> (...) aboriginal Savaras of Shāhābād make images of him which differ from the orthodox Hindu type; and the Bhiyās of Keonjhar revere him under the title of Bīr, that is, Vīra or Mahāvīra, 'great hero'. ... In Western Bengal the first duty of the founder of a hamlet is to erect an image of Hanumān, which is kept duly decorated with daubs of vermilion. He is regarded as typifying the virile element, and thus, as the protector of crops and cattle, is conceived to stand to the Earth-Mother in the relation of consort. (1909: 486)

> His image is found guarding the entrances of town and villages, as well as the shrines of the gods, and all the forts erected in the Deccan by Sivāji may be known by his image placed inside the main gate. He is also the impersonation of virile strength, one

> of the many consorts of the Earth Mother. Women smear his image with oil on Saturday, his day, and those who are barren go to his shrine at dawn, strip themselves naked and embrace him.[13] In the Deccan when a patient is possessed by a spirit he is seated in front of Hanumān's image, and his brow is marked with ashes taken from the pot of incense which burns before him. He is believed to be closely connected with human beings, and in the Central Provinces and elsewhere his position seems to rest on the belief that the monkeys were the aboriginal lords and owners of the soil before man came on the scene. The Jethwa Rājputs trace their descent from him ... and the wild Bhuiyas call themselves Pavanbans, 'children of the wind', an allusion to his name Māruti. (1926: 175)

The special kind of heroism associated with Hanumān in the village situation is not just his heroic feats in the rescue of Sītā. Although of course this is well known, his heroism is more clearly associated with special, supernatural powers. The priest of Siddha Bābā used the expression *vīr vidyā* in connection with exorcism. He also linked this with the idea of the eighty-four *vidyās* or kinds of esoteric knowledge. This is the special knowledge that Hanumāṇ possesses, which makes him a *vidyādhara.* There is a class of supernatural beings also known as Vidyādharas ("possessing spells") and Siddhas ("perfect beings"), who live in the Himalayas, and have magical powers. According to Daniélou, they "resemble men but have magic powers and change form at their fancy. They are aërial spirits, generally benevolent. They live in the northern mountains, where they have cities and kings. ... When warriors fight with courage Vidyādharas shower a rain of flowers on them (*Mahābhārata* 2.408)" (Daniélou 1964: 304).

However, in lowly Jamnā Kheṛā, these grand powers are restricted to the power to banish *bhūts* from possessed people, and the power to keep the village settlement free from supernatural, and also natural harm. In the words of one of the participants in the worship of Hanumān on Nāg Pañcamī, they do it so that "*unhā̃ī ke iṣṭ se śānti raihai gā̃v mẽ*" ("by his will there may be peace in the village"). It is a much less macho version of Hanumān than that encountered in Bhojpurī villages, but with the same range of activities. His protective rôle is one he shares with the village goddess. In their association, it is as if she, as earth mother, is more concerned with the land itself, whereas Hanumān is more concerned with what is above the land but that affects the land.

NOTES

1 The anthropological fieldwork that is the main source of these data was carried out in 1966–67 in a Bundelkhaṇḍī-speaking, multi-caste, peasant village of about 1200 people in Sagar District, Madhya Pradesh.

2 *Cf. infra* p. 62.

3 The association of Hanumān with Śiva is not confined to this region. In the *Jñāneśvarī*, I.141, Jñāneśvar speaks of him as an incarnation of Śaṅkara.

4 I shall be giving here much ethnographic data from my field work (Duncan 1972), since it is not otherwise readily accessible. I adopt in this account the convention of the "ethnographic present".

5 *Guniyā* is the Bundelkhaṇḍī word for that religious functionary who is not a Brāhmaṇ, who knows spells and charms and may from time to time become possessed by one of the village deities and enter a trance condition. However, Hanumān was never recorded as a deity who would possess his worshippers.

6 The *brahmarandhra*, one of the *cakras* or psychic vortices, is situated by traditional yogic physiology at the crown of the head. The most frequently cited source of information on the *cakras* is Woodroffe's *The Serpent Power* (1931).

7 Jacobi has written "... there were *popular* wind-gods, variants of Vāyu as it were, who in epic language were therefore styled sons of Vāyu or Māruta. One of them is Hanumat, the valorous monkey of the *Rāmāyaṇa* ... he is now the tutelary god of all village settlements. The writer ... believes that he is connected with the monsoon ..." (Jacobi 1909: 806). If this statement be interpreted as implying that Hanumān has some power to bring the monsoon, then on this evidence Jacobi would be slightly mistaken.

8 The trident is conventionally a *śaiva* symbol, and in some contexts the tongs or *cimṭā*, which are regularly carried by *sādhus*, are taken to be *vaiṣṇava*, but in this example both items may be read together as representing the power associated with renunciation, a widespread theme in Hindu practice – see, for instance, Eliade (1958: 88–89).

9 Here celibacy is, of course, understood in its specifically Hindu nature of *brahmacarya*, the place of which is widely discussed. See, for example, Ghurye 1964: 17ff.

10 A local Brāhmaṇ claimed that this temple was one of the *pīṭha-sthānas* originating from the various pieces of the goddess Sati's body, slain at the sacrifice held by Dakṣa, but neither name – Rāngir or Harsiddhī – appears in the *Pīṭhanirṇaya*, the text describing the fifty-one *pīṭhas*, nor in any other similar text (see Sircar 1948 for the text and the story of Dakṣa's sacrifice), nor in the *Devī Māhātmya* (Agrawala 1963).

Despite Prabhūdesāī's claim (1968: 355) that Harsiddhī is the correct name of the goddess at the *pīṭha* in Ujjain (Sati's elbow is said to have fallen at this place), the local story of Rāngir Harsiddhī definitely removes her from any connection with Dakṣa's sacrifice, as she is said to have revealed herself to a local ruler in a dream, asking him to pull her image from a river, which he awoke and did.

11 In Bundelkhaṇḍ a special kind of folk song known as a *laguriyā̃* is used in the worship of Hanumān (Pāṇḍey 1975: 475). Pāṇḍey writes, "Lagur is one of Hanumān's names. Through these songs, prayers are addressed to Mātā Durgā and Mahāvīr Hanumān together, which is in accordance with the *śāstras* [*śāstrasammat*]. Women also worship these images" (loc. cit.).

12 This association surfaces in another figure in Jamnā Kheṛā. Just beyond the outskirts of the village is a hillock on top of which is a shrine dedicated to Ādhār Bābā, a local folk hero of the Ahīr (Milkman) caste around whom a small cult has developed. During the field work period, the only collective worship at his shrine was a hymn-singing session for rain, as the monsoon had been late arriving.

13 *Cf. supra* p. 47.

REFERENCES

Agrawala, V.S. 1963. *Devī-Māhātmya: the Glorification of the Great Goddess.* Varanasi: All-India Kashiraj Trust.

Babb, Lawrence A. 1970. Marriage and Malevolence: the Uses of Sexual Opposition in a Hindu Pantheon. *Ethnology* 9.2: 137–48.

Briggs, G.W. 1938. *Gorakhnath and the Kanphata Yogis.* Calcutta: Y.M.C.A. Publishing House.

Bulcke SJ, C. 1950. *Rām-Kathā* (in Hindi). Prayāg: Hindī Pariṣad Viśvavidyālaya.

Citrāv, S. Śāstrī 1964. *Bhāratavarṣīya Prācīn Caritrakoś* (in Hindi). Pune: Bhāratīya Caritrakoś Maṇḍal.

Courtright, Paul 1985. *Gaṇeśa: Lord of Obstacles, Lord of Beginnings.* New York: Oxford University Press.

Crooke, William 1909. Bengal. *Encyclopaedia of Religion and Ethics*, vol. 2, 479–501, ed. James Hastings. Edinburgh: T. and T. Clark.

———. 1912. Dravidians (North India). *Encyclopaedia of Religion and Ethics*, vol. 5, 1–21, ed. James Hastings. Edinburgh: T. and T. Clark.

———. 1926. *Religion and Folklore of Northern India.* London: Oxford University Press.

Daniélou, Alain 1964. *Hindu Polytheism.* London: Routledge and Kegan Paul.

Dowson, J. 1950. *A Classical Dictionary of Hindu Mythology and Religion, Geography, History, and Literature.* London: Routledge and Kegan Paul (7th edn.).

Duncan, Ian R. 1972. The Structure of Village Religion and its Relationship to the Social Structure of a Village in Madhya Pradesh. Ph.D. thesis submitted to the University of Poona.

Eliade, Mircea. 1958. *Yoga: Immortality and Freedom.* New York: Pantheon Books.

Elwin, Verrier. 1958. *Leaves from the Jungle.* Bombay: Oxford University Press (2nd edn.).

Ghurye, G.S. 1962. *Gods and Men.* Bombay: Popular Book Depot.

———. 1964. *Indian Sadhus.* Bombay: Popular Prakashan.

Hopkins, E.W. 1968. *Epic Mythology.* Delhi: Indological Book House (1st pub. 1915).

Jacobi, Hermann 1909. Brahmanism. *Encyclopaedia of Religions and Ethics,* vol. 2, 799–813, ed. James Hastings. Edinburgh: T. and T. Clark.

———. 1913. Heroes and Hero-gods (Indian). *Encyclopaedia of Religion and Ethics,* vol. 6, 659–61, ed. James Hastings. Edinburgh: T. and T. Clark.

Jay, P. 1965. The Common Langur of North India. In *Primate Behaviour: field studies of monkeys and apes,* ed. by I. DeVore. New York: Holt, Rinehart and Winston, 197–249.

Jones, E. 1948. *Papers on Psycho-Analysis.* London: Baillière, Tindall and Cox.

Mathur, K.S. 1964. *Caste and Ritual in a Malwa Village.* Bombay: Asia Publishing House.

Mayer, Adrian C. 1960. *Caste and Kinship in Central India: a Village and its Region.* London: Routledge and Kegan Paul.

Motichandra n.d. Some Aspects of the Yakṣa Cult of Ancient India. In *Ghurye Feliciation Volume,* ed. K.M. Kapadia. Bombay: Popular Book Depot, 244–65.

Pāṇḍey, Śrīrāmavallabh 1975. Bundelī lok-sāhitya mẽ Śrīhanumān (in Hindi). *Kalyāṇ* 49 (Śrī Hanumān aṅk), 474–75.

Prabhudesāī, P.K. 1968. *Ādīśaktīce Viśvarūp, arthāt Devī Kośa,* vol. 2 (in Marathi). Pune: Ṭiḷak Mahārāṣṭra Vidyāpīṭh.

Russell, R.V. (ed.). 1906a. *Central Provinces District Gazetteers: Saugor District.* Allahabad: Government Press.

———. (ed.). 1906b. *Central Provinces District Gazetteers: Narsinghpur District.* Bombay: Government Press.

Sircar, D.C. 1948. The Śākta Pīṭhas. *Journal of the Royal Asiatic Society of Bengal.* 14, 1, 1–108.

Tulsi Das. 1966. *The Petition to Rām; Hindi Devotional Hymns of the Seventeenth Century.* A Translation of Viṇaya-patrikā with Introduction, Notes and Glossary by F.R. Allchin. London: George Allen and Unwin.

Vogel, J.Ph. 1926. *Indian Serpent Lore or the Nagas in Hindu Legend and Art.* London: Arthur Probsthain.

Wolcott, Leonard T. 1978. Hanuman: the Power-dispensing Monkey in North Indian Folk Religion. *Journal of Asian Studies* 37, 4 (August), 653–61.

Woodroffe, Sir John. 1931. *The Serpent Power (Ṣaṭcakranirūpaṇa and Pādukāpañcaka).* Madras: Ganesh and Co.

Zimmer, H. 1962. *Myths and Symbols in Indian Art and Civilization.* New York: Harper and Bros.

Two Clever Heroes of Tamil Folk Narrative

GABRIELLA EICHINGER FERRO-LUZZI

Introduction

ON HEARING the term "hero" most of us first think of a great warrior. In a wider sense of the term any man admired for his great achievements and noble qualities may be called a hero. There is no dearth of war heroes in Tamil literature. Like ancient literary works in other parts of the world, ancient Tamil poetry reserves much space for the man of extraordinary valour. For instance the *Puṟanāṉūṟu* (1983), a collection of four hundred poems dealing with public matters composed in the first centuries of our era, abounds with heroes who value fame and honour more than their lives. The Tamil admiration for the war hero is not limited to the works of professional poets, it is a strand running through folk narrative as well. It appears, for instance, in historical ballads that flourished in the last few centuries. These folk ballads describe "the resistance of local Tamil warlords and petty rulers to superior powers that may be – the Nāyaks of Madurai, the Nawāb of Arcot and the English East India Company" (Filipský 1990: 113).

The ordinary man admires exceptional courage and physical feats but he also admires exceptional mental feats. I shall deal with this second type of exemplary character: with the clever folk hero. Folk narrative everywhere speaks of both clever and stupid characters who are sometimes shown in a comic light. It has been my study of Tamil humour (Eichinger Ferro-Luzzi 1992: 155–59) that has attracted my attention to the clever folk heroes to be discussed. There seems to be a relatively greater interest in cleverness in Tamil folk narrative than in its Western counterparts. German fairy tales sometimes inspire sympathy with the fool who may, of course, be more naive than genuinely stupid. For instance, in the tale of *The Poor Miller's Son and the Cat* the foolish protagonist is rewarded by marrying the princess. The story ends with the words "Therefore nobody should say that a fool cannot succeed in life" (Grimm 1937: 336).

In my corpus of hundreds of Tamil folk stories there is none that draws this conclusion. The Tamils either enjoy the fool being punished for his stupidity or they enjoy foolishness for its own sake without making any value judgement. But the Tamil villager seems to delight even more in a character's cleverness that he himself might be unable to match. Cleverness in Tamil folk narrative rarely serves to solve abstract problems; it rather is practical cleverness that mostly consists in outwitting one's fellowman who may be stupid but more often is a person endowed with ordinary mental faculties.

To illustrate the Tamil folk view of cleverness I shall deal with two clever heroes situated at opposite sides of law and order. One is a judge called Mariyātai Rāmaṉ (The Honorable Rāma), the other is a master thief whose name we never learn. In the following I shall examine the cognitive strategies each of them employs to achieve his ends. On the basis of their actions and reasonings I shall then try to draw some inference about the Tamil and more generally the Indian view of morality and mind.

The Clever Judge

Stories of Mariyātai Rāmaṉ first appeared in print at the beginning of the 19th century (Dhamotharan n. d.) but the motifs found in them are certainly much older. The judge's name is patently connected with that of Tenāli Rāmaṉ, court jester of Krishna Devaraya who reigned over the Vijayanagara kingdom in the 16th century. The figure of the judge is probably as legendary as that of the court jester, but if one gave credit to the fact that Mariyātai Rāmaṉ was judge to an unspecified Cōḻa king this historical clue would make him several centuries precede the court jester and perhaps place him in the 11th or 12th century at the height of Cōḻa power. Though it may be possible to document the first appearance of the judge's name, the same cannot be said of stories about him. Folk stories do not diffuse as inviolable wholes, as it is sometimes assumed, but any motif no matter how it is conceived may be combined with any other motif (Eichinger Ferro-Luzzi 1987). Since several motifs of the Mariyātai Rāmaṉ stories have parallels in other parts of India and the world trying to pinpoint the origin of an individual story is a vain enterprise.

Both Mariyātai Rāmaṉ and Tenāli Rāmaṉ are emblems of cleverness but apart from their different professions they have strikingly different characters. Tenāli Rāmaṉ may employ his cleverness to mete out well deserved punishment and help others, but he may also put it to purely selfish uses. Sometimes his tricks are needlessly cruel to man and beast (Ramaiya 1976). Conversely, Mariyātai Rāmaṉ, as a rule, pronounces mild verdicts, he never acts selfishly and is only concerned with the triumph of justice. But justice and truth in his eyes are not the abstract concepts of the West; the ends justify the means. He does not hesitate to resort to lies and bluffs to outwit the culprit. This is not really surprising since 13 out of 20 cases he has to decide (in the collection of his tales *Mariyātai Rāmaṉ Kataikaḷ* 1986 examined here) lack testimony, so he somehow has to induce the guilty one to admit his guilt. Rather than applying torture he uses his wits.

Lawsuits Lacking Testimony

Some lawsuits Mariyātai Rāmaṉ unambiguously decides on the basis of Sherlock Holmes-like serendipity by keenly observing the sites and circumstances of the crime. At other times he uses his psychological knowledge. In the case of a theft where all circumstances seem to favour the thief Mariyātai Rāmaṉ orders the plaintiff and the defendant to pass the night in two different temples before he will pronounce the sentence. As he had correctly foreseen, feeling remorse and fearing the punishment of the god the thief in the morning confesses his theft and asks forgiveness. So he is only sentenced to paying a fine (1986: 69–76). Frequently Mariyātai Rāmaṉ bluffs the culprit into betraying himself as when he tells the cattle thief the animal stolen by him is branded, which it is not (1986: 61–66).

Strategies such as these are devised by clever persons anywhere. More interesting may be those relying on culture-specific features. Mariyātai Rāmaṉ is able to guess people's minds but also excels at guessing what they may or may not know. Illiterate villagers' knowledge in their own field of competence may be striking. At least this is what the story of the clever judge tells us. To prove the superior knowledge of an experienced herdsman whose best cow has been stolen Mariyātai Rāmaṉ makes him and the presumed thief eat a meal of vegetables divided into three parts. One part has been fertilized with cow dung, another with goat dung and a third has been grown without fertilizer. The three parts have then been cooked separately in cow's milk, goat's milk and buffalo's milk. The experienced herdsman, who has many cows and therefore need not steal just one, is able to distinguish all three types of vegetables exactly while the thief finds no difference (1986: 94–104).

One case that the clever judge has to decide obliges him to take into account the superior qualities not of a man but of a god. A minor god who feels slighted by a farmer decides to teach him a lesson. For this purpose he takes on the farmer's semblance, so the latter's wife finds herself with two identical husbands she cannot distinguish. Since also Mariyātai Rāmaṉ is unable to distinguish the two men he seemingly invokes divine judgement through an ordeal. The true husband must be capable of entering a pot and leaving it through a tiny opening. The human husband protests that this is impossible but the god in disguise declares himself ready to perform the feat. When told by Mariyātai Rāmaṉ that he betrayed himself the god is not angry but praises the judge for his cleverness and blesses him.

Some lawsuits Mariyātai Rāmaṉ decides on the basis of cultural associations of ideas. Since he has already guessed who is telling the truth and who is lying, the fact that his argument sounds plausible only in his cultural context and might not be accepted elsewhere does not invalidate the justice of the verdict. One such culture-specific association of ideas obtains between shamelessness and other types of opprobria.

A man's young second wife unwittingly suffocates her child whose crying disturbed her during a tryst with her lover. She then puts the blame on her barren co-wife. Mariyātai Rāmaṉ decrees that she who swears after having walked naked around the court hall three times will be considered innocent and she who refuses to do so will be condemned for murder. The older wife would rather die than act in such a shameless way; the younger wife has no qualms to fulfil the judge's order. Arguing that a shameless person is capable of any crime Mariyātai Rāmaṉ gives the murderess a life sentence.

Lawsuits on Questions of Opinion and Common Sense

In seven of twenty lawsuits brought before the judge no liar needs to be discovered but since one party intentionally misuses reason the judge gives him tit for tat. In one case the guilty person does tell a lie but contrary to the lies considered so far, which might have been true, his lie is absurd and hence immediately recognized as a lie.

An iron-monger claims the iron rods entrusted to him by a friend have been eaten by rats. To make him retract his absurd assertion and give back the iron Mariyātai Rāmaṉ advises the friend to invite the iron-monger's ten-year-old son to his house and then claim to have seen a vulture carry him away. If rats can eat iron a vulture can carry a ten-year-old boy (1986: 46–49).

Absurdity cancelling absurdity is a very effective narrative device that has parallels both in stories of Tenāli Rāmaṉ and in other parts of the world including Europe. Therefore such stories seem to be more the result of a cross-cultural form of reasoning than of diffusion. A particularly interesting mental strategy employed by the clever judge consists in looking at things from different angles. Already in his youth he was able to adopt this not very common type of reasoning which earned him his future high position. Four thieves put their hoard in a closed water pot and entrusted it to an old woman enjoining on her to hand it out only if all four of them would ask for it together. One thief managed to trick the old woman and his companions so the former gave him the pot with which he escaped. The then judge to the king accepted the remaining three thieves' claims that the old woman had to compensate them for their loss but a young farmer's son, Rāmaṉ by name, disagreed. He argued the old woman must indeed give them back their belongings if all four of them asked for it together, which would of course never happen. Delighted at the lad's cleverness the king appointed him new judge to his court and bestowed on him the honorary title *mariyātai* (1986: 6–13).

Later in his career the judge is once more called to decide a case by a similar shift of perspective. Four cotton merchants jointly buy a cat to protect their cotton bales from rats assigning to each one of them the care for one of the cat's legs. When the cat hurts itself in one leg its owner bandages it but the bandage soaked in oil catches fire. The desparate cat jumps on the bales and thus causes their destruction. The owner of the bandaged leg pleads for a deplorable accident but his partners hold him responsible. Mariyātai Rāmaṉ, however, argues: since the cat could not walk on the injured leg the other three legs caused the damage so their owners have to compensate the defendant (1986: 21–24).

Some culprits intentionally disregard implicit meanings or use other linguistic tricks promptly countered by the judge in a similar way. For instance, wherever the concept sample exists it is an accepted convention that the price stated for the sample applies to a larger quantity. In one of the lawsuits brought before the judge a rich landlord denies this obvious implication. He claims the price he told a merchant applied to the sample, a little basket of rice rather than a sack of rice. Mariyātai Rāmaṉ asserts he needs one month to investigate the matter during which time the landlord must live in the merchant's house and take his food with him. As instructed by the judge the merchant first eats in the kitchen and then shares one rice grain with his guest. When the latter complains to the judge he is told that the merchant has agreed to give him food but had not said how much. If his sale of rice to the merchant was right so is the food the latter gave him (1986: 76–82).

The Master Thief

The master thief's exploits are set in Madurai, capital of king Tirumalai Nāyakkar who ruled over the Pāṇṭiya kingdom in the 17th century. Rajanarayanan (1984: 214–307), a contemporary Tamil writer from Tinnelveli district, has written down the life story of the master thief by fusing the countless oral versions he had heard since his childhood. He draws attention to connexions with the Sanskrit story of Vikramāditya leaving it open as to the direction in which diffusion might have occurred. In my mind, however, some details of the story such as the maternal uncle's concern for his sister's child are clearly Dravidian. In any case the figure of the master thief is not peculiar to India; it rather belongs to the folklore of the world. The thief of Baghdad, for instance, has even become a Western film hero.

Childhood and Apprenticeship

Mariyātai Rāmaṉ is an instance of individual upward mobility in the caste system. A farmer rises to a position much above his ascribed status. The master thief, conversely, is a high caste person who takes up a low caste profession, at least for a while. The future master thief is the nephew of a general belonging to the royal dynasty. Having no children of his own the general adopts his sister's charming little boy and takes care of his education. Though intelligent the boy does not like school and prefers to play truant. One day when roaming around he is kidnapped by a Kaḷḷar (thief) because of the jewellery he is wearing and eventually adopted by him. The Kaḷḷar introduces his foster child to the subtleties of his trade with the help of stories such as that of the all-round thief (*pakkātiruṭaṉ*) and his three sons pertinently called quarter (*kāl*), half (*arai*) and three-quarter (*mukkāl*) thieves. Like the exploits of the future master thief the episodes of this side story consist of a triad arranged on a rising scale. This is a very common structural element of folk narrative including myths ignored by the structural theory of myth that is only concerned with triads in the form of binary opposites and a mediator (Eichinger Ferro-Luzzi 1987: 167–69). The father thief in the side story asks his three sons for birthday presents that prove their skill. Starting with a piece of coconut shell tied into his lower garment as if it were a rupee coin the youngest son manages to bring his father a great amount of stolen silk cloth. The second son succeeds in obtaining a heap of jewellery from no lesser person than the town watchman whom the king has ordered to catch the first thief. Learning of the trick played on the town watchman the king convinces himself that he alone will be able to catch such a clever thief. The three-quarter thief, therefore, promises his father that as a birthday present he will punish the king for his arrogance. He disguises himself as a merchant who conducts an evening bazaar in a dilapidated *maṇṭapam* (pillar hall) at the outskirts of town. Pretending to wait for clients he sings devotional songs. Informed of his presence the king goes to see him and is deeply moved by the religious songs. He thus readily forgives the presumed merchant who admits to be selling to thieves and to be waiting for one who has recently put the town in uproar. With precious gifts the king tries to induce the merchant to help him catch the thief. The merchant feigns to agree but stipulates that the king alone must stay with him, the guards must wait at a distance. He then suggests that the ornaments the king is wearing might be a hindrance in a possible fight with the thief so he better take them off and put them into a sack. Jokingly he puts the king into the sack too, but then immediately ties it fast and rides off on the king's horse.

Mastership

Educated in this way the Kaḷḷar's foster child soon outdoes all members of the Kaḷḷar colony in his capacity to go "hunting". But he longs for his own parents and relatives and eventually finds them. They are overjoyed to have him back but dismayed at his profession. His uncle, the general, peremptorily orders him to give up stealing; the master thief finally agrees to do so on condition that his uncle catches him red-handed. The general thus challenges his nephew to steal his horse from the stable heavily guarded during the night. The master thief easily passes this trial by disguising himself as an old woman selling sleep-inducing food and drink to the guards. Since the uncle tries to minimize this feat pointing out that it does not take great cleverness to steal from sleeping drunkards, the nephew proposes that he will next steal from his uncle while he is awake. The uncle thus challenges his nephew to steal his silk blanket and his wife's emerald ring warning him that in doing so he will risk his life and will be treated like any other criminal. The nephew, however, remains convinced that he will be able to steal his life even from the god of death. To fulfil the trial the master thief first steals a corpse from the stake. He then props up the corpse to receive the dagger his uncle hurls at the figure that seems to enter his bed room through the window. The general then buries the corpse face down as it is customary with males. Tormented by remorse for having killed his nephew the uncle wanders through the garden of his palace. The master thief thus has time to call his superstitious aunt from below the window – imitating his uncle's voice – to throw down the silk blanket and ring which he will bury together with the corpse. Only in this way will they escape from being harrassed by the vengeful ghost of the deceased. Seeing that his nephew has successfully passed the second trial the uncle no longer tries to minimize his deed. He announces, however, that he will give him a third trial after consulting the king. The king greatly enjoys the story of the master thief and challenges him to steal some gold from the spire of Srirangam temple, which is protected against thieves by a fatal machine of rotating knives. The uncle tries to dissuade his nephew from accepting this trial since it is a great sin to steal from the god. The nephew, however, replies that this theft like the preceding ones have not been his own decision, so the blame does not fall on him.

From the uncle's reluctance to speak about the artisan who made the machine the nephew guesses that the uncle must know much. The nephew therefore turns to his aunt. Exploiting her gossiping habit he extracts from her the secret that the artisan has been banished to Sri Lanka after having made to swear he will never tell anybody how his machine can be stopped. The master thief promptly travels to the island, finds the artisan and tricks him into giving him a clue about banana plants. On his return he stops the machine by throwing on it a great number of banana trunks. He climbs up the spire, pinches off some gold from it and takes it to the king. Wanting to use the extraordinary talents of the youth for the benefit of his country the king appoints him chief of police.

Change of Profession

The responsibility and dignity of his high office operate a change in the young man's character. He wishes to fulfil, to the best of his ability, the first task given him by the king. This task consists in catching a dangerous criminal who poses as a Śaiva devotee. To discover the whereabouts of the criminal the ex-thief disguises himself also as a devotee of Śiva (the third religious disguise in the story replete with redundance, cf. Eichinger Ferro-Luzzi 1987, ch. B IV) and thus easily finds him in a dilapidated Śiva temple in the forest. The disguised chief of police hears the disguised criminal preach to his disciple about how to reach Śiva's heaven without leaving one's body. He also notices that the criminal constantly repeats Śiva's holy name and concludes that he must have become a true devotee of the god. With the help of his men the chief of police could have caught the criminal right away but he should like to do so alone and carry him to the king in a sack (note the repetition of the sack motif also figuring in the side story).

While reflecting on how to put his plan into action his aunt happens to tell a story that gives him an idea. This second side story which really is a story within the story is connected with the main one through motifs of the thief and the religiously motived night watch. The aunt's story is about *ekādaśī*, 24 hours sacred to Viṣṇu on which his devotees fast and renounce sleep. Those who succeed in staying awake may receive the boon to go to Vaikuṇṭha, Viṣṇu's heaven, in their bodies. Once Viṣṇu sent his messengers to bring him such faithful devotees but they found everybody asleep except an old woman who used to steal chicken, cook and eat them during the night. Though she did not even remember it was *ekādaśī* night the fact that she deprived herself of sleep was enough for Viṣṇu's messengers to grant her the joy of going to heaven in her body.

On hearing this story the chief of police decides to catch the criminal disguised as a Śaiva religious mendicant on *Śivarātri*, Śiva's holy night. He starts by training a white bull to carry him and a heavy load. On *Śivarātri* he approaches the criminal in the disguise of a *gaṇa*, one of Śiva's demon servants, riding on a Nandi-like white bull and blowing the conch shell. To make the atmosphere more suggestive still he previously released dozens of crabs to which backs he had fixed candles so they seem to be roaming lights. The false *gaṇa* announces to the awestruck criminal devotee that his lord has ordered to take him to Kailāsa in his body despite all the sins he committed because he has constantly pronounced the divine name and remained awake during Śiva's holy night. However, since human beings cannot ride the bull the chosen one has to be carried to heaven in a sack. In ecstasy the criminal gets into the sack; the chief of police thus carries him before the king.

Final Remarks

The Clever Folk Heroes' Cognitive Strategies

Mariyātai Rāmaṉ and the master thief have become Tamil folk heroes thanks to their intelligence and resourcefulness. Comparing the cognitive strategies each of them employs to achieve his ends reveals both differences and similarities. The thief is above all a man of action, the judge relies on thought alone; at most he advises others what to do. The thief is past master in the art of disguise, the judge would probably think it beneath his dignity to resort to disguise. In his youth the judge gave proof of courage when he dared criticize the then judge to the Cōḻa king but later in his career he has no need to show courage. The master thief, like his similars in the side stories, constantly risks his life and limbs given the severe punishments imposed on criminals at his time, which included impaling and the amputation of one arm and one leg at opposite sides of the body. He thus constitutes a bridge between the hero in his more typical acceptation of a man endowed with exceptional valour and the clever hero.

Tiruvaḷḷuvar (1976, ch. 71, 702) speaks highly of the person who possesses psychological knowledge. The one who can guess the mind he compares to the gods. Both the judge and the thief excel in guessing people's minds, in foreseeing their reactions, in exploiting their weaknesses. They are familiar with the stereotypes of certain categories of people, which as stereotypes are not true at all times but have a great likelihood to be so. The judge, for instance, correctly foresees the fine gustatory distinctions only an experienced herdsman can have (the story does not, of course, pretend to be realistic); while the master thief, for instance, correctly foresees low caste guard's drinking habit.

Both the judge and the master thief do not hesitate to exploit people's religious beliefs and superstitions for their purposes. This does not mean that they are atheists or skeptics; it rather points to a more nonchalant attitude towards the divine than is normally tolerated in the West (cf. Eichinger Ferro-Luzzi 1990: 95–111). In outwitting a god or a human devotee they prove to know well their religious mythology. The power of the god to diminish his size in one of the stories about the judge is connected directly and by opposition with the myth of the demon devotee Bali who was trodden down to the underworld by Viṣṇu's dwarf *avatāra* Vāmana expanding in size. This motif of supernatural change in body size is not limited to India. One may remember that in Wagner's opera based on Germanic mythology Wotan by tricking the dwarf Alberich into transforming himself into a toad was able to snatch away from him the magical ring.

The judge has more opportunity than the master thief to devise linguistic and logical snares but also the latter is capable of sophism. When warned of the dire consequences stealing from a god might have he argues that a commissioned theft is no theft. Hence he need not worry about being punished by the god. (It does not occur to him, however, to refuse the commission.)

The Clever Folk Heroes and Morality

Rajanarayanan has entitled the story of the master thief *The Art of Thieving.* Though thieving does not seem to be one of the traditional Indian 64 arts, he states in the introduction, all who have heard the story will agree that it should be counted as the 65th art. Rajanarayanan's comical point is clear but it disregards the fact that in numerical groupings, as I have argued elsewhere (Eichinger Ferro-Luzzi 1977: 512–13) the favourite number seems to be more important than the things grouped under it. Different authors tend to list different components especially in larger groupings. In my mind it would have been more likely for stealing to be included in the 64 arts, (since these comprise magical tricks meant to cheat people) than to be counted as the 65th art. Contrary to the number 64 the number 65 has no status in India while 64 appears, for instance, also in Śiva's 64 sports.

Rajanarayanan's favourable attitude towards the clever thief is not peculiar to him, yet it may be more natural in Tamil culture than elsewhere. Tamil castes comprise the Kaḷḷars who used to be professional thieves as their name implies. Thus when stealing they perform their caste duty and cannot be morally condemned. The aunt of the newly appointed chief of police in telling her nephew about thieves who profit by people's proneness to fall asleep expresses this cultural view of stealing. She remarks that god has created all professions and seems to have given the thieves the boon to make people fast asleep whenever they arrive. Her observation reflects the well-known relativity of Indian values.

Moral relativity also appears in the stories of the clever judge. Unlike the master thief, Mariyātai Rāmaṉ is only concerned with upholding justice and morality. But he has no qualms to use lies and bluffs to achieve his ends. He thus acts according to Tiruvaḷḷuvar's dictum that falsehood must be considered like truth if it produces the good of truth (1976, ch. 3, 2). This pragmatic view of truth and morality is deeply rooted in Tamil culture. The modern Tamil writer Sundara Ramaswamy also espouses it in one of his short stories. Unable to prove a scoundrel's misdeeds the police put liquor bottles into his car to be able to lock him up for awhile under the prohibition law (1977: 137–43).

Mariyātai Rāmaṉ and Sundara Ramaswamy's police use dubious means with good intentions. But one need not always have good intentions to be rewarded by the gods for one's actions. This magical automatic view of morality and religious merit is not unknown in Christian legends (Thompson 1957, V 254) but certainly more common in Hindu religion. The chicken thief receives the boon to go to heaven in her body simply because she has stayed awake during Viṣṇu's holy night, even though she did so for criminal reasons and did not remember that it was *ekādaśī*. Indian lore contains many similar stories but the closest parallel is found in the Śaiva legend about a hunter's unintentional austerity performed during Śiva's holy night. He could not sleep on the *bilva* tree he had climbed for safety's sake; his movements made Śiva's favourite *bilva* leaves fall on the Śivaliṅgam hidden at the bottom of the tree and water dripping from his bottle kept bathing the god. This threefold unintentional worship induced Śiva to grant liberation (*mokṣa*) to the hunter. In one version of the legend it also produced in him a change of heart and made him give up the desire to kill.

This additional positive effect of an unintentional action again reveals the Indian belief in the automatic power of actions which has been given philosophical-religious elaboration in the theory of *karma*. The conviction that right actions by a sort of feedback produce right intention is not limited to folk narrative, it also lies at the basis of the process of Sanskritization though, in this case, it is applied intentionally. The wisdom coming with age may at times induce a criminal to change his ways. But in the story of the master thief this is not so. Rather, it is explicitly stated that it was the high office bestowed on him obliging him to change his outward behaviour that induced his change of heart. The same motif appears a second time in his story. His last victim, the disguised criminal, became a true devotee of Śiva by first pretending to be one.

Just as other redundances in folk narrative also this one obviously does not serve to reveal deeper meanings as structural students of myth claim. The cultural meaning is quite clear as it stands. The motif rather seems to be repeated because it appeals to the folk artist and his audience. The fascination it exerts on the Tamil mind can be assessed by the fact that it has been repeatedly given literary expression. In a short story Akilan (1976: 43–53) presents a false holy man who similarly transforms himself into a true one. In another short story by Vimala Ramani (1983: 33–41) a young non-Brahmin poses as a Brahmin. By giving up non-vegetarian food and accompanying his old Brahmin landlady on pilgrimages his character also changes for the better.

At the beginning of this paper I have presented the judge and the thief as clever folk heroes at opposite sides of law and order. Due to the thief's change of character their opposition disappears, but it has not resulted in a synthesis or mediation as dialecticians from Hegel to Lévi-Strauss have claimed oppositions are resolved. This is not really surprising because the triad thesis, antithesis, synthesis or two binary opposites and a mediator according to structuralist terminology are mental constructs with little or no relation to reality. In real life opposites almost never fuse completely because we tend to make a hierarchical distinction between the two poles. In the Tamil and Indian hierarchy of values the clever judge as the guardian of law and order always ranks higher than the clever thief no matter how much people may enjoy his feats and how leniently they may judge his crimes.

The Clever Folk Heroes and the Mind

There is nothing surprising in the fact that the Tamils attribute high value to the mind; we all do so. Descartes has made thinking the proof of our existence; archaeologists have chosen the same criterion to name our species. More recently they have redundantly stressed it by calling us *Homo sapiens sapiens*. However, just as all people speak but not all are equally interested in language so all people think but not all are equally interested in thought. In ancient times mainly the Greeks and the Indians were given to intellectual speculations. The stories of the clever judge and the master thief are folk versions of this traditional Indian interest in the mind. The thief gives above all proof of imagination. Purified of its selfish intent this mental quality may lead to artistic creations. The first action of the newly appointed chief of police already has traces of the free play of fantasy characteristic of art. Though he could have immediately arrested the criminal posing as a devotee of Śiva he prefers to create a colourful theatrical performance complete with actors and stage setting.

The judge uses both imagination and reason with emphasis on the latter. The tricks he performs may not strike us as very difficult. But most solutions seem simple once we know them, to find them is another matter. Besides, in my view, some of his cognitive strategies have a potentially much wider application. His idea to make an absurdity apparent with the help of another absurdity exemplifies reasoning by analogy which is an important element in scientific discoveries. The sophisms he employs to decide the cases of the old woman and the four thieves as well as the damage caused by the cat consist in a shift of perspective. The relativity of truth and its dependence on the perspective taken has long been recognized in Indian culture. In the West it has become grudgingly accepted only in this century.

Tamil culture and Indian culture in general are much concerned with right action and with thought but if a hierarchy were to be established between the two primacy might be given to the latter. Rajanarayanan tells us that the king rewarded the master thief with precious gifts for stealing his uncle's silk blanket and his aunt's emerald ring in a heavily guarded palace, because he appreciated cleverness no matter in whom he found it. In a very different non-criminal context another contemporary Tamil writer makes a similar morally indifferent point. One of Ramamirtham's characters remarks: "Neither merit nor sin is important, thought alone is so" (1972: 151).

REFERENCES

Akilaṉ. 1976. *Nantic cittar* (The Nandi Holy Man). In: Akilaṉ's *Nellūr arici* (Nellore Rice), 43–53. Madras: Paari Puthaka Pannai.

Dhamotharan, A. n. d. *Der Tamilroman.*

Eichinger Ferro-Luzzi, G. 1977. Ritual as Language: The Case of South Indian Food Offerings. *Current Anthropology* 18: 507–13.

———. 1987. *The Self-milking Cow and the Bleeding Liṅgam: Criss-cross of Motifs in Indian Temple Legends.* Wiesbaden: Harrassowitz.

———. 1990. Humorous Hinduism: Non-blasphemous Tamil Joking on Religious Matters. In: *Rites and Beliefs in Modern India.* Edited by G. Eichinger Ferro–Luzzi. Delhi: Manohar, 95–111.

———. 1992. *The Taste of Laughter: Aspects of Ṭamil Humour.* Wiesbaden: Harrassowitz.

Filipský, Jan. 1990. History Motivated: Historical Ballads in Tamil. In: *Language versus Dialect: Linguistic and Literary Essays on Hindi, Tamil and Sarnami*. Edited by M. Offredi. Delhi: Manohar, 113–26.

Grimm. 1937. *Märchen der Brüder Grimm*. Selected by K. Hobrecker. Berlin: Th. Knaur.

Puṟanāṉūṟu. 1983. With Tamil explanations by Puliyur Kesikan. Madras: Paari Nilaiyam.

Rajanarayanan, K. 1984. *Tāttā coṉṉa kataikaḷ* (Grandfather's Tales). Sivaganga: Annam.

Ramaiya. 1976. *Teṉālirāmaṉ*. Madras: Paari Nilaiyam.

Ramamirtham, L.S. 1972. *Cāṭci* (The Witness). In Ramamirtham's *Paccaik kaṉavu* (The Green Dream), 149–73. Madras: Kalainyan Pathippagam.

Ramani, Vimala. 1983. *Eṅkiruntō vantāṉ* (He Came from an Unknown Place). *Ananda Vikatan* 21.8: 33–41.

Ramaswamy, Sundara. 1977. *Mey + poy = mey* (Truth plus Falsehood is Equal to Truth). In: Sundara Ramaswamy's *Piracātam* (The gift of god), 137–43. Madras: Tamil Puthakalayam.

Tamilvanan, Lena. (ed.). 1986. *Cirikka cintikka mariyātai rāmaṉ kataikaḷ* (Stories about Mariyātai Rāmaṉ to Make you Laugh and Think). Madras: Manimekalai Piracuram.

Tiruvaḷḷuvar. 1976. *Tirukkuṟaḷ*. With Tamil prose rendering by Puliyur Kesikan. Madras: Pumpukar Piracuram.

Thompson, Stith. 1955–58. *Motif-Index of Folk-Literature*. 6 vols. Copenhagen: Rosenkilde and Bagger.

Kālī – A Hero between Tradition and Progress

About the Novel *Dhartī, dhan na apnā* by Jagdīsh Candra[1]

MARGOT GATZLAFF

AN INDIAN PROVERB says: "The peasant is India, and India is the peasant." Despite the enormous industrial advance in India since its liberation from British colonial rule, this saying has not lost much of its expressiveness. Indeed, three quarters of all Indians still live in villages.[2]

Since the publishing of Premcand's (1880–1936) classic novel *Godān* (The Gift of a Cow)[3] in 1936, in which, as in many of his short stories too, he denounced the miserable, hopeless position of the Indian smallholders in north India, there has been no shortage of literary discussion about conditions in the villages. I mention here such famous authors as Mulk Raj Anand (1905–2004), writing in English and depicting in his stories and novels such as *The Village* (1939), *Across the Black Waters* (1940), *The Sword and the Sickle* (1941), the circumstances in Pañjāb. Another author to write in English is Kamala Markandaya (1924–2004), who paints in her novel *Nectar in a Sieve*[4] a deeply moving picture of the plight of peasants in southern India. Not to be forgotten should be also Takaḻi Śivaśaṅkarappiḷḷa (born in 1914), who, writing in Malayalam, depicts in stories and especially in his novel *Raṇṭitaṅṅaḻi* (Two Measures of Rice, 1949) problems of south Indian villages.

However, Hindī literature after Premcand also contains other important books dealing with problems of the Indian countryside. In the early 1950s a literary movement developed known as "Āñcalik Upanyās" (Regional Novel). The outstanding representatives of this movement are Phaṇīśwarnāth Reṇu (1921–77) and Nāgārjun (born in 1911). Reṇu, as everyone knows, dedicated his entire literary output to the village in Bihar and wrote such remarkable novels as *Mailā āñcal* (A Dirty Veil, 1954) and *Partī parikathā* (About Fallow Land, 1957). Nāgārjun displayed a greater breadth of themes, dealing in particular in his two novels *Balcanmā* (1952) and *Bābā Baṭesarnāth* (1954) humorously and satirically with social problems of the north Indian rural population. Exactly this movement of Āñcalik Upanyās is characterized by commitment for reality and exposing the detrimental mechanisms of traditional structures, whose roots are especially deep in the rural districts.[5] Āñcalik Upanyās writers favoured a concrete manner of depiction by electing a certain region, a certain social group and a certain time, and tried to produce the impression of authenticity by describing the smallest details of geographical, historical and other specific facts, even including linguistic peculiarities of the region described.

Jagdīś Candra (1927–96), who takes his place in literature with his novel *Dhartī, dhan na apnā* (We Have Neither Land nor Property, 1972 and 1980),[6] grappling with the Indian countryside, does not direct his attention to a certain village or a certain time. His chief concern lies in showing typical, widespread social conditions, especially by highlighting grievances in the north Indian village based on these social relations. His intention is to shake up the readers and to inspire them to fight against these conditions. In a personal conversation a couple of years ago Jagdīś Candra told me in actual fact his novel could take place at any time in any north Indian village. His two other village novels *Kabhī na choṛẽ khet* (Never Shall We Give up Our Land, 1976) and *Ghās godām* (The Haystack, 1985) took a similar tack. Consequently Candra rejects the 'Here and Now' of the Āñcalik Upanyās writers and turns towards 'Everywhere and Ever'. He makes use of a plain, unvarnished, rather sober and reporting narrative manner, which avoids the inclusion of dialectal and regional words, but does not relinquish sharp expressions or spicy curses.

Accordingly our author is more closely associated with the literary movement of "Pragatīvād" (Progressivism), which arose in India in the thirties and led in 1936 to the foundation of the Association of Progressive Indian Writers[7] under the presidency of Premcand. The Pragatīvād, whose most outstanding representative was Yaśpāl (1903–76), demanded that literature should address everyday reality, a cause it shared with the well-known and important literary movement "Naī kahānī" (New Story), of which the Āñcalik Upanyās is the rural component. However, the approach it called for was to tackle general problems instead of describing specific details. We do not find in it an authenticity "carried to extremes", as Konrad Meisig wrote in the concluding remarks to his German translation of short stories by Mohan Rākeś.[8] Despite its commitment to reality, Pragatīvād is above all concerned with elaborating characteristic features and general validity. Jagdīś Candra feels bound by this approach too, but he does not openly proclaim his loyalty to it. This becomes evident among other things in his preamble to the Hindī edition of the novel, in which he mentions that childhood experience led him to create this novel:

> Thanks to the social position and the affiliation to high caste of my family I myself did not experience the grievous existence of an untouchable. However my courage secured me the opportunity to observe the life of the untouchables at close quarters. Thus I have now tried, without wanting to force upon anybody my opinion and my views, to show impartially some aspects of the Indian reality. (pp. 8–9)[9]

In spite of all his tendencies to generalization, which are also accompanied, of course, by a certain temporal and local haziness, the author could not avoid establishing his novel in temporal and local respects, otherwise it would have been set in a vacuum. Considering the temporal respect some details – such as some remarks by the general practitioner and communist Dr. Biśandās about the Second World War and Russian partisans' struggle against the fascist invaders, and his failure to mention the newer developments in India such as mass-migration from the countryside to the cities, the penetration of modern mass media even in the Indian rural regions, particular political and historical events, especially the British colonial system and others – give reason to believe that the events of the novel happen in the time during or shortly after World War II. Moreover, the author does not refer to a bigger period in his depiction as Premcand does in *Godān* or Nāgārjun in *Balcanmā*. Jagdīś Candra concentrates the plot on a period of less than one year. Consequently he does not put his hero's process of maturity at the centre of his novel, focusing it instead on the increasing gravity of the situation during the rainy season, so that the plot starts shortly before the beginning of the rainy season and ends a few months after it.

Geographical indications are also few and far between, and even vaguer. The action takes place in the village of Ghoṛewāhā, which evidently largely corresponds to the birthplace of the author. It is located in the north-west of the Union State Pañjāb; to the north of it there lie the Śivālik-Hills, a southern promontory of the Himalaya. Near the village flows a small river named Co, which has a crucial impact on the fate of the village and the whole action of the novel. Following these preliminary remarks and before speaking about the concept of the hero in Candra's novel, I shall outline the plot.

After an absence of six years the *camār* Kālīdās, for short Kālī, has returned to his home village. Poverty and misery had forced him away when he was very young. He found a job in a textile factory in Kānpur and managed to save some money there. But loneliness and the longing for family life induced him to return to his village, where his aunt Pratāpī, his sole remaining relative, lives. She had brought him up after the death of his parents, her own five sons and her husband died of hunger and malnutrition or of a contagion. When Kālī comes back to the village he finds it has hardly changed. The *jāṭ*-peasants still exploit and oppress the *camārs*. The newly arrived Kālī becomes the witness of a thrashing. On a field belonging to the village chairman Harnāmsingh some cows have eaten the unharvested corn, and now he seeks a scapegoat to take responsibility for driving the cows into the field. Therefore the chairman, as usual, has all the *camārs* line up and chooses one of them, on whom he vents his fury. The other *camārs* stand by and silently watch the spectacle. Nobody dares to stop Harnāmsingh and help his caste brother. Kālī is certainly full of indignation, but he does not interfere either.

Since Kālī has saved some money, he has the idea of replacing his aunt's old, half-decayed mud hut by a solid house with brick-walls – a completely new and for a *camār* scandalous venture, which evokes in some of his caste brothers enthusiasm and in others jealousy. The village authorities cannot do anything against it, but they know very well that this Kālī with his new ideas is a source of disruption in the village. Kālī's plan to build a solid house brings him together with different people in the village, with Chajjū Śāh, the merchant and moneylender, with Dīnū, the potter, with Santāsingh, the carpenter, with Munśī, the owner of a brickyard, and others. He meets his neighbours, former friends and so on. In this way many aspects of village life are examined closely and the reader is acquainted with them. At the same time the love of our hero for the girl Gyāno develops. Gyāno also belongs to the caste of the *camārs*, but Kālī cannot marry her, because it is a traditional custom to take a marriage partner from a different village.

Thus the novel begins, despite some adversities, promisingly and optimistically for the hero. He is at home, he is no longer alone or isolated, he has some money, the villagers receive him kindly, he plans to improve his living conditions by building a solid house with brick-walls and Gyāno makes him happy. The changes start with the rainy season. Although the particular events happen independently of each other, all in all they change the position of Kālī. His aunt Pratāpī dies without giving away her nephew in marriage. Kālī himself, busy with the house-building, had postponed this necessary matter. The house is not yet ready either. He is again alone now. Somebody steals the rest of his money. Heavy rainfalls make the River Co swell and burst its banks, threatening to overflow not only the fields but also the inhabited houses in the village. The necessary rescue operations and later on the clearing works lead to an open conflict between the *jāṭ*-peasants and the *camārs*. Though the *camārs* have since ancient times worked without payment on the farms of the *jāṭ*-peasants – each peasant only has to feed his particular *camār* or *camārs* and to provide them with the most necessary things – now they believe they should be paid a daily wage for all the work connected with the flood disaster and its after-effects, because work exceeds the daily task they usually have to do. After three days they learn that the *caudhrīs* are not willing to pay them. With Kālī at their head they refuse to carry on working. Both sides start to boycott each other. The *camārs* do not go to work on the farms of the *jāṭ*-peasants, and the peasants do not provide the *camārs* with food and do not allow them to work on the fields. Kālī asks for help first from the communists, then the Christians and finally the wrestler Lālū, but all in vain. The *camārs* cannot maintain the boycott for long, because they have neither food nor money. Moreover, the *jāṭ*-peasants need the workers, because they cannot do work alone – not to mention the fact that they are loath to deal with such vulgar things in the long term which caste privilege allows them to escape. The harvest is ruined. Thus a compromise is inevitably reached. The *camār*s eat humble pie, and the peasants are glad to get their workers back and pay them a small consideration for their work on the embankment.

Involuntarily all persecution is directed now against Kālī, who increasingly becomes an outsider. His house-building has to be stopped, for the little he had has been stolen. His love for Gyāno displeases the whole village, because it flies in the face of both tradition and morals. But they cannot bear to part and meet in secret. Finally Gyāno gets pregnant. All efforts to induce a miscarriage do not have any effect, therefore her mother Jasso is at her wit's end and poisons her daughter to save the honour of the family. Kālī, who has not found a job since the boycott, leaves the village again. It remains uncertain whether Maṅgū, the brother of Kālī's beloved, stooge and talebearer of the village mayor and opponent of Kālī from the very beginning, has killed him, as threatened, or whether Kālī just has run away.

As optimistically as the novel starts with Kālī's trust in his own strength, with his right to happiness and a human future, it ends tragically with the failure of the hero due to traditional social structure in the village, the old customs and the jealousy of his neighbours. The figure of the hero Kālī in this novel is placed between these two poles, between progress and tradition. Now I will turn towards a closer analysis of this figure.

In line with the intention of the author to denounce the misery of the untouchables in the village, the hero of the novel is an untouchable. He is at the centre of the structure of multifarious social relations, which are introduced to the reader, illustrated and individualized with the help of this figure. Unlike the story-tellers of *Naī kahānī* (compare stories by Mohan Rākeś as *Zakhm – The Sore* or *Ek ṭhaharā huā cāqū – The Knife* or the story by Rājendra Yādav *Birādarī bāhar – A Foreigner Among Others* and others),[10] J. Candra depicts the traditional social structure as intact. It still completely subjugates people to itself, whilst it is already disintegrating in the cities and leaves the individual with his new experiences alone. Whereas the authors of *Naī kahānī* portray the isolation of the individual via urban social conditions in the city, the destruction of traditional social bonds and family structures, and lay the blame for the decadence of the individual on the decadence of the traditional community, Jagdīś Candra describes how the village community closely connected to the caste system ruins the individual, because it still functions in the traditional manner, resists the efforts of the individual for change, does not give him the chance to develop, does not allow him free play and cuts a person down to size, consequently cramping and finally expelling him should he overstep the limits too frequently or too far. Accordingly the development of the hero's character is not pursued in the novel; instead the impact on his life of external circumstances is shown. Consequently the hero of this book is not a dynamic personality, but rather a static figure, whose acting is determined more by events, by external influences, than by his own perceptions, experiences and own will. All the events in the book are in one way or another connected with Kālī; there are only a few chapters (7 out of 49) in the novel in which Kālī does not appear personally. Village life is formed by the two social groups opposed to each other: the unpropertied *camārs* and the landholding *jāṭ*-peasants. Let us start with the social relations of our hero with his own caste.

As everybody knows the *camārs* are on the lowest rung in the social caste hierarchy. They belong to the "untouchables", who have to be avoided by the twice-borns; only the work they do is "clean". The only people lower than the *camārs* in the village are the *bāzīgārs*, the jugglers and mat-weavers, who live on the other shore of the River Co. Every *jāṭ*-peasant has his own *camār* or *camārs*, who do all the agricultural work, such as tilling the fields of their peasant, tending the cattle and performing all necessary work on the farmstead. The women and girls, the *camārins*, clear away dung and other filth and help do the housework. For their work the *camārs* get as a rule only natural produce, and occasionally a little money. Therefore they lead a miserable life. They live in wretched mud cottages in a separate quarter in the village without running water or electricity. For water they have their own separate well. The sewage is drained off out of the huts in open gutters along the village streets and lanes, nature is relieved on the fields. Jagdīś Candra describes the *camārs* as men with red eyes without eyelashes, which constantly run with tears. They are wrapped up in dirty, ragged clothes and stink of sweat. Their snotty children run around naked and barefoot (pp. 17, 19). Their lack of income guarantees their full dependence upon the rich village peasants. The money they need for certain occasions such as the marriage of children, illness and death of close relatives, has to be borrowed from their peasant or from moneylenders, who extract enormous interest. It is not unusual for those concerned to be plunged into debt for years, which is even passed on to their sons and grandsons. Thus the *camārs* are closely tied to the village. In the novel for instance Maṅgū, the brother of the heroine Gyāno, is in inherited debtor's bondage to the head of the village Harnāmsingh. This total dependance of the *camārs* on the mercy of the rich people, the total absence of rights of which they are constantly reminded by ill-treatment and humiliations, in addition to their ignorance and lack of education, supported by the Hindu doctrine of *karma*, which assigns to every individual the fault for his miserable life due to his sins and crimes in his former existence, has formed over the centuries in these people the unconscious conviction that they cannot undertake anything against their miserable life, that they are completely in the clutches of their masters and that they have to tolerate their fate with humility and readiness for suffering. Rebellion would be useless and also contradictory to the traditional order. This outlook, conclusively drawn already by Premcand in the novel *Godān* with his hero Horī, is expressed in Candra's novel by the old Phattū, the speaker and representative of the *camārs* in the village-*pañcāyat*, who continuously endeavours in all conflicts to act as a mediator, to point to the traditional order and to restore it. Indeed he even accuses the *jāṭs* of deviating from this order in moral regards and not respecting the dignity of the *camārs*, so that conflicts in the village arise. When one of the *camārs* has stolen a melon from the field of a *jāṭ*-peasant and the *pañcāyat* has to assemble to pass judgement upon him, Bābā Phattū, asked for his opinion, delivers the following speech:

> Why did you call us if you want to decide the punishment alone? We are *camārs*, your farm-hands. You are the *caudhrīs*, our masters. We have to accept every punishment you give us, no matter how it turns out. He who lives in the river cannot start fighting with the crocodile! ... You and we have lived together in this

> village since time immemorial. You are our *caudhrīs*, and we are your *camārs*. Our task is to serve you and to work for you. Your task is to care for us, to help us in case of need. I am already more than seventy years old and have spent my whole life in this village. I still can remember those times when the *camārs* and the *caudhrīs* lived harmoniously in the village and respected each other. Then there was no quarrel. No *camār* would have dared even to look askance at a *caudhrī*. The whole muddle has come into being since you *caudhrīs* started to trample upon the honour of the *camārs*, since the blood of peasants and farm-hands started to mix with each other. (pp. 172, 256 and 257)

Thus the *camārs*, unpropertied, exploited and oppressed, themselves observe and maintain the traditional order instead of being keen to change it. The reason has to be seen in their hopeless situation. Therefore they defend with might and main the only thing they have, and this is their imaginary "honour", based on traditional ideas of morality. Even when it came to open conflict with the *jāṭ*-peasants because they refuse to pay money to the *camārs* for working on the embankment, the *camārs* want only to assert their legitimate interests in getting paid but do not try to revolt against the whole social system. We do not notice either any collective effort to link up with other oppressed and backward groups – something which has been ardently called for over the past few years in India; I have in mind the Bahujan Samaj Party, which was founded by Kanśī Rām on the fourth of April in 1984 at Delhi.[11] This party aims to link up all the dalits, tribesmen and religious minorities (Muslims, Christians, Sikhs and others) and wants "to change the slaves of India into rulers".

Of course there are individual attempts to avoid the preordained lot. But they find expression as a rule in the wish to convert to a religion proclaiming the equality of men. In the novel this is demonstrated by the shoemaker Nandsingh, who, born as a *camār*, thus as a Hindu, first converts to Sikhism and later to Christianity. Talking to our hero Kālī he explains the background to his decision:

> I do not like life in the village, because here a poor man, especially an outcast is not respected. Only those

> who have land and property are respected. Yes, yes! Land and power! This is the point! All other things are of no account! ... The worse thing is to be a *camār*. This is the most ghastly stigma. The poorest peasant is superior to the *camār*. ... How I hate this word *camār*! I hit the ceiling if I am called by this word. ... (pp. 190, 284)

Again the *camār*s themselves, this time in the figure of Tāyā Basantā, defend the social order and rebuke the shoemaker. He says:

> My goodness, Nandsingh! I am surprised that horns haven't yet grown out of your head! How one can be so stupid! You can do whatever you will, but a *camār* remains a *camār*! It isn't religion that determines to which caste you belong, but birth. If you don't like this, you should have crawled out of the belly of another woman. (pp. 200, 299)

The author draws in many ways the picture of people, who in their dependent position are helplessly and defencelessly surrendered to the arbitrariness of others, whose life takes via cruel exploitation and constant humiliation a sorrowful and cheerless course in misery and need, in ignorance and dread, but who cannot imagine for themselves another way of life either. For this reason the *camār*s are those in the novel who in their entirety as a caste within the untouchables stand up for the maintainance of the tradition and who thus are its active supporters. They themselves adhere to the ancient social order and oppose every change. But change is necessary for the idea of progress, as Jawaharlal Nehru states in his book *Discovery of India*, when he speaks about the idea of progress and about the idea of safety and stability, which are more or less mutually incompatible.[12] A certain change and thus also a certain progress in the village involves the reappearance of Kālī. He shakes the traditional bonds. Contrary to his caste-brothers he passed four forms at school, whereas most of the others rarely manage one. Through his six years absence from the village he "has seen the world", whilst most of the other *camār*s have hardly emerged from the village, certainly going no further than the next district town. Having worked in a textile mill in Kanpur,

Kālī has earned money and brought with him some savings, which ensures him at least initially a certain independence and respect. And all this on the other hand gives him the idea of spending the money on building a brick house – a completely unusual desire for a *camār*, who since ancient times has only had the right to live in a shabby mud cottage. Indeed, the construction of a solid (*pakkā*) house is the dream of every *camār*. The old Phattū, for instance, tells how he has toiled all his life and did not allow himself even to sleep, but that his dream of a brick house failed (pp. 45, 63).

Jagdīś Candra describes his hero as tall and impressive. Kālī nearly touches the roofs of the huts with his head. He is stronger and more robust than the other *camār*s. His friend Jītū, who is of the same age, looks emaciated and dried up (pp. 16, 18). Compared to him Kālī has a broad chest, a muscular, well-formed and well-nourished body, gleaming like old rosewood (pp. 41, 57). He is always tidily and cleanly dressed, behaves modestly, but self-confidently and with dignity. He does not allow others to treat him unfairly or to provoke him. Whereas most of the other young men of his age already have families with three or four children, he is not yet married. The character of Kālī is described as honest and faithful. He esteems his elders and protects them from ill-treatment. He is kind to women and girls, he loves his aunt Pratāpī and does everything for her. Besides this he is ready to help, has a keen sense of justice and does not like quarrels (for instance chapter 12, when Nikkū and Prīto pick a quarrel with him on account of his building a house). Consequently he differs in many aspects from his caste-brothers. On the other hand he is a *camār* as they are, too, and therefore he succumbs to all the restrictions and obligations connected with caste membership. Like the others he does not own land, livestock or a plough. They are all have-nots. Socially he is tied to his caste as all the others are too. But he has family ties only to his aunt Pratāpī. When she dies, he feels himself uprooted; only his love for Gyāno keeps him in the village, which on the other hand ruins his social support.

In the beginning the *camār*s receive Kālī with some pride because he has done better than them. Therefore his friend Jītū addresses him only with "Bābū-jī" (Sir). This emphasis also produces an attitude of some uncertain expectation among the *camār*s. Spontaneously they see in Kālī their leader. And from their leader they expect deeds of the type usually performed by "heroes". Therefore they are really pleased to hear that Kālī has dealt properly with Maṅgū, who, though also a *camār*, is due to debts a bondman of the village head and acts as his talebearer and instrument. He often sets himself up as a master towards the other *camār*s, his caste fellows, he humiliates and persecutes them worse than the *caudhrī*s themselves, and that is why he is hated by everybody. Maṅgū becomes Kālī's adversary. Even when playing *kabaḍḍī* Kālī turns out to be a powerful, skilful and quick player, who is more than a match for *caudhrī* Hardev. In the end Hardev can only beat Kālī by foul play. When due to the threatening flood the embankment of the river Co has to be broken through to save the village from flooding Kālī again helps. At first Kālī lives up to the expectations of his caste mates. He is their hero, who performs heroic deeds in their eyes and who, by opposing the *caudhrī*s (albeit only in small matters) and not putting up with injustice, takes revenge indirectly for much of the humiliation and ill-treatment meted out to the others.

Little by little the tide turns. Robbed of all his savings Kālī loses his already very insecure independence. Previously he did not need to work for a peasant, but now he must earn a living at first by selling grass to the shopkeepers of the village and later on as a farm-hand with the *jāṭ*-peasant Lālū, who was a famous wrestler in his early years. Thereby Kālī loses imperceptibly his authority. His friend Jītū sees in him now a person like himself and does not address him any more by "Bābū-jī". Kālī's importance as the hero of the *camār*s diminishes.

Finally the expectations of the *camār*s are disappointed during the decisive conflict with the *jāṭ*-peasants. Following Kālī's example, the *camār*s refuse to carry out the repairs to the embankment after the flood without wages. They expect of course far-reaching decisions from Kālī, resulting in their victory in this conflict. But Kālī turns out to be a person who cannot escape the dictates of his *camār*ese existence any more than the others. His revolt against the arbitrariness of the *caudhrī*s originates from a rather spontaneous sense of justice and not from knowledge of the social and economic conditions or the pursuit of a political aim. With no experience or allies, he has nothing which could have helped him in this situation. Kālī asks the communists, the village parson and the wrestler Lālū to support the starving *camār*s with foodstuff, so that they can endure the conflict. But each of them has a different reason to refuse support. The communists like Doctor Biśandās and Ṭahalsingh, a *jāṭ*-peasant from the neighbour village, enter hair-splitting ideological quarrels and consider the *camār*s to be opportunists, because they are not ready to starve "a little" and to take upon themselves sacrifices to the death for the sublime idea of class warfare. The parson only wants to help Christians and by doing so indirectly to convert all *camār*s into Christians, so that he can show to his authorities the success of his pastoral care. And the wrestler Lālū feels linked to his caste, to the *jāṭ*-peasants, whom he does not want to stab in the back, in spite of his sympathy for the *camār*s and especially for Kālī. Therefore Kālī does not manage to get support for the *camār*s who now have to eat humble pie in this conflict. In this respect Kālī cannot live up to his leading role, which finally decides the change in the attitude of the *camār*s to him. They stop looking at him with admiration and pride. Full of desperation they turn away from him, because he has plunged them into unnecessary discord with their masters, which yielded for them only a few days of starvation. Thus, Kālī failed as an hero. Hence the picture of our hero changes: from an admired model he becomes an ostracized outsider.

His relations with the girl Gyāno, disapproved by the whole village, also contribute to this change. He rattles also morally at the traditional barriers. As long as Kālī's aunt Pratāpī was alive, Gyāno could go into Kālī's hut without causing offence, because officially she came to visit aunt Pratāpī. It was during these visits that their mutual affection developed. Gyāno felt attracted by this young and strong man, who supports justice and tries new things; carried away by her feelings she laughs away conventional customs and prescriptions. Kālī likes the bright pretty young girl with the supple figure and the elastic walk, who takes care of him and is the only person close to him after the death of his aunt. By degrees their meetings, especially when Pratāpī is no longer alive, cause public scandals. The annoyance of the village is directed against both, but more against Kālī, because he is seen as the seducer. The *jāṭ*-fellows in their turn are annoyed, because Gyāno successfully resists their advances and now call her "Kālī's pea-hen" (*Kālī kī mornī*).

The attentive reader cannot fail to notice the double morality shown here by the author. Generally speaking, the reputation of all girls and women in the caste of the *camār*s is closely observed.

None of the *camār*-fellows is allowed to commit indecent assault on them. Again and again it is drummed into their heads that they have to regard the girls of the village as their sisters and the women as their mothers. When someone dares to violate this unwritten law quite openly as Kālī does he will be outlawed by his caste. In chapter 47 Kālī is caught meeting by chance Gyāno, who is now engaged to a man from another village, and all the villagers pounce upon him. Tāyā Basantā and Bābā Phattū try to intercede and ask Kālī to pronounce in public that Gyāno is for him only a sister. Kālī refuses and is therefore condemned. On the other hand the whole village tolerates that the *jāṭ*-peasants and their sons are after the *camārins* and gratify their sexual desires with them. Maṅgū, Gyāno's brother, jealously guards the reputation of his sister, beats her because of her relationship with Kālī and wants to kill him, himself drives a *camār*-girl to Hardev, the nephew of the village chief, and advises him what to do in order to rape Laccho after luring her into a store-room. Such events are very frequent and belong to the established rights of the *caudhrīs*. This is also illustrated in other places of the novel. For instance in chapter 12 the two *camārins* Pratāpī and Prīto fly at each other when the ground plan of Kālī's house is measured. They reproach each other over which *caudhrīs* they had intercourse with in their youth. In his speech, dealt with above, the old Phattū indicates the results of such relationships, which lead to the fact that fair-skinned children appear between the dark-skinned *camārs*.

Light still remains to be thrown on Kālī's relations with the *caudhrīs*, otherwise the social concept of the main figure in this novel would be incomplete. As everybody knows, *caudhrīs* include all those in the village who are respected through property or knowledge, religious or worldly, if they belong to the upper castes. First of all these are the *jāṭ*-peasants, who own the land and are the real antipole of the *camārs*. They have land and livestock, they live together with their relatives in multi-storey solid brick-houses. The *camārs* (as mentioned above) depend on them completely. They only get the most basic essentials if they work for the *jāṭs*. They can earn a little money by mowing grass and selling it to the storekeepers and other people of the village, who do not possess land, but keep cows. In the beginning Kālī believes that he is independent, because he has some money and does not work for a peasant. Therefore he protests proudly and self-confidently against the defamation and injustice to him. The *caudhrīs* know very well that this behaviour alone is enough to cause unwanted trouble in the village for they profit most of all by the traditional village order. Therefore they are interested in its maintenance and enforce it with all means up to physical terror. In depicting such brutalities the novel still remains far behind those atrocities reported again and again within the last few years in the Indian newspapers.

Kālī brings restlessness into the village just with his behaviour. He has trouble with his neighbour Nikkū, who, set up against him by Maṅgū, accuses him of erecting the foundations for his house on a part of his ground and makes furious scenes, so that the whole village comes out. Kālī is not intimidated by this, and finally it comes out that the walls of Nikkū's house stand on Kālī's ground. All the time Maṅgū acts as the opponent of Kālī, which especially dramatizes and sharpens the conflicts. Maṅgū tries to stop Kālī from digging clay near the village pond, which is allowed to everybody, and slanders him in front of the village chief. Again and again Kālī succeeds in settling such quarrels, in asserting his rights or in proving his innocence. But this makes him unliked by the peasants.

Jagdīś Candra does not involve his hero Kālī into his own direct conflicts with the *jāṭ*-peasants. The conflicts he has with them are conflicts of all *camārs* in the village in which Kālī plays a special role. It is not the aim of the author to fabricate special conflicts of Kālī with them, because he wants to demonstrate the functioning of the traditional social structure and to show how it crushes the individual. Therefore it is sufficient to bring some movement into the paralyzed relations, to threaten their stability by a little bit of progress in the form of very simple, natural and human intentions in order to make evident their whole harmfulness and depravity. Kālī's isolation comes less through operations of the *caudhrīs*, but more through the functioning of the existing relations themselves. Tradition wins out over progress.

With the help of his hero the author also points out to the reader that it is not enough to possess money to break out of the caste order. Since his savings do not suffice for building a house, Kālī has to go to one of the shopkeepers and usurers of the village, whose name is Chajjū Śāh. He impresses our hero with his gentle and kind manner, but he does not lend any money to

Kālī, because Kālī is not an owner of land, which he could have pledged. More than this, Chajjū Śāh even explains to Kālī that the ground on which Kālī's cottage is built does not belong to him, but to the village and is let out to Kālī and to his family for inheritable usage. If the family dies out, the ground reverts to the village. But the shopkeeper makes use of the chance and collects from Kālī outstanding debts of his uncle, who died long ago. On the other hand Kālī witnesses, how the shopkeeper haggles with the district revenue officer Faujāsingh, assisted by the village chief Harnāmsingh. Faujāsingh also wants to borrow some money from the usurer for his daughter's wedding and in the end gets a bigger amount by depositing wasteland as security. The seeming kindness of the shopkeepers towards the *camārs* has its reasons, because the *camārs* are the best customers of the village shopkeepers, who sustain the business with their small money. On the other hand the shopkeepers, due to their caste affiliation and to their property, do not belong to the lower classes of the village; they belong to the *caudhrīs*. Therefore in the conflict with the *camārs* during the embankment repairs they side, as do all the other village authorities, with the *jāṭ*-peasants, who provide them in this case with grass for their cattle.

Politically Kālī feels attracted to the communists in the person of Doctor Biśandās, who in his young years sought Kālī as an interlocutor and lectured to him on his revolutionary ideas. But his dogmatic attitude in the central conflict of the *camārs* and the *jāṭ*-peasants shows that the doctor is unable to put these ideas into practice and to make use of them in village life. On this account Kālī eventually feels disgusted with them. During his stay at Kānpur he was obviously not involved politically. Asked by Doctor Biśandās he said that he was not even a member of a trade union, since he did not like their internal squabbling. Statements or hints about other Indian parties are completely lacking, the Indian National Congress is not mentioned at all, thus this important aspect of Indian reality is fully neglected in the novel.

In conclusion I want to say that the hero in this novel by Jagdīś Candra is designed more statically than dynamically, there is no development of his character. As a member of the *camār*-caste he is subjected to the conventional laws, prescriptions and customs bound up with tradition. But the stay in the city has formed his views, wishes and ideas, and now they go a little beyond the narrow caste-thinking. For that reason Kālī is keen to change his life, bound by common human rights, thus representing a certain progress in comparison with the poverty, misery and the readiness for sorrows of his caste-fellows. But Kālī is not bent on general basic change. On this account he stands between tradition and progress. Back in his home village Ghoṛewāhā he inevitably gets into conflict with the village community, whose traditional stability and order have not yet experienced a drastic shock, for which the villagers are not yet mentally ready either. Therefore, his social and moral notions, which are "progressive" at least as compared to the notions of the villagers, make Kālī a victim of tradition.

In the preface to his novel the author affirmed that he wants to remain impartial and to abstain from personal statements. This gave occasion to Lothar Lutze to judge Jagdīś Candra as follows: "What the author promises in his preface he keeps in the novel. His artistic action in the reality depicted is confined to its arrangement in the development of the plot."[13] But I do not think that this judgement, though it is broadly speaking true, can be made absolutely. For besides all intended impartiality the author succeeds in sketching a manifold picture of the Indian village and unveils the social evils and defects merely via the artistically clever arrangement of the story. In this way he wakes in the reader solidarity for the burdensome fate of the *camārs*, arouses him into action against it and evokes in him the conviction that these conditions need whole-hearted change. For this reason the author does not remain impartial, but values reality and takes his stand with the help of the plot which he artistically arranges in a very clever manner. The novel fascinates by its plainness, by the dramatic development of the events, by the beautiful scenes of village life and appealing portrayals of Indian rural reality. Critically and emotionally it brings the reader closer to a bit of Indian everyday life. The author succeeds in comprehending his hero Kālī as an individual and social being in all his different relations with the environment and captures thereby the typical character of *camār*-existence. He shows in an impressive and feeling way that in India there is still a very long way to go until realization of the vision of Jawaharlal Nehru, the first Prime Minister of this country, who in his time wrote: "... in the social organisation of to-day it [caste] has no place left. If merit is the only criterion and opportunity is thrown open to everybody, then caste loses all its present-day distinguishing features and, in fact, ends."[14]

NOTES

1 Rājkamal Prakāśan, Nayī Dillī and Paṭnā, 1972, 284 p.; German translation: *Unberührbar* (Untouchable), translated and edited by the present author, published by Kiepenheuer Publishing House, Leipzig and Weimar, 1991, 458 p.

2 The All-India Census of 1981 counted a rural population of 525 million out of a total of 685 million, or 66.5 per cent. Among them were 92.5 million cultivators and 55.5 million agricultural labourers (*Statistical Outline of India 1984*, Tata Services Lmtd., Bombay 1984, pp. 29, 41 and 44).

3 German translation by Irene Zahra: *Godan oder die Opfergabe*, Manesse Publishing House, Zürich, 1979.

4 In German: *Nektar in einem Sieb*, Aufbau-Verlag, Berlin, 1956.

5 One of my Berlin colleagues, Hannelore Lötzke, dealt with this literary movement in her dissertation *Das indische Dorf im Spiegel der modernen Hindi-Literatur – Menschen- und Gesellschaftsbild in ausgewählten Hindi-Romanen nach 1947* (The Indian Village in the Mirror of Modern Hindi-Literature – the Portrait of Man and Society in Selected Hindi Novels after 1947), unpublished Ph.D. thesis Humboldt University of Berlin.

6 The novel *Dhartī, dhan na apnā* was translated into Urdū in Pakistan, into Pañjābī in Pañjāb and into Russian in 1980 in the Soviet Union. In 1975 the novel was broadcasted as a radio play by All India Radio in Delhi. For many years it has also been required academic reading for Hindī students at several Indian universities.

7 The Association was renamed in its conference in 1975 at Gaya 'National Association of Progressive Writers'.

8 See: *Groß stadtgeschichten* (Stories of Metropolitan Societies), edited and translated by Konrad Meisig, Otto Harrassowitz Publishing House, Wiesbaden, 1990, p. 127.

9 Here and in the following quotations the first page-number refers to the Hindī-text, the second one to the German translation (cp. note 1).

10 See for this the German translation *Die Wunde* of *Zak͟hm* (The Sore) and *Das Messer* of *Ek ṭhaharā huā cāqū* (The Knife) in *Groß stadtgeschichten*, ib., pp. 87–122, and *Fremd unter andern* of *Birādarī bāhar* (A Foreigner Among Others) in the journal *Sinn und Form*, vol. 21, no. 4 (1969), pp. 839–52, ed. Deutsche Akademie der Künste, Rütten & Loening Publishing House, Berlin.

11 Utterance of Kanśī Rām in Dalit Voice, 16–31 October 1988, p. 4, quoted by Dagmar Ansari in her article "Efforts of Uniting Indian Muslims and Dalits in the 1980s", in: *Archiv Orientální*, vol. 58, no. 1 (1990), p. 40.

12 *The Discovery of India*, London 1946, passim.
13 See: "Armut und Reichtum in indischen Gegenwartsliteraturen", in: *Aspekte sozialer Ungleichheit in Südasien*, Beiträge zur Südasien-Forschung der Universität Heidelberg, Wiesbaden, vol. 17, pp. 206f.
14 *The Discovery of India*, 1946, p. 448.

Hero and King

Śivājī and His Tutelary Goddess Bhavānī

ROLAND JANSEN

Introductory Remarks

IN THE COURSE of this seminar the question as to what actually constitutes the (Indian) hero has been raised again and again. I would thus like to begin this paper with a quotation from the British historian Carlyle, who remarked upon what we, having met with a variety of different heroes in the course of this seminar, might call the heroic or, in a broader sense, the political hero. Carlyle says: "A hero is both the creature and the creator of the times he lives in" (Sardesai 1957: 45). This attempt at a definition is of course minimalistic, but might serve as an appropriate introduction to the hero of this paper: Śivājī, the well-known 17th-century Marāṭhā leader. We are going to take a look at a significant event in his life and discuss the way in which we find this depicted in traditional sources of Marāṭhā history. Also, we shall ask ourselves how the presentation of Śivājī's heroic exploits was shaped by historical and ideological forces at work at the time. Finally we are going to look at the position these sources attribute to the goddess, the Bhavānī of Tuljāpūr,[1] in relation to the hero – a constellation which may be found as a pattern in more than one context of Indian history.

The Historical and Geographical Environment

It was in the 12th and 13th centuries that India, especially south India, went through changes which were to become significant in political as well as in religious terms. Burton Stein (1974: 77ff.) has shown how in parallel with the crumbling of great empires like that of the Cholas and the rise of local rulers (*nāṭṭār*) another, in this case a religious change took place. With the passage of time the religious significance of the large temple complexes (such as Kanchipuram and Chidambaram) declined and small temples, dedicated to deities of not more than local importance, rose to prominence. Had the large temples been dedicated to deities of the pantheon of the Purāṇas or even the Vedas, the gods that now surfaced were *grāma devatās*, which were to a large extent female: an age-old loyalty of the rural population to these deities had not been disturbed by a few centuries of royal patronage to deities of a brahmanic background. The reason for the growing importance of these cults of local gods and goddesses is not hard to account for: the rising local chieftains not only remained loyal to the cult their family had been following for generations, but also popularised it, sometimes by making it the central cult of the new state.

Accompanying this trend (in south India as well as in other parts of the country) was a growing interest in the devotional aspect of religion, to which the newly popular gods lent themselves better than the old ones: their emotional rather than intellectual appeal made them more accessible to the common people who did not know Sanskrit.

The nature of these gods and goddesses can be appropriately described by the terms *ugra* (powerful, fierce, savage, wrathful; also a name of Rudra) in Sanskrit or even better through the Marāṭhī *kaḍak*, an approximate translation of which would be: rough, fierce, ardent, impetuous (as a disposition). The Marāṭhī-word also carries another shade of meaning: "dry, crisp, hard and stiff from dryness" (Molesworth). This may be taken as a perception of the natural habitat of these deities – the dry areas, suffering from lack of rain and thus displaying a hard and often fissured soil. Both terms moreover indicate sharpness, pungency, heat and acridity – qualities which are even today found in the food prepared in these areas. They were less cultivated (in terms of agriculture and state culture) and dangerous to travel through. The Sanskrit term *durgam* (difficult to approach) is used for the type of goddesses prevalent in this area and is clearly an indication of their nature and their geographical and ecological environment as well.[2] This correlation between the character of the goddess, the landscape she "lives in", and the nature of the people who worship her may become clear from a quotation of Pamela Price:[3]

> Goddess worship was appropriate for areas of dry cultivation, areas which saw warrior control in relatively small and unstable domains (...). The power to claim resources was not rooted in and justified by one's status in the caste system and, thus, the purity of one's habits. The strength to fight and kill were predominating themes in popular religious worship of these drier areas.

And:

> In an unstable political world, one of opportunities for an ambitious soldier to establish a ruling lineage, a deity who represented the power of skill and force rather than the protection of a hierarchical structure (...) held considerable appeal.

Often these goddesses serve as family-deities, *kuladevatās*, or *kulasvāminīs* to families who may have their residence at a considerable distance from the original site (*mūlpīṭh*) of the deity. The regularly conducted pilgrimages to these sites indicate that their power is dependent on their location. As Maxine Berntsen (1988: 18) once remarked, the names of these (*kaḍak-*) deities are always, at least in Marāṭhī, mentioned along with their place of residence – thus one would speak of *jejurīcā khaṇḍobā* or *tuḷajāpuracī bhavānī*. This is the place where the god is alive (*jagṛt*) and grants boons, mostly as the result of a vow (*navas*). It is again the location which probably is responsible for the fact that these gods and goddesses of the "centers out there" (Turner) are the family deities of certain groups of people, frequently those, who were roaming these areas. The Bhavānī of Tuḷjāpur for instance is, besides being the *kulasvāminī* of the Marāṭhās, also worshipped by the gypsies of India, the Lambāḍīs or Bañjāras, and by groups like the Rāmośīs (Sontheimer 1976: 85–89), and 'Bhavānī' was worshipped by the infamous Thugs,[4] whose name has become synonymous with highway robbery and strangling.

The following similarities in the religion of so-called predatory groups and Kṣatriyas should be noted: They share the worship of goddesses, often of the *durgā* type. These goddesses are usually given the position of the family deity (*kulasvāminī*). Their mythology makes the battlefield their favourite haunt, their cult caters to their strong liking for non-vegetarian offerings, for blood and alcohol. Many Kṣatriya dynasties are known to have come from obscure origins. The Bhosales, of whom Śivājī is the outstanding member, are no exception to this rule. The worship of the *kuladevatā*, to whom the credit for the successful rise of the dynasty is usually attributed is continued, even if the family had to migrate to a new capital at a considerable distance. The most spectacular occasion for a study of this phenomenon is of course the Dasarā festival, where not only the king receives the authorization of his rule along with his weapons from his family goddess, but the different groups of worshippers meet and merge. The Dasarā festival is often metaphorically described as a battle without weapons. Moreover this is traditionally the occasion for heroes to show their feats of bravery.

The function of the goddess whereby she provides warriors or heroes with the necessary *śakti* or inspiration for their heroic undertakings is probably a very old and certainly a wide-spread pattern. A very good historical example of this is the biography of Śivājī.[5] His is, to my knowledge, the first case in which we can draw on historical sources to reveal a process that may lend itself as a historical pattern: An able ruler from a nondescript family-background stakes his claim in a larger political context and legitimizes this claim successfully. How this was achieved will concern us in the following.

The Killing of Aphjul Khan

The example I have chosen to illustrate this pattern is a famous one: the killing of Aphjul Khan. This episode in the history of Maharashtra has continued to stimulate the imagination of historians for roughly 330 years[6] now. To a large extent this is probably due to the controversial character of this event: the argument centers around the question who first tried to murder the other at a meeting that was arranged as a diplomatic one. This longstanding controversy will never be resolved, it indicates that most probably neither trusted the other[7] and Śivājī happened to have more luck and presence of mind.

The historical background needs a brief sketch. In the years preceding the event, Śivājī, son of a *sardār* in the services of Bijapur and Ahmednagar, had conquered large areas of territory belonging to the Sultan of Bijapur (mainly in North and south Konkan) and plundered shipments of taxes, also destined for Bijapur. While the Moghuls were concentrating on affairs in Delhi (Aurangzeb followed his father on the throne in July 1658) the Bijapuris thought the time ripe to teach Śivājī his lesson. Aphjul Khan, a general in the Bijapur army, volunteered for the job and set off with a large army to confront Śivājī.

Connected with this outset in September 1659 is another controversial episode in the history of Maharashtra. On the way from Bijapur to Wai, where negotiations were to take place, the Khan travelled past the most sacred places of pilgrimage to the Hindus in this area, Paṃdharpūr and Tuḷjāpūr. What happened at the instance of his visit to Tuḷjāpūr is open to conjecture – the reports in the *bakhars* are as contradictory as they are biased: all of them were written by Marāṭhās and, therefore, reflect their point of view. Whether the Khan was successful in destroying the temple and the idol of Bhavānī in Tuḷjāpūr or whether the priests managed to remove and hide the *mūrtī* in time is hard to decide.[8] For our purpose it is more interesting to see how the event is portrayed in the traditional sources, the *bakhars*, than attempting to trace a historical truth. In the *bakhar* of Sabhāsad (2, 20) we read about Aphjul Khan's visit to Tuḷjāpūr:

> Then the army came to Tuḷjāpūr. They made a night halt there. Having broken Bhavānī, the *kuladevatā* of the Mahārājā, they put her in a quern and powdered her. In the instant Bhavānī was broken, a heavenly voice (*ākāśavāṇī*) was heard to say: "Hey, Aphjul Khan, lowly creature, within 21 days your head will be chopped off and your army, completely routed, will satisfy nine crores of *cāmuṇḍās*!"

Also interesting for us is the fact that the Khan seems to have known of the central importance of Tuḷjā Bhavānī, the *kulasvāminī* in the life of Śivājī. Whether his act was intended to inflict terror on Śivājī or whether he calculated that the chances for a success of his mission would be better after the destruction of Śivājī's *śakti* is open to speculation.[9]

Through envoys the two opponents arranged a meeting at the foot of Pratāpgaḍ, a fort which Śivājī had captured three years earlier and then fortified in order to make it his new headquarters.

It is situated in the Sahyādris on a high mountain, and controls one of the main passes over the Western Ghāṭs which connects the Konkan and the Desh lands. The Khan agreed to leave his camp at Wai (some 37 km to the east of Pratāpgaḍ) and, accompanied by not more than an eighth of his army, made the way through what were at that time densely forested and impassable mountains to the appointed location.

Though this move put Śivājī in a strategically advantageous position, it was no doubt a very dangerous situation for him, who saw himself for the first time in a head-on-confrontation with one of the main powers on the Dekhan. From several accounts in the traditional sources of Marāṭhā history, the *bakhars*, we know of this situation. Śivājī, as usual in times of crisis, turns to Bhavānī for help and counsel. We find the following description in the *bakhar* of Śivadigvijayakār:[10]

> In a discussion on politics, namely which means should be applied in the case of Aphjul Khan, Jijābāīsāheb [Śivājī's mother] orderd him thus: "until today the success [of your policy] was brought about by *parameśvara* as it was your wish. And [as if] he will bring it about in future, so it should be done. Address a prayer to Śrī. The acting [which is] in accordance with her order should be done." When this idea was accepted by all and Śrī was asked, the answer was: "'He [Śivājī] shall go to the meeting and there [I shall take him] as a captive,' that is his [Aphjul Khan's] plan. [That he wants] to conduct negotiations about sovereignty is not true. As the sweet words of a mainabird or as the noble ideas of a hypocrite, such is his kind. Therefore do not go. Having brought *him* into the meeting *his* sovereignty shall be taken. And you will obtain great wealth."

This, as well as all the other accounts in the *bakhars* were, of course, written after the event, and we can easily see how the writers tried to give the impression, the destruction of Aphjul Khan was preordained. If the main point in the description by this author seems to be the warning and advice given to Śivājī, the next account puts the emphasis on a slightly, but significantly different point. Citragupta, the author of another *bakhar*, tells us (Kulkarni 1920: 81):

> With great firmness [of purpose] the Mahārājā remembered Śrī Ambā. At this moment Śrī became favourable and entered into the body (*mahārājāṃceṃ aṁgī prasanna hoūn saṃcār karūn*) of the mahārājā and spoke thus: "You don't need to be worried, Śivājī. At this moment I myself stand on your earth. Having confused the Khan, I bring this Mahiṣa (*mhaisā*) before you. Then you, with fearless mind, will effect his killing and, having cut off his head, will place it before me. [Then] applying a ṭīkā of his blood as an ornament of prowess on [my] forehead and having [thus] given this excellent Mahiṣa (*mhaisādā-ṇīs*) [to me] you effect my satisfaction." Having spoken in such a way Śrī Tuḷjā Bhavānī became invisible.

Here we find the ensuing duel portrayed in terms of a buffalo sacrifice to the goddess. Aphjul Khan has become the buffalo, the sacrificial animal (the term *mhaisādāṇā* seems to suggest: "a fine specimen of a Mahiṣa") which is to be sacrificed in front of the goddess, as it is the custom at the climax of the Dasarā or Navarātra festival, where, according to the famous myth in the *Devī Māhātmya*, the goddess finally overcame the buffalo demon Mahiṣāsura. Aphjul Khan is thus practically identified with Mahiṣāsura. It should also be kept in mind that *Vijayādaśamī* is the occasion for another famous victory: that of Rāma over Rāvaṇa.[11] We shall return to this later.

The other extraordinary point about this version of the story is that the author mentions the goddess entering the body of the Mahārājā. The phenomenon (*aṁgāt yeṇe*) is well known and widespread in the folk religion of Maharashtra. Yet one is surprised to hear of a king becoming possessed by a goddess. Nevertheless the *bakhars* are quite explicit about this. Śivadigvijayakār gives us a short description of what seems to have been a regular occurrence (Kulkarni 1920: 80):

> At the time when Śrī was expected to come into the body of the Mahārājā, only Bālājī was to be present. Questions which were to be asked had to be told to

> him before. After he had invoked Śrī (*to Śrīs prārthana karūn*) he had to ask the question [and] if there was an answer he had to write it down. Later he had to show it to the Mahārājā. According to that scheme (*betāpramāṇe*) they would have to act.

Although there are other cases where we hear of an intimate relationship between a king and his family goddess,[12] Śivājī's is to my knowledge the only case where a king becomes possessed by his *kulasvāminī*. Moreover, if one follows the *bakhars* it appears that political decisions were taken in accordance with the oracles the goddess gave through the medium of the king. In any case the strategy proved to be successful – not only, but particularly so in the case of Aphjul Khan.

The meeting was arranged in a tent a little below the fort. Apart from one or two bodyguards for each of them nobody was to be present. According to Sardesai (1957: 130–38) the situation developed as follows: When Śivājī entered the tent, the Khan stood up and went to embrace him, thereby trying to push a dagger in Śivājī's back. This failed, for Śivājī wore a chain mail under his clothes. Making use of the embrace, Śivājī ripped open the Khan's bowels with an instrument known as *vāghnākhas* (tiger-claws)[13] and thrust a short sword after it, bringing him to the ground immediately. When the bodyguards rushed to the assistance of their fallen master they were cut down at an instant. In the ensuing fight Śivājī received a blow on the head, but as it turned out, he wore a metal cap under his turban. Then, before the body of Aphjul Khan could be carried away, Śivājī's men cut off his head and exhibited it on a high pole from the topmost bastion of the fort. A preconcerted signal was given and the Bijapurī soldiers were cut down to the last man. The following day the Marāṭhās attacked the camp of the Bijapurī army at Wai, routed them and returned with a tremendous amount of plunder.

This, in a much abbreviated form, is one reconstructed version of the chain of events that instantly brought Śivājī to the notice of every ruler near and far in India. It is moreover the outstanding as well as by strict moral standards dubious heroic feat that probably laid the basis for his later reputation as a "wily mountain rat" and for his fame as a hero at the same time. We need not be surprised, therefore, that the writers (or composers as I have called them above) of traditional Marāṭhā history in the *bakhars* and *povāḍas* were inspired by the fabulous character of the event and probably exaggerated in their narrations quite a bit. In other words, one might say they rendered the story in a way that reflects their own ideas of an ideal hero. And in doing so they are in essence not very far from the writers of biographies in Sanskrit, the *caritas*. As Romila Thapar has remarked when discussing the continuity between hero and king in the *Harṣacarita* and the *Vikramāṅkadevacarita*, the biography "encapsulates the current notions of what constitutes the great king".

Thus, one is well advised to bear in mind that: "The sources for the study of the legendary hero Śivājī are many and varied, far more numerous than for the 'historical Śivājī'" (Laine 1995: 3). Furthermore it has to be borne in mind that all narrations of the event come from Marāṭhā sources: I do not know of a single account of the event from Muslim sources. Thus, all the narrations make the Muslim the wicked man of evil intentions in a plot, where distrust and treachery seems to have been a strategy resorted to by both opponents.

I would like to focus our attention on the way in which this was achieved. Citragupta has, as we have seen, portrayed the conflict in terms of a buffalo sacrifice to the goddess, as it can still be seen in some parts of the country at the Dasarā festival. This is in analogy to the slaying of Mahiṣa by Durgā in the *Devī Māhātmya* (Adhy. II & III).[14] Anyone who has experienced those ten days at a centre of worship for the goddess Durgā, knows of the tremendous emotional tension building up over this period which culminates and finds its release in the sacrifice of one or more animals. Usually it is the head or the first drop of blood of the animal that is offered to the goddess and is said to satisfy her. Thus one feels justified in saying that, in the case of Aphjul Khan's killing, the release of tremendous political tension was seen by the composers of the *bakhars* as having been effected through the sacrifice of the Muslim – Śivājī in a way becomes the sacrificer who satisfies his goddess with the head of a sacrificial "animal".[15]

Two more examples will help to show that the analogy between the fight and the sacrifice is not at all an arbitrary one. The sacrifice of a buffalo or a he-goat (Marāṭhī: *bokaḍ*) to the goddess is still a common feature of her worship. In two *povāḍas*[16] we find a reference to Aphjul Khan as the *battīs dāṃtāṃcā bokaḍ*, the "he-goat with 32 teeth" (or in other words a human sacrificial goat), whose head was offered to the Bhavānī of Pratāpgaḍ.

The other clue is the fact that after this event a new temple for Bhavānī was built on the fort. The temple faces towards the east, as in Tuḷjāpūr. The location of the temple is exactly opposite the *Aphjul buruj*, the bastion where the head of the Khan was displayed after his gruesome end. The bastion and the tomb which Śivājī is said to have erected for the Khan, are both to the east of the temple: this layout does therefore resemble that of the temple in Tuḷjāpūr, where the goats are sacrificed over a pit a few yards to the east of the temple of Bhavānī (also facing east). The temple on Pratāpgaḍ deserves one more remark. In the beginning we have said that goddesses of this type are to be found in areas which are dry, 'uncivilised' and dangerous, and that the power of such goddesses is dependent on their location in this area. This goddess would seem to be an exception to the rule. Tuḷjā Bhavānī and her cult have been transported and reestablished a couple of times: to Nepal, where she is worshipped as Taleju Bhavānī (the circumstances of which need not concern us here), to Pune, to Wai, to Hubli (in Karnataka), all of no historical significance, and to Pratāpgaḍ, where is her secondmost famous temple. The reason for this is political. The traditional environment for heroes in Maharashtra, the drought-prone pastoral areas south-east of Pune where Tuḷjāpūr itself is located, were not open to Śivājī. This country had come under direct control of either Bijapur or Ahmednagar, and therefore not only was the pilgrimage to the place a dangerous undertaking but, as the Aphjul Khan incident has shown, the safety of the goddess herself could no longer be guaranteed. The strategically safest areas for Śivājī were the Sahyādrīs, the densely forested mountains separating the Desh from the Konkan lands. Numerous passes wind their way through these mountains and all the trade between the Deccan plateau and the coastal areas with their oversea harbours had to be carried over these passes, thus offering rich and easy booty. Moreover, this is an area where large armies, such as those of the Muslim rulers, were of no use, as has become evident from the fate of the army of Aphjul Khan. Śivājī knew the terrain well and he enjoyed the sympathy as well as the support of the local people, the *Māvaḷīs* being a well known example.[17] The decision to erect another temple for Bhavānī at his favourite fort was an unusual step and received much attention in the writings of the times. It is interesting to note that all reports in the *bakhars*[18] attribute responsibility for this step to the goddess herself: she appears to Śivājī in a dream and orders him to have a *mūrtī* made for her and to arrange for her establishment (*sthāpana*) in his kingdom. As if to preempt any doubts in the devotee whether the new *pīṭh* would be *jagṛt* (alive) too, all the *bakhars* make it a point to mention that the goddess does fulfil the vows made to her if visited at her new place. *Pūjā*, offices, *navas* and *yātrā* were arranged in the same way as in Tuḷjāpūr. According to Sabhāsad (3, 25) the goddess even appeared to those people who were (still) going to Tuḷjāpūr in their sleep and told them

> "I am at Pratāpgaḍ [now]. You should go there, take *darśan* and do your *navas*." So said the Devī. A big *jagṛt* place had come into being.

Looking at those two temples of Bhavānī today, one must say that in spite of all the advertising in the *bakhars* and in the writings of Rāmadāsa, the *śakti* seems to have stayed where it had probably always been: While the temple on Pratāpgaḍ has practically declined to little more than a tourist attraction, the worship of Bhavānī in Tuḷjāpūr continues to flourish.[19]

Ideological Integration: Svāmī Samartha Rāmadāsa

A very good example for the embedding of some of the events in Śivājī's life into a religious frame of reference is provided by Svāmī Samartha Rāmadāsa (1608–80), known as the religious guru and political adviser of our hero. By many he is seen as the man behind the scenes of political developments in the second half of the 17th century in Maharashtra. The *deśasthā* brahmin Rāmadāsa is particularly famous for two things: 1. his unshakable devotion to Rāma, and 2. the creation and advancement of an idea known as *Mahārāṣṭra dharma*. This is both a religious and a political movement, based firmly on traditional, brahmanical values and meant to supply a new cultural and moral self-esteem to the Marāṭhās who had, according to Rāmadāsa's perception, fallen into a state of deep moral decay.

The family deity of Rāmadāsa was the Bhavānī of Tuḷjāpūr. Even after he had become a *saṃnyāsī* and a devotee of Rāma his devotion to Bhavānī, whom he often addresses as "Mother", continued. She, as the *kulasvāminī* of Maharashtra, was of great importance to him and he in turn promoted devotion to her by composing several hymns and *āratīs* in praise of her. It has to be noted here that the most important epithet of Tuḷjā Bhavānī is that of Rāmavaradāyinī: she who grants a boon to Rāma. This epithet originated in a story that is well known in Maharashtra from various sources and in various versions.[20] A summary of the story runs as follows:

> When Rāma and Lakṣmaṇa were wandering through the *daṇḍakāraṇya* in search of Sītā they suddenly saw Sītā standing in front of them. While Lakṣmaṇa enthusiastically welcomes Sītā, Rāma understands that this is a trick, played by the universal mother's *māyā* in order to test him. He thus addresses her: *tū kā āī?* (Is it you, mother?) And she answers: *mīc tukāī!* (I am Tukāī [one of Bhavānī's epithets]). Satisfied with Rāma's passing of the test Bhavānī grants them a boon. They both wish for the successful rescue of Sītā, which the goddess promises. At first they do not believe her, but then, from a high place half a mile to the south of Tuḷjāpūr [where the meeting took place], the goddess grants them a vision of Lanka.

In the *bakhars* we come across a number of different accounts of the meeting of Śivājī and Rāmadāsa. It does not come as much of a surprise that Śivadigvijayakār (Kulkarni 1920: 87) has Bhavānī as the arranging agency for this meeting. She appears to Śivājī in a dream, when he spends a night sleeping in her temple. Then she directs him to the shelter of Svāmī Rāmadāsa, who, according to her, is an *avatār* of Śrīmāruti, having taken a physical form for his support.

Hanumān is known as Māruti in Maharashtra and Rāmadāsa ("servant of Rāma" is the translation of his name) naturally felt a great affection for Hanumān/Māruti, whose *bhakti* to Rāma is proverbial. Rāmadāsa fostered the popularity of Māruti by erecting eleven temples to him in southern Maharashtra. Hanumān is known from the *Rāmāyaṇa* for both his physical strength and sucleverness – he can carry mountains and outwit numerically superior opponents, as was demonstrated in the burning of Lanka.

Māruti in Maharashtra is appropriately known as the god of athletes (and of bachelors) and hence was perfectly suited as the embodiment of what we would call 'a concept' that suited Rāmadāsa: a physically strong body in combination with a discriminating intellect, what he considered essential for the new type of selfconfident Hindu/Marāṭhā, embodying what he saw as traditional, but unfortunately forgotten ideals of the proper way to conduct one's life.

For Rāmadāsa, the battle between Rāma and Rāvaṇa was anything but an event in a distant past. He gained the inspiration for both his religious and political ambitions from classical literature, the *Rāmāyaṇa* naturally being the most important to him. Not unfrequently in his writings one finds him challenging the gods, reminding them of their mythological deeds and calling upon them to repeat them here and now.[21] He thus gave a new dimension to the political and social conflicts of his time by interpreting them as part of the eternal cosmic struggle between good and evil, the gods and the demons, as known from the mythology of the epics and the Purāṇas. In other words, he tried to bridge the gap between epic struggles, the dichotomy of *suras* and *asuras* or *devas* and *daityas* or *dānavas*, and that of the Marāṭhās and the Muslims or Śivājī and Aphjul Khan and later Aurangzeb.

Three verses of Rāmadāsa's hymn to Rāmavaradāyinī may throw some light on this:[22]

I had heard a lot
That you gave a boon to Rāma
I am the servant of Raghunātha
Be a *varadāyinī* [giver of boons] for me also! (9)

Now I have only one thing to ask of you
Grant it for my cause
Nourish this king of yours
Soon, while I am watching. (17)

You have killed the vile people in the past
I have heard of that a lot
But [please] show me directly
Your original power! (18)

Another sample, this time from Rāmadāsa's *Ānandavanabhuvana*, his apocalyptic vision called the *Region of Bliss*, in the translation of R.D. Ranade (1982: 367):

> A great evil has fallen upon the Mlecchas. God has become the partisan of the virtuous in the Region of Bliss. All evil-doers have come to an end. Hindusthan has waxed strong. Haters of God have been destroyed in the Region of Bliss (...) The power of the Mahomedans is gone (...) The Mother Goddess who had bestowed a boon upon Śivājī has come with a bludgeon in her hand, and has killed the sinners of old in the Region of Bliss. I see the Goddess walking in the company of the King, intent upon devouring the wicked and the sinners. She has protected her devotees of old, and she will again protect them today.

Conclusion

A process one might feel tempted to call "Rāmaization" seems to have been at work in the religious history of Maharashtra and possibly larger areas of south India from mediaeval times onwards. The epic hero Rāma served as a model to be emulated – if not for the king or hero himself then at least for those people who were concerned with the "making" of history, i.e. the composers of historical records, the *bakhars* in Maharashtra.[23] In Rāmadāsa's *Ānandavanabhuvana* it was "The Mother Goddess who bestowed a boon upon Śivājī (...)" The Rāmavaradāyinī has thus turned into a *Śivājīvaradāyinī*. The perception of Śivājī's intimate relationship to the goddess expresses itself through the employment of the same metaphor that has been used to describe the relationship between Rāma and the goddess.

Remembering Carlyle's statement we may concludingly say that Śivājī had, no doubt, been a creator of his times and can thus aptly be called a hero according to Carlyle's use of the term. Although we did not discuss the historical consequences of his acts, we may say so from looking at the effects his image had on traditional historiography in Maharashtra. His acts, when portrayed by authors of *bakhars* or singers of *povāḍas*, seem to fit effortlessly into a traditional framework of ideas, which he again helped to reinforce. Not only did he provide the stuff for legends: he moreover gave an opportunity for traditional ideas to be applied on the political situation of his times. Without him Aphjul Khan and Aurangzeb would not have been equated with Rāvaṇa for lack of the Rāma-like counterpart. And without him Tuljā Bhavānī would not have attained to the prominence she enjoys today. One might even go as far as to suggest an analogy between Maharashtra and Sītā ("the furrow"): it had not been abducted, but had certainly been occupied by a foreign power and was in need of rescue.

NOTES

1 Instead of 'Tuḷajā' I prefer the spelling 'Tuḷjā' in accordance with its pronunciation.

2 It should be noted here that another meaning of *durgā* is "a difficult or narrow passage, a place difficult of access, citadel, stronghold" (Monier Williams). Since the term for this type of goddess and a fort is identical, we need not be surprised that so many of her temples are situated on the top of fortified mountains. For a detailed discussion of the goddess associated with the protection of a city or a fort in India and West Asia, see Parpola, "From Ishtar to Durgā". In Sontheimer and Murty (forthcoming).

3 Price: "Villages and Royal Courts in south India". In Sontheimer and Murty (forthcoming).

4 Sircar (1973: 15) writes: "It is well known that the Thuggees (both Hindus and Muslims), many of whose organizations belonged to Western India and the Deccan, were followers of the goddess Bhavānī, irrespective of their personal religious beliefs." Although this is true it must, however, be said that the Thugs' worship of Bhavānī was not directed to Tuḷjāpūr but to the goddess Vindhyavāsinī (her temple is situated a few miles southeast of Mirzapore, c. 36 miles southeast of Benares) – a goddess of very similar characteristics.

5 In my opinion a very good illustration of this configuration is the famous, and in Maharashtra ubiquitous picture illustrating the legend of how Śivājī received his famous sword from Bhavānī. See Jansen 1995.

6 The date for this event given by Sardesai is Thursday, 10 November 1659.

7 Moreover, there are quite a few references to their relationship having suffered as a result of earlier events. Thus Aphjul Khan is said to have distinguished himself at the arrest of Śivājī's father Śahjī eleven years earlier and to be responsible for the death of Śivājī's elder brother Sambhajī by failing to render assistance in a military campaign. Cp. Sardesai, 1957: 84 and 87.

8 For a detailed discussion of this event see Jansen 1995.

9 Meadows Taylor in his historical novel *Tara, a Maratha Tale* has

it, that Aphjul Khan went via Tuḷjāpūr because he had heard of a conspiracy meeting at the temple – he describes the destruction of the temple as an unintentional conseqence of a fight that ensued at the arrival of the party.

10 Quoted from Kulkarni (1920: 81). Unless stated otherwise all translations are by the author.

11 The *Kālikāpurāṇa* (62: 24–32) gives a short description of the fight between Rāma and Rāvaṇa: on the first day of the bright half of the month of Āśvin the goddess went to Laṅka where, though remaining herself hidden, she caused Rāma and Rāvaṇa to be engaged in battle for seven days. After she had caused Rāvaṇa to be killed by Rāma on the ninth day, all the gods held a special *pūjā* for her. On the tenth day she was dismissed with Śabara festivals. See van Kooij, 1972: 109.

12 An interesting historical detail comes from Nepal, where Tuḷjā Bhavānī is worshipped under the name 'Taleju' as the goddess of the royal family. Allan (1975: 16–17): "An important feature of all these tales is that Taleju is consistently represented as a beautiful goddess who once maintained an intimate relationship with her worshipping King. Then one day an event occurred which so offended her that she no longer appeared in physical form. In some versions the King himself committed the offence by breaking the rule that he must not see her when he came to visit her; in others the offenders were suspicious female members of his family, either his wife or his daughter. But whatever the version, there is always the implication, which is sometimes made explicit, that the King developed a strong desire to sexually possess the goddess."

13 It is a weapon carried in a similar fashion as brass knuckles ("knuckle dusters") with the addition of four sharp, inwardly curved knives running along the inside of the fingers and imitating claws. The tiger is, it should be remembered here, the *vāhana* of the goddess Durgā.

14 Another reference to the *Devī Māhātmya* is found in the *Śivabhārata*, a Sanskrit biography of Śivājī by a contemporary court poet. Here we come across the verse: "By him, who behaves badly and whose lustre is like that of Niśumbha (*niśumbhasamatejasā*) the goddess living in Tuḷjāpūr was insulted." (see Apte and Divekar (eds.) 1927: Adhy. XVIII, 19). The story of the slaying of Niśumbha forms Adhy. IX. in the *Devī Māhātmya.*

15 In another context we come across a reference where Śivājī calls himself the *bhope* of his goddess (Ḍhere 1966: 94). "Bhope" (possibly etymologically related to Skt. *bhūpāla* – king) is the family name of the priests of Bhavānī in Tuḷjāpūr.

16 Ḍhere (1966: 93) quotes Śāhir Agindās: *pratāpgaḍcī bhavānī / śir vāhile jagadaṃbelā // battīs dāṃtāṃcā bokaḍ mātlā ge hotā / āhuti dilī abdulyācī //* Laine refers to the *Afzal Khān Vadha Povāḍā* of Ajñāndās in Kelkar 1928: 1–23 and id. 1961: 321–28.

17 Sontheimer (1985: 133) writes: "Wie auch sonst bei aufstrebenden Herrschern, rekrutierten sich die treuesten Gefolgsleute Śivājīs aus der bergigen Waldregion ('kuṟiñci') der angrenzenden westlichen Ghats."

18 For the relevant passages in the *bakhars* of Ciṭṇis, Sabhāsad, and Citragupta see Kulkarni 1920: 174–76.

19 In fact the story of Bhavānī's migration to Pratāpgaḍ is more complex. Another goddess, the Rāmavaradāyinī of Pār, is worshipped in a village nearby. She was the family deity of the Mores, an important and powerful Kṣatriya family which Śivājī defeated in 1656. How the Rāmavaradāyinī of Pār and the newly established Tuḷjā Bhavānī on Pratāpgaḍ got along with each other, i.e. whether the cults contributed to or borrowed from each other or remained distinct, can not be said at the moment.

20 Besides constituting a portion of the Tuḷjā Māhātmya (in both Sanskrit and Marāṭhī), the story appears in the *Bhāvārtha Rāmāyaṇa* of Ekanāth (see Ḍhere 1966: 87ff.), in the hymns of Svāmī Rāmadāsa, and in the *Śrīrāmavijaya* of Śrīdhāra (Kulkarni 1920: 19–22). Similar stories, connecting the abduction of Sītā through Rāvaṇa and Rāma's journey to Lanka with the Bhavānī of Tuḷjāpūr appear in Nepal. Cp. Wright (1877: 106) and Allan (1975: 15). According to Uerbach a similar story appears in Adhyāya 16, 25–28 and 30 of the Nepāla Māhātmya: they contain a "summary" of the *Rāmāyaṇa*. Unfortunately, I have not yet been able to secure the text.

21 *duṣṭa saṃhārile māgeṃ / aiseṃ aise udaṃḍa aikto // paraṃtu rokaḍe kāṃhīṃ / mūḷa samartha dākhavī //* "You have destroyed the vile people in the past/ I have heard of that a lot. But [please] show me directly/ Your original power." Pangarkar 1925: 389.

22 The translation is the outcome of a session with Dr. Tulpule in Pune, February 1989. My thanks are due to him. For the text see Pangarkar 1925: 57.

23 The process is reflected in a growing interest in the *Rāmāyaṇa* from the 16th century onwards. The Tuḷjā Māhātmya is, of course, hard to be dated. The meeting between Rāma and the Devī, which I consider the nucleus of the work, is a story that probably existed and still exists in many oral versions before it was committed to writing. The first more or less datable appearance of this version of the *Rāmāyaṇa* story in Marāṭhī literature is in the *Bhāvārtha Rāmāyaṇa* of Ekanāth (according to Ḍhere [1966: 87] in the Araṇyakāṇḍa: 20.64–65) which remained incomplete at his death in 1599. Secondly, there are a number of references to Rāmavaradāyinī in the compositions of Svāmī Rāmadāsa, i.e. from the 17th century. And finally there is the Śrīrāmavijaya, a Marāṭhī *Rāmāyaṇa*, composed by Śrīdharasvāmī in the 18th century. (See Kulkarni 1920: 19.)

REFERENCES

Allan, Michael R. 1925. *The Cult of Kumari. Virgin Worship in Nepal.* Kathmandu: Madhab Lal Maharjan (2nd edn.).

Bakhar of Sabhāsad. Edited by S.N. Jośī. 1960. Pune: Citraśāḷā Prakāśan.

Berntsen, Maxine. 1988. One Face of God. In: *The Experience of Hinduism.* Edited by Eleanor Zelliot & Maxine Berntsen. New York: State University of New York Press.

Ḍhere, Rā. Ciṃ. 1966. Pratāpgiricethāyī, ādiśakti virājate. In: Id., *Rāmarājyācī sphūrtikeṃdre*. Pune: Lalitavaibhava Prakāśan [in Marāṭhī].

Jansen, Roland. 1995. *Die Bhavānī von Tuljāpūr*. Religionsgeschichtliche Studie des Kultes einer Göttin der indischen Volksreligion. Beiträge zur Südasienforschung, Band 168, Südasien-Institut der Universität Heidelberg. Franz Steiner Verlag, Stuttgart.

Kelkar, Y.N. 1928–61. *Aitihāsika povāḍe*, 3 vols. Pune: Tilak Mahārāṣṭra Vidyapīṭh [in Marāṭhī].

van Kooij, K.R. 1972. *Worship of the Goddess according to the Kālikāpurāṇa*. Bd. I. Leiden: E.J. Brill.

Kulkarni, D.M. 1920. *Mahārāṣṭrācī kulasvāminī śrītuḷajābhavānī*. Pune [in Marāṭhī].

Laine, J.W. 1995. Śivājī as Epic Hero. In *Maharashtra: Culture and Society*. Edited by G.-D. Sontheimer. Delhi: Manohar.

Pangarkar, L.R. (ed.). 1925. *Samartha Sañjīvanī*. Pune [in Marāṭhī].

Parpola, Asko (forthcoming). From Ishtar to Durgā: Sketch of a Prehistory of India's Feline-riding and Buffalo Slaying Goddess of Victory. In: Sontheimer & Murty (forthcoming).

Price, Pamela (forthcoming). Villages and Royal Courts in South India: Continuities and Discontinuities in the Worship of the Goddess. In: Sontheimer & Murty (forthcoming).

Ranade, R.D. 1982. *Mysticism in Maharashtra*. Indian Mysticism. Delhi: Motilal Banarsidass (repr. 1st edition: Pune 1933).

Sardesai, G.S. 1957. *New History of the Marāṭhās*. Vol. I: *Śivājī and his Line*. Bombay.

Sircar, D.C. 1973. *The Śākta Pīṭhas*. Delhi.

Śivabhārata of Paramānanda. Edited by D.V. Apte and S.M. Divekar. 1927. Poona: Bhāratīya Itihās Saṃśodhak Maṇḍal [Sanskrit].

Sontheimer, G.-D. 1976. *Birobā, Mhaskobā und Khaṇḍobā*. Wiesbaden.

———. 1985. Cāturvarṇya, Bhakti und der Aufstieg von Volkskulten in Maharashtra: Religionsgeschichtliche Skizze einer Region. *Regionale Traditionen in Südasien*. Edited by H. Kulke & D. Rothermund. Heidelberg: BSAF, Bd. 104.

Sontheimer, G.D. & Murty, M.L.K. (eds.) (forthcoming). *Durgā and the Buffalo Demon*. Heidelberg/Delhi: South Asian Studies.

Stein, Burton. 1974. Devī Shrines and Folk Hinduism in Mediaeval Tamil Nadu. In: *Studies in the Language and Culture of South Asia*. Edited by E. Gerow & M.D. Lang. Seattle and London.

Vīramāla Sīvājīcā. 1966. Edited by N.B. Jośī. *Aitihāsik Saṃkīrṇa Nibaṃdha* (Quarterly of the Bhāratīya Itihās Saṃśodhak Maṇḍal). Pune: 9–18 [in Marāṭhī].

Wright, Daniel (ed.). 1877. *History of Nepal*. Translated from Parbatiya by Munshi Shew Shunker Singh and Pandit Sri Gunanand. Calcutta: Susil Gupta (India) Private Ltd. 1958 (reprint).

The Frustrated Hero

The Image of the Hero in Contemporary Urdu Stories

CHRISTINA OESTERHELD

WITH regard to the contemporary Urdu short story, the term "hero" should be used in a restricted sense only since it implies a judgement distinguishing it from more neutral terms as "central figure" or "protagonist". Very often, however, these three terms are treated like synonyms, and in this sense I shall use "hero" in the present paper.

While the hero in older Urdu literature, e.g. in the *dāstān*, despite of his often unheroic behaviour at least fights for a noble aim and represents the principle of good *versus* evil, the image of the hero in modern Urdu literature – as in many other contemporary literatures – is much more differentiated and shows a strong tendency towards the anti-hero. One should therefore more aptly speak of the concept of man rather than the concept of the hero in contemporary Urdu literature. The present study attempts to analyse this concept of man in the context of the conditions under which literature is produced and received as well as of the literary strategies used in the modern Urdu short story.

To provide a background for this analysis, let me first give a short review of the development of the Urdu short story in India. The status of Urdu in independent India as a language recognised in the constitution but of rather small importance in the political, administrative and commercial sector brought about a continuous shrinking of the market for Urdu literature. (Only in regard to mass literature the contrary can be stated). Works of literature are published in small editions (500 to 1000 copies); second editions are rare and often much belated. Thus, literary or other journals offer the promptest and most effective opportunity for publication, since they are cheaper than books and therefore sell better. Even renowned writers like Iṣmat Cuğtā'ī had their texts published in popular journals like "Bīsvī̃ ṣadī" or "Śama". The literary journals are dominated by poetry and short stories, serialised novels are a rare feature. Since the number of stories published in journals is immense, the examination of this material would require extended field studies. Besides some good texts a vast number of mediocre writings would have to be gone through, because for getting a piece published, connections are often more decisive than literary standard. Over the last years, a number of critical writings on short prose have come out in India summing up the development of the last 35–40 years and drawing first conclusions. A valuable contribution to the research in this field are the published materials of a Indo-Pak seminar on the Urdu story which was held at the Jamia Millia Islamia in Delhi 1980. The following survey is based on the analysis of short stories and secondary literature from the 1970s and early 1980s.

The fundamental changes in the political and social framework in independent India caused far-reaching transformations in literature, too. The All-Indian Progressive Writers' Association which had been the leading force in the literary scene of the 1930s and 1940s, gradually lost its influence under the new conditions until in 1956 it ceased to function – at least in the field of Urdu literature. The Progressive Movement had given a special boost to the Urdu short story. Authors like Kriśan Candar, Ṣaᶜādat Ḥasan Manṭo, Iṣmat Cuġtā'ī, later Aḥmad Nadīm Qāsimī and Rājindar Singh Bedī and others took up pressing social problems and treated them each in their own way. They continued the tradition of Premcand[1] and of the stories collected in "*Aṅgāre*"[2] and developed it further. This critical-realistic line was quite diverse in subject matter and formal structure. On the other hand, from the end of the thirties on there had been an organized movement of predominantly aesthetically oriented literature whose representatives viewed committed literature with more or less strong reservations. After independence this movement became concentrated in Pakistan, discussions on committed literature, on the social function of literature and its formal-aesthetic realization, however, increased in the first half of the 1950s in India as well and led to fierce controversies about humanist middle-class writers on the one hand and writers like Kriśan Candar on the other. He and other progressives were criticized for superficially propagandistic writing, lack of form-consciousness and a too limited choice of subjects.

Some of these accusations were justified – the very prolific writer Kriśan Candar, for instance, did not always produce masterpieces, and especially from the fifties onwards he tended to self-repetition and formulaic writing, but they ignored the great contributions of these writers, their literary innovations, which opened new vistas for Urdu literature. On the other hand, progressive writers often failed to respond to the altered circumstances or to understand the reaction of younger writers to changed social conditions. The break-up of the anticolonial united front, the disillusionment caused by the results of independence, the forced capitalist development and the shift to the right in domestic policies not only increasingly withdrew the basis for an organized literary movement, it had an impact on the writers' objectives and their views on the functioning of literature as well. The possibility of a direct, operational intervention in social conditions through works of literature became unlikely. Urgent social problems remained unsolved, but it was not possible to deal with them in the same fashion again and again without effecting aversion. The overall social conditions led to the choice of new subjects and to a more subjective presentation centred around the – in most cases middle-class – individual. In the 1950s, the term "*jadīd afsāna*" (new or modern story) was coined for this type of story which concentrated on the working of the consciousness and the intellectual and emotional processing of the experiences of life. The term "*jadīd*" is quite ambiguous; it has also been interpreted as "modernistic".

In the beginning, the "new" story showed certain reductions – the social environment of the characters and the social roots for their psychological problems were widely omitted, and no story in the real sense was told. However, these reductions did not occur in all texts to the same extent. Instead of breadth, more depth was gained, new dimensions were opened up. This line, too, had a tradition – authors like Sajjād Ẓahīr or Qurrat-ul-ᶜAin Ḥaidar had written in a similar fashion in the 1930s and 1940s already, but only in the 1950s this trend could develop into a full-fledged school. Though most of these "new" stories were realistic, they were inconsistent with the narrow, normative concept of realism of the fifties, which implied a linear narrative and concrete representationalism.

In the 1960s, within the "new" story the trend of the symbolic or abstract story (*ᶜalāmatī* or *tajrīdī afsāna*) arose which was extremely heterogeneous. The term "abstract story" has never been defined. The Indian critic Vaḥīd Aḵẖtar rightly remarked that the term as such is absurd because it is specific for fiction to clothe the most abstract facts in a concrete, sensory form (see Vaḥīd Aḵẖtar: 21). The term was used for texts operating with non-literary sign languages (from mathematics or chemistry, for instance), but also for symbolic or parable-like stories having a plot abstract in time and space. This trend included writers who chose forms of symbolic encoding, of the parable or of mythological narration to tackle a complex reality full of contradictions and to achieve a generalizing presentation. This type of literature aimed at comprehending and criticizing reality and stimulated the reader's activity. On the other hand, some writers brought their stories to such a high level of abstraction or to such a symbolic obscurity that the representative character of the narration was totally lost and communication with the reader became rather impossible. Even within a chosen circle of people having literary education this kind of short story was finally rejected. Texts of this type proved to be either unreadable or so boring that the reader put them away after a few lines. Moreover, this school began to show tendencies towards imitation, formulaic repetition and formal experiments for their own sake. In the 1970s, this development ceased to exist as an independent trend. Symbolic presentation became one possibility among others. The majority of writers returned to an approach facilitating reception. In the meantime, reading habits had developed, too, so that author and reader met halfway.

At the same time, many authors continued the critical-realistic tradition – taking into account the new social conditions and introducing various structural innovations. Some prominent names in this line are Rājindar Singh Bedī, Iṣmat Cuğtā'ī, Qurrat-ul-ᶜAin Ḥaidar, Jīlānī Bāno, Jogindar Pāl, Rām Lāl, Kartār Singh Duggal and Śaukat Ḥayāt. The Urdu short story of the 1970s and 1980s presents a colourful, lively picture. Most authors use an individual, distinctive style, but it has become difficult to distinguish between particular trends or schools because the writings of a single author often reveal a broad spectrum of subjects and formal techniques. A common feature of the contemporary Urdu short story is a deep sense of artistic conscience. The contemporary writer is not less committed than his predecessors of the

1930s and 1940s. Subjects like corruption, hypocracy and double standards, the decline of intellectual and moral values are of central importance to modern writers as are social contradictions in the country and the cities, unemployment, the unpleasant living conditions of the lower middle-class, the as yet suppressed position of women and perennial themes like love, death, war and peace. Urdu writers respond to contemporary issues – the emergency or communal riots, for instance – without getting agitative or propagandistic. Even such highly political subjects are treated in their effect on the individual in a very subtle, personal and at the same time generalizing manner.

As I have already mentioned, most of the heroes of contemporary Urdu literature come from the urban middle-class – like the producers and readers of this literature who are journalists, teachers, office workers or civil servants. In spite of all diversity in approach, the texts reveal certain basic patterns of human behaviour:

1. The type of the ruthless opportunist and social climber. As a rule, he is depicted from the outside in objectified narration by a non-personal narrator.

2. The type of the conformist suffering from his conformity. He is often depicted from the inside, in interior monologue or stream of consciousness-technique.

3. The type of non-conformist or drop-out. He is depicted from the inside and/or outside, mostly in linear narrative.

This scheme is of course simplified and should be taken as an aid for orientation only.

One type is conspiciously absent from this list – the type of the idealist, the rebel or reformer. This type is very rare in contemporary Urdu literature in India, only elements of it are recognizable in some figures. In regard to Pakistan's Urdu literature, things are quite different. Especially under the military dictatorship of Zia-ul Haq, a number of stories were written which contained clear social and political utopian dreams and propagated the type of the rebel and revolutionary. The most prominent representative of this line is Anvar Sajjād, who in symbolic coding sharply criticized the conditions prevailing in his country and tried to provoke the reader to action. The stronger political and ideological repression in Pakistan led to a politicized literature that could create more definite concepts of an enemy and more concrete objectives than the Indian Urdu literature. The complexity of the situation in India with its vast social, religious, ethnic and caste divisions does not allow for such clear-cut messages. There are, however, certain exceptions. In "*Mukālama*" (The Dialogue) by Aḥmad Yūsuf, for instance, the story is set in the world of fairy tale. The hero – in the original meaning of the word – is a kid drinking from a spring, side by side with a lion. (The picture of the kid and the lion drinking from one spring is symbolic of a situation where law and order and the rights of the weak are guaranteed by a just ruler.) Defying the lion's threats, the kid continues to drink and is consequently eaten by the lion. When the lion returns to the spring he finds another kid drinking at the same place. The story repeats itself again and again until the lion is completely exhausted. The end of the story remains open, but the final victory of the weaker seems inevitable (see Aḥmad Yūsuf: 207–08). It is certainly no coincidence that this story encouraging self-assured, upright behaviour is written in the form of a parable – on the level of everyday-experience this message would have been much more difficult to relate.

Characters of the first type for whom social advancement and material gain are more important than all other values and who cast off love, friendship, solidarity and compassion in the process get negative evaluations from all writers. They describe either the process or its results, that is the behaviour of such characters towards others. As a rule, stories having main characters of this type are written in the traditional critical realistic manner; some of them contain sentimental social criticism in Kriśan Candar's style.

Characters of the second type are depicted with much more differentiation and authorial empathy. They either adjust themselves after attempted rebellion or right from the beginning lead a conformist life without finding peace of mind. Characters of this type are among the most interesting in Urdu literature. They can be central figures in stories written in the traditional critical-realistic mode or I-figures in subjectively structured narration. These characters clearly show the frustration, the loneliness, the loss of identity, the helplessness and existential fear of the individual in modern society which in India, too, leads to alienation, levelling down, to the predominance of commercial values and the decline of received moral concepts. The hero of this type is a victim of the circumstances but in a certain sense also partly responsible for them – through his passivity and conformity. A good example for this kind of hero is the main figure of the short story "*Khūn bahā*" (Blood Money) by Salām bin Razzāq (Salām bin Razzāq 1981: 223–37). The story is about the murder of a young farm labourer who had organized his workmates in a struggle for the minimum wages. The murder is committed by goondas employed by the landowner. This incident is not described directly, however, but as mirrored in the recollections and feverish ravings of the village teacher who happened to witness the murder. This teacher is the central figure of the story, his pangs of conscience form the main subject. The police officer in charge of the investigation stays with the landlord and is clearly on his side. The teacher, too, is paid by the landowner. But out of the fear to be murdered himself the teacher not only remains silent about what he has seen, but also fails to reject the hush-money the landlord slips him. This money he unnoticedly passes into the cradle of the victim's son. Then he leaves the village. This story which is convincingly and impressively told by the I-figure (the teacher) leaves no doubt about it that the hero will nevertheless not be able to escape from his conscience.

The motif of conscience is of central importance in the modern Urdu short story. One of the basic patterns is to describe how a person's conscience dies while he or she is successful in making a career and in rising in the social order. The Indian writer Kumār Pāśī points out the difference between the presentation of the moral decay of society by the older writers (Premcand, Manṭo) and by the younger ones (after 1960) as follows: With the older writers, the guilty hero has to die or to be reformed; with the younger writer only his conscience dies (see Kumār Pāśī: 9). In the story mentioned above the outcome of the hero's moral conflict remains open, his conscience is alive and makes him suffer terribly, and yet he is unable to act according to his conscience so that the practical result is the same as if he had silenced his conscience.

The story is told entirely from the hero's point of view without any authorial comments or judgements. This highly subjective presentation makes the story very compelling. The author's attitude towards his hero contains elements of identification as well as detachment, of understanding and sympathy as well as a critical assessment of the hero's failure. He thereby includes that class into his social criticism which is the main producer and perceiver of contemporary Urdu literature.

In his story "*Anjām-i-kār*" (The final Result), Salām bin Razzāq uses similar literary devices – with the difference that here he depicts the development from rebellion to resignation (Salām bin Razzāq 1974: 19–26). A comic version of the same theme is Qurrat-ul-ᶜAin's short story "*Faqīrõ kī pahāṛī*" (The Faqirs' Hill) (Qurrat-ul-ᶜAin Ḥaidar 1982: 123-37).

While Salām bin Razzāq uses forms of mimetic narration, the writer Qamar Aḥsan prefers symbolic modes of presentation. This author who like Salām bin Razzāq entered the literary scene in the seventies, tends to put his figures into extreme, often deadly situations – one of his characters is locked up in a room getting filled with smoke and flames and cannot find the exit, another one, a leper, has been banished from the village community and languishes in the wilderness. In every case the author intends to expose the mercilessness of the circumstances and of individuals in exaggerated form. One of the most striking examples for this method is "*Taᶜāqub*" (The Chase), the story of a family fleeing from cruel pursuers in a not specified war. To save his own life, the father sacrifices his three children. In the mother, the maternal instinct wins over the instinct of survival – after having lost two children, she comes to the third's rescue and is captured herself (Qamar Aḥsan 1980: 155). More interesting in regard to the second type of hero is another short story by the same author, representing a special case of this second type – "*Yā Muṣtafā*", a stream of the author's reflections deploring his cowardice and inactivity. He dreams of a violent revolt, of radical changes, but does not have the courage to act accordingly and is in doubt about the potential of his writings to create any impact: "I'm quite an unimportant prose writer. If even Allāma Iqbāl was unable to turn anybody into a true believer, how could I bring about a revolution?" (Qamar Aḥsan 1980: 151). The story ends: "What I want to say may be quite serious and important, but my literary expression is weak. Thus I get lost in the tangles of narration and remain a helpless spectator." (Qamar Aḥsan 1980: 157). The introspection of the author here goes beyond the scope of a short story and becomes rather essayistic. Stories of this kind are quite a common feature in the highly subjective Urdu prose related from the hero's point of view. Often such texts resemble lyric outpourings and are long-winded and boring. Qamar Aḥsan's texts face another danger. Most of them are quite incomprehensible, their components – motifs from different mythologies, from the history of Islam, especially from Schiite traditions, pieces from *dāstān*-literature, etc. – sometimes fail to form an integrated whole, time and place remain abstract. Formal experiments often seem to be an end in themselves – as a means to gain innovativeness and originality at any rate. The short story mentioned above shows that the author is to a certain degree conscious of this problem. The doubt expressed by him regarding the effectiveness of his literary expression points to the fact that he is searching for modes of expression facilitating literary communication. At the same time, the story is a compelling depiction of the conflict between the urge to act and bring about changes on the one hand and toleration and the retreat into the private refuge on the other hand. The same conflict is depicted in Kunvar Sen's short story "*Is bār nahī̃*" (Not This Time). The narrator-hero sensitively registers the signs of the times, realizes the necessity to act, but in view of the consequences of active involvement he retreats with the words: "No, not this time, not again and again!" He justifies his retreat referring to the failure of his previous attempts: "What was the result of my last sacrifice? The situation is much worse than before!" (Kunvar Sen 1980: 76–81). This is an expression of bitterness created by the fruitlessness of social involvement – a disillusionment born in the 1950s which has been growing ever since. The hero justifies himself with the excuse that active intervention doesn't change anything, and yet he is tormented by his bad conscience because he as an intellectual realizing the need for changes more clearly than others feels a special responsibility.

The third type is linked with the motif of travelling or wandering, one of the oldest literary motifs which is of central importance especially in the *dāstān*. In modern Urdu prose this motif is particularly common in narrative-symbolical texts. The journey may have a destination which is never reached, however, or which proves to be deceptive. The aim may be one's own identity, the meaning of the individuals' existence or a better, fuller life. The heroes are in search of something without knowing the way to their destination. Often their journey rather is an attempt to escape circumstances felt to be unbearable. This escape can be more important than the destination which often remains unknown. In one of Qamar Aḥsan's short stories a character confesses: "Why after all did we set out for this journey? The problems there won't diminish after we have gone, and what will we gain by this journey?" (Qamar Aḥsan 1980: 167–80). The sense of the journey is questioned by the travellers themselves – in contrast to the attitude of the hero of the *dāstān* which the title of this story – "*Ṭilismāt*" (Magic) – clearly refers to. The three heroes of this story actually are fleeing from themselves and searching for themselves to be confronted at the end, after reaching the supposed destination, with their own old-age images into whom they finally merge. In the story "*Ātmakathā*" by Ḥusain-ul-Ḥaq, too, the escape into a better world fails because life's misery is the same everywhere. To be able to survive the hero has to cut off his head – a symbol for complete mental and moral submission. The destination of the journey in Akhtar Vāṣif's story "*Zamīn mẽ gaṛe pā'o*" (Feet Sunk into the Earth) remains unknown (Akhtar Vāṣif 1980: 130–32). The story depicts a half realistic, half dream-like train journey through the desert. The motif of the journey here is contradicted by the title of the story clearly pointing to the fact that this journey actually leads nowhere. The hero with his perceptions and impressions feels completely lonely in the crowd of travellers. There is no communication between him and the others. The situation fills him with fear and apprehension. This impression is heightened by the image of the desert around. The same motif of a journey through the desert is used by Sājid Raśīd in his story "*Ret ghaṛī*" (The Hour-glass) – here too symbolic of emptiness, lifelessness, monotony (Sājid Raśīd 1980: 87–92).

The general decline of values, opportunistic attitudes, greed and selfishness affect the female characters not less than the male ones. The heroines, however, are often reduced to the role of the victim, especially in stories written by women. In contrast to their male counterparts they are not only the victims of general social circumstances, but of men, often of their husbands. This, too, is due to patriarchal conditions which don't allow women to develop their individuality, to gain self-determination and to fully realize their sexuality. In varying gradations, these restrictive social norms bear on men as well. They enjoy more freedom than women, but they too have to submit to the rules of the community if they don't want to become outcasts.

If one looks at the characters of modern Urdu short stories it becomes obvious that the most common and the most interesting character is the anti-hero. The clerk, the teacher, the unemployed academician or – as in symbolic prose – the nameless and shapeless "*vah*" (he) are victims of alienation and isolation, of a helpless frustration; they have lost their identity (therefore the abstract heroes!) and their orientation. The hero experiences his living circumstances as depressing and ponders about his unhappiness and restlessness, he longs for another life without finding the strength to bring about a change at least in his own life. Where the hero acts he as a rule escapes from his old life and searches for a new, better one without ever succeeding in his search. Mostly this situation is depicted in gloomy colours from a subjective point of view, often without any detachment of the author. A detached, ironical or satirical point of view is rather rare because the author himself is too involved to find the necessary detachment. And yet the fact that the "frustrated hero" critically reflects his situation, that he is unable to accept it without resistance, that he sometimes tries to escape it carries a glimmer of hope since it proves that the longing for a fullfilled existence and the free development of the individual's potentials, for humanity, warmth and solidarity is still alive. This humanistic potential is an essential component of contemporary Urdu fiction.

NOTES

1 Premcand (1880–1936), one of the best-known prose writers of Hindi and Urdu, is understood to be the first critical realist in both literatures. He depicted the life of Indian villagers and, to a lesser degree, of the lower urban middle class in a partly realistic, partly idealistic and romantic manner. Premcand was one of the mentors of the Progressive Writers' Movement.

2 The collection of short stories "*Aṅgāre*" (Live Coals) was published by a group of young writers in 1931–32. In a very outspoken manner – influenced by Marxian and Freudian ideas – they condemn social and religious oppression and hypocrisy. The publication of this rather slim volume provoked strong reactions from different orthodox quarters, and the book was finally recalled by the government.

REFERENCES

Aḥmad, Yūsuf. 1981. Mukālama. *Alfāz, Afsāna nambar*: 207–09.

Ājkāl. Delhi: Publications Division.

Akḫtar, Vaḥīd. 1981. Sukḫangustarāna bāt. *Alfāz̤, Afsāna nambar*: 14–26.

Akḫtar, Vāṣif. 1980. Zamīn mẽ gaṛe pāo. In: *Nayā urdū afsāna*, 130–32.

Alfāz̤, Afsāna nambar. Aligarh: Educational Book House, Jan.–Apr. 1981.

Ḥaidar, Qurrat-ul-ᶜAin. 1982. *Rośnī kī raftār*. Aligarh: Educational Book House.

Kumār Pāśī (ed.). 1980. *Nayā urdū afsāna – iḥtisāb aur intiḵẖāb*. Delhi: Modern Publishing House.

Qamar, Aḥsan. 1980. *Āg, alāo, ṣaḥrā*. Ilāhābād: Śab ḵẖūn kitābghar.

Raśīd, Sājid. 1980. Ret ghaṛi. In: *Nayā urdū afsāna*, 87–92.

Razzāq, Salām bin. 1974. Anjām-i-kār. *Ājkāl* 8/74: 19–26.

———. 1981. Ḵẖūn bahā. *Alfāz̤, Afsāna nambar*: 223–37.

Sen Kunvar. 1980. Is bār nahī̃. In: *Nayā urdū afsāna*, 76–81.

From Sacrificer to Hero

PETER D. SAKHAROV

THE present essay concerns the earliest Sanskrit mythological narratives, in which a man – not a god – acts as a protagonist. Sporadically, narratives of this kind are found as early as in the Brāhmaṇas, but a real multitude of them appears in the epic and the Purāṇic texts. In order to trace the prehistory of monoheroic narrative I undertake the comparative analysis of a typical Purāṇic example – a well-known Hariścandra myth, found in the *Mārkaṇḍeya-purāṇa*, cantos 7–8.[1]

The story goes like this: A virtuous king Hariścandra incurs the anger of a sage, Viśvāmitra. The king is ready to satisfy the sage. Viśvāmitra demands the fee appertaining to the *rājasūya* sacrifice (though there is no mention that this sacrifice was performed). Hariścandra gives up to Viśvāmitra his kingdom, but the sage demands an additional payment. After a month's deferment, Hariścandra sells his wife, Śaibyā, and his son Rohitāsya (in some versions, Rohitāśva), to a *brāhman*. Finally, he sells himself to a *caṇḍāla* (in fact, the god Dharma, in the guise of a *caṇḍāla*). As the *caṇḍāla*'s servant, Hariścandra works at a burning-ground and endures terrible sufferings. One day Rohitāsya is bitten by a snake and dies. Śaibyā takes his corpse to the burning ground; there she meets Hariścandra. Both resolve to immolate themselves on their son's funeral pyre, but Indra, Dharma and other gods interpose and restore Rohitāsya to life. Indra calls Hariścandra to heaven; Hariścandra ascends with his wife and all his people. Viśvāmitra enthrones Rohitāsya.

In order to find out the origin of this myth I tried to compare it with epic and Vedic (mostly, Brāhmaṇic) records about king Hariścandra. The information in the *Mahābhārata* is scanty. Hariścandra is mentioned as an inhabitant of the celestial palace of Indra. During his earthly life he was a great sovereign. Having conquered the whole earth, he performed a *rājasūya*. After the sacrifice he gave enormous gifts to *brāhmans*. That is why he has gained more glory and majesty than other kings.[2] There are some obvious similarities between epic and Purāṇic accounts, such as Hariścandra's sovereignty over the whole earth, his generosity, and his dwelling in Indra's celestial abode. It is also noteworthy that both texts mention the *rājasūya*: The *Mārkaṇḍeya-purāṇa* merely as a pretext to demand the fee, the *Mahābhārata* as the great merit of Hariścandra. It is warranted to suppose that by the time of the formation of epic and Purāṇic literature the *rājasūya* was not practiced as a rite. Therefore, these texts never explain the reason for performing this sacrifice.[3] Its name remains just as an unaccountable attribute of the heroic age.

Some more parallels to the Purāṇic myth can be found in the Brāhmaṇic Śunaḥśepa myth, which is narrated in the *Aitareya-brāhmaṇa* (VII. 13–18) and the *Śāṅkhāyana-śrautasūtra* (XV. 17–28). Its contents are as follows:

A childless king, Hariścandra, makes a vow that on obtaining a son he will sacrifice him to the god Varuṇa. A son is born to him named Rohita. But Hariścandra puts off on various pious pretexts the fulfilment of his vow, and when at length he consents to perform it, his son refuses to be sacrificed and retires to the forest. Varuṇa punishes Hariścandra by causing him to be afflicted with dropsy. After six years of wandering, Rohita purchases Śunaḥśepa, the son of a poor seer, Ajīgarta, to serve as a substitute. Varuṇa agrees to accept Śunaḥśepa as a sacrifice, because a *brāhman* is more suitable as an offering than a *kṣatriya*. The *rājasūya* is commenced, celebrated by certain divine seers (including Viśvāmitra). Śunaḥśepa is tied up in order to be immolated. He addresses various gods, and after his praise of the goddess Uṣas his fetters become untied. At the same moment Hariścandra is cured of his dropsy. Viśvāmitra adopts Śunaḥśepa as his son. If this myth is compared with the epic narrative concerning Hariścandra, only one similarity is found: the reference to the *rājasūya*. There are, however, numerous parallels between the Brāhmaṇic and Purāṇic myths besides *rājasūya*, such as similar names, actual or potential death and resurrection of a son (or his substitute), necessity to fulfil a vow, its deferment and consequent wandering, and a penalty for Hariścandra and restoration of his original state; moreover, in both narratives Viśvāmitra rewards the hero (celebrates the *rājasūya* and enthrones his son). But there is also a profound similarity of these two myths which corroborates the supposition that they have a common source. The plot of the Brāhmaṇic Śunaḥśepa myth consists of two parts: the first one concerns the events before the *rājasūya*; the second one, the *rājasūya* itself. The two parts are analogous structurally and semantically: a person who seeks some benefit must reduce himself (give up the things he seeks); as a result he gains the proper reward. In the first part, the king, who seeks a son, must sacrifice the same son. The second part has a similar meaning, though not one that is expressed explicitly. A king who performs a *rājasūya* symbolically gives up everything he possesses (i.e. by observing of the complicated ritual symbolism he sacrifices his whole kingdom and himself); as a result he gets back his royal prosperity.[4]

It is sufficient that in both parts the god Varuṇa plays a significant role. In the first part Varuṇa satisfies Hariścandra's wish for progeny; he also punishes the king by giving him dropsy. Varuṇa's role in the second part is more latent: the whole rite of the *rājasūya* in most of the Vedic texts is connected with the name of Varuṇa par excellence. Consequently, the association of Varuṇa with the sky implies the idea that the final reward of a king for performing a *rājasūya* is heaven.[5]

The Purāṇic Hariścandra myth has the same outline: the king sacrifices his prosperity, his son, and himself; through this he gets back everything he has given up and also attains heaven as a highest reward. If so, it is reasonable to suppose that either this myth has developed from the Śunaḥśepa myth or both myths have originated from a common source.

The evolution of Varuṇa's role in the development of this cycle of myths deserves special notice. As for the Purāṇic myth, the part of the gods is minimal: they play secondary roles. Careful comparative analysis of the Hariścandra myth indicates that the functions of Varuṇa are distributed among other dramatic personae. The majority of Varuṇa's functions is inherited not by a god but by the priest, viz., Viśvāmitra. Like Varuṇa, the most ambivalent of Vedic gods, Viśvāmitra is ambivalent for the hero: he tests and saves. Much more surprising is another thing, which is not expressed explicitly in the Hariścandra myth but appears in many related myths: Viśvāmitra does not merely test and save a hero, but also suffers himself or participates in the sufferings of a hero.

Three groups of such myths may be marked. The first group includes different variants of myths about Triśaṅku,[6] in which sufferings of the king are paralleled by those of Viśvāmitra;[7] at last, Viśvāmitra helps the hero to obtain benefits and to ascend to heaven.

The second group of myths demonstrates situations of obvious reduction of Viśvāmitra: during the cosmic disaster he wanders and endures hunger; as a result he conduces to the universal good.[8]

The third group is the most notable: it is represented by myths in which, at first, Viśvāmitra is tested by some supreme being. Through that test he, a *kṣatriya* by birth, becomes a *brāhman*. After this, he puts someone else to a test and grants rewards.[9]

All the listed mythological situations indicate that Viśvāmitra possesses double ambivalency: he tests and benefits – on the other hand, he tests and is tested. This suggests once again the idea of the sacrifice – especially the *rājasūya* – as the source of myths mentioned above. In essence, a sacrificer, a sacrifice and a priest were somehow identified with one another by the Brāhmaṇic ritual mentality. Moreover, the symbolism of the *rājasūya* definitely emphasizes this identification.[10] With regard to this peculiarity, it may be noticed that the change of social position of Viśvāmitra is typical of these myths. In many of them he, being a *kṣatriya*, becomes a *brāhman*; or, quite the reverse, he shares the destiny of a *caṇḍāla*. A similar change of *varṇa* position happens to some other characters in these myths, especially to kings: as a rule their social status becomes much lower, but is restored by the end of a story. It is not likely to be a mere coincidence that one of the most important episodes of the *rājasūya* is the temporal translation of a king who performs a sacrifice, to the state of a *brāhman* and the consequent recovery of the original position of a *kṣatriya*.[11]

This remarkable feature of the Brāhmaṇic royal ritual seems to be manifested also in two types of mythological situations. The first one is represented by myths in which one of the kingly gods (as a rule, Indra or Rudra) is excommunicated from a numinal sacrifice.[12] Another is represented by numerous myths about earthly exile kings. Some certain peculiarities may be noticed in myths of this type: a king is deprived of his kingdom in the very beginning of his rule, the exile lasts twelve years, the king obtains his kingdom and heaven at the end of the story. All the listed peculiarities are present in the Hariścandra myth (the period of twelve years appears not in the actual duration of Hariścandra's sufferings, but in the hero's dream). Another vivid example of this type is the story of the Pāṇḍavas in the *Mahābhārata*.[13] It is quite possible that both types of mythological situations have originated from some archaic practice, ritual or social, which is not witnessed adequately in available texts. The relationship between the *rājasūya* sacrifice and the Hariścandra myth (no less than other myths mentioned above) may also be corroborated by the functional analysis of some characters. As I have already mentioned, the most significant role in the *rājasūya* was that of Varuṇa. In the Purāṇic myth his functions are inherited mostly by Viśvāmitra, as was noted above, but also by some other deities. Dharma is the most evident among them. Like Viśvāmitra, he is ambivalent for the hero: he exploits the hero and then (together with Indra) invites him to heaven. The part of Dharma, the comparatively late deity, may be explained by the fact that some of his features are similar to those of Varuṇa. It is Dharma who possesses Varuṇa's functions as the custodian of the cosmic order and moral law. Just like Varuṇa, Dharma is known to be "king".[14] It remains to be added that the whole Brāhmaṇic *rājasūya* sacrifice symbolized the release of the sacrificer from Varuṇa's fetters; in the Hariścandra myth Dharma, in a similar way, captures and releases the hero. Another heir of Varuṇa in the later mythology is Yama, the king of the dead. The Yama of the epics and Purāṇas does not have much in common with the Vedic Yama.[15] Some features of his appearance and behavior copy those of Varuṇa.[16] But, as a rule, Yama does not test and save a hero explicitly, as Dharma does. In some myths he is absent and his part is substituted for by the motif of death. Thus, in the Hariścandra myth the motif of death appears repeatedly, though each time the actual death of the hero does not happen. It is substituted, for instance, by the death of Hariścandra's son and by Hariścandra's ascending the funeral pyre. Quite typical is Hariścandra's triple loss (kingdom, wife and form), which may be considered a "pseudo-death".[17]

Similarly, the motif of death manifests itself in the *Mahābhārata*, in which it assumes even more complicated forms. For instance, just before the end of twelve years dwelling in the forest, a mysterious temporal death of Pāṇḍavas happens, after which they are restored to life.[18] Then comes the thirteenth year, the most dangerous one for the Pāṇḍavas, when they have to dwell unrecognized among people. With this purpose the Pāṇḍavas change their appearence and social status. The text of the *Mahābhārata*, describing the thirteenth year, repeatedly identifies the state of the Pāṇḍavas with the embryonic one, i.e. the state which is to be followed by a new birth.[19] There is also an episode of the real death of the Pāṇḍavas in the end of the epic; they visit hell and, after that, ascend to heaven. Indra, who meets them, explains that every king must see hell before ascending to heaven.[20]

All the above-mentioned parallels – and many other ones[21] – lead to a conclusion that epic and Purāṇic myths about exiled kings have originated from an archaic complex of solemn royal sacrifices (probably, inauguration or para-inaugurational rituals). In the Brāhmaṇic period some of the related rites – among them, definitely, *rājasūya* and *aśvamedha* – were not strictly esoteric: the number of their participants was not confined to members of the royal family and a multitude of *brāhmans*, but spread over the various strata of society of those days.[22] Perhaps these sacrifices provided a favourable environment for the development of storytelling. Something of that kind is known, for instance, to have taken place at the *aśvamedha*: it is witnessed by several texts commenting on the horse-sacrifice, in which "*itihāsa*" (the term later applied to the *Mahābhārata*) and "*purāṇa*" are mentioned.[23]

Generally, the Vedic terms "*itihāsa*" and "*purāṇa*" (or compound "*itihāsa-purāṇa*") were obviously used as collective nouns, which implied some verbal production – initially, heroic songs and stories, royal panegyrics and glorifications of genealogies. This verbal production was in use at solemn royal rites or had a close connection with them, and it was addressed to kings.[24] It may be more or less safely inferred that the principal element of the archaic ritual prototypes, analyzed above – and, consequently, of myths connected with them – was the reduction and exile of a king.[25] The differences among myths of this cycle may be explained by differences of functions and contexts. Thus, the Brāhmaṇic Śunaḥśepa myth, which represents the early level of the narrative actualization of ritual, appears no more than a detail in the mechanism of interpretation of the *rājasūya*. On the contrary, in the Purāṇic myth the ritual is superseded by the outlying area of the narrative. It remains to be added that the same mythological model passed through many other kinds of development; for instance, its two different forms, enormously expanded, are represented by the two great Indian epics.

It is reasonable, however, to mark the phases of the evolution: the latest phase is represented by fully developed mythological stories about kings; these are found in the epic and Purāṇic literature, which is functionally narrative. An earlier phase consists of complete mythological narratives about kings found in the Brāhmaṇas and the ritual Sūtras; such stories were instruments of ritual, because their principal function was interpretation of ritual. To their number belongs the Śunaḥśepa myth, no less than nameless "*itihāsas*" and "*purāṇas*", mentioned in the context of *aśvamedha*. An even earlier phase is represented by incomplete and fragmentary mythological information, which is multiple in the Brāhmaṇic codices, as it accompanies every moment of ritual. This mythological information, already fixed as a sacred text, declares the whole set of symbolic identifications to be known by a performer of a ritual – "who knows thus" – in order to make sacrifice successful.[26] It may be supposed that the earliest phase of this process was represented by some archaic ritual prototypes, not witnessed textually.

But how could it happen that some ritual paradigms have been transformed into complete narratives? An answer may be but tentative. The mythological fund of the Vedas had two aspects: the universal one (cosmology and pantheon) and the individual one (ritual). Each rite, though associated with the cosmic process, was performed for a certain sacrificer. A sacrificer formed the nucleus of a sacrifice, in which he passed through different stages, each one with its complicated symbolism and some concise mythological information. Very fragmentary in early Brāhmaṇic time, this mythological information gradually grew and, as a result, developed into complete myths to be narrated at a ritual. In those myths a sacrificer (king) was replaced by a hero (protagonist). The deeds of the latter doubled the symbolic actions of the former; the stages of a ritual, passed through by a sacrificer, were paralleled by the episodes of a narrative, which actualized previously formless mythological information to a certain plot, constructing and vivifying its originally dispersed elements.

Unfortunately, the extant texts give no explicit information concerning the evolution of story-telling. Moreover, I do not state that this was the only mode of its formation. The present hypothesis claims to explain just one possible way of herogenesis in ancient Indian literature.

NOTES

1 The Bombay edition of the *Mārkaṇḍeya-purāṇa* contains the fullest version. The best English translation was produced by F.E. Pargiter (1904); it is based on another version, which is slightly different and omits some verses.

2 *Mahābhārata* II. 7: 13; 12: 10–19. References to the *Mahābhārata* are given according to the Bombay edition of the Vulgata version.

3 There are various theories concerning the purpose of the *rājasūya* (e.g. Weber 1893; Heesterman 1957; Falk 1984). I am not going to dispute any of them, because each one contains a number of valuable observations. At the same time, I am not sure whether singers of fully developed epics and Purāṇas knew much more about the purpose of *rājasūya* than we do.

4 Cp. *Śatapatha-brāhmaṇa* V. 5.2; for interpretation see Heesterman 1957: 22–23.

5 See Weber 1893: 7–8; Heesterman 1957: 7, 22, 211. The recent study by B.K. Smith has indicated that a king who performed a *rājasūya* symbolically ascended to heaven and returned back right at the time of the sacrifice; anyway, his posthumous dwelling in heaven was the final purpose (Smith 1985: 292, 297–98).

6 One of the early variants is the Triśaṅku myth in the Rāmāyaṇa I. 57–60. The further development of this story is found in the Satyavrata legend, contaminated with the Triśaṅku myth. Among other Purāṇic versions, *Harivaṃśa* I. 12–13 seems to be the earliest.

7 Usually, Viśvāmitra practices austerities, which are simultaneous with the sufferings of a hero (as in Triśaṅku myth) or precede them (in the story of Hariścandra). In the Triśaṅku myth this motif is added by that of sufferings of Viśvāmitra's family: his wife, starving, tries to sell her son. (Cp. the similar situation in the Śunaḥśepa myth: the name of Śunaḥśepa's father – Ajīgarta – literally means "he, who has nothing to swallow").

8 E.g.: *Mahābhārata* XII. 141; *Brahma-purāṇa* 93.

9 A vivid example is the Gālavacarita in the *Mahābhārata* (V. 106–20). Cp. also *Mahābhārata* I. 71; IX. 40.

10 The *rājasūya* symbolism implies, at the same time, the identity of a king and his son (e.g. *Śatapatha-brāhmaṇa* V.4.2: 5–9; cp. also Heesterman 1957: 124–26; Falk 1984: 118–19, 135). The identity of a sacrificer, a sacrifice and a priest in the *rājasūya* is declared vividly in the *Aitareya-brāhmaṇa* VII. 26. For additional arguments see Heesterman 1957: 192; Falk 1984: 123. Remarkable observations concerning the similar identity of a sacrificer and a priest in the Brāhmaṇic ritual in general were made by the late Vsevolod Semencov in his valuable work dealing with ritual symbolism; unfortunately, it is still available only in Russian (Semencov 1981: 30–31, 117–18).

11 See *Aitareya-brāhmaṇa* VII. 23–24 (cp. VII. 19).

12 E.g., *Aitareya-brāhmaṇa* VII.28; *Mahābhārata* III.124; V.9–18; X.17–18; XII.124, 285, 343.

13 It is not a contradiction that I take the story with five heroes as monoheroic one, because, in fact, five Pāṇḍavas form one collective protagonist of the *Mahābhārata*'s general plot (though in certain episodes any of them (along with ascension to heaven) may act as a separate protagonist). The twelve-year period of disaster, exile or austerities (along with ascension to heaven) may be found in the Satyavrata-Triśaṅku myth and in several sub-stories of the *Mahābhārata* (e.g. I.171–73; 213–18). In some cases, this figure is corrupt: e.g. the sufferings of Nala begin after the twelfth year of his rule; the duration of Rāma's exile is fourteen years, etc. An interesting ethno-historical study concerning the twelve-year cycle in Indian culture was undertaken by Yaroslav Vasilkov (Vasil'kov 1972).

14 For additional evidence see Gonda 1971. In the *Mahābhārata* there are numerous situations in which Dharma, having changed his appearance, tests somebody. Thus, in the Gālavacarita he assumes the shape of Vasiṣṭha to test Viśvāmitra. He follows Yudhiṣṭhira to heaven in the shape of a dog (XVIII.2–3). Cp. also: *Mahābhārata* I.63; III.313; XII.127, 273; XIV.90–91. A curious situation is found in the medieval version of the Hariścandra myth, included in the *Devībhāgavata-purāṇa*: Viśvāmitra assumes the shape of a *brāhman*, who purchases Hariścandra's wife (VII.22: 8); on the other hand, it is declared at the end of the story (VII.27: 19) that Dharma himself wore the forms of all malefactors (i.e., the *brāhman*; a *caṇḍāla*, who has purchased Hariścandra; and a snake, who has bitten his son). I suppose that this contradiction is quite natural: in this case, mythological functions of both Viśvāmitra and Dharma are thus unified, because originally they were of similar semantics. It is also noteworthy that the medieval Bengali modifications of the Śunaḥśepa myth put Dharma in Varuṇa's place: in order to obtain a son, Hariścandra builds a temple dedicated to Dharma, and then he sacrifices his son to Dharma (see Dasgupta 1946: 464–66).

15 The Yama of the early Vedic texts is merely the first mortal. Though the Vedas call him "king", his position there is not that of the lord of the dead, as in the epics and Purāṇas. The role of Yama in the royal myths deserves attention, if one takes into consideration the reconstruction by B. Lincoln (1981) concerning the Proto-Indo-European prototype of Yama as the first king, who has murdered and sacrificed his twin-brother.

16 See Kuiper 1979: 12, 67–74.

17 This is my translation of the Russian term, widely used by Dr. Pavel Grincer in his monograph concerning the origin and typology of Indian epics (Grincer 1974). The typical triple loss (and its consequent recovery) in the *Mahābhārata* was previously indicated by Vladimir Romanov (1985); he has analysed the role of subconscious associations of such ideas as "property", "body" and "wife" in the Indian epic. The triple loss (and, moreover, the loss of memory) is quite explicit in the Hariścandra myth: cp. *Mārkaṇḍeya-purāṇa* 8: 171–73 (in F.E. Pargiter's translation verses 169–70).

18 *Mahābhārata* III.312–14. Only the four Pāṇḍavas and Draupadī pass this temporal death; Yudhiṣṭhira remains alive. This makes the "death" of the Pāṇḍavas exceedingly incomplete.

19 The symbolism of this period of the Pāṇḍavas' life is analysed in detail by A. Hiltebeitel (1980: 149–61). As J.C. Heesterman (1957) has pointed out, the embryonic symbolism is typical of the whole *rājasūya*, which implies the idea of the king's new birth.

20 *Mahābhārata* XVIII.3: 12–14. Again only four Pāṇḍavas and Draupadī die, but Yudhiṣṭhira still remains alive. So, this death is once again incomplete.

21 For additional details see Sacharov 1987; id. 1991: 64–85.

22 The problem of whether some stages of the *rājasūya* and *aśvamedha* were accessible to lower strata of society deserves special study. But, at any rate, Vaiśyas were definitely present at certain moments of the *rājasūya*.

23 E.g. *Śatapatha-brāhmaṇa* XIII.4.3. 12, 13; *Śāṅkhāyana-śrautasūtra* XVI.2. The idea concerning the *aśvamedha* as the common source of the *Mahābhārata* and the Purāṇas was previously suggested by R.C. Hazra (1955).

24 It is remarkable that the *hotṛ*-priest had to narrate the Śunaḥśepa story to a king at the *rājasūya* (see the colophon at the end of the Śunaḥśepa section of the *Aitareya-brāhmaṇa*). For more details concerning the original meaning of the terms "*itihāsa*" and "*purāṇa*" see Sacharov 1991: 18–19, 21–22, 108–09 (nn. 22, 29).

25 Indeed, the archaic prototype of a sacrificer was not a king in the common sense, but a tribal chief (or, probably, a warrior). It is quite probable, too, that the royal ritual originated as a result of transformation of archaic initiation practices and rites. But, anyway, the ritual prototypes implied the idea of obtaining the proper social status (along with prosperity) and heaven. If so, Brāhmaṇic social practice – viz., the *brahmacārin* and *vānaprastha* stages – represents another branch of its transformation. In fact, the goal of the former period of life (its prescribed duration is twelve years!) is the position of a householder, and that of the latter is heaven. The parallels between these two stages, pointed out by W.O. Kaelber (1978: 78; 1981: 88–96), may suggest both typological and genetic explanations.

26 The "who knows thus" principle was carefully studied by V. Semencov in his monograph mentioned above (Semencov 1981).

REFERENCES

Aitareya-brāhmaṇa (Aitareya Brahmanam of the *Rigveda*), Ed., transl., and expl. by M. Haug, 2 vols. 1863. Bombay: Government Central Book Depot; London: Trübner (in Sanskrit and English).

Brahma-purāṇa (Brahmapurāṇam) Ānandāśrama Sanskrit Series 28. 1895. Poona (in Sanskrit).

Dasgupta, S. 1946. *Obscure Religious Cults as a Background of Bengali Literature*. Calcutta: University of Calcutta.

Devībhāgavata-purāṇa (Devībhāgavatapurāṇam) 1889. Bombay: Veṅkaṭeśvara Press (in Sanskrit).

Falk, H. 1984. Die Legende von Śunaḥśepa vor ihrem rituellen Hintergrund. *Zeitschrift der Deutschen Morgenländischen Gesellschaft* 124.2: 115–35.

Gonda, J. 1971. The Vedic Mitra and the Epic Dharma. *Journal of the Royal Asiatic Society*, 120–33.

Grincer, Pavel A. 1974. *Drevneindijskij epos. Genezis i tipologija.* Moskva: Nauka (in Russian).

Harivaṃśa 1927. Bombay (in Sanskrit).

Hazra, R.C. 1955. The Aśvamedha, the Common Source of the Origin of the Purāṇa Panca-lakṣaṇa and the *Mahābhārata*. *Annals of the Bhandarkar Oriental Research Institute* 36: 190–203.

Heesterman, Jan C. 1957. *The Ancient Indian Royal Consecration.* 's Gravenhage: Mouton & Co.

Hiltebeitel, A. 1980. Śiva, the Goddess, and the Disguises of the Pāṇḍavas and Draupadī. *History of Religions* 20.1/2: 147–74.

Kaelber, W.O. 1978. The 'Dramatic' Element in the Brāhmanic Initiation: Symbols of Death, Danger and Difficult Passage. *History of Religions* 18.1: 54–76.

———. 1981. The Brahmacārin: Homology and Continuity in the Brāhmanic Religion. *History of Religions* 21.1: 77–99.

Kuiper, Franciscus B.J. 1979. *Sanskrit Drama.* Amsterdam: North-Holland Publishing Company (= Verhandelingen der Koninklijke Nederlandse Akademie van Wetenschappen. Afd. Letterkunde. Nieuwe Reeks. Deel 100).

Lincoln, B. 1981. The Lord of Dead. *History of Religions* 20.3: 224–41.

Mahābhārata 1890. Bombay (in Sanskrit).

Mārkaṇḍeya-purāṇa Mārkaṇḍeyamahāpurāṇam. 1890. Bombay: Veṅkaṭeśvara Press (rpt. 1911. Bombay: Kṛṣṇadāsa) (in Sanskrit).

Pargiter, F.E. 1904. *Markandeya Purana.* Transl. with notes by F.E. Pargiter. *Bibliotheca Indica* work 125. Calcutta: The Asiatic Society (rpt. 1981, Varanasi).

Rāmāyaṇa Rāmāyaṇa of Valmiki with the comm. (Tilaka) of Rāma. Edited by K.D. Parab. 1888. Bombay: Nirnaya-Sagara Press (in Sanskrit).

Romanov, V.N. 1985. Iz nabl'udenij nad kompozicijej 'Machabcharaty'. Drevn'aja Indija. Jazyk. Kul'tura. Tekst. Moskva: Nauka, 88–104 (in Russian).

Sacharov, P.D. 1987. Genezis mifa o Chariśćandre (Markandeja-purana, 7–8). Literatura i kul'tura drevnej i srednevekovoj Indii. Moskva: Nauka, 74–87 (in Russian).

———. 1991. *Mifologićeskoje povestvovanije v sanskritskich puranach.* Moskva: Nauka (in Russian).

Śāṅkhāyana-śrautasūtra (Śāṃkhāyana Śrauta Sūtra). Together with the commentary of Varadattasuta Ānartīyā. Edited by A. Hillebrandt, 3 vols. 1888–97. Calcutta (in Sanskrit).

Śatapatha-brāhmaṇa (Śatapatha-Brāhmaṇa) in the Mādhyandina-śākhā with extracts from the commentaries of Sāyana, Harisvāmin & Dvivedaganga. Edited by A. Weber. 1855. Berlin: F. Dümmlers Verlagsbuchhandlung, London: Williams & Norgate (in Sanskrit).

Semencov, Vsevolod S. 1981. *Problemy interpretacii brachmanićeskoj prozy.* Ritual'nyi simvolizm. Moskva: Nauka (in Russian).

Smith, B.K. 1985. Gods and Men in Vedic Ritualism: Towards a Hierarchy of Resemblance. *History of Religions* 24.4: 291–307.

Vasil'kov, Ja. V. 1972. *12-letnij cikl v drevnej Indii*. Soobšćenije ob issledovanii protoindijskich tekstov. Moskva: Nauka, 305–37 (in Russian).

Weber, A. 1893. Über die Königsweihe, den *rājasūya*. Berlin: Verlag der Königlichen Akademie der Wissenschaften.

The Hero in the Junjappa Epic

T.N. SHANKARANARAYANA

Introduction

THE discourse on the concept of hero in classical epics in Sanskrit and other Indian languages has a long history. But it is only since three decades ago that Indologists and Folklorists have realised how important it is to understand the concept of hero in Indian folk epics. Under the guidance of D.D. Kosambi, the German Indologist Günther-Dietz Sontheimer tried to understand the folklore of Maharashtra, to get a comprehensive picture of the culture of Maharashtra. "Sontheimer firmly believed that the ritual and mythology of Hinduism represented a composite tradition in which regional, tribal, pastoral and agrarian elements were interwoven in the very process of its growth" (Jutta Jain-Neubauer, 1992: 18). His famous book *Pastoral Deities in Western India* (1989) is a major contribution in this direction. Folklorists in different Indian languages have collected and published folk epics in their respective languages and have discussed the difference between folk and classical epics. They are of the opinion that to understand Indian epics it is very important to understand Indian folk epics also. Some micro studies by American scholars like Brenda Beck (1982), Gene Roghair (1982), Peter J. Claus (1987), Stuart H. Blackburn (1986) and others, from the point of view of text, context, performance, structure and ideology, are significant contributions to this area of scholarship. There are some important research papers in *Another Harmony* (ed. Stuart H. Blackburn and A.K. Ramanujan, 1986) and *Indian Folklore*, vol. II (ed. Peter J. Claus et al., 1987), which deal with folk epics. But a major breakthrough in this area of scholarship is the publication of *Oral Epics in India* (1989), which deals with some individual folk epics and also contains a comparative study of Indian folk epics. The concept of the hero in Indian folk epics is also discussed. The epic of Junjappa is just mentioned and not elaborated in this book. The purpose of the present paper is to discuss the concept of the hero in this epic in detail.

Kāḍugollas and their Deities

Junjappa is a popular deity and a cultural hero of the Kāḍugollas, a Kannada-speaking community in transition from pastoralism to agriculture, living in the south-central part of Karnataka State. Kāḍugollas live separately in settlements called *haṭṭi*, which are surrounded by fences of thorns, away from the villages. Earlier they were cowherds when there were abundant pasturelands for grazing cattle; but because during the past decades the pasturelands have been converted into agricultural fields, the Kāḍugollas have become mainly shepherds and agriculturists. They still maintain their tribal identity to the extent possible. Their tribal deities are Citradēvaru, Kāṭamadēvaru, Kētēdēvaru, Pātedēvaru, Ettappa, Junjappa and many more such as Vīranāgaṇṇa, Vīrakariyaṇṇa, etc. They also worship female deities like Māramma and male deities like Puralahaḷḷi Bhūtappa etc. which are worshipped by other communities also. Junjappa is a deity of Kāḍugollas in general and of the Māranavaru and Kambiyavaru clans in particular. Junjappa has become their deity by a process of death and deification. An elaborate epic on Junjappa has been developed and an annual fair called *jātre* is also held. The epic of Junjappa does not exist in any written form. It is oral in composition, performance and transmission. The narrative on Junjappa is considered an epic as an analytical category for academic purposes but as an ethnic genre it is called *Junjappana pada/hāḍu* (Song of Junjappa) or *Junjappana kathe* (Story of Junjappa). Usually only some episodes of this narrative are performed but the entire epic is also performed by some singers, as with any other Indian epic.

Epic of Junjappa

The epic of Junjappa is concerned with the intra-tribal conflict between two clans of Kāḍugollas, viz., Māranavaru and Kambiyavaru, and also with the inter-tribal conflict between Kāḍugollas and Myāsabeḍas (hunters). It is a story of three generations: the life of Junjappa; his father, Kenguri Mallegauḍa; and his grandfather, Dēvara Dayamāra; all belong to Māranavaru clan. The story begins with the life of Dēvara Dayamāra. In the first generation story, Dēvara Dayamāra married Kambakka of Ajjiyavaru clan. But his concern for his cattle was irresistible and he left his wife and went to the grazing lands to take care of his cattle. Unable to bear the torture of the members of the joint family, Kambakka left her home and joined her husband with great difficulty. She spent some time with him and became pregnant. Both of them went to a thick forest. Kambakka gave birth to a male child. Both husband and wife died of starvation as they could not get any food. The child was blessed by Īśvara and Pārvatī and was nurtured by Baḍachittamma, the child's maternal aunt. The child was named Kenguri Mallappa. Being an orphan, he was also ill-treated by his own uncles and aunts and was driven out of the house. Fortunately, he was supported by Honnahaṭṭi Ālegauḍa, an agriculturist of the Aḷuvinavara Vokkaliga caste. Honnahaṭṭi Ālegauḍa developed confidence in Kenguri Mallegauḍa and entrusted to him the responsibility of taking care of his cattle. In this process, both Ālegauḍa and Kenguri Mallegauḍa became very prosperous.

Kenguri Mallegauḍa was married to Cinnamma, who belonged to the Kambiyavaru clan. By the blessings of Lord Īśvara, through the mediation of a female family deity called Gaurasandrada Mārakka, Junjappa was born in an unusual way, out of the backbone of his mother, Cinnamma. He performed miracles when he was in the womb of his mother and also after his birth. Cinnamma also gave birth in the natural way to two male children called Māranna and Mailaṇṇa and a female child called Mārakka. The birth of Mārakka was believed to be inauspicious and Kenguri Mallegauḍa died because of a breach of tribal convention.

Junjappa became an adult. Because he was poor, his seven maternal uncles supported him by giving him seven calves. Junjappa worked hard and his cattle wealth increased to seven hundred cows. The maternal uncles became jealous and planned to kill his cattle by poisoning the water in a tank. They took the help of a sorcerer, who buried a calf alive as a part of the ritual. Junjappa found out that the calf belonged to his maternal uncles. But they refused to acknowledge the deed. Junjappa brought back the calf and nurtured it with love and affection. It became a very powerful bull and was named Baḍamaila by Junjappa; this bull became his assistant. Since Junjappa was an incarnation of Vīrabhadra (a classical Hindu deity and a son of Īśvara), he became very powerful and aggressive. He competed with his maternal uncles and was successful in increasing his cattle wealth. The maternal uncles became very jealous and thought of various methods to pull him down. They allied with the local chieftains, called Pāḷeyagāra, such as Sirā Ranganṇa, Cēḷūru Ranganṇa, Maraḍi Ranganṇa of the Myāsabeḍa tribe to bring about Junjappa's ruin. Junjappa fought and won battles against them.

The maternal uncles finally thought of killing him by means of food poisoning. Junjappa's sister was married to the youngest of the maternal uncles. The maternal uncles invited Junjappa to attend a festival in their home and forced Mārakka to serve poisoned food to him, much against her conscience. Junjappa knew this. Before he dutifully ate the food, he made it clear to the people gathered there that his maternal uncles had planned to kill him by poisoning. After that, he went inside a haystack; by the fire of his third eye, he burnt the maternal uncles and their settlement. Finally, he, too, was consumed by fire, but in order to honour a request of his mother, he did not burn his sister Mārakka and, instead, blessed her that her progeny would continue to prosper. After his death Junjappa was deified by the Māranavaru and Kambiyavaru clans and they began to worship him. Even after his death he performed many miracles. His own paternal grandfathers became his priests and gradually other clans among the Kāḍugollas also began to worship the deity Junjappa.

This epic is full of descriptions which are valuable from the point of view of cultural and literary studies. The hardship of the female characters, the jealousy and conspiracy of the maternal uncles and the Pāḷeyagāras, the heroism and adventures of Junjappa are also all described in the epic in detail. Prof. J.S. Paramashivaiah is the first scholar in Kannada who has collected and introduced this epic to Kannada readers (1971, 1979). The present author (1982) and Dr. Kāḷegauḍa Nāgavara (1985) have also worked on this epic.

Ritual Tradition of Junjappa

The tradition of Junjappa includes ritual performance during annual fairs and also narrative performance of the epic. The staunch devotees of the deity Junjappa are called Gaṇeyavaru or Kāṇikeyavaru. They are religious bards who go from place to place to the devotees and collect offerings in the form of money called *kāṇike* and also small images of gold- and silver-plated serpents or scorpions as vows called *harake*. They follow the bull of Junjappa, called Junjappana Basava, and carry the image of Junjappa which is in the form of an ornamented *gaṇe*, the top of which is covered by the image of a serpent-hood made of silver plate and decorated with peacock feathers and coloured cloth. A *gaṇe* is a three-foot long, one inch wide bamboo flute.

Junjappa is believed to cure snake bites and scorpion bites. People take a vow to pay *kāṇike* or *harake* if they are cured of snake bite or scorpion bite. Gaṇeyavaru/Kāṇikeyavaru are supposed to help the devotees by taking their *kāṇike* to the temple of Junjappa, thus relieving them of their burden. The bull is identified with the bull Baḍamaila described in the epic. The devotees treat the bull and the Gaṇeyavaru with respect. The Gaṇeyavaru sing some portions of this epic when they stay in devotees' houses.

Junjappa as a Cultural Hero

Junjappa emerged as a cultural hero because of intra-tribal and inter-tribal conflict. He fought against his own maternal uncles, who belonged to the Kambiyavaru clan, while he belonged to the Māranavaru clan among the Kāḍugolla tribe. He is depicted as a ferocious, angry young man. He is believed to have been born from the backbone of his mother in a supernatural way with the blessings of Īśvara. He was not supported by his paternal elders because of his suspicious supernatural birth. His maternal uncles supported him after his father's death, but they expected him to be subservient and faithful to them. It was not possible for him to do so because of his self-respect. He had certain other constraints also. His two young brothers were too innocent and mild. To compensate for this deficiency, he nurtured and trained a bull called Baḍamaila. He took proper care of the seven calves given to him by his maternal uncles and his cattle wealth increased to seven hundred cows. The uncles never expected that Junjappa would prosper, become rich and rival them. When he became powerful, they tried to pull him down. They decided to kill his cattle. They went to a sorcerer and requested him to poison the water in a tank, hoping that Junjappa's cattle would die soon after drinking the poisoned water. But Junjappa could easily understand this strategy by his special powers of perception. By his supernatural power he not only cleansed the water in the tank, but also raised the calf to be a powerful ally, the bull, Baḍamaila, which became his very important assistant. It could command all the cattle of Junjappa and fought against local chieftains in his absence. It may be noted that the status given to the animal is not that of a *vāhana* (vehicle). Junjappa did not use the bull for riding. Instead, he used it as a commander to fight against enemies. This is a clear deviation from the *prāṇi vāhana* stereotype such as Śiva-Nandi, Viṣṇu-Garuḍa, Gaṇapati-Mūśaka, etc. Here the role of the animal is not a vehicle for the deity but an ally of a cultural hero. This is a very important point, showing how much importance is given to an animal in this epic which highlights pastoral culture.

There are important distinctions to be made between Junjappa and his maternal uncles. Junjappa was only a cowherd, living in the forest, grazing his cattle and leading a quiet life. On the other hand, his maternal uncles were not only cowherds but also businessmen who used to sell cattle products and earn money and who, in this process, were exposed to the outside world. Junjappa belonged to the Māranavaru clan, which is supposed to be the earliest clan formed among Kāḍugollas, but the clan of the maternal uncles, called Kambiyavaru, was formed at a later stage, when people from other communities were converted and taken into the fold of the Kāḍugolla tribe. There was a conflict between the Māranavaru and Kambiyavaru clans. Probably the Kambiyavaru were not ranked high by the people of the Māranavaru clan. In this epic, Junjappa's maternal uncles are depicted as rich. Junjappa became very poor soon after the death of his father and he did not get any support from his paternal forefathers. Unfortunately his two younger brothers were very weak and he also was very young. His sister was also married to the youngest of his maternal uncles and thereby they had become strong. Junjappa became aggressive in order to counteract the strategies of his maternal uncles and he established supremacy over them. The maternal uncles became very jealous, and finally they thought of a plan to kill him. They invited Junjappa and persuaded his sister Mārakka to serve poisoned food to her own brother against her conscience. Before dying he opened his third eye and burnt the maternal uncles and their settlement. Having understood the helplessness of his sister, he did not kill her and blessed her, saying that her progeny would continue to live and prosper.

Now we come to inter-tribal conflict. We have to understand why Junjappa fought against the local chieftains, who belonged to the Myāsabeḍa tribe.[1] Kāḍugollas and Myāsabeḍas are supposed to have a common descent. According to a legend, there were two brothers who belonged to the Kāḍugolla tribe. One brother cut off the leg of a calf and used it as food; but the other brother strongly opposed this and did not follow him. The descendants of the brother who had cut off the leg of the calf became hunters in addition to cowherding but the descendants of the other brother, who had opposed that act, continued to do cowherding only. These two tribes live side by side and, since there is a difference between these two tribes, the conflict is obvious. This has found expression in their respective epics also. A section of the Myāsabeḍas became warriors and, in turn, they became local chieftains called Pāḷeyagaras during the Vijayanagara empire. After the downfall of the Vijayanagara empire, these Pāḷeyagāras became independent and ruled over small kingdoms. The Pāḷeyagāras mentioned in the Junjappa epic are of this type. All the grazing lands in their kingdom were their property and they levied taxes on them. In order to graze the cattle in the grazing fields one had to pay a grass tax called *hullu banni*. Junjappa opposed this type of taxation, probably because, being a tribal person who was very close to nature, he thought that one should not pay tax for grass, which grows naturally. But the Pāḷeyagāras thought that Junjappa was challenging them by refusing to pay the tax, and hence the conflict between them started. Junjappa had to establish his supremacy by defeating them. It should also be borne in mind that the maternal uncles played a significant role by instigating these Pāḷeyagāras to fight against Junjappa. Throughout the short span of his life Junjappa struggled hard and succeeded in establishing supremacy of his clan against his maternal uncles on the one hand and against the Pāḷeyagāras on the other. In this process he became a cultural hero.

His death is also unique because he did not die in a battle; but he was poisoned by his own maternal uncles through his own sister, who served poisoned food to him against her conscience.

Let us think of what this epic conveys. Kāḍugollas are a mild and easy-going people. But if this goodness is misunderstood as weakness then the tribe has to protect itself. If there is aggression by outsiders like Pāḷeyagāras one should fight against them. If there is aggression by another clan then also the Kāḍugollas should protest. The three-generation story of Junjappa conveys a message. There is a gradual development of the concept of heroism in this epic. In the first generation Dēvara Dayamāra was good and mild; he was a professionally devoted cowherd. But what did he achieve in his life? He was deserted by his own kinsmen. He and his wife died unnoticed of hunger and thirst in the forest. He suffered all this because he was mild and innocent. In the second generation the situation improves. Kenguri Mallegauḍa was also a mild and innocent cowherd. He did not get support from his kinsmen and hence went out of his tribe; sought the protection of Honnahaṭṭi Ālegauḍa, a man of an agriculturalist caste; worked hard and became a rich man. Then his kinsmen compromised and respected him. He became an important person in his tribe. People respected him. He died for the honour of his family. This was possible because he emerged as a powerful person. But even then he was only a human being, not superhuman.

Dēvara Dayamāra and Kenguri Mallegauḍa were married persons. They had to spend their energy and time to protect their families and could not protect the interest of their clan or tribe. Hence they are not treated as cultural heroes either by their clan or tribe. In the third generation the concept of hero changes. Junjappa is not only human but also superhuman. He could devote himself fulltime to protecting his interests and those of his clan and tribe. In this process, Junjappa established his personal identity, and restored the identity of his clan and the identity of his tribe. Junjappa could achieve what his father and grandfather could not. Thus we find that this epic is basically a clash of egos at different levels. This could possibly be a well reasoned inference. Conflict at different levels becomes necessary to establish different identities. Stuart Blackburn's remark regarding Indian epics is worth quoting here: "What Kalevala did for Finnish nationalism in the nineteenth century, oral epics continue to do for caste, language and groups in India today" (Blackburn, 1987). Blackburn's remark is true in the case of Junjappa epic also.

Junjappa as a hero differs from other cultural heroes of the Kāḍugollas. There are more than twenty different clans among the Kāḍugollas and each clan has a cultural hero, such as

Kāṭappa, Cittappa, Ettappa, Ajjappa, Siriyaṇṇa, Vīranāgaṇṇa, Vīrakariaṇṇa, etc. Kāṭappa is depicted as a very mature and saintly type of hero. Cittappa is very aggressive. He marries Gange Māḷamma of the Myāsabeḍa tribe and has to suffer a lot because of inter-tribal rivalry. Ettappa is famous for his devotion to his wife. He refuses to elope with a prostitute called Guḍḍada Bōri of the Muccalōra Nāyaka community. Ajjappa, Siriyaṇṇa, Vīranagaṇṇa, Vīrakariyaṇṇa and other heroes are famous for their valour and courage. They protect women and cattle from enemies and wild animals. They are human and not superhuman. But Junjappa is unique among all the cultural heroes of the Kāḍugollas. The epic of Junjappa is the most elaborate of all the epics of the Kāḍugollas. It is the only one which consists of a story of three generations and a large number of adventure episodes. Ettappa, Kāṭappa, Cittappa and other heroes are cultural heroes for their respective clans only. But Junjappa is a cultural hero for two clans. This is an important point which distinguishes Junjappa from other cultural heroes.

Junjappa as a Pastoral Deity

It is found from this study that Junjappa is a very important pastoral deity of south India in general and Karnataka in particular. Among other things, Junjappa is represented iconographically as a serpent, and his worship is actually serpent worship. The serpent has been worshipped in the form of a snake, a termite mound etc. Ettappa, Kāṭappa, Cittappa and many other deities are also worshipped in the form of snakes. Hence, we can say that serpent worship is a general feature among Kāḍugollas. The epic of Junjappa is only a recent addition. Junjappa is also represented by a sword, by a *gaṇe* (three-foot long bamboo flute), a stone, a termite mound, a serpent and a *liṅga* kept in a basket called *Junjappana peṭṭige*, etc. He is represented as a hero sitting on a horse made of bronze. The *utsavamūrti* (the idol which is taken out in procession) is made of silver and placed on a wooden platform with small umbrellas and many horses. With the equation of Junjappa with Vīrabhadra we find a process of upgrading to the level of classical deities. This appears to be a later development. The image of Junjappa in the form of different idols is not according to the description given in the text. He is believed to be sleeping on a serpent, which again resembles the classical deity Viṣṇu lying on

Ādiśeṣa, the mythical seven-hooded serpent. During the course of the present study, nowhere could the author find Junjappa presented in the image depicted in the text of the epic. The picture of Junjappa as depicted in the text of the epic is fascinating, but the actual iconographic representation does not accord with it. Junjappa is worshipped because he is heroic and ferocious. Curiously, Junjappa is not an affectionate name among Kāḍugollas, who do not normally name their children after him.

For the Kāḍugollas Junjappa is a cultural hero, but for people of other communities he is only a deity who can save them from snake bites and scorpion bites. Junjappa is closely associated with serpent imagery in the epic. "New social groups accept the hero as a god and not simply as the deified dead because they have no close link to him by blood or locale" (Blackburn, 1989: 33). The fact that people of other castes accept and worship Junjappa supports the observation of Blackburn. Dr. Sontheimer comes to the following conclusion in his study of the pastoral deities of western India: "All three gods, Birobā, Mhaskobā and Khaṇḍobā, have their origin in the forest and pasture region. They are based on a deity who was once found all over south India and who still exists in his original form even today. This is a deity of forest and pasture, who appears in the form of a snake, and who lives on the mountain, in the termite mound, and in trees. The original, formless deity of forest tribes and pastoralist groups first took form according to the ideas of these people" (1989: 205). This statement holds good for Junjappa also. Junjappa is believed to represent as well as control serpent.

Why is Junjappa believed to be an incarnation of Vīrabhadra? According to Hindu mythology, Vīrabhadra was created from a handful of Śiva's hair in order to kill Dakṣa. Vīrabhadra is known for his ferociousness, ruthlessness, vengeance and destructive tendency. The same traits are ascribed to Junjappa also. Kāḍugollas needed a cultural hero of their own tribe who would protect them from others. Junjappa fulfils the needs of his tribe. He lived only sixteen years. His mother Cinnamma had to choose between an ordinary son with full lifespan and an extraordinary son with only sixteen year's span. We are reminded of Abhimanyu in the *Mahābhārata* who lived only sixteen years.

Kāḍugollas consider Kṛṣṇa to be a member of their own tribe. The conflict between Junjappa and his maternal uncles resembles the conflict between Kṛṣṇa and Kaṃsa. Folk epics take different incidents, characters, motifs and images from classical mythology and literature to suit their needs. The process of making of the folk epics includes all these elements. The epic of Junjappa belongs to the Śaiva tradition. Kāḍugollas worship Junjappa. At the same time, they are also aware that Śiva is a greater god. They worship their tribal deities as well as those of pan-Indian folk epics. Dr. Sontheimer has observed this process aptly: "An essential characteristic of Indian culture makes itself felt: new notions and images, often those belonging to an upwardly mobile dominant group, are taken over without the old ones being given up. ... Thus a Dhangar can believe in the individual identity of his *kulasvāmī* Bīroba, but at the same time know that Bīroba is only a local or individual manifestation of Śiva, the Mahādev (great God) who rules over all" (1989: 205). This is true in the case of the Kāḍugollas also.

The epic of Junjappa follows the 'Death and Deification' pattern. That is, if a cultural hero meets with a violent, premature death then he is deified. A legend develops about him. "Historically a tradition begins with the final narrative event (a death), proceeds by adding an event that is prior to the death (a supernatural birth), and finally adds a state that is prior even to that (divine existence through association with a god). ... To follow the narrative we read the epic forward, but to trace the development of the tradition we must read it backward. ... Narratives expand through this backward-building process by providing causes for present events. ... The narrative sections describing the lives of the hero's parents and grandparents surely were added later in historical time than the narrative sections centering on the hero's own life "(Blackburn, 1989: 31). Blackburn explains the process of epic development in this way. The epic of Junjappa might have developed according to this process but it needs further study to confirm this statement.

Junjappa as an Identity Symbol

The scholars who have worked on the Kāḍugollas and Junjappa have thought that Junjappa is an identity symbol for the Kāḍugolla community as a whole. The present research shows that Junjappa is an identity symbol for the clans of Māranavaru and Kambiyavaru only. Kāḍugollas belonging to other clans pay only casual respect but they do not identify themselves with Junjappa. Hence, of more than twenty clans of Kāḍugollas, Junjappa is a cultural hero for only two clans. Other clans have cultural heroes like Vīranāgaṇṇa, Vīrakariyaṇṇa, Ajjappa, Siriyappa, Ettappa, etc., and hence none of these deities, not even Cittappa or Kāṭappa, are common to all Gollas. For socio-economic-political reasons different types of Gollas are uniting under the pan-Indian umbrella of the Yādava community, who consider Kṛṣṇa as their identity symbol. The pan-Indian Yādava community is more Sanskritized and has a classical background. And hence, the educated Kāḍugollas today are not so much interested in cultural heroes like Junjappa, Ettappa, etc. For them, to be associated with Akhila Karnataka Yādava Sangha and Akhila Bhāratha Yādava Sangha (All Karnataka Yadava Society and All India Yadava Society) is more beneficial. Hence there is a tendency among them not to emphasize and encourage further subgroups among themselves. This is another reason why Junjappa cannot continue to be an identity symbol for Kāḍugollas.

Junjappa does not have an exclusively independent existence. He is believed to be the strongest among all the cultural heroes of the Kāḍugollas and the epic of Junjappa is the most elaborate epic when compared to the epics about other Kāḍugolla deities such as Ettappa, Citradēvaru, etc. But he is always associated with senior deities like Cittappa, Kāṭappa and Ettappa. During his battle with local chieftains like Ceḷūru Rangaṇṇa, Maradi Rangaṇṇa, etc., he is assisted by a female deity, Mārakka, and a male deity, Bhūtappa. He is also assisted by Baḍamaila, which indicates the support he gets from animals. The position of Junjappa is like an important younger member in a joint family system. In some religious centres of Kāḍugollas, Junjappa is not important at all. In some other centres, he is only a minor deity. But there is scope that at least in a limited area Junjappa may become an identity symbol. The audio cassettes of the epic of Junjappa are sold on a commercial basis. Here the songs are edited and repetitions are deleted, but there is no distortion in the text with modernisation and commercialization. Junjappa may become an identity symbol for a small group of Kāḍugollas in a limited area, but may not continue as an identity symbol for the whole Kāḍugolla community.

Conclusion

The present paper confirms some general observations of Stuart H. Blackburn about Indian oral epics and also of G.-D. Sontheimer about pastoral deities in western India. It is also observed in this paper how classical mythological motifs are selectively used in the creation of the folk epic of Junjappa to express the identity of the Kāḍugolla tribe in general, and of two clans in particular. Junjappa has emerged as a cultural hero because of inter-tribal and intra-tribal conflicts. The importance given to an animal, Baḍamaila, by depicting it as an assistant to Junjappa in the capacity of a commander as an identity symbol of pastoral culture, and thereby deviating from the *paśu-vāhana* stereotype in Indian mythology, is a unique factor in the concept of hero in Indian culture. The present paper is only a modest attempt in the interpretation of this epic.

Acknowledgements

The present paper has been prepared out of material collected in a research project entitled 'The Epic of Junjappa: Text and Performance'. Thirty male and twenty female versions of this epic, which range from half an hour to fourteen hours in different performance contexts, have been collected. The total recording in audio cassettes is 250 hours; this includes prose and poetry versions and also interviews with the performers and audience.

I am thankful to the Regional Resources Centre for Folk Performing Arts (RRC), Udupi, Karnataka, and the Ford Foundation, USA. My thanks are due to Prof. K.S. Haridasa Bhat, Prof. Peter J. Claus and Prof. G.T. Marulasiddappa for their encouragement and suggestions. I am also thankful to Sri S.A. Krishnaiah, Sri A.V. Navada and Sri Harshavardhan Bhat of RRC, Udupi, and also to my research assistants Dr. M.N. Venkatesh and Sri Sannahanumappa and to my wife, Smt. Nagalakshmi.

NOTES

1 Editor's note: *Myāsa* is cognate with Telugu *mēsa*, to graze. The Beḍa are known in Andhra as Bōya, a large community in Western Andhra Pradesh, where they have a tribe-like identity and some sections are associated with hunting. See Thurston, vol. I (1975: 185).

This information has been recently confirmed by Peter J. Claus (oral communication).

REFERENCES

Blackburn, Stuart H. 1988. *Singing of Birth and Death: Text in Performance.* Philadelphia: University of Pennsylvania Press.

Blackburn, Stuart H. and A.K. Ramanujan. 1986. *Another Harmony.* Delhi: Oxford University Press.

Blackburn, Stuart H. et al. 1989. *Oral Epics in India.* Berkeley: University of California Press.

Beck, Brenda E.F. 1982. *The Three Twins: The Telling of a South Indian Folk Epic.* Bloomington: Indiana University Press.

Claus, Peter J. 1987. *Tuḷuva Darśana* (Vision of Tulu Culture), tr. by Navada A.V. and Subhash Chandra. Kundapura: Pradeshika Vyāsanga.

———. 1983 (unpublished report). *A Study of Social Structure and Epic Songs of the Gollas.*

Claus, Peter J. and Frank Korom. 1991. *Folkloristics and Indian Folklore.* Udupi: RRC, MGM College.

Claus, Peter J., Jawaharlal Handoo and D.P Pattnayak. 1980. *Indian Folklore,* vol. II. Mysore: Central Institute of Indian Language.

Jain-Neubauer, Jutta 1992 (Aug./Sept.). Dr. Günther-Dietz Sontheimer: An Indologist with a Difference. *German News,* 18–19.

Nanjundaiah, H.V. and Anantha Krishna Aiyer. 1926. *The Mysore Tribes and Castes,* vol. III. Bangalore: Mysore Government Press.

Nāgavāra Kāḷegowda 1985. Ondu Budakaṭṭina Haṭṭi, (Settlement of a Tribe), unpublished Ph.D. dissertation, Bangalore University.

Paramashivaiah, J.S. 1971. *Janapada Kāvya Kathegaḷu* (Folk Narrative Poetry). Mysore: Suruchi Prakashana.

———. 1979. *Dakṣina Karṇātakada Janapada Kāvya Prakāragaḷu* (Genres of South Karnataka Folk Poetry). Mysore: Prasaranga, University of Mysore.

Roghair, Gene H. 1982. *The Epic of Palnadu: A Study and Translation of Palnati Virula Katha, A Telugu Oral Tradition from Andhra Pradesh, India.* New York: Oxford University Press.

Shankaranarayana, T.N. 1982. *Kāḍugollara Sampradāyagaḷu mattu Nambikegaḷu* (Customs and Beliefs of Kāḍugollas). Mysore: Prasaranga, University of Mysore.

Sontheimer, Günther-Dietz. 1989. *Pastoral Deities in Western India.* New York: Oxford University Press.

Thurston, Edgar. 1975 (1909). *Castes and Tribes of Southern India,* vol. I. Delhi: Cosmo Publ.

Leadership in Maharashtra during the British Raj

CHRISTOPHER SHELKE

Introduction

IN THIS PAPER I would like to investigate how two great Maharashtrian leaders rose to all-India standing and what was their impact on social and political spheres of Maharashtra and that of India as a whole. The first leader is Mahadev Govind Ranade, commonly known as "Nyayamurti" Ranade and the second is Balwant Gangadhar Tilak, popularly known as "Lokmanya" Tilak. The first leader was a public and government servant throughout his life, and the latter refused to accept any government appointment. Ranade saw his role in educating and informing the people so that they unite themselves as one nation and uplift themselves. The British rule for him was ordained by God because the Indian people had forgotten certain civil and moral virtues. He never tried to be a leader but only a companion and through his companionship he fostered high ideals among his colleagues. On the contrary, for Tilak the British rule was a colonial and foreign rule. It was a hindrance to the growth of the nation. By his craving for collecting masses for political action he indirectly fostered the hero-worship and thereby he won for himself the title "Lokmanya". These two leaders came in conflict with each other only once. However, the conflict of their ideas still continues in Maharashtra and in India today.

Birth and the Years of Turmoil

Ranade was born in 1842 in a small town called Niphad in Nasik district, 24 years after the fall of the Maratha Kingdom and six years before the abduction of the Maratha King in Satara. Tilak was born on the 23 July 1856 at Ratnagiri, a town on the coastal

Maharashtra, a year before the first battle of the Independence, generally called the mutiny of soldiers by British historians. Tilak was about 13–14 years younger than Ranade.

The battle of Kirkee in 1817 and the battle of Koregaon in 1818 brought the Maratha Empire to an end (Bhattacharya 1967: 582). The downfall of the Maratha Empire evoked different feelings in different people. There were people who praised the role of the British in the downfall of the kingdom and who were happy because the cursed and tyrannical rule of the Brahmin Peshwas was brought to an end. But the majority of the people were stunned and had not known how to react. This stunned reaction brought not only in Maharashtra but throughout India, not only among the Hindus but also among the Muslims, the uprising of 1857. Some historians state that the uprising was spontaneous and unorganized, however its leaders, like the exiled Peshwa Nanasaheb fighting for his enthronement and Rani Laxmibai of Jhansi fighting for the recognition of her adopted child as an heir, were certainly fighting for their personal interests. The personal interests of different *Rajas* and *Sultans* and the interests of their kingdoms and their *prajā* were certainly not to be separated.

Reaction to Turmoil

Mahadev G. Ranade and Balwant G. Tilak were children of this turmoil and a stunned generation. Ranade, a towering personality, a leader clear, cautious, and circumspect in his thinking proclaimed his faith in these turmoil years saying,

> "This country of ours is the true land of promise. This race of ours is the chosen race. It was not for nothing that God has showered His choiced blessings on this ancient land of Aryavarta. We can see his hand in history. Above all other countries we inherit a civilization and a religious and social polity, which have been allowed to work their own free development on the big theatre of time. There has been no revolution, and yet the old condition of things has been tending to reform itself by the slow process of assimilation. The great religions of the world took their birth here, and now they meet as brothers prepared to welcome a higher dispensation, which will unite all and vivify all. India

> alone, among all the countries of the world, has been so favoured and we may derive much strength of inward hope from such a contemplation, change for the better by slow absorption. This has been the characteristic feature of our past history." (Ranade 1915: 125–26)

This proclamation of Ranade's faith elucidates his tenacious and amiable character, with which he approached the problems of the society, i.e. individual freedom, widow-marriage, eradication of child marriage, the *purdah* system, and caste atrocities, and education of the common man. Ranade laboured vehemently for the cause of the Indian widow. He joined the Widow-Marriage-Association, which had been founded in 1861. Together with six other leaders he was publically excommunicated by the Shankaracharya of the western India in 1869. After the excommunication he was the one who refused to repent and he continued the agitation for the uplift of widows.

Ranade the Public Servant

In 1866, Ranade secured the LL.B. degree with first class honours and then pursued further studies in Edinburgh. Before his appointment as First Class First Grade Subordinate Judge in Pune 1871, he served the government as oriental translator, as administrator of the state of Akkalkot, as judge in the native state of Kolhapur and as professor of English and History at the Elphinstone College in Bombay. Despite these various appointments and devoted service to the *Raj*, the Government of India looked upon him with suspicion, and it took him twenty-three years to rise to the position of High Court Judge.

Tilak's Education

In 1873, Tilak enrolled at the Deccan College in Pune and soon advanced in Mathematics and Sanskrit. In 1876, he took his B.A. and in 1879, his LL.B., devoting special attention to Hindu law. This shows that Tilak was preparing himself for a legal career, like the sons of many rich and influential Indians of the times.

Tilak, the son of a primary teacher, who had risen to Assistant Deputy Inspector, got the opportunity to study in Pune, and here, through Fergusson College, first as a student and later as a teacher, he came into contact with Maharashtra's intelligentsia that was represented in the *Sarvajanik Sabha*. This intelligentsia had started playing a prominent role in the cultural, social, and political life of the Presidency of Bombay.

As a young man Tilak was high spirited, willful, not easily amenable to discipline, and not readily agreeable to routine. He developed an independent, precise, and analytical intellect, which can be seen in his renowned book *Gitarahasya*, a commentary on the *Bhagavadgita*, applauding the *karmayoga*. His endurance and impertubability were equally remarkable. Therefore, the founder of the newspaper *Kesari*, i.e. 'The Lion', could roar against the cruel English rule saying, "*Swarajya* is my birth right and I shall have it." He was the first Indian leader who called for "total freedom".

The Newspapers

He not only roared like a lion but as a pragmatist he gathered masses and activated them for the cause he had proclaimed. Therefore, he was called the leader of "*Telitamboli*", i.e. the leader of workers. In order to influence the masses this born teacher along with another active reformer, Gopal Ganesh Agarkar, started two newspapers, *Maratha* in English and *Kesari* in Marathi. These newspapers undertook the job of educating the public on current political questions. Naturally, their views were not pleasant to the colonial power.

The *Maratha* kept in view the Indian intelligentsia as a whole, while the *Kesari* catered to the Maharashtrian public in general, to "the mass of ignorant population who usually have no idea of what passes around them and who, therefore, must be given the knowledge of such topics as concern their everyday life by writing on literary, social, political, moral and economic subjects" (Tahmankar 1956: 27).

Imprisonment of the Editors

The *Raja* of Kolhapur had been deposed by the British. People demanded the reinstatement of the *Raja* to his throne. Masses of Hindus and Muslims gathered and demanded the enthronement of their king. Two years previous to this event the rebellion of peasants under the leadership of Vasudev Balwant Phadake had been suppressed by the British. Tilak and Agarkar through the articles in the *Kesari* and the *Maratha* supported the enthronement of the *Raja*.

> "The *Maratha* wrote in 1881: There appears nothing of special interest in the case, except that the case is made out to be a conspiracy against Her Majesty the Queen, Empress of India. The well-known mad patriot with a handful of Ramoshies wished to establish a republican form of government and now an attempt is reported to have been made to reinstate Chimaji Apa on the Kolhapur *gādī* [throne]. We have nothing to say on this point, except that we wish our readers and our benign rulers to fancy for a moment a handful of half-starved men making an attempt at subverting the British Raj." (*Times of India*, 22 Jan. 1881; see also Reisner and Goldberg 1966: 34)

The article in *Maratha* also disclosed Barve, *Diwan* of Kolhapur and puppet of the British resident at Kolhapur, who was brazenly plundering the treasury and in everyway defaming the *Raja*. Tilak and Agarkar had tried to expose the *Diwan* and support the deceived *Raja*. The colonial rule could not see the plundering of the treasury by Barve and the defamation of the *Raja*, but rather saw the defamation of the *Diwan*. After a trial Tilak and Agarkar were sentenced to four months' imprisonment each. Naturally, the public regarded Tilak-Agarkar's action as patriotic and commendable. After their release from jail both were lauded with enthusiastic receptions by the public in Maharashtra.

Differences with Colleagues

Pragmatist Tilak always wanted to gather masses. Political freedom was his primary aim, and it could not be achieved without the mobilisation of the masses. He believed strongly that 'social' or rather 'domestic reforms' could divert attention from the direct struggle against the alien rulers. On account of religious reform Tilak feared that the masses could be further alienated from the leadership and be divided among themselves. Besides, according to him, by pressing religious reforms the reformists were giving opportunities to the foreign rulers to interfere in the religion of the natives and in the daily affairs of the people. Agarkar was more of an agnostic and of a strong rationalist character. He could not bear with Tilak. He felt that Tilak was merely paying lip-service to reform and was actually siding with the orthodoxy. After the tea-party at the Panch Haud Mission the orthodox Brahmins demanded from those who were present at the tea-party that they do penance. Many of the reformers had refused either to do penance or to be purified, stating that they had not done anything wrong by taking biscuits and tea from the missionaries. But Tilak was among the few others who apologized and offered to take the penance from the Brahmins.

After seeing Tilak's attitude towards reform, Agarkar started his own paper with the title *Sudhakar*, i.e. 'Reformer' (1888). In *Sudhakar* Agarkar wrote: "Tilak, with lack of conviction, pays only lip-service to reform, in order to catch the wind of popularity" (Mehra 1985: 722). The differences between Agarkar and Tilak came to the climax on the issue of "remarriage of child widows" and on the bill of "Age of Consent" (1891). With the help of reformers the government sought to raise the consummation age of marriage from ten years, as it was fixed by the act of 1860, to twelve. For Agarkar, the bill itself was highly conservative. The liberals and strong reformists wanted the age to be fourteen years. The bill was prepared with the consent and help of the reformers. However, Tilak opposed the bill in *Kesari* and attacked the reformists.

Tilak's anti-reform stance has made his critics label him a reactionary, a revivalist, and a communalist. Tilak's prime motivation was to unite all Indians; he advocated social and religious reform not through legislation but through peaceful evolution, which he thought would not alienate the masses from the political struggle for freedom. Tilak argued that once the country was free, social and religious reform would automatically follow.

Educational Activity

Agarkar, Tilak and four others opened a "New English School" in Pune on 1st January 1880. They saw the importance of private schools on the model of missionary institutions, especially the American Marathi Mission's high schools in Ahmadnagar, and St.

Xavier's High School and St. Xavier's College in Bombay. This initiative of new English schools within a few years developed into the Deccan Education Society. Tilak wrote about the ideal underlying this establishment:

> "Our mission has been to establish an educational institution at Pune after the model of missionary societies for the purpose of making English education indigenous by placing it on a popular basis. It was necessary for that purpose that we should form ourselves into a society of Indian Jesuits, and this all of us had voluntarily consented to do. It was our determination to devote ourselves to the work accepting only bare maintenance." (Limaye: 15)

The founding members of the Deccan Education Society had agreed on the principles of self-reliance, self-sacrifice, and simplicity of conduct. Later on, the society raised monthly honoration from Rs. 35 to 75 and members were also allowed to take up outside work. Tilak disagreed with the increase of honor and allowing members to do work outside. He wrote:

> "Of late, I see a marked tendency in our body to deviate from the principles we originally accepted for our guidance, and which have brought us so much success. At everytime when the tendency displayed itself, I have protested against it; but nothing has ensued except heart-burning and bitter repartees. Under the circumstances, I feel it my duty to withdraw." (Kelkar 1928: 528–60; see also Reisner 1966: 55)

The members of the Deccan Education Society had not lacked in any way in self-sacrifice or self-reliance. It is most astonishing to know that when Agarkar passed away as principal of Fergusson College he was a poor man living in extreme poverty. A small purse containing merely Rs. 30 was found in his room with a note on it: "For my funeral".

Separation from the Deccan Education Society

It is appropriate to know that the membership of the Deccan Education Society increased from the initial five. It developed divergent views, especially in the matter of social reforms, renewal of religious customs, and attainment of political freedom. In political reform there were extremists and moderates. Tilak found himself in the minority and feeling that he could no longer follow the cause of forced compromises he preferred to break with the creation he was initially involved with and therefore withdrew.

Tilak's break with the Deccan Education Society aggravated his relations with the Sarvajanik Sabha, a most influential organization in western India. Differences arose in this organization too. However, Tilak and his followers enrolled new members and outvoted Ranade and his companions. The new committee naturally opposed social reform and started using the Sabha as an instrument for their nationalist, revivalist outlook. After the withdrawal from the Deccan Education Society and some years later from the Sarvajanik Sabha, Tilak acquired sole proprietorship of *Kesari* and *Maratha.* He devoted himself to journalism and politics. He invented a new method of appealing to the masses by celebrating the festivals of Shivajayanti and Ganapati.

Ranade the Reconciler

With the advent of Tilak, the educated classes became divided into "moderates" and "extremists", "liberals" and "nationalists". Now, Maharashtra had gained its selfconfidence and its sociopolitical aims were quite clear. However, its leadership was divided.

It was against this background that Ranade reiterated the directives for the Deccan Sabha and gave a new perspective to the Maharashtrian intelligentsia:

> "Liberalism and moderation will be the watchwords of this Association. The Spirit of Liberalism implies a freedom from race and creed prejudices, and a steady devotion to all that seek to do justice between man and man, giving to the rulers the loyalty that is due to the law they are bound to administer, but securing at the same time to the ruled the equality which is their right under the law. Moderation imposes the condition of never vainly aspiring after the impossible or after remote ideals, but striving each day to take the next step in the order of natural growth by doing the work

> that lies nearest to our hands in a spirit of compromise and fairness. After all, political activities are chiefly of value not for the particular results achieved, but for the process of political education, which is secured by exciting interest in public matters and promoting the self-respect and self-reliance of citizenship. This is no doubt a slow process, but all growth of new habits must be slow to be real." (Ranade 1896: 2)

Through the efforts of Ranade the unity and activity of the Deccan Education Society was preserved. Another younger colleague who realised this spirit of liberalism and gradual progress and that of individual freedom was none other than Gopal Krishna Gokhale, who called Ranade his *guru*. After a few decades we find Mohandas Gandhi follow the precepts and advice of liberal Gokhale and call him to be his political mentor. In this way Ranade became the 'grand preceptor' of the non-violent movement of Gandhi.

Socio-religious Festivals

Pragmatist Tilak, in order to reach out to the people, started the celebrations of Ganapati (1894) and of Shivaji's birth (1896). The Hindus and the Muslims joined in the celebrations. But his extreme pragmatism failed to see that the same celebration could bring conflict between the Hindus and Muslims. The man who stood for the unity of the Indian masses, without consideration of caste and creed, actually became the cause of separation on account of his crazy striving for masses.

The first Shivaji festival was organized on 5 April 1896 at Raigad, where Shivaji had been consecrated as king in 1674, and where his grave is situated. In the following year, the feast was celebrated to mark the anniversary of his coronation. Soon the festival extended to other towns and villages in Maharashtra, providing a forum for discourses on Indian culture, religion and nationalism. Tilak began the festival of Ganesh so that he could metaphorically explain to the people the demonic activity of the British rulers.

Tilak desired the support of the Muslims also. He realized how the British authorities pressed and seized the chance to brand the Cow-Protection Association as an inspirer of Hindu-Muslim strife, and how in 1893 the Government had refused to investigate the riots and thereby had sheltered those who had started the riots. Tilak advocated Hindu-Muslim unity. He wrote in September 1895 asking the Muslim community to see the real intentions of the British rulers: "It is no use being puffed up by the partiality of the Government. When the time comes, the Hindus and the Muslims alike will equally be a prey to them" (Kelkar 1928: 237–38). The Shivaji festival and Ganesh-feast-celebrations soon gained popularity all over Maharashtra. As the Hindus were taking part in the Moharam celebrations, so also, initially, the Muslims joined the celebrations. The Shivaji festival and the Ganesh festival movement gradually spread beyond the frontiers of the Bombay Presidency. Many discerned in it a fresh and successful attempt to rally large sections of the population to the idea of liberation of their country, as an idea embodied in the image, familiar and dear to many Indians, of the founder of the independent Maratha state. The festival found a strong echo in Bengal and in North India. The most pacifistic Christian Sanyasi, Brahmobandhu Upadhyaya, was till 1907 propagating the celebration of Shivaji's birthday in Bengal (Animananda 1946: 148–55).

The Rift between Hindus and Muslims

However, past history could not be changed. Shivaji's valorous deeds against the Bijapur Sultanate and against the *Badshah* Aurangzeb could not be avoided to be spoken of. Praises of these valorous deeds not merely caused hurt feelings among the Muslims, but made them insecure. In such insecurity the Muslims identified patriotic and national movements as Hindu revivals. Tilak and his followers lacked tact and failed to interpret the history in more suitable terms for their time. We understand why, in the trial of 1908, Jinnah refused to take the advocacy of Tilak, that later was taken by a Christian, known by a nickname, Kaka Baptista. However, Tilak's magnanimity, pragmatic approach, and desire for unity by bringing the Muslims in the main national stream could be seen in the Lucknow Congress, where he strongly advocated separate constituencies for the Muslim community. He supported the Khilafat movement (Mehra 1985: 727). This activity of Tilak is enough proof that he was not a communalist.

Ranade's Attitude towards Festivals

On the other hand Ranade, a man of deep insight, feared along with some close friends, that the Ganapati-celebrations and Shivaji-festivals by arousing the communal consciousness of Hindus were bound to provoke a reaction from the Muslim community. Besides for Ranade it was not of primary importance whether the Government was partial or impartial to one or another community on contentious issues like processions in public places, music before mosques, and cow-slaughter. Ranade was interested that India satisfied and solidified herself into a "single nation, unified in thought, in feelings and charged with a sense of a common destiny," otherwise India was to invite chaos and disruption in the name of independence.

Ranade also looked towards Shivaji as an ideal that could be put before the generations of Indian people. He wrote *The Rise of the Maratha Power*, the first volume of the unfinished *History of the Maratha People*. Here in the introduction he acknowledged that the religious movement commencing with Jnaneshwar tended to "raise the nation generally to a higher level of capacity both in thought and in action". He sought to illustrate how the rise of the Maratha Kingdom "was a genuine effort on the part of Hindu nationality and how the success achieved was due to a general upheaval, social, religious and political of all classes of population". Ranade saw with the insight of a *rishi* that India required not merely revival or a revolutionary change, but comprehensive reform, complete remoulding of the entire life of the nation. Ranade wrote:

> "It cannot be easily assumed that in God's Providence, such vast multitudes as those who inhabit India were placed centuries together under influences and restraints of alien domination, unless such influences and restraints were calculated to do lasting service in the building up of the strength and character of the people in directions in which the Indian races were most deficient. Of one thing we are certain, that after lasting over five hundred years, the Mohammedan Empire gave way, and made room for the re-establishment of the old native races in the Punjab, and throughout Central Hindustan and Southern India, on founda-

> tions of a much more solid character than those which yielded so easily before the assaults of the early Mohammedan conquerors.
>
> Both Hindus and Mohammedans lack many of those virtues represented by the love of order and regulated authority. Both are wanting in the love of municipal freedom, in the exercise of virtues necesssary for civic life, and in aptitudes for mechanical skill, in the love of science and research, in the love and daring of adventurous discovery, the resolution to master difficulties, and in chivalrous respect for womankind. Neither the old Hindus nor the old Mohammedan civilization was in a condition to train these virtues in a way to bring up the races of India on a level with those of western Europe, and so the work of education had to be renewed, and it has been now going on for the past century and more under the Pax Britannica with results – which all of us are witnesses to in ourselves."
>
> (Moon 1989: 232–33)

The Democratic Revolutionary Movement

Pandit Nehru called Tilak "Father of Indian Revolutionary Movement". Often Tilak is considered to be advocating violent methods and encouraging violence. However, Tilak was actually opposed to violence. In order to do justice to Tilak, one must call him to be the "Father of the Indian Democratic Revolutionary Movement". Despite famine and plague, and when people were suffering hunger and scarcity, the British Government had been determined to celebrate, and it had celebrated the Diamond Golden Jubilee of Queen Victoria's rule. "The celebration was performed in Pune in such a way that the whole country became ablaze with the act that electrified the Indian People." Damodhar Chapekar and his brother were sentenced to death. When Yasudev B. Phadake declared himself to be the prime minister of Shivaji II and tried with the help of a handful teachers, *Kulkarnis*, *Patils* and *Ramoshis* to establish a form of republican government, the Government not only suppressed the movement but hanged the culprit and his companions (Keer 1988: 1, 332, 481). Tilak-Agarkar had condemned the violence, calling such methods foolish attempts. Both of them had supported the claim of the *Raja* of Kolhapur but had also warned people not to be violent. Tilak was very clear about the causes of violence in India. For him, it was the bureaucracy and the cruel rule that was causing the violence. He warned the colonial Government saying,

> "The authorities have to conduct themselves in subservience to public, in proportion to the rights of *Swarajya* acquired by the people. That power should remain in the hands of such authorities as may be approved by the people and that it should be taken away from the hands of such authorities as may not be liked by the people; this itself is called the exercise of the rights of *Swarajya*. If *Swarajya* is exercised, there will be no bombs." (Reisner & Goldberg 1966: 558)

He made a clear distinction between the violence that was taking place in Europe and the violence that was taking place in India, especially in Bengal, pointing to the atrocities that Lord Curzon was conducting in Bengal. The Government failed to examine its conscience.

> "There is a wide difference between the bombs in Europe desiring to destroy society and the bombs in Bengal as between the earth and heaven. There is an excess of patriotism at the root of the bombs in Bengal, while the bombs in Europe are the product of hatred felt for selfish millionaires." (Reisner & Goldberg 1966: 557)

Advocating Bloodless Revolution

Tilak was not in sympathy with the violent revolutionaries, but he understood their despair. He advocated a revolution which was non-violent, a revolution that brought change in the bureaucracy. He didn't preach violence but asked of his followers readiness for the suffering and sacrifice for the sacred cause of *Swarajya*. Tilak said in 1907, a year before his deportation for six years to the prison in Mandalay,

> "It's true that what we seek may seem like a revolution. It is a revolution in the sense that it means a

> complete change in the theory of the Government of India as now put forward by the bureaucracy. It is true that this revolution must be a bloodless revolution, but it would be a folly to suppose that if there is to be no shedding of blood there are also to be no sufferings to be undergone by the people. This suffering must be great. You can win nothing unless you are prepared to suffer. An appeal to the good feelings of the rulers is everywhere discovered to have but narrow limits. Your revolution must be bloodless, but that does not mean that you may not have to suffer or to go to gaol." (*Maratha*, 4 July 1908; see also Reisner & Goldberg 1966: 557)

Abhinav Bharat Society

It is not on account of Tilak's activity and pragmatism that violence came into Indian politics. The causes of violence were the British attitude and the spirit of the younger generation which went to London for study but was working for the freedom of India. Vinayak Damodar Savarkar, a young student from Nasik, came to Pune in January 1902, just a year after the death of Nyayamurti Ranade. Before Savarkar came to Pune he had arranged in Nasik a small group of friends, boys mostly below fourteen, who had used violence against the Muslims by throwing stones against the mosque. After joining the Fergusson College Savarkar came under the influence of Tilak, R.P. Paranjape and Agarkar. Savarkar advocated revolution among the students and he also asked fellow students to hit back at the "foreigners". Savarkar was cautioned by the elders and was even fined by Principal Paranjape. Tilak admired his zeal, yet he too cautioned him. However, Tilak admired his readiness for self-sacrifice. Tilak was all taken up by the fact that Savarkar was refusing to take any government-job, though initially he had thought of joining the Indian Civil Service. Savarkar desired nothing now, but to serve the cause of freedom. Tilak recommended him, on account his selfless desire to serve, for the scholarship, and Savarkar went to London in 1906.

In the British Capital, Savarkar came to know about the violent revolution that was advocated by Joseph Mazzini. He studied

Mazzini and his writings. Here Savarkar was inspired to write the history of the battle of 1857 under the title *The Indian War of Independence*. Here he came in contact with the Russian revolutionaries and revolutionary literature. Savarkar and other students studying in London immediately started the *Abhinav Bharat Mandal*. The London-based *Abhinav Bharat Mandal*, seeing the international situation and hoping that the support of French and Russian revolutionaries would help to develop violent methods, such as preparing bombs, making pistols and using guns, aspired violently for the freedom. They gathered literature and dispatched it to India. It was through the contact with the western revolutionaries, Savarkar and his other friends turned into violent reactionaries (Keer 1988: 14–35). In later years, even after serving many years imprisonment due to the Government ban, Savarkar could not take part in Indian politics and started working for social and religious reform. Then, he wrote his famous treaty, *Hindutva*, giving a philosophical basis to the Hindu Mahasabha. He resisted the non-violent non-cooperation of Gandhi. It was for him, merely, "a jail-seeking programme". Absolute *ahimsa* he regarded as absolutely immoral because it was "anti-human" (Keer 1988: 277–78). From this Mahasabha came the assassins who murdered Gandhi.

Ranade's Importance

Nyayamurti Ranade, a true visionary like a *rishi* of ancient India, who penetrated into the future and also a thorough realist, who never allowed himself to be carried by short and timely gains, remains even today a guide for India, stating that reform has to be comprehensive, taking all classes of society together. According to Ranade, it is not primarily political activity that brings change but the activity of an individual that respects the freedom of the other man and uplifts him. The value and importance of Nyayamurti Ranade's thought is especially great today, when the nation is finding itself beset by conflicting ideas.

Today, India is tormented by various conflicts and problems. The states are seeking more autonomy, Hindus feel threatened by the rights of minorities, the minorities feel insecure by the revival of extreme Hindu fundamentalism; there are separatist movements in Punjab, Kashmir, and in the northeastern states; atrocities are being perpetrated against scheduled castes, against women, children, and the poor. These conflicts show that it is neither merely the political reform nor the social reform that brings stability. Therefore, even today Ranade's warning is of importance for India.

> "You cannot be liberal by halves. You cannot be liberal in politics and conservative in religion. The heart and the head must go together. You cannot cultivate your intellect, enrich your mind, enlarge the spheres of your political rights and privileges, and at the same time, keep your hearts closed and cramped. It is an idle dream to expect men to remain enchained and enshackled in their own superstitions and social evils, while they are struggling hard to win rights and privileges from their rulers. Before long these vain dreamers will find their dreams lost." (Moon 1989: 223)

References

Animananda, B. 1946. *The Blade*. Calcutta.

Bhattacharya, Sachchidananda. 1967. *A Dictionary of Indian History*. New York.

Keer, Dhananjay 1988. *Veer Savarkar*. Bombay.

Kelkar, N.C. 1928. *Life and Times of Lokamanya Tilak*. Madras.

Limaye, P.M. 1935. *The History of the Deccan Educational Society*, Part III.

Mehra, Purushottam. 1985. *Dictionary of Modern Indian History*. Oxford.

Moon, Vasant (ed.). 1989. *Dr. B.R. Ambedkar: Writings and Speeches*, vol. 1. Bombay.

Ranade, M.G. 1896. *Manifesto Constituting the Deccan Sabha*. Pune.

———. 1915. *Miscellaneous Writings of the Late Honorable, Mr. Justice M.G. Ranade*. Bombay.

Reisner, I.M. and N.M. Goldberg. 1966. *Tilak and the Struggle for Indian Freedom*. Delhi.

Tahmankar, D.V. 1956. *Lokamanya Tilak*. London.

Tilak, Balwant Gangadhar (ed.). 1881. *Maratha*, 22 Jan.

———. (ed.). 1908. *Maratha*, 4 July.

On Heroes in the Karakoram

HUGH VAN SKYHAWK

The beginning of almost all true epical traditions should be sought at the point at which the tales of the gods touch the earth and attach themselves to historical remembrances in a daring mixture of the sensual and the spiritual. If one follows the further development of such traditions it becomes clear how they cause the figures of gods to vanish more and more behind human heroes, and put real circumstances in the foreground. Events that exerted a powerful influence on the spirit of a people and made a living impression on them, form their primary subject matter. At the same time, these very historical events, though stripped of their mythical shimmer, gradually enwrap themselves as they are told from generation to generation and disappear into the distance in a wondrous twilight, like that in which the memories of youth are seen in later life. (...) If, in the end, an individual undertakes to apply the final creative hand to the material that has been passed down to him, then only he will be able to fulfil his task to the fullest whose consciousness is still at one with that out of which the ancient world of the sagas grew, but who, together with this unconditional devotion to the sensibility of his people, at the same time combines a clear vision with creative power in order to unify the traditions and songs of the saga he treats into an inseparable whole, and melt them into an organic work of art.

Adolf Friedrich Graf von Schack,
the faithful pupil of Eugène Burnouf and Christian Lassen[1]

On Oral Traditions in the Karakoram

SOME FIFTY YEARS ago a similar paper in a volume about the hero in South Asia would certainly have dealt with the intricate network of inter-relationships linking the oral versions of the epic of Gesar/Kesar in Ladakh, Baltistan, and the valleys of the Karakoram to one another and to the written sources in Tibetan. Today, such an undertaking must be viewed differently: How does an oral epic that has developed over centuries change when the cultural area in which it developed is rent asunder, and the new society that emerges in its wake no longer draws its narrative themes from previous sources? How is the narration of the epic perceived in the new cultural context? Which themes live on? Which are discarded? Specifically: How is the story of the pre-Buddhist culture hero *par excellence* modified to satisfy the minimum normative demands of a Semitic scriptural religion?

Though, today, oral traditions are narrated far less frequently in the Karakoram than fifty years ago, it cannot be said that they are about to vanish completely. The majority of the population is still non-literate and have not yet succumbed to the de-education inherent in being mere passive recipients of the programming of electronic communications media (television, radio, tape-cassettes). In numerous villages functional dialogues between narrators and their immediate audiences still take priority over pseudo-dialogues with a distant broadcaster one seldom if ever sees and who can never respond to the immediate reactions of his audience.[2]

While for the Western-educated younger generation the belief in supernatural beings (spirits, witches, fairies) is more of a curious hang-over from their grandfather's generation, there are still numerous agriculturists and herdsmen who practice the cult of the fairies and fear the predations of the witches. In April 1992, I observed a shepherd from Karimabad who carried a container of goat's milk up to the Ultar Glacier as an offering to the fairies when the water that was urgently needed for irrigation did not melt and flow down into the fields on time. A similar contrast can be observed with regard to the oral traditions in which supernatural beings play a predominant role. While a politically active village schoolmaster, who had lived for several years in Karachi and Rawalpindi, considered traditional stories to be a waste of time and, even worse, yet another machination of his arch-enemy the former king of Nager [Burushaski (hereafter: bu.): *míir*] to keep the population ill-informed and uneducated, a hotel owner in Altit requested me repeatedly to take his photograph next to the irrigation channel that Kisár had had built by his protective spirits (bu. *ráaçikuyo*) in one night. The name of his hotel "Kisar Inn" betrays a living belief in the existence of the ancient hero of our epic.

Though in Híspar, the village at the end of the old caravan path from Baltistan over the Híspar Glacier, there is now no one who knows an extensive version of the epic of Kisár – the last narrator, who knew a version that was narrated on three successive evenings, died some ten years ago (late 1980s) –, there are any number of people who would like to hear a narration of the epic again. This became clear when a story-telling afternoon that was arranged at my request spontaneously grew into a story-telling festival that lasted for three days during which approximately twenty men from 14 to above 90 years of age narrated and dramatized their favourite stories.

On the Narrator of the Present Version of the *Kisár-nimás*

The narrator of the present version of the *Kisár-nimás*, Zawáar Dáado (Mahamát Alí, Ġośóṭkuċ), is now (1999) approximately 72 years old, father of six children and grandfather of four. Until the abolition of the monarchy in 1972, he had been a member of the bodyguard (bu. *baaḍigáar*) of the *tham* or *míir* of Nager. Since childhood he has been a dedicated hunter. At various times in his life Zawáar Dáado received ibexes from Kisár as a reward for narrating the hero's deeds in the "right" way, that is, in the right spirit. Even today Zawáar Dáado's belief in Kisár's existence remains unshaken: Kisár is indeed alive and well and has the power to damage or destroy his enemies or to help the deserving.[3]

In narrating Kisár's story Zawáar Dáado breathes life into an ancient ancestor and experiences his presence. As in the hero-cults of ancient Greece, in which a demonic ancestor was conjured up bodily by the singing of a song of praise, Zawáar Dáado invokes Kisár by giving life again to his deeds (Baeumler 1965: 68–74; quoted in Hübner 1985: 217 f.). However, it must be admitted that, for the majority of his audience, the direct experience of a mythical arché has been supplanted by the vicarious experience of aesthetic enjoyment of the narration of an exciting story.

On the other hand, Zawáar Dáado has gone on pilgrimage to the holy places of Twelver Shiism in Iraq and Iran and is considered to be an exemplary Shiah. With his steadfast belief in the autochthonous spirits of the Nagérkuċ, his intimate knowledge of the sacred traditions of Shiism, his familiarity with Persian folk-literature, and his direct experience of the "verity of the myth" (ibid.), Zawáar Dáado embodies the archetypal epical poet of whom von Schack wrote a hundred years ago. For, in his performance of the epic of Kisár one perceives no decline in epical style. The ancient story of Kisár is not sung to death by Zawáar Dáado. Rather, it is appropriated anew as a living text at each re-telling.[4]

On the Sources of the *Kisár-nimás* of Zawáar Dáado

On the basis of comparisons with the versions of the Kesar epic from Ladakh published by Silke Herrmann (1991: 127), we can show that the Nager version of the epic corresponds substantially with one or more of the Muslim versions of Kesar current in Southern Ladakh. Of the 90 possible narrative segments from which Silke Herrmann has constructed an "ideal Kesar" for Ladakh, the Nager-version contains the leitmotifs of 33 narrative segments. This is especially striking when one considers that the most comprehensive Kesar version in Ladakh contains only 70 narrative segments, and is performed in three sessions of eight, eleven, and three hours, while the *Kisár-nimás* of Zawáar Dáado is narrated in about two and a half hours.

Despite the adaptation of the basic narrative structure of versions of the Kesar-epic current in Ladakh, it becomes clear in the first segment of the Nager epic with what fantasy and sensitivity the Shiahs of Nager have made the epic of Kisár their own. From the very outset of the narrative, in the story of the circumstances of Kisár's birth, the Nager epic varies clearly from all other versions of Kesar that have been documented in north-west India and Pakistan up to the present time. Kisár is not conceived when his mother swallows a hail stone, or eats a dish of yoghurt, rather, he is conceived as a human being is normally conceived. He is not born as the son of the supreme deity (as in the Tibetan and Mongolian versions of the epic), but as the son of a famous *pahalwān* (paladin, wrestler) by the name of Abúu Drumbú, who then abandons Kisár's mother before his birth, but not without giving her a signet ring by which he will one day recognize his son. Up to this point our tale does not correspond to any of the extant versions of Kesar in north-west India and Pakistan. Then follows the story of Kisár's birth, childhood, and humiliation as a bastard.[5]

Following the humiliation of the boy-hero there comes a segment in which Kisár forces his mother to reveal his father's name by pressing red-hot pebbles onto the palm of her hand. This segment also occurs in the Balti-Stak and the Muslim versions of the epic from Southern Ladakh and is important because it introduces the theme of the son's search for his father. In the versions from Baltistan and Ladakh, however, Kisár's mother does not know his father's name because she became pregnant by swallowing a hailstone (or by eating yoghurt). Only in the version of the epic from Nager does Kisár's mother reveal his father's name and give Kisár instructions for finding his father.[6]

At this point in the Nager version the narrator then digresses on the similarity of Kisár's story with a story from the life of Ḥażrat ʿAlī. The story concerns ʿAlī's "third son", Muḥammad ibn al-Ḥanafiyya (d. AD 700), ʿAlī's son by the "woman of the Banu Ḥanīfa", and not by Fāṯimā, the daughter of the Holy Prophet, who subsequent to Ḥusain's death at Kerbala in 49/680, claimed the imamate for himself, and contested the claims of Zayn al-'ābidīn, Ḥusain's elder son. The conflict was resolved by no lesser authority than the *Ka'ba* itself whose voice loudly proclaimed Zayn al-'ābidīn's right to the imamate. According to Zawáar Dáado, ʿAlī contracted a temporary marriage (Urdu and bu. *mut'ah*) with the "woman of the Banu Ḥanīfa" by whom his "third son" was born.[7]

From the allusion to the story from Ḥażrat ʿAlī's life Zawáar Dáado shifts smoothly to the description of the battle between Kisár and Abúu Drumbú, who fails to recognize his own son. Especially striking here is the tactic Abúu Drumbú uses to save his life: According to the ethical code of a *pahlawáan* the victor should give the first battle to the vanquished. Kisár, being young and inexperienced, believes this ruse and lets his opponent get up again. The two heroes then fight anew, and Kisár loses the second battle. Instead of having mercy on him, Abúu Drumbú draws his dagger and prepares to cut Kisár's throat. Kisár then sighs and Abúu Drumbú reproves him saying that a *pahlawān* should not beg for mercy. A conversation between the two heroes then ensues in the course of which Abúu Drumbú realizes that the young hero whose throat he is about to cut is none other than his own son. Kisár then takes his rightful place among the sons of Abúu Drumbú and the first chapter of the epic ends happily.

What we have just heard in summarized form is an example of the fruitful encounter of three cultural traditions of Central Asia in a remote valley of the Karakoram. For, the unusual first chapter of the Nager version of the epic of Kisár derives from no less a source than the *Šāh-nāma* of Abu'l Qāsīm Mānsūr Firdausī. In the famous Persian *Book of the King* the episode that deals with Rustam's sign of recognition is narrated in the seventh book, chapters two and three. But in the *Šāh-nāma* the story of Sohrāb's childhood is similar to, but not identical with, the story of Kisár's childhood in the Nager epic. While Sohrāb is not humiliated as a bastard, and only threatens his mother with dire consequences if she does not reveal his father's name, Kisár actually tortures his mother, thus making her endure the pain he has endured as a result of being humiliated as a bastard.

The narrative thread of our epic then leads to the battle between Kisár and Abúu Drumbú. The corresponding battle between Sohrāb and Rustam represents a major theme of the *Šāh-nāma*, and can be found in book 7, chapters 19 and 20. Particulary striking in this context are three points: (1) the motif of the ring or jewel as a sign of recognition; (2) the trick that Rustam uses to save his life when he loses the first battle with Sohrāb, namely, that the victor spares the vanquished in the first battle, as in the Nager Kisár-epic; (3) Sohrāb's threat that Rustam would revenge his death. As in the *Šāh-nāma*, Kisár taunts Abúu Drumbú that he would not have the courage to sit on his chest if Kisár's father were there. The tragedy of the *Šāh-nāma* is, of course, that Rustam does not recognize Sohrāb, and that he does not show his victim the same mercy that he himself had been given. Rustam immediately kills Sohrāb and recognizes too late that the young hero who lies dying before him, is none other than his own son. The core of this sublime story is recounted in the first chapter of the Nager version of the Kisár epic in the following form:[8]

> Once upon a time there was a certain *pahlawáan*, who lived in a certain region of Baltistan. He was one of the heroes who lived in those times (i.e. *in illo tempore*) in the twelve kingdoms of Baltistan. He lived in a certain kingdom and his name was Abúu Drumbú. Being a

pahlawáan, he would wander from city to city. One day as he wandered he reached a certain city. It was his habit (...). He was a *pahlawáan*, and lived from the booty that fell to his share by fair means or foul. The lustre of his body could be seen from afar.

In this city there lived a certain woman by the name of Máni. She was very beautiful. He contracted a temporary marriage (*mut'ah*) with her.[9] He prayed, and soon she was in a family way. After some time he didn't feel at ease there and set out again in search of battles. Before departing he said to Máni: "I'm going to a certain city. If you give birth to a daughter, then it should go according to your wish. But, if you bear a son, give him the name Libí Kisár." After saying this he gave her the ring that he wore on his finger and said: "If he should ask where his father is when he is grown up, bring him to that road over there and put this ring on his finger. He will come to me."

Some time passed. On the other hand, she was pregnant. She was near her time, and there was only one sister there to help her. She lived in that city, and apart from her there was no one to help her. Seven months had passed, and finally the time came for her delivery. The labor pains began, and a voice arose in her womb: "Oh! Oho! Am I to be born here? I am sacred! Oho! Shall Libí Kisár be born here? I am a spirit! I will be born in a pure place! I will be born on beautiful water! I will be born on the stony riverbed!" When the voice inside her arose the poor thing rolled on the ground in pain. And, in that city there was no one apart from a sister who could help her. She had been married to a man from over there (Baltistan) and lived far away from Máni. When she had gone from the mountain peak to the riverbed, a voice arose again in her womb: "Shall I, Libí Kisár, be born here? On the mountain tops, among the fairy-flowers will I be born! Among the ibexes will I be born!" After hearing this she took her staff in her hand and staggered toward the mountain top. After she had been brought there, the voice

> called out again: "Shall I be born here? I will be born on the water!" Again he forced her down. Twelve times to the riverbed and twelve times to the mountain top did he force her!
>
> Finally, on the summit there were some caves. Faint and exhausted she rolled herself into a cave, and Libí Kisár came out of her womb. When he had emerged from the womb, he became a spirit. Just in front of him, on the rocks, there were some beautiful ibexes. He went there and mounted one. And under her he laid a mortar and pestle[10] and went away, didn't he?

Already at his birth an important characteristic in Libí Kisár's personality emerges clearly: even more than the Kesar of Hunza, Baltistan, Ladakh, or Mongolia, Libí Kisár of Nager is a "trickster" who has his 'fun' with human beings – and not only with evil human beings as this episode clearly shows. This rather cruel treatment of his mother during his delivery serves to emphasize Kisár's supernatural origin: a *diwaáko* (spirit, demi-god) is not to be judged by the standards applicable to ordinary mortals. On the one hand, he embodies the very essence of manly virtues. On the other hand, he violates a duty which is binding for all men: to honour and protect his mother, and that even at the time of his own birth.[11]

> What happened then? When the poor sister realized that the time of delivery must have come she said: "The poor thing must be in childbed by now! What has become of her?" She went and searched for her. She lay unconscious in the cave. When her sister shook her, she stood up. She wept loudly and said: "The people will ridicule me! 'Where did you get that bastard from?' they will say. But I haven't given birth to a child. Under me there was only this grinding stone." Her sister was very clever. She said: "May someone molest your daughter!"[12] After she had said that, her sister became very wise: "May you be possessed by a demon![13] Where has that to which you have given birth actually gone? Come with me! I'll show you your son!" She looked up, and saw him playing polo on

an ibex on a cliff above them. "Look up there!", she cried. "Are you possessed by a demon? How did my son get up there?" (asked Máni astonished). "Hey! Come on!", her sister said. She tied a silk shawl around her neck and drove the horses onto the barren field. After walking back and forth on the barren field, she found some horse droppings. She took the droppings and made a fire and some smoke.[14] After lighting the fire, she went under a big boulder and called out: "Oh, you venerable spirit! Who are you? What shall I and my sister say when we go out into the world? You have done this to us and have gone away. 'This woman has given birth to a mortar and pestle.' That's what they'll say. At least do whatever it is that you intend to do and get it over!" They pleaded in this way and held on tightly to the boulder. When they did this, he became an infant and wimpered *"kiá, kiá"*, and fell into the silk shawl that Máni and her sister held open for him. They wrapped him in swaddling clothes, took him home and kept him with them.

They took care of him for a long time. When he had become seven years old, because of his agility in wrestling, anyone who fought with him fell down and anyone who collided with him while playing children's polo[15] was injured. One day the boys were playing polo on a certain barren field and the grandson of a certain old woman was there. He collided with Kisár. When they collided, he fell down and broke his arm. In tears he ran home to his grandmother and said: "That guy hit me!" She rushed to the scene and said: "If you had known your father, what would have happened? You, a mere bastard, have injured my grandson, haven't you?" Cut to the quick, Kisár said "I'm sorry", and went home.

As he was about to sit down his mother asked him: "What happened?" "I'm hungry", he replied. "Just sit down. I'll cook something for you", she said. He went out of the house, smashed some flintstones, and returned. He ground them down into fine pebbles, took a frying-pan, made a fire, and heated them. "Hey! What are you doing?", his mother asked. "I got hungry. So I made some roasted kernels (bu. *khaní*)." "O no!", she said. "Just sit down. Are you possessed by a demon? Are you making *khaní* from these pebbles?" "Yes, from these." His hand darted quickly into the frying-pan and he took a mouthful and began chewing loudly. When he did that his mother said: "What kind of kernels are you frying? Give me some!"

When she said that he darted his hand into the pan again, snatched some hot pebbles, put them on the palm of his mother's hand, and rolled her hand into a fist. When the skin on her hand began to peel off, she cried out in pain: "Did I raise you so that you could do this to me one day? After I had carried you twelve times to the mountain top and twelve times to the riverbed, I raised you." "Enough of that! If you've done all that for me, then tell me who my father is. Am I a bastard, after all?" "Oh no! Your father is not of this world. He is a *báadśaa* (king, emperor). Your father's name is Abúu Drumbú. He is a great *pahlawáan*. I'll show you who he is." He let go of her hand. Then he rubbed it with his saliva, and her hand healed instantly.[16] Then his tone became hard again. "I'm going to go on a journey now." Then his mother said: "I will tell you all about your father." Then she told him everything. "When my son has grown up and wants to find me, put this ring on his finger and show him that road over there and let him go. He will come to me." "Fine", he said. "What will you need in the way of provisions?", he asked. "When you are gone there won't be anything I can get without trouble. I need wood, water, and something to eat." "Don't worry", he said. Then he brought a big load of wheat-flour and poured it out (into the storage bins). He made the necessary provisions for her. He gave orders to his protective spirits (bu. *ráaçikuyo*). He ordered them like this: "Bring brushwood and fireword from our alpine meadow. Collect big logs and put them in the nearby gorge." When the provisions were ready, he said to his mother: "Give me leave to go now, o Mother!" "Very well", she said and went to him and put the ring on his finger. "Walk in that direction. Somewhere you will see your father."

In short, the prince walked for many stages (bu. *basámiṅ*). After many days, he finally became weak from hunger. Then he suddenly came upon a city, a certain city in Baltistan where there are twelve kingdoms – that's what the people say. There, among those people, wrestling matches and other martial competitions often took place. When he had reached a certain garden, his glance fell inside. All around this garden there was a high compound. The walls bristled with steel spikes. It was impossible to get into the garden. When he looked inside he saw so many date palms.[17] In the garden, a man was climbing up a date palm – there isn't much difference between this story and the one about Ḥaẓrat ʿAlī, is there (à part to the audience)? The man climbed up the date palm and shook it. Underneath two boys were eating the dates. When Kisár saw that he became angry. Hunger conquered him. "I'm sorry. But I should get some of these fruits too!" After saying this, he jumped over the wall and ran straight toward the two boys. Libí Kisár was very clever, as clever as clever can be. And besides that, he was a great *pahlawáan*. He was very shrewd and very naughty to boot! When he jumped into the garden, the two boys cried out: "*Babá*! He won't let us eat!" From up in the date palm Abúu Drumbú shouted down: "O boy! Whoever you are, I will satisfy your hunger. Don't worry. Just let go of my sons!"

One boy's name was Phuqtún and the other boy's name was Ç̣huqtún. They were from one of Abúu Drumbú's other wives. He didn't let go, and the boys began to cry. When they began to cry, Abúu Drumbú was stunned: "Who dares to prevent my sons from eating?", he shouted and jumped down the tree in a flash. In the meantime Kisár had filled his belly and lusted for battle. When Abúu Drumbú asked "Who are you?", they grabbed each other and began wrestling. Kisár was very young. But still their feet pressed deep into the earth. Neither fell under the other. But, finally, Abúu Drumbú fell under Kisár. When he fell under him, he said: "O boy! It's the custom of *pahlawáans* to give the first fall to the enemy."[18] Prior to this battle Libí Kisár had had no real experience in wrestling. When he had heard what Abúu Drumbú had said, he stood up. After both had stood up, they grabbed each other again. After a long struggle Abúu Drumbú pinned Libí Kisár to the ground.

He had given the first battle to his enemy. But now Abúu Drumbú drew his dagger and said: "I'm going to cut your throat!" Libí Kisár sighed. When he sighed Abúu Drumbú said: "That's not fitting for a *pahlawáan*." When he said that Libí Kisár spoke: "O uncle! I didn't sigh out of fear that you would kill me. I sighed because I didn't reach my goal." "What was your goal, o boy?", asked Abúu Drumbú. "What has my goal got to do with you? Pursue your own goal! God did not grant my wish. You are sitting on my chest now and have drawn your dagger. I had only come to see if I have a father." "Who is your father? What is his name?", asked Abúu Drumbú. "If my father were here now, would you be sitting on my chest? Kill me now! If my father were here, would you be in a position to kill me? How much courage would you have then, if he were here?" "Just tell me, who is your father?", asked Abúu Drumbú. When he said that Kisár explained. "My father's name is Abúu Drumbú. I had come to see him. But without having seen him, I have become your victim."

Now it all became clear to Abúu Drumbú and he stood up from Kisár's chest. When he looked at him, he saw his own signet ring on Kisár's finger. He kissed him and wiped the dust from his face. He climbed up the date palm again, shook the dates down and fed his three sons. Then he took them with him to his own castle.

> When they had reached the castle, they held wrestling matches with each other. Kisár was still young when he mastered the art of wrestling completely. At that time Abúu Drumbú went to his final abode. When he had passed away Libí Kisár took over his 'work'.

The final example of the cultural range in the first chapter of the Kisár-epic of Nager is the brief episode that tells of Kisár's wrestling matches and polo games with his childhood friends. Neither Zawáar Dáado nor his audience know the origin of this episode. It may ultimately stem from an epic that is now at home only in India, the *Mahābhārata*. As mentioned above, the motif of the humiliation of the young hero as a bastard does not occur in the *Šāh-nāma*. But, in the Ladakh and Balti-Stak versions of the Kesar-epic the young Kesar is humiliated as a bastard by his playmates. It is significant in this context that the Ladakh versions of Kisár are known throughout Zanskar down to Lahūl in the South where Kesar is identified with Bhīma, the Pāṇḍava. For, it was the young Bhīma who injured the Kaurava boys as often as they collided with him (*Mahābhārata*, 1.119). The motif of the humiliation as a bastard in the story given above (p. 183) may be a folk variant in which the story of Bhīma injuring the Kaurava boys is combined with the well-known story of Karṇa's humiliation as a bastard at the hands of Bhīma (*Mahābhārata*, 1.127).

A connection between the folk traditions of Bhīma and Gesar/Kesar seems more plausible when one considers a fragment of a Kesar-tradition that was narrated by Raja Fazl Ali Khan to Karl Jettmar in Rondu in 1978. The passage that is most significant in this context concerns Kesar's Herculean characteristics, which are not developed in the Nager version of the epic. However, when one compares the fragment from Rondu with the episode dealing with Kisár's youth in the Nager version it becomes evident that the Nager version is a trimmed down variant of the Rondu tradition, in which Kesar's prowess as a fighter is equalled by his prowess as an eater, thus moving him much closer to Bhīma at the great banquet table of epical heroes. In the Nager version of the epic Kisár only takes food from Abúu Drumbú's other two sons because he was overpowered by hunger, whereas it is the habit of the Kesar of Rondu to steal the food of his playmates:

> (...) In two years Kesar became a strong young man. He became a shepherd and took his sheep and goats along with the other boys. Relations with the other boys were good initially, but later Kesar prepared a huge trap made of wood for his companions. He sat on the wooden trap and said: "We do not need to walk to the mountain top, we can fly with this machine." The boys refused, and Kesar started beating them hard and chased them up the mountain. He stole away all their food. He would beat them and then eat their food. There was an old woman who lived there with a son (or nephew) named *Api-phara-so*. He was one of Kesar's companions. Gradually, all the boys, including *Api-phara-so*, became weak through Kesar's beatings and from lack of food. One day his mother asked him: "Why have you become so weak?" He replied: "Kesar takes us up the mountain and beats us and takes our food." She advised her son: "Next time Kesar tries to take your food away from you, you should resist him and ask him who his father is." Accordingly, he resisted Kesar on the next day and said to him: "Tell us who your father is before you start beating us." At this Kesar became ashamed and ran home (...)[19]

Similarly, Bhīma's prodigious appetite has inspired the imagination of folk narrators of the *Mahābhārata*, as, for example, in the tradition narrated by "Ramtchund" (Paṇḍit Rāmacandra, Sir William Jones's teacher) to Lt. Col. Antoine Louis Henri de Polier in the 1780s. According to the tradition of Ramtchund, subsequent to Draupadī's *svayaṃvara*, Kuntī instructs her new daughter-in-law in the proper portioning of the meals in the Pāṇḍava-household. The food was to be divided in two equal parts: one for Bhim and one for his four brothers, which included an extra portion for unexpected guests.[20]

The development of the Nager version of the epic was influenced most decisively by the adherence of the royal family of Nager to the ancient Iranian ideals of kingship as described in the *Šāh-nāma*. Moreover, the narration of the epic of Kesar formed a part of the ideal upbringing for princes at the court of the Amachas of Shigar, who were related to the royal house of Nager.[21] The addition of material from the seventh book of the prestigeous *Šāh-nāma* was yet another in a long series of appropriations to the folk traditions, which, according to Karl Jettmar (1990: 264 f.), go back to the source of the epic of Gesar/Kesar that August Hermann Francke had seen in the pre-Buddhist traditions in Ladakh.

Cultural Geography

Prior to the partition of British India the cultural area to which the Gesar epic belongs had extended from Central Asia through the Himalayas and the Karakoram to the Kulu Valley and Lahūl. Since 1947, the versions of Kesar in Baltistan, Nager, and Hunza have been cut off from the main stream of the tradition by the ceasefire lines that presently form the boundaries between India and Pakistan. As a consequence of this truncation the fruitful give-and-take among the ethnic groups of the Western Himalayas and the Karakoram has been interrupted. However, the rich cultural mosaic of previous centuries – the result of the merger of the influences of Islam, Hinduism, Buddhism, autochthonous spirit cults, and Iranian notions of the ideal king – is still evident in the character of Kesar, the folk hero *par excellence* of the Karakoram.

Moreover, Kesar's development as a folk hero reflects processes of great significance in the development of the cultures of the Hindu Kush and Karakoram, as, for example, the perception of woman as an ambivalent creature with dangerous powers, in contradiction to the exemplary image of woman in Shiism – in this connection one thinks at once of the obedient and self-sacrificing Fāṯimā –, or notions of caste among the people of Nager – one thinks immediately of Kisár's decision to reconcile himself with his treacherous favourite wife because she was born in a high caste – in contradiction to the egalitarian teachings of Islam. Mention should also be made of Kisár's marriage with a goldsmith's daughter, who is of a low caste, and of the generous portions of bucolic humour in the narration of Kisár's courtship of his brides. Moreover, the similarities in the traditions of Kisár in Hunza and Nager with the stories that are spread throughout South Asia concerning a warrior-king (who is also a folk deity) and his marriages to a wife from a high and a wife from a low caste are striking. In this connexion, one is reminded of Khaṇḍobā, a pastoral folk deity of the Deccan, and his two principal wives, Mhāḷsā and Bāṇāī, who come from a high and a low caste, respectively (Sontheimer 1989: 7-62).

The dense overlayering of cultures evident in the formation of the hero Kesar can best be understood when one considers the unique geographical situation of the Karakoram. Here, near the southern route of the Silk Roads, at the crossroads of Tibetan, Turkic, Iranian, and South Asian cultures, where even geologically, India and Central Asia meet, there has been from time immemorial a lively exchange of goods, ideas, and – how could it be otherwise? – of stories.

As early as 816 an Arabian offensive reached the kingdom of Bolor in the area of present-day Chitral. In the ninth century Gilgit came under the control of the Indian princes of Khotan, who styled themselves "the lords of the Tibetans and the Turks". They named the province to which Gilgit belonged a "*Khrom*", or military district, which is ultimately a corruption of the word "Rome", or "Rūm", which to the ethnic groups of Central Asia meant Byzantium (Uray 1985: 541 f.). In the writings of the *rÑiṅ-ma-pa* scholar Lo-čhen Dharmaśrī (1654–1717), Khrom is synonomous with 'Bru-ža (Tsering 1979: 183 f.), which both Helmut Hoffmann (1950: 187 and 211) and Giuseppe Tucci (Heissig and Tucci 1970: 100) equate with the region of Gilgit, the language of which, according to Hoffmann (1969: 143) and Rolf-Alfred Stein (1962: 35; cf. Stein 1959: 59 f.), was Burushaski.[22]

A name similar to that of our epic hero, *Phromo Kesaro*, is mentioned in several Bactrian inscriptions of the Šāhī-dynasty of Gandhāra as the name of a Bactrian king who ruled between 738 and 745 and who was the father-in-law of the king of Khotan, Bijaya Saṅgrāma.[23] It is possible that the story of Khrom Gesar was brought to the Karakoram by the Turkish mercenaries of Khotan (Jettmar 1990: 264). In one traditional account Gesar is said to have conquered the Hunza valley and established a dynasty of kings that ruled before the Traqhanáatiṅ kings of Gilgit (Müller-Stellrecht 1979: 100 and 106 f.). The sagas woven around the hero Gesar/Kesar may thus represent the most ancient living traditions of the Karakoram.

NOTES

1 *Heldensagen des Firdusi*, vol. 1, Stuttgart [Verlag der J.G. Cotta'schen Buchhandlung] 1893: 11 and 13f.; translated from the German by the

present author. Von Schack acknowledges his debt to "his masters, Burnouf and Lassen" on page nine of his introduction to the *Šāh-nāma*.

2 On formal dialogues that are not functional dialogues see Tedlock and Mannheim (eds.): 1995: 4.

3 In Hunza Kisár is believed to be the apical ancestor of the Dirámitiṅ clan. In order to propitiate him, goat's milk and butter (*maltáṣ*) were formerly sacrificed before beginning work on any new house. Cf. Müller-Stellrecht 1973: 137; 1979: 100.

4 The question of the sinking of epical level caused by the incorporation of new material and the adjustment of the epic to the changed expectations of a modern audience was the subject of a significant discussion between Arthur Thomas Hatto and Walter Hinck following an Academy of Sciences lecture in Bonn in 1990. Cf. Hatto 1991: 28f.

5 In the version of Ali Madad of Hunza, which was published by D.L.R. Lorimer in 1935, Aba Dumbu is nominally but not biologically Kiser's father as Kiser's mother becomes pregnant by ingesting a raindrop in which Aba Dumbu's brother, who had been given to Fasan Karaski of the land of Yal Butot, had promised to return to his father, Dungpā Míru. Cf. D.L.R. Lorimer, (Lt. Col.), "The adventures of Kiser" in: *The Burushaski language.* Volume II. *Texts and translations*, Oslo [H. Aschehoug and Co.] 1935: 103–11. The name Abúu Drumbú may ultimately derive from the Sanskrit *Dhruva*, the north or pole star, and is the name of an ancient hero in the region of Kargil, Agu Drumba, as was noted by August Hermann Francke on visiting the village of Shargola in 1909 (cf. Francke 1972: 102 and n. 3).

6 In versions of the epic from Hunza this theme does not occur, as the hero grows up in an intact family with mother and father. Cf. Söhnen 1981: 496f. and nn. 52 and 54.

7 On the traditions concerning the equality of ʿAlī's "three sons" see Watt and Marmura (eds.) 1985: 32, 38, 41ff., 45, and especially 49. Historically, ʿAlī is said to have been the father of fourteen sons. But only three, i.e. Ḥasan, Ḥusain, and Muḥammad ibn al-Ḥanifiyya, played a significant role in the history of Islam.

8 For a more detailed discussion of the *Kisár-nimás* and a complete linguistic transcription of Zawáar Dáado's performance of it, see van Skyhawk (ed.) 1996.

9 In the Balti-Recension Kisár is the Dajjal (Arabic: *daǧǧāl*, Balti: *dajjāl*) the Islamic Anti-Christ (Sagaster 1983: 341-48), while in the versions from Hunza no statement at all is made about Kisár's religion. In contrast to the Balti and Hunza versions, the characters of the heroes in the Nager version (e.g. Abúu Drumbú) are fashioned in such a way that their conduct is in harmony with the minimal demands of Shiism, or, they are even compared with the *imāms* of the Shiahs. By such minimal 'Shiization' of the hero Kisár, and by omitting any mention of his pre-Islamic origins, the narrator succeeds in highlighting Kisár's manly virtues, such as courage, valor, presence of mind in dangerous situations, love of adventure, and sense of justice, so that the Nagérkuċ, who are pious *ithnā 'ašariyya* (Twelver Shiahs),

can identify with him as an exemplary hunter and fearless warrior with no misgivings and experience his deeds anew, that is, *in illo tempore.*

10 In the West Tibetan version of the epic Gesar's mother, *Gog bzang lha mo*, gives birth to a number of creatures, and finally to a miscarriage that "looks like a lizard (...)" Horrified, she hides it under a stone. But the grandmother, *A ne bKur dman mo*, discovers and rescues the infant Gesar (Hermanns 1965: 307). The motif of the mortar and pestle appears to be a variant of the lizard-motif of the west Tibetan epic.

11 Geoffrey Samuel has drawn attention to Gesar's trickster personality: "(...) He is not a figure of conformity to authority but someone who can act outside any kind of established authority and who by his actions continually plays with and creates structures of authority." In his note to this passage Samuel points out the similarity of Gesar's personality with the personality of the universally beloved trickster of popular Hinduism, Kṛṣṇa: "His Indian analogue, if there is one, is more Krishna than either Rama (with whom he is compared in the *gLing tshang*-edition) or Bhima (with whom he overlaps in the Kulu valley and Lahuli folklore)." Samuel 1992: 720 and n. 27. On Kṛṣṇa as "trickster" see Apte 1985: 218ff. Classic studies of the "trickster" can be found in Boas 1898: 1-18 and 1914: 394ff. The first and, for a long time, only scholar to take notice of Gesar's trickster personality was G.N. Potanin 1893: 127 and 1899: 198, 200, 487, 748 (cited by Stein 1959: 6). Though Matthias Hermanns did call attention to Gesar's "tricks", he did not discuss the theme of the "trickster" with regard to Gesar. Cf. Hermanns 1965: 310.

12 A favourite curse in Hunza and Nager.

13 Another popular imprecation.

14 It is no coincidence that Máni's sister uses horse droppings for her smoke sacrifice. For, the smoke of cow's dung would not please the *diwaáko* as the cow and its products are despised by pure spirits, especially by fairies, from whom the *diwaáko* are said to descend. Cf. Müller-Stellrecht 1973: 219f. and Frembgen 1985: 169 and n. 429. There are two occurrences of the smoke-sacrifice in the Nager version of the Kisár epic: 1. by Máni's sister in order to propitiate the *diwáako* and 2. by Kisár himself when he first sees the magic ibex (*iskébum haldén*).

15 bu. *gaṭál bulá.* That is, on foot with sticks but without horses.

16 The first reference in Islam to the healing power of saliva (in this case that of a holy man) is found in the traditional account of the Battle of Qamūs (May-June A.D. 628), in which the Holy Prophet is said to have stopped the pain in ʿAlī's wounded eye by rubbing his saliva on it (cf. Rizvi 1986: 15). This incident does not occur in other Kisár-versions and is an example of the influence of Shiism on the *Kisár-nimás.*

17 The fact that date palms do not grow in Baltistan does not disturb the audience in their enjoyment of the story.

18 Abúu Drumbú's trick has some similarity to the episode in the Mongolian Gesser epic in which Gesser becomes involved in a humorous wrestling match with his indomitable wife, Adschu Mergen. But, the

further development of that bout reminds one more of Kṛṣṇa's sport with the clothes of the bathing *Gopīs* than of the battle of Sohrāb and Rustam in the *Šāh-nāma*. Adschu Mergen, dressed as a man, sets out to compete with Gesar in the hunt: "(...) So wie Gesser erkannte, daß es ein Weib sei, sprang er auf und rang mit ihr. Einmal warf sie den Gesser auf die Knie; da sprach Gesser: 'Kämpfen die Männer nicht dreimal hintereinander? Klopfen sie nicht viermal den Staub aus?' Abermals begann der Ringkampf und Gesser warf sie nieder. Gesser sprach: 'Ich nehme dich zum Weibe!' Als Adschu Mergen einwilligte, sprach er weiter: 'Wenn dem so ist, wirst du meinen kleinen Finger ablecken?' Adschu Mergen war auch damit einverstanden, worauf Gesser sich in den kleinen Finger stach und sie das Blut ablecken ließ. Nun gingen die beiden zum großen See, um Wasser zu trinken. Als sie zum Wasser kamen, sah Gesser das Abbild eines Pfeiles im Wasser schimmern und sprach: 'Hinter mir war niemand mit gespanntem Bogen.' Als er nun hinter sich schaute, erblickte er Adschu Mergen mit gespanntem Bogen und fragte sie: 'Was hast du vor?' Adschu Mergen antwortete: 'Auf dich habe ich den Bogen nicht gespannt; es gilt einem Fisch im See.' In der Tat rötete sich das Wasser von dem getroffenen und getöteten Fisch. Als beide an das Ufer des Sees gelangt waren und getrunken hatten, zog Gesser seine Kleider aus, sprang in den See und schwamm an das jenseitige Ufer. Adschu Mergen, erhitzt und in Schweiß, konnte nicht ruhig bleiben, sondern zog ebenfalls ihre Kleider aus und sprang in den See. Dies wußte Gesser, er pfiff, und es entstand ein Wirbelwind, der ihre Kleider in die Höhe hob, wo sie an der Spitze eines Baumes hängenblieben. Nachdem Gesser zurückgekehrt war und seine Kleider wieder angelegt hatte, kam Adschu Mergen, der es fröstelte, und setzte sich auf Gessers Schoß (...)" (Schmidt 1925: 83f.).

19 I am grateful to Professor Dr. Karl Jettmar for making me aware of and generously giving me access to the material quoted above.

20 De Polier's *Mahābhārata* was edited and published by his cousin, Canoness Marie-Elizabeth de Polier, about twenty years subsequent to her cousin's violent death at the hands of brigands during the chaotic times that followed upon the French Revolution. It is bitterly ironical that de Polier's throat was slit because the brigands believed that he had brought back the legendary diamond Koh-i-nūr from Golconda to France. Cf. Polier 1809, cited by Dumézil 1989: 43ff., 112ff.; cf. also Schwab 1984: 155ff. Owing to devastating philological criticism (cf. Schwab 1984: 157), de Polier's version remained virtually unknown until Georges Dumézil drew attention to it in his erudite analysis of the epic from the point of view of an indigenous Sanskrit *paṇḍit* of the 18th century.

21 Karl Jettmar has drawn attention to the similarities in the story of the killing of the man-eating king Shiri Badat and the death of Rustam in the *Šāh-nāma*. The slayer was said to be a "(...) grandchild of the queen of Shigar and a refugee prince from Persia (...)" Cf. Jettmar 1975: 241 and n. 226.

22 Most recently, Kevin Tuite (1997: 450) has evaluated the outcome of previous research on the question of a relationship of *Bru-zha*

and Burushaski as being indecisive: "(...) the attested fragments of the language referred to as *Bru-zha* in late 1st millennium CE Tibetan sources, despite its promising resemblance to the ethnonym *Burusho*, might be unrelated to any known language of the area (...)" Notwithstanding the difficulty of demonstrating a genetic relationship between the extant fragments of *Bru-zha* and Burushaski, the question still remains: How did it come to pass that the Tibetans called the region of Gilgit *Bru-zha*, the people of this region came to be known as Burusho, their language became known (to outsiders) as Burushaski, but, strangely, these very similar ethnonyms are only similar in name but not in content? While Tuite has not yet been able to resolve this question either, he has pointed the way toward further research on "*quasi-genetic resemblances*" between Burushaski and the linguistic phylum "Macro-Caucasian" on the basis of "(...) resemblances of structure and vocabulary that do not prove genetic relatedness in the standard sense but certainly suggest a possible connection at a level slightly deeper than the comparative method can reach" (Tuite 1997: 467).

23 Uray 1985: 534; Humbach 1966: 20-23 and 64f.; Harmatta 1969: 409-412 and 431f.; Jettmar 1990: 264f.

REFERENCES

Amoretti, Biancamaria Scarcia. 1990. Die historische Entwicklung der Sekten im Islam. In: *Der Islam III. Islamische Kultur. Zeitgenössische Strömungen. Volksfrömmigkeit.* Edited by Schimmel, Annemarie. Stuttgart: Kohlhammer Verlag, 100–56.

Apte, Mahadev. 1985. *Humor and Laughter. An anthropological Approach.* Ithaca and London: Cornell University Press.

Baeumler, Alfred. 1965. *Das mythische Weltalter. Bachofens romantische Deutung des Altertums.* München: C.H. Beck'sche Verlagsbuchhandlung.

Boas, Franz. 1898. Introduction to James Teit, 'Traditions of the Thompson River Indians of British Columbia'. *Memoirs of the American Folklore Society* 6: 1-18.

———. 1914. Mythology and Folk-tales of the North American Indians. *Journal of American Folk-Lore* XXVII: 394ff.

Dumézil, Georges. 1989. *Mythos und Epos. Die Ideologie der drei Funktionen in den Epen der indoeuropäischen Völker.* Frankfurt/New York: Campus Verlag. (Translated from the French by Hornig, Diether; original title: *Mythe et épopée. T. I: La Terre soulagée.* Paris: Éditions Gallimard, 1968); 5th edn., Paris.

Francke, August Hermann. 1968. *Der Frühlings- und Wintermythos der Kesarsage* (Beiträge zur Kenntnis der vorbuddhistischen Religion Tibets und Ladakhs. Mémoires de la Société Finno-Ougrienne, XV). Helsingfors 1902; reprinted in Osnabrück: Otto Zeller Verlag.

———. 1972. *Antiquities of Indian Tibet.* Part 1:*Personal Narrative* (Archaeological Survey of India. New imperial series, XXXVIII). Calcutta, 1926; reprinted in Delhi: S. Chand and Co.

Frembgen, Jürgen. 1985. *Zentrale Gewalt in Nager (Karakorum). Politische Organisationsformen, ideologische Begründungen und Veränderungen in der Moderne* (Beiträge zur Südasien-Forschung, published by the South Asia Institute of Heidelberg University, 103). Wiesbaden: Franz Steiner Verlag.

Harmatta, J. 1969. Late Bactrian Inscriptions. In: *Acta Antiqua Academiae Hungaricae*, Part XVII/3–4: 297–432. Budapest.

Hatto, Arthur Thomas. 1991. *Eine allgemeine Theorie der Heldenepik* (Vorträge. Rheinisch-Westfälische Akademie der Wissenschaften). Opladen: Westdeutscher Verlag.

Heissig, Walther, and Tucci, Giuseppe. 1970. *Die Religionen Tibets und der Mongolei* (Die Religionen der Menschheit, 20). Stuttgart: Verlag W. Kohlhammer.

Hermanns, P. Matthias. 1965. *Das National-Epos der Tibeter Gling König Gesar*. Regensburg: Verlag Josef Habbel.

Herrmann, Silke. 1991. *Kesar-Versionen aus Ladakh* (Asiatische Forschungen. Monographienreihe zur Geschichte, Kultur und Sprache der Völker Ost- und Zentralasiens, 109). Wiesbaden: Otto Harrassowitz.

Hoffmann, Helmut. 1950. *Quellen zur Geschichte der tibetischen Bon-Religion* (Abhandlungen der Geistes- und Sozialwissenschaftlichen Klasse. Akademie der Wissenschaften und Literatur Mainz, Jahrgang 1950, Heft 4). Wiesbaden: Franz Steiner Verlag.

———. 1969. An Account of the Bon Religion in Gilgit. *Central Asiatic Journal. International Periodical For the Languages, Literature, History and Archaeology of Central Asia*, XIII.2: 137–45.

Hübner, Kurt. 1985. *Die Wahrheit des Mythos*. München: C.H. Beck'sche Verlagsbuchhandlung.

Humbach, Helmut. 1966–67. *Baktrische Sprachdenkmäler. Mit Beiträgen von Adolf Grohmann*, Parts I and II (illustrations). Wiesbaden: Otto Harrassowitz.

Jettmar, Karl. 1975. *Die Religionen des Hindukusch* (Die Religionen der Menschheit, 4.1). Stuttgart: Kohlhammer Verlag.

———. 1990. Das Westtibetische Zentrum der Kesarsage. In: *Wissenschaftsgeschichte und gegenwärtige Forschung in Nordwest-Indien*. Edited by Lydia Icke-Schwalbe and Gudrun Meier. Dresden: Staatliches Museum für Völkerkunde, 259–65.

Lorimer, David Lockhart Robertson (Lt. Col.). 1929. The Supernatural in the Popular Belief of the Gilgit Region. *Journal of the Royal Asiatic Society*, July 1929: 507–36.

———. 1931. An Oral Version of the Kesar Saga from Hunza. *Folk-Lore* XVII: 105–40. London.

———. 1935. *The Burushaski Language*, vol. II: *Texts and Translations*. Oslo: H. Aschehoug and Co.

———. 1938. *The Burushaski Language*, vol. III: *Vocabularies and Index*. Oslo: H. Aschehoug and Co.

Müller-Stellrecht, Irmtraud. 1973. *Feste in Dardistan. Darstellung und Kulturgeschichtliche Analyse* (Arbeiten aus dem Seminar für Völkerkunde der Johann Wolfgang von Goethe-Universität Frankfurt am Main, 5)

———. 1979. *Materialien zur Ethnographie von Dardistan (Pakistan). Aus den nachgelassenen Aufzeichnungen von D.L.R. Lorimer. Teil I: Hunza.* Graz: Akademische Druck- und Verlagsanstalt.

———. 1980. *Materialien zur Ethnographie von Dardistan (Pakistan). Aus den nachgelassenen Aufzeichnungen von D.L.R. Lorimer. Teil II: Gilgit.* Graz: Akademische Druck- und Verlagsanstalt.

———. 1980. *Materialien zur Ethnographie von Dardistan (Pakistan). Aus den nachgelassenen Aufzeichnungen von D.L.R. Lorimer. Teil III: Chitral und Yasin.* Graz: Akademische Druck- und Verlagsanstalt.

Polier, Marie-Elisabeth de (ed.). 1809. *Mythologie des Indous, travaillée par Mdme la Chnesse de Polier, sur des manuscrits authentiques apportés de l'Inde par feu Mr. le Colonel de Polier, Membre de la Société Asiatique de Calcutta.* Roudolstadt and Paris, in two volumes.

Potanin, G.N. 1893. *Tangutsko-Tibetskaya okraina Kitaya i Central'naya Mongoliya*, vol. II. Saint Petersburg.

———. 1899. *Vostočniê motiviê v srednevyekovom europeiskom eposye.* Moscow.

Rizvi, Sayid Athar Abbas. 1986. *A Socio-Intellectual History of the Isnā-'Asharī Shī'īs in India*, vol. I. Canberra/Delhi: Munshiram Manoharlal.

Sagaster, Klaus. 1983. Kesar, der islamische Antichrist. In: *Documenta Barbarorum. Festschrift für Walther Heissig zum 70. Geburtstag.* Edited by Klaus Sagaster and Michael Weiers. Wiesbaden: Otto Harrassowitz, 341–48.

Samuel, Geoffrey. 1992. Gesar of Ling: The Origins and Meaning of the East Tibetan Epic. In: *Proceedings of the Fifth Seminar of the International Association for Tibetan Studies.* Edited by Shōren Ihara and Zuihō Yamaguchi (Narita, 1989). Narita: Naritasan Shinshōji, 711–21.

Schack, Adolf Friedrich Graf von. 1893. *Heldensagen des Firdusi*, vol. 1. Stuttgart: Verlag der J.G. Cotta'schen Buchhandlung.

Schmidt, Isaac Jacob. 1925. *Die Taten Bogda Gesser Chan's, des Vertilgers der Wurzel der zehn Uebel in den zehn Gegenden.* Berlin: Auriga Verlag (1st published in St. Petersburg and Leipzig, 1839).

Schwab, Raymond. 1984. *The Oriental Renaissance. Europe's Rediscovery of India and the East, 1680–1880.* New York: Columbia University Press (translated from the French by Patterson-Black, Gene, and Reinking, Victor; original title *La Renaissance orientale.* Paris: Éditions Payot, 1950).

Söhnen, Renate. 1981. On the Stak Version of the Kesar Epic in Baltistan. *Zentralasiatische Studien* XV: 491–511.

Sontheimer, Günther-Dietz. 1976. *Birobā, Mhaskobā und Khaṇḍobā. Ursprung, Geschichte und Umwelt von pastoralen Gottheiten in Mahārāṣṭra* (Schriftenreihe des Südasien-Insituts der Universität Heidelberg, 21). Wiesbaden: Franz Steiner Verlag.

———. 1989. The Myth of the God and his two Wives. In: *Living Texts from India.* Edited by Richard K. Barz and Monika Thiel-Horstmann. Wiesbaden: Otto Harrassowitz, 7–62.

Stein, Rolf-Alfred. 1959. *Recherches sur l'épopée et le barde en Tibet* (Bibliothèque de l'Institut des Hautes Études Chinoises, XIII). Paris: Presses Universitaires de France.

———. 1962. *Tibetan Civilization.* London.

Tedlock, Dennis and Bruce Mannheim (eds.). 1995. *The Dialogic Emergence of Culture*. Urbana and Chicago: University of Illinois Press.

Tsering, Pema. 1979. Historische, epische und ikonographische Aspekte des gLiṅ Gesar. In: *Die Mongolischen Epen. Bezüge, Sinndeutung und Überlieferung (Ein Symposium)*. Ed. Heissig, Walther (Asiatische Forschungen. Monographienreihe zur Geschichte, Kultur und Sprache der Völker Ost- und Zentralasiens, 68). Wiesbaden: Otto Harrassowitz, 158–89.

Tuite, Kevin. 1997. Evidence for Prehistoric Links between the Caucasus and Central Asia. In: *The Bronze Age and Early Iron Age Peoples of Eastern Central Asia. Volume one: Archaeology, Migration and Nomadism, Linguistics*. Edited by Victor H. Mair, Philadelphia: The Institute for the Study of Man in collaboration with The Unversity of Pennsylvania Museum Publications, 448–75.

Uray, Geza. 1985. Vom römischen Kaiser bis zum König Ge-sar von Gliṅ. In: *Fragen der mongolischen Heldendichtung*, Teil III. Edited by Heissig, Walther (Asiatische Forschungen. Monographienreihe zur Geschichte, Kultur und Sprache der Völker Ost- und Zentralasiens, 91). Wiesbaden: Otto Harrassowitz, 530–48.

van Skyhawk, Hugh (ed.). 1996. *Libi Kisar. Ein Volksepos im Burushaski von Nager. Mit Beiträgen und Ergänzungen von Hermann Berger und Karl Jettmar* (Asiatische Forschungen. Monographienreihe zur Geschichte, Kultur und Sprache der Völker Ost- und Zentralasiens, 133). Wiesbaden: Otto Harrassowitz.

Watt, W. Montgomery and Michael Marmura (eds.). 1985. *Der Islam II. Politische Entwicklungen und theologische Konzepte*. Stuttgart: Verlag W. Kohlhammer.

Of Kings as Heroes

ROMILA THAPAR

THE hero of early times, the *vīra*, was associated with a genre of literature, the epics, which by the mid-first millennium A.D. had become a part of what was believed to be the narrative of the past. Thus the *Mahābhārata* is referred to as *itihāsa* and the *Rāmāyaṇa* as the *ādi-kāvya*. But the hero as a model was not discarded. He was woven into the category of "hero" which superceded the *vīra*. This was the king in the context of the court. The context had changed but there were strands which still meandered back to earlier heroes. The term *rājā*, previously used for chiefs of clans characteristic of chiefdoms, continued to be used for rulers of kingdoms and thereby perhaps sub-consciously provided a link. Frequently the king took the exalted title of *mahārāja* or the even more exalted *mahārājādhirāja*, and these titles marked a departure from the simple clan chief or *rājā* (Thapar 1984).

Epic heroes such as Rama in the *Rāmāyaṇa* and Arjuna in the *Mahābhārata* remained familiar to later times. Nevertheless in the Purāṇas of the mid-first millennium A.D. they were relegated to distinctly earlier periods – such as the Treta and Dvāpara *Yugas* – the more distant time cycles. The initiation of the fourth and final Kaliyuga of the present times, after the Mahābhārata war (*Viṣṇu Purāṇa*, 4), introduced the time cycle associated with dynasties. The succession of rulers in each dynasty constitutes the narrative of the past in the genealogical section of the *Viṣṇu Purāṇa*. The king now emerges as the focus of heroic activity, the protector of his subjects and the one who ensures the prevalence of law in society. How this was to be done differed from the time of the epic heroes, but nevertheless the values which they had endorsed were still reiterated even if their meanings had changed to some degree. Elements of these values are evident in later redactions and interpolations of event and statement in the epics. But the more extensive exploration of the king as hero and the mutations undergone by such heroes were developed in the *carita* literature or the royal biographies associated with various royal courts. The earliest of these dates to the seventh century A.D. but they came to be associated with many royal courts from the eleventh century A.D.

Such biographies are in the main of kings and to a lesser extent of persons in political authority such as ministers. The term *carita* refers literally to the activities of a person. Such texts use themes which were part of the genealogical section of the Purāṇas although their subject is not the lineage or the clan but the individual. They relate ancestral origins which often involve an association with deities. They narrate the early history and antecedents of both the author and the subject. The focus is on the actions of those in political authority and involves justifying in particular, actions which deviate from earlier norms. Such explanations often derive from the remembered tradition of the past where comparison with earlier heroes is implicit. Their significance has also to be seen in a changed historical situation in that they centre on the king's relations with his subordinate chiefs and functionaries.

The political legitimacy of lineage and caste which were important to these biographies was expressed in various ways: through genealogical patterns underlining the importance of birth, through dynasties indicating the declining authority of the *kṣatriyas* and the opening of political power to other castes with the growth of state systems and monarchies, through an emphasis on marriage alliances as the public acceptance of status using at times the ceremony of the *svayaṃvara* and the symbolism of the *digvijaya* from earlier times. At the *svayaṃvara* the princess chose her husband from among a gathering of eligible suitors. The *digvijaya* encapsulated the conquest of the four quarters, not necessarily as a statement of actual conquest but as a claim to political power. These features, associated with an earlier tradition, although transformed in meaning were nevertheless carried over into the courtly culture of the later monarchies.

The biography had its antecedents in earlier forms particularly the narratives in praise of clan heroes. Linked broadly with these were a number of inscriptions eulogising the actions of kings. Kharavela in the first century B.C. ruling in eastern India provides a chronological resumé of his reign.[1] From western India the Queen-mother of a Sātavāhana ruler refers to her son in a miniaturised *carita* text, the inscription containing elements which later characterised historical biography.[2] Samudragupta in the fourth century A.D. is eulogised as the conqueror par excellence, the model for the *digvijayin* or world conqueror.[3] These are statements about the individual ruler elaborating on the bare lists of kings available in the early *Purāṇas*.

Heroes from earlier literature were the subject of *kāvyas* or lengthy poems and as individuals became the prototypes for *caritas*. The popularity of Rāma for instance, encouraged kings in their claims to being, like him, incarnations of Viṣṇu. This is reflected in part in the constant rewriting of the *Rāmāyaṇa* in the regional languages and incorporating local episodes. Biographical writing was also influenced by the treatment of the lives of kings and monks in Buddhist and Jaina texts. The biography of the Buddha, the *Buddhacarita* of Aśvaghoṣa, was doubtless influential even if not directly referred to by *Brāhmaṇa* authors.[4]

The eulogistic function was also the result of a courtly style of literature, comparable to similar literature from other parts of the world.[5] There was a selected core of information on contemporary events around which was woven a framework of hagiography composed in elegant courtly language replete with linguistic virtuosity and sophisticated allusions to classical learning. It was the formal picture of the ideal king according to existing canons. To some extent the subject of the biography was an exemplar. This was particularly important where dynasties came from newly established families anxious that they be respected. These texts were not associated with an oral tradition, but were essentially the texts of a literate society. They were not intended as critical historical writing for such a category did not exist. They were *kāvyas*, creative literature, except that they related to the exercise of power and claimed that they were presenting the past as it actually happened and narrating the present.

Prior to this the tradition had drawn on kingship as a form of authority and those in power were the protectors of society preventing a condition of anarchy. We are told that in the absence of a *rājā*, lawlessness prevails and, as in conditions of draught, the big fish eat the little fish.[6] Protection lay both in defence against external aggression and in upholding the social and moral order of society. The latter was encapsulated in brahmanical sources as the *varṇāśramadharma*, the social order seen as sacred duty, although Buddhist and Jaina texts define it differently. But the legitimacy of the ruler had also to be established, for, an unlawful king could be the cause of disasters. Earlier this legitimacy had derived from connections by birth and often endorsed through Vedic sacrificial rituals, such as the *rājasūya* where the *yajamāna* or patron of the sacrifice emerged with enhanced political authority, or the *aśvamedha* which was an assertion to territorial control and status apart from its association with fertility. Recognition was now increasingly given to an additional type of authority. The reality of political power drew less on the earlier rituals and more on the recognised structures of powerful dynasties. Political power was said to lie in conquest and in the appropriation of resources. Marriage alliances could underline status as also affirmations of association with divinity. All these were seen as culminating in the authority of the king.

The legitimation of this authority grew out of the various hierarchies within the state, the need for legitimacy arising from the existence of inequality and competition. Nevertheless the intermeshing of control through a serried ranking from clan chiefs to kings was a change from the earlier kingdoms which had registered a greater flexibility in their formal insistence on hierarchy. The presence of intermediaries of many categories, from *aṭavi-rājās* (forest chiefs) to the *sāmantas* and *maṇḍaleśvaras* (feudatories and tributary allies), was more proximate in the countryside than was the distant control by the king.[7] The intermediaries acted as an integrative network to support the polity of the state.

One of the results of local initiative meshing with administrative control was the coming into importance of new castes, largely functional and jostling for status. The acculturation of Sanskritic culture in areas new to it required the accomodating of clans and occupations in the caste hierarchy. In the settling of status some theoretical conformity to the normative texts was expected. Hence the need for those in authority to claim *kṣatriya* status. This was also a reflection of an increasing transition in many of these new areas opened to settlement, where a clan dominated society with a relatively more equitable distribution of resources was gradually included within a state system with a pressure on producers. The post-Gupta state did not try and uproot local authority but encouraged a new role for this category by suggesting links with earlier lineages.

However distant the centre may be the producers of revenue had to be kept under control by the intermediaries and this required a political balance between them and the king. The heightened significance of the king whether symbolic or actual became more central as the court evolved into a gathering of competing intermediaries, sometimes competing with the sovereign ruler as well. References to *sāmantas* of various categories increase from this period. Some held ministerial appointments, others were there as loyal subordinate rulers, their loyality having to be continually put to the test. This made personal relations more immediate than lineage links as is reflected in the biographies. The impact of legitimation was not restricted to the status of the king, but crystalised a view of temporal power and its effects on a temporal domain. This in turn involved the bringing together of many facets of contemporary ideology to lend support to temporal power.

The first major royal biography claiming to be historical was the *Harṣacarita*, a biography of the king Harṣavardhana, written by Bāṇa-bhaṭṭa in the seventh century A.D.[8] Harṣa was the sole ruler to give prominence to a short-lived dynasty. The text carries the usual characteristics of the *carita* literature. It begins with invocatory verses to the deity. This is followed by a narration of the antecedents of the author who, as a Bhṛgu *brāhmaṇa* would have been especially familiar with the historical tradition. Not surprisingly he makes particular mention of the reading of the *Vāyu Purāṇa*, one of the early Purāṇas and adds that it was also recited by a bard. There is an affectionate description of the *agrahāra* (the royal donation of a village), where his family resided. We are told that Bāṇa was specially requested to write the biography by the king, Harṣa himself.

The text then moves to the life of the king. The home base of the family was modern Thanesar north of Delhi. The ceremony of legitimation of an early ancestor is described. A Śaiva ascetic, Bhairavācārya, a preceptor of the king, performs the *mahākāla* rite in the cemetery assisted by his three disciples and the king. Whilst Bhairavācārya stands on a corpse, a being arises from the earth, the Nāga Śrīkaṇṭha. The king uses a magic sword to vanquish the Nāga, but does not kill him as he notices him wearing a sacred thread. The sword then turns into a radiant woman, the goddess of good fortune, Śrī, who offers him a boon. He asks for the success of Bhairavācārya's rite. Pleased with his magnanimity she prophecies that he will be ancestor to a line of heroic kings of whom the foremost, predictably, will be Harṣa. This myth draws on both a Śaiva ritual, perhaps because Thanesar was the centre of a Pāśupata Śaiva cult, and also involves Lakṣmī the consort of Viṣṇu. This is a legitimation rite significantly different from the Vedic sacrificial rituals of earlier times, required of *kṣatriya* heroes. Part of the reason for this deviation may have been that the family was not of *kṣatriya* but of a lower *vaiśya* origin.

The scene then shifts to the childhood of Harṣa. The valour of his father is described in resounding phrases which become part of the conventional rhetoric of a king's conquests. He was, "... a lion to the Hūna deer, a burning fever to the king of the Indus land, a troubler of the sleep of the Gurjara, a bilious plague to that scent-elephant, the lord of Gandhāra, a looter to the lawlessness of the Latas and an axe to the creeper of Mālava's glory."[9] We know from inscriptions that his father dropped the simple title of *mahārāja* to use the more grandiose, *paramabhaṭṭāraka-mahārājādhirāja*.[10] The title marked a distinct change of status and the royal biography was also meant to underline the change.

Grief at the death of their father overwhelms Harṣa and his elder brother. It is hinted that Harṣa was the more ambitious and that there was some rivalry regarding the succession. Other sources indicate that his brother was appointed successor, a fact which Bāṇa ignores. Further bad news informs them of the kidnapping of their sister and the killing of her husband, the ruler of Kanyakubja or Kannauj, as well as an impending attack on their own capital, Thanesar. Harṣa's brother leaves to defend the kingdom but is treacherously killed by the enemy. At this point in the text there is a lengthy digression on earlier kings, who were assassinated in various ways by disgruntled officers and courtiers. This was either a comment on the inefficiency of Harṣa's brother or was meant to warn Harṣa against court intrigue. Harṣa now assumes the kingship and declares his wish to conduct a *digvijaya* or conquest of the four quarters.

Harṣa's immediate concern is to find his sister and he sets out with his army in the direction of Kannauj. This becomes something of a *digvijaya* as well, for we know that he eventually shifted his capital to Kannauj as being more strategically located.

At this point the king of Kāmarūpa, Assam, also recently risen in status, requests a treaty with Harṣa for he too is battling against their common enemy, the king of Gauḍa.

The scene shifts again to a village in the heart of the Vindhyas where Harṣa arrives and meets the young chiefs of the Śabara and other forest tribes. These are areas which are yet to be touched by Sanskritic culture-ways and the description is therefore valuable in depicting the non-caste, "tribal" societies, still extensive in this region. Harṣa makes enquiries about his sister and is directed to the hermitage of a Buddhist ascetic. This turns out to be the habitat of persons with various religious affiliations including Buddhists, Jainas, Bhāgavats, Śaivas, Lokāyatas teaching materialism, alchemists, reciters of the Purāṇas and grammarians, suggesting so wide an intellectual range as to be a sign of the weakening of the doctrine. However the references are generally sympathetic to the Buddhists though some satire is irresistable as in the statements that even the parrots were expounding texts and the tigers had given up eating meat!

Harṣa's sister is eventually found and the text ends with the happy return home of brother and sister and the coronation of Harṣa. It has been argued that the sister is also to be seen as allegorical and represents the goddess Śrī, the goddess of good fortune (Pathak 1966: 30–55). The episode is therefore symbolic of the settling of good fortune on Harṣa and to that extent completes the function of the biography. At a more mundane level the rescue of his sister was essential to his ambition as without her he could not have claimed sovereignty over Kannauj, earlier held by his brother-in-law, and which was to become significant to political control over the Ganga Valley. The attempt in the biography was not to cover the events in the life of the kings, but to focus on the acquisition and establishing of power. The *Harṣacarita* is a precursor of the genre. While it draws on some elements of the continuing tradition, it does not touch on *kṣatriya* legitimation, so characteristic of later biographies. Harṣa's reign was close enough to the period when such legitimation was not required and his personal involvement with Buddhism would have encouraged him to perform Vedic rituals.

Among other biographies of this genre is that of Vikramāditya VI, the Cālukya king, written by Bhaṭṭa Bilhaṇa in about A.D. 1088 and entitled the *Vikramāṅkadeva-caritam*. (*VC*)[11] Of its eighteen cantos the last is a brief biography of Bilhaṇa himself. These short biographies of the authors are in striking contrast to the anonymous authorship of the earlier tradition. Bilhaṇa is from Kashmir, from an *agrahāra* on the banks of the Jhelum located in the midst of saffron fields and vineyards: a nostalgic description of a distant home (*VC*, 18.73–81). Bilhaṇa's family were Bhṛgu *brāhmaṇas* and hailed from central India from where they had been brought to Kashmir. As a young man he travelled in many parts of northern India in search of a patron. He was finally appointed at the Cālukya capital at Kalyāni by Vikramāditya VI where he wrote the biography of the king.

The opening canto associates the origin of the Cālukyas with a deity. Indra complains of the decline in sacrificial offerings caused by the popularity of other religions, presumably a reference to the Jainas. The ancestor of the Cālukyas, created to restrain the spread of these other hostile religions, was born from the water in the cupped hands, *culuka*, of Brahmā, and so called Cālukya. This being a grammatically incorrect derivation has been taken as a literal Sanskritization of a non-Aryan name. Like a second Rāma he conquered in every direction and established the rule of the righteous. Śiva is then invoked, the invocation in keeping with the religious loyalty of the author's patron who moved from Jainism to become a patron of Śaivism in later life, a shift which creates a further link with the origin myth.

We are told that the Cālukyas were *kṣatriyas* of Ayodhya, the capital of Rāma, and after having ruled there for fifty-nine generations began a southward migration. Is migration from afar an attempt to cover up an obscure origin? A genealogy of the family follows. His father seeks legitimation through the performance of an *aśvamedha* but also prays to Śiva for sons. Śiva appears before him and predicts that he will have three sons of whom the middle son, Vikramāditya, will achieve the distinction of the earlier heroes of the Sūryavaṃśa, thus reiterating the dynasty's claim to be among the best of *kṣatriyas*. At the birth of each son gold is gifted to the bards who sing the praises of the family. We are also told that Vikramāditya's father was keen to declare him, Vikramāditya, as the crown-prince, but the son objects, insisting that his elder brother be given priority in accordance with the norm.

Later, while campaigning, news reached him of his father's

death. His elder brother succeeded to the throne but reigned only briefly, for the throne was usurped by Vikramāditya. Bilhaṇa's version concedes this but justifies the act as the command of Śiva who had been angered by the elder brother's evil ways and misrule. Vikramāditya was eventually also to have problems with his younger brother who organised a revolt of the intermediaries but was imprisoned.

Vikramāditya's successful campaigns particularly against the major powers of the peninsula – the Coḷa, Drāviḍa, Kerala, Koṅkan and Kuṇṭala – are frequently recited. The inscriptions of the Coḷas who are the pre-eminent enemy, predictably give a contrary version. Bilhaṇa's list begins to take on the tones of rhetoric as such lists also do in inscriptions. Claims to victory add up to a tally of frequent confrontations among a number of well-matched kingdoms competing for supremacy. Five cantos take up the narrative of how Vikramāditya wooed and won the Vidyādhara princess at a *svayaṃvara*. A multitude of poetic images are used for the occasion and the romance implicit in this alliance. The biography ends on the happy note of more conquests and the birth of sons.

Bilhaṇa's biography draws on elements of the perception of the past as well as on the *carita* literature both of which are reflected in the inscriptions issued during the reign of various Cālukya kings. One of the most oft-quoted of these, the Gadag inscription from Dharwar district, dated to A.D. 1098 and therefore later than the biography provides a complementary source (*EI*, 15, No. 24, 349ff.). In recording a grant it also endorses the high status of the grantee and provides a summary of the official version of the activities of the king. It acts as a back-up of the biography and by the same token contradicts the inscriptions of those who were opposed to Vikramāditya.

The opening verses are a eulogy on the succession of Cālukyas, the *vaṃśa*. This is followed by a genealogy of the seven generations preceding Vikramāditya. His elder brother is described as being neglectful of his subjects and infatuated by pride and in this echoes the biography, both of which contradict the positive personality of the elder brother as suggested in his own inscriptions. The Gadag inscription also informs us that Vikramāditya ceased to use the current Śaka era and started his own Cālukya-Vikrama era coinciding with his coronation. As is the case with many inscriptions, the date is recorded with precision, mentioning the day, the lunar fortnight, the month and the year of the era, corresponding to Monday 17 May 1098.

Bilhaṇa's concern was with contemporary politics. He was defending both Vikramāditya's usurpation of the throne and the succession of his son rather than his younger brother. These actions were obviously regarded as controversial and a convincing official version was required. Bilhaṇa therefore argues that Vikramāditya was destined to succeed his father through the instructions and intervention of the god Śiva whom he could not disobey. It has been argued that the significance of Śiva was also tied into the current ideas of some Śaiva sects – the preordination of the course of human life through the grace of Śiva, the divinity of kings associated with Śiva and divine instructions received in dreams (Pathak 1966: 70). Such association with divinity places the hero and his deeds above human criticism. One could add here that these would be recognised conventions and were probably intended less for current contemporary consumption and more for tracing claims to political legitimacy on the part of the sons and successors of Vikramāditya. The law of primogeniture was prominent in the earlier texts, the breaking of the law being associated with long periods of drought and other calamities as mentioned in the narratives of the brothers Devāpi and Śantanu.[12] Even during these later times although elder sons were superceded the act required to be defended. This in part explains the need for an official version in both biographies discussed here.

In the case of Vikramāditya, the supercession of his younger brother had also to be justified. The Gadag inscription suggests that brother-to-brother succession was familiar to the earlier Cālukyas. Inscriptional evidence suggests that the younger brother was removed from office and replaced by Vikramāditya's son. A defence of his action is to be found in yet another text, the *Vikramāṅka-abhyudaya*, an incomplete biography of Vikramāditya by this very son and successor, Someśvara III (Pathak 1966).

Someśvara's biography of his father differs from that of Bilhaṇa. The inspiration is substantially Vaiṣṇava with Viṣṇu incarnating himself twice over in the family. Vikramāditya's father, desirous of a son, is said to have had a vision in which it was revealed to him that Viṣṇu himself would be born to him but not as his eldest son. The intervention of divinity determines the character of the sons and the sequence of events. Echoing an earlier myth, that of

Pṛthu Vainya, the first born is associated with everything evil and inauspicious and is put aside. The second son was an incarnation of divinity and it was predicted of him that he would surpass the great heroes of old. He was declared heir apparent and set off on his *digvijaya* and here the text comes to an end.

Someśvara's biography is also staking his own claims as the rightful successor by giving such an exalted status to his father. He makes no mention of his paternal uncle preceding his father. Such an omission suggests that the descendants of his uncle may well have been organising support for their claims. The choice of the Vaiṣṇava incarnation requires an explanation. It can be suggested that Someśvara was a Vaiṣṇava and was addressing Vaiṣṇavas. But this contradicts Bilhaṇa's appeal to Śiva as the deity who intervened. In a recent analysis this has been linked to the politics of the ruling houses of the time, in that Viṣṇuvardhana Hoysala, a neighbour, but by now an avid and successful rival against Cālukya power, claimed to be an incarnation of Viṣṇu. This occasioned Someśvara's counter-claims that his father was also an *avatāra* of Viṣṇu (Pathak 1966). Divinity leant itself easily to political manipulation. Far from the Divine Will directing history, the political ambitions of rulers tended to give shape to the intervention of deities. The king being an incarnation of Viṣṇu had many familiar resonances. Viṣṇu has as his symbol the *cakra* or wheel which is suggestive of the *cakravartin*; the *vijigīṣu* or the one desirous of victory is positioned in the hub of the wheel of the *maṇḍala* circle and powerful feudatories and competing kings can be seen to represent a circular movement; Viṣṇu's wheel is symbolic of controlling the universe; and in the concept of the *trimūrti*, Viṣṇu is the one who preserves and sustains, a function also required of the king.

The *carita* literature as a new genre may be viewed in terms of historical change in the post-Gupta period. Both the *Harṣacarita* and the *Vikramāṅkadeva-carita* draw on the tradition of *itihāsa* or the perception of the past (Thapar 1986: 353–83). The juxtaposition of the biography of the author with that of the subject reinforces the idea that the choice of the author cannot be arbitrary. Appending the biography of the author is a means of legitimising the subject as well. The author, as Bilhaṇa puts it, provides the nectar of immortality to the king's body of fame when the drum of the eternal departure sounds (*VC*, 18.106).

The caste of the royal family being appropriate was seen as

necessary, at least in theory, and particularly so in a period when obscure families were aspiring to power. Thus origin myths became central and *kṣatriya* status was sought by linking the family if possible to one of the two major *kṣatriya* descent groups, the Sūryavaṃśa or the Candravaṃśa or an equally appropriate origin. Yet the variations in genealogical linkages would also seem to suggest the use of genealogies in balancing political factions.

The performance of Vedic sacrificial rituals had been another mechanism of claiming status, but these were now on the decline. Epigraphical evidence for the performance of the *aśvamedha* ceases after the ninth century A.D. It had in any case changed in form and meaning. Territorial conquest was no longer sandwiched within the rites and was a separate activity unconnected in most cases with the ritual. The *digvijaya* is now less a prelude to the *rājasūya* and is often invoked by itself. It takes on other meanings although the rhetoric of conquest retains a formal link with its earlier associations.

Legitimation by ritual involved the performance of rites but did not require the invocation of the past or any notion of causation. This was now being replaced by an invocation of the past through genealogical links and heroic paradigms and by suggesting that the deities of the Purāṇic religion motivated the action of the king. This legitimation was a function increasingly sought by *brāhmaṇas.* The *yajña*s or sacrificial rituals gave way to the *mahādānas* or great gifts, gifts of gold and grants of land made to the *brāhmaṇas.* These could be the gifting of the *hiraṇyagarbha* or golden womb from which the king was born symbolically or the *tulāpuruṣa* where the king was weighed against gold and the gold gifted, or equally commonly the gifting of land and villages to *brāhmaṇas* as *brahmadeyas* or *agrahāras.* Not only is the contractual element more evident in the gift than in the ritual, but the relationship with the Purāṇic deity tends, to some extent, to demystify kingship.

In the conventions associated with the biographies two features not only drew upon earlier forms but became important to the ideology of kingship. The traditional *digvijaya* or conquest of the four quarters was part of the rhetoric of kingship. Thus skirmishes and raids could well be poeticised into campaigns (*VC*, 3. 62–68). But conquest held other meanings as well. War would symbolise collecting wealth through booty or through the settling of conquered lands which would then yield revenue. The practice of the granting of land by kings and intermediaries required constant access to new land. Campaigns became a synonym for the acquisition of resources. Alternatively, the listing of campaigns need not have referred to actual warfare for such a list could also be a claim to status among contending powers and be read as indicating political rank or aspirations. Some among these powers are singled out for repeated and special mention, representing the more realistic relations.

Yet conquest alone does not make a universal monarch; there must also be the association with good fortune in the form of the goddess Śrī (Pathak 1966: 84ff.). This is often depicted as the king acquiring a worthy consort. The action involves a *svayaṃvara*, the essence of which is the competition between rival rulers and the success of the one who is chosen. It subsumes warfare and political alliances. Possibly this idea was also influenced by two other developments of this time. One was the pervasive notion that Śakti, personified as the female principle or deity, was necessary to the fulfilment of any action and the other was the concept of the female consorts for major deities. Marriage into a family which had already been accorded high status was crucial to those claiming such status, for their acceptance would be concretised in such marriages and this in turn would endorse their claims to land and political power. Where the *svayaṃvara* resulted in marrying a woman of higher status, there it could even be a subvention of caste rules. For the Cālukyas, marrying a Śilāhāra princess whose family claimed descent from the Vidyādhara provided them with a higher status, a status particularly respected by the not insignificant group among their subjects, that of the Jainas. The *svayaṃvara* then was an underlining of legitimacy through status.

The ultimate in power was the *cakravartin* or universal monarch. Buddhist and Jaina texts emphasised to a greater extent the image of the *cakravartin* as upholding the moral order. Buddhist tradition extolled the virtues of the Mauryan emperor Aśoka who is a mere name in the list of kings as given in the Purāṇas (Pargiter 1975: 28). The concept in the Purāṇas differed in that a *cakravartin* was said to be born in each age as a manifestation of deity, to both conquer territory and protect the subjects. The ideal *cakravartins* in this tradition were the ancient *kṣatriya* heroes who were both patrons of the sacrifice and conquerors.

The notion of the *cakravartin* in the post-Gupta period laid less emphasis on status through ritual and more on conquest. Its importance grew with the increase in the number of kingdoms as well as the influence of the political theory of *maṇḍala*. A *maṇḍala* was a circle of territories held by intermediaries or independent rulers. The theory as a political construct referred to relations between territories and rulers. This assumed that each king desirous of victory, the *vijigīṣu*, was ringed around by circles of allies and enemies. Politics was a competition for supremacy. There was no fixed centre and the balance shifted with each major campaign or with the outcome of the politics of conciliation. The focus was the aspiration of a king to being recognised as a *cakravartin*. The aspiration often accounted for the rhetoric of hostility so characteristic of this age. What was fixed was the perspective as seen from a particular region.

That the *cakravartin* could be a manifestation of deity doubtless encouraged aspirants to conquest in their claims to be incarnations of deity. Where the king was transgressing a norm, this claim made it easier to explain away the transgression. The frequency of claiming such incarnations as a political manoeuvre does suggest that the appeal to divinity had multiple utility. Part of the reason may have been the Bhṛgu authorship, for some of the myths of earlier Bhṛgu sages depict them as being on a par with the gods (Goldman 1977).

The use of incarnations and divine intervention also had to do with the shift from the centrality of Vedic Brāhmaṇism to the Purāṇic religion. The latter availed itself of some aspects of Brāhmaṇism, partly for purposes of legitimation, but was essentially different. It incorporated Bhāgavatism and the new *bhakti* or devotional forms of worship and elements of the Śākta cults and subsumed aspects of Śramaṇism. Among the significant changes was the attitude of the individual to salvation. Whereas previously the focus had been on the importance of *karma*, the effect of one's actions in a former life on the present, there was now through *bhakti* the mediation of the deity as well, in fact almost a reliance on the deity for the attainment of *mokṣa* or freedom from rebirth. This could be achieved through devotion and loyalty to the deity and a sharing in the deity's grace, a relationship which paralleled that of the political hierarchies of the period. All this added significance to biography.

The heroic ethos is further elaborated in the clusters of hero stones in various parts of the subcontinent (Settar and Sontheimer 1982). These commemorate death on the battlefield or in protecting the village or herd of cattle. The hero, whose religious sectarian affiliation is also depicted, is taken up to heaven by celestial maidens, the *apsarās*. For him there is no *karma*, no rebirth, only an eternity in heaven. Such hero-stones generally commemorate not kings, but persons of lesser standing, and are based on the belief that a heroic death is rewarded with *mokṣa* which in this case takes the form of heaven (Thapar 1981). The narratives of these actions were again influenced by the activities of epic heroes but they also carry traces of those values which were associated with royal heroes, the emphasis being on the king's role to protect his subjects. The centrality of the action covers a brief spell of time.

The writing of historical biographies was also set in a time frame which was brief and linear and therefore very different from the elaborate cosmological cycles of time, familiar from the Purāṇas (Thapar 1996). Notions of time however continued to be multiple, coeval in the same society but varying with different functions. The span of cosmological time continued to be the cyclic *mahāyuga* as described in the Purāṇas in the vast figures of a cosmological frame. The tendency now was to refer to the current Kaliyuga and therefore implicitly to cosmological time, but there was greater frequency in references to the more manageable time spans such as the sequence of generations where each was a unit of reckoning, or the short span of part of a lifetime as covered in the biographies. Even briefer was the precisely measured, exact time in the dating of inscriptions, following in many cases, a known chronology with established eras and virtually a linear concept. Familiar eras such as the Vikrama, Śaka and Laukika *saṃvat* were used, except when a reigning king wished to proclaim his status by departing from these and commencing a new era with a major event of his reign. Doubtless the precision of dating in inscriptions was because they were official documents and often recorded grants. Time therefore not only involved a sequence of changes but the category of time measurement indicated the recognition of these changes.

Cyclic time is not emphasised in the biographies, possibly because in the association of time with the moral order, the sequence of the Kaliyuga prophecies a period of decline. The biography projects the reverse, a movement up towards a golden age with the reign of the king destined by deity to be invested with prosperity and power. Legitimacy also becomes crucial where the *varṇāśramadharma* or the moral order, and the *rājanīti*, the royal polity, have to be upheld as part of the function of kingship. The king himself has therefore to be seen to conform to the moral order.

The authors of these biographies were employees of the court, as court poets or additionally as ministers and advisors in various capacities. The authors therefore were different from the bards who are associated with the epics and the early Purāṇas. The status of the bards of earlier times, the *sūta* and the *māgadha*, was by now unambiguously low in court circles. They are said to be the progeny of marriages which are not approved of for they are inter-*varṇa* marriages (*Nāradasmṛti*, 12.106–16). There was now an inter-locking of dynasty, court and chronicler. Biographies were tied to courtly culture and were subject to handling, different from the epic tradition. Genealogies are memories of social relationships and they are renewed and change over time. Courtly literature remains frozen and a difference of opinion requires not the adjustment in an existing composition but a new text. There is less possibility of transmuting the past. Among the reasons for this change was the role of literacy.

Literacy in an oral society, it has been argued, can have an enabling effect, with a dependence on the literature for interpretation, identification and order (Goody 1968). The carriers of the courtly culture and its interpreters were largely *brāhmaṇas*. There is a cultural difference between *brāhmaṇas* learned in the *Vedas* and emphasising ritual and the oral tradition, and those who recognised the uses of literacy in the context of the court. There are references to the *akṣapaṭalādhikṛta* in inscriptions of the Gupta period and to a keeper of state documents in Chinese accounts of India.[13] Royal seals indicate the use of literacy in administration. Inscriptions with genealogical information required a functioning keeper of records as indeed did the lengthier inscriptions with information officially vetted, on the ruler, the dynasty and the purpose of the record. Some inscriptions, such as the Madhuban Copper-plate of Harṣa, carry linguistic mistakes suggesting that either the author or the engraver was not fully conversant with Sanskrit.[14] This inscription also mentions an earlier forged record which in itself indicates the availability of literacy. That copies of the grants were maintained at the court is suggested by the repetition of verses from earlier grants in those of later rulers and by the fact that the engraver's work may also sometimes have been hereditary given that occasionally a son is recorded as succeeding his father (*EI*, 15: 293–301).

One of the by-products of the granting of wealthy *agrahāras* was the increase in the number of educated *brāhmaṇas*. They travelled over long distances seeking employment as is evident in the case of Bilhaṇa's family. This coincided with the increase in courts and the seeking of *brāhmaṇa* retainers as court poets and chroniclers. The *carita* literature was part of the formal education of those who claimed to be learned. The currency of the *Harṣacarita* is evident from echoes in later compositions and from the frequency of authors from later centuries who, in the biographies which they wrote, spoke of themselves as the "new Bāṇas".[15] The court poet as an employee of the king changed the relationship between political authority and its legitimiser. Although there continued to be a mutual dependence between the poet and the ruler, the balance did tilt in favour of the latter particularly where the court poet was also a functionary. The bard was not an employee. This gave him the freedom to criticise the king should he wish to, as is recorded for a state in Rajasthan in the fourteenth century.[16]

To appreciate the role of the king as "hero" depicted in the historical biographies requires some familiarity with the delineation of the epic hero in the *Rāmāyaṇa* and the *Mahābhārata* and in the legends narrated in the early Purāṇas. However these kings did not merely continue the roles of the earlier heroes. The context of their activities was different and the social background to their functioning had changed. Not only were kings set in the mosaic of courts which were dissimilar from the gatherings of clan-dominated chiefdoms, but from the perspective of literary genres as well, the initially oral epic form had given way not only to the epic as a literary composition, but also to the biography which was inspired largely by the highly literary court tradition. Thus not only did the concept of the hero change, but so too did the literary form in which he was portrayed. These two aspects were intertwined in the projection of the king as the new hero.

Notes

1 Hathigumpha Cave inscription, *Epigraphia Indica* (*EI*), 20.72ff.
2 Nasik Cave inscription of Gotami Bālāsrī, *EI*, 8.59ff.
3 Allahabad Stone Pillar inscription, Fleet 1888: 6ff.

4 Aśvaghoṣa, *Buddhacarita*, ed. E.B. Cowell, Oxford, 1893.
5 Southern 1970: 20, 173–96; 1971: 21, 159–79; 1972: 22, 159–80; 1973: 23, 243–63. Brandt: 1966.
6 *Mahābhārata*, Śāntiparvan, 67.17. *Śatapatha Brāhmaṇa*, 11.1.6.24.
7 This is demonstrated for example in the widespread setting up of hero-stones to commemorate local heroes and defenders of village and community (Thapar 1981).
8 See Parab 1925; Cowell and Thomas 1929.
9 *Harṣacarita*, 4.132. Cowell and Thomas 1929: 101.
10 Banskhera inscription, *EI*, 4.208.
11 Bhaṭṭa Bilhaṇa, *Vikramāṅkadeva-caritam* (*VC*), ed. G. Bühler, Bombay 1875. trans. S.C. Banerji and A.K. Gupta, *Bilhaṇa's Vikramāṅkadevacaritam*, Calcutta 1965.
12 *Ṛg Veda*, 10.98; *Nirukta*, 2.10; *Rāmāyaṇa*, 2.110.36; *Mahābhārata*, 1.85.22.
13 Fleet 1888: 190; Watters 1973: I.154.
14 E.g. The Madhuban Copper-plate of Harṣa, *EI*, 1.67–75.
15 A.K. Warder, *An Introduction to Indian Historiography*, Bombay 1972, 117.
16 N. Ziegler, "Marwari Historical Chronicles", *Indian Economic and Social History Review*, April-June 1976, 13, 2, 219ff.

REFERENCES

Aśvaghoṣa. *Buddhacarita*, see Cowell (ed.).

Bāṇa. *Harṣacarita*, see Cowell and Thomas (tr.) and Parab (ed.).

Bhaṭṭa Bilhaṇa, V. *Vikramāṅkadeva-caritam*, see Bühler (ed.) and Banerji and Gupta.

Banerji, S.C. and A.K. Gupta. 1965. *Bilhaṇa's Vikramāṅkadevacaritam*. Calcutta.

Bhattacharya, B. and Romila Thapar (eds.). 1986. *Situating Indian History*. Delhi.

Brandt, W.J. 1966. *The Shape of Medieval History*. New Haven.

Bühler, G. (ed.). 1875. Bhaṭṭa Bilhaṇa, *Vikramāṅkadeva-caritam*. Bombay.

Cowel, E.B. (ed.). 1893. Aśvaghoṣa, *Buddhacarita*. Oxford.

Cowell, E.B. and F.W. Thomas (tr.). 1929. *The Harṣa Carita of Bāṇa*. London.

Fleet, J.F. 1888. *Corpus Inscriptionum Indicarum*, The Inscriptions of the Guptas, vol. III.

Goldman, R. 1977. *Gods, Priests and Warriors*. New York.

Goody, J. 1968. *Literacy in Traditional Societies*. Cambridge.

Humphreys, S.C. and H. King (eds.). 1981. *Mortality and Immortality: The Anthropology and Archaeology of Death*. London.

Parab, K.P. (ed.). 1925. Bāṇa-bhaṭṭa, *Harṣacarita*. Bombay.

Pargiter, F.E. 1975 (rpt.). *The Purana Text of the Dynasties of the Kali Age*. Delhi.

Pathak, V.S. 1966. *Ancient Historians of India*. Bombay.

Settar, S. and G.-D. Sontheimer. 1982. *Memorial Stones*. Dharwad.

Southern, R.W. 1970–72. Aspects of the European Tradition of Historical Writing. In: *Transactions of the Royal Historical Society*.

Thapar, Romila. 1981. Death and the Hero. In: Humphreys and King 1981, pp. 293–316.

———. 1984. *From Lineage to State*. Delhi.

———. 1986. Society and Historical Consciousness: the Itihasa-Purana Tradition. In: *Situating Indian History*, ed. S. Bhattacharya and Romila Thapar. Delhi, 353–83.

———. 1996. *Time as a Metaphor of History: Early India*. Delhi.

Warder, A.K. 1972. *An Introduction to Indian Historiography*. Bombay.

Watters, T. 1973. *On Yuan Chwang's Travels in India*. Delhi (rpt.).

Ziegler, N. 1976. Marwari Historical Chronicles. *Indian Economic and Social History Review*, April-June, 13, 2.

Heroes in the *Caritra-Bakhar*, *Povāḍā* and *Ākhyāna* of Seventeenth and Eighteenth Century Mahārāṣṭra

N.K. WAGLE

THIS paper deals with the concept of heroes found in seventeenth- and eighteenth-century Marāṭhī historical biographies known as the *caritra* or *bakhar*, the *povāḍā*, historical ballads, and lastly the *ākhyāna*, the genre of literature which incorporates myths, legends and exploits of the heroes of antediluvian days with exploits of the known historical figures. The heroes described in this paper are real human beings; they are not the heroes of the dramas and novels which may or may not have a historical basis. Of the heroes covered in this paper, Śivājī was the founder of the Marāṭhā kingdom; the Peśvā family extended the limits of the Marāṭhā empire; Tānājī Mālusare died while capturing Sīṃhagaḍ fort for his king Śivājī; Bājī Pālaskar was an aristocratic "Lord of the Manor"; and Mālojī Yādav was a lineage founder of the House of Yādav Deśamukhs of Māṇḍavagaṇ.

Caritra-Bakhar

In his *Introduction to Indian Historiography*, A.K. Warder has clarified the concept of "universal history" of the Purāṇas as being representative of traditional Indian concepts of history. The *avatāra* theory, which is descent of the gods to earth to restore order, is a recurrent motif of the Purāṇas. We should not expect to find, as Warder cautions us, the real historical happenings associated with events, although there is always an element of historical reality in purāṇic depiction of known historical dynasties of ancient India. The eighteenth-century Marāṭhī biographical literature which is known as *bakhars* or simply as *caritras* appears to be working within the parameters of the traditional purāṇic motif that the *yuga puruṣas*, the purāṇic epoch making heroes, appear on earth periodically to protect and restore *dharma* in peril.[1] This point is illustrated in seventeenth century *Mahikāvaticī Bakhar*:

> The *yavanas* multiply and prevail. The people have disowned their pride in their self rule (*rājya*). Discarding their weapons, they toil in their fields. Some have chosen servitude. Others have perished. Many have forgotten their customs. They cannot remember their *gotra*, *pravara*, and *kulaguru* [collectively to be taken as representing family traditions]. The goddess became aware of this situation and, appearing before Nāyakobā in a vision, gave him instructions to protect the *dharma* of Mahārāṣṭra. (Keśavācārya 1924: 53; 5–6)

The *Saptaprakaraṇātmaka Caritra*, a biography of Śivājī composed in 1811, directly alludes to the purāṇic motif.

> The entire *dharma* was overturned. The *brāhmaṇas*, cows and [holy] sacrifices were annihilated. In olden days, when Earth agonized at the end of the *yuga*, the gods took on human forms. They became great sages and the gods on earth (*bhūdevas*) and established *dharma*. The great Śiva Prabhū (Śivājī) acted in a similar manner. (Malhār Rāmrāv Ciṭṇīs 1924: 1)

In the *Śrī Śivadigvijaya*, Śivājī is referred to as the *aṃśa* (essence) of God (*īśvarāṃśa*) and as the true *avatāra* of the god Śiva (*pratyakṣa śivācā avatāra*).[2] In the *Sabhāsad Bakhar*, the god Śiva, pleased with the water tank constructed near his temple by Mālojī Bhosle (Śivājī's grandfather), gave him a boon (*vara*), reaffirming it thrice (*trivāra vacana karūna vara dilā*):

> I will take birth in your lineage [as Śivājī], protect the brāhmaṇas and cows and destroy the *mlecchas*.[3]

Historians of Mahārāṣṭra like Rājvāḍe (1929: 348–49) and Hervāḍkar (1957: 8–9) have acknowledged the indebtedness of the *caritra-bakhar* to the Purāṇas. Śridhar Kulkarṇī, in his *Prācīna Marāṭhī Gadya Preraṇā āṇī Paraṃparā*, observes that the *caritra-bakhar* writers, in the manner of the Purāṇas, roused

Mahārāṣṭrians' regional identity and pride by extolling their heroes. The readily available purāṇic model of eulogizing the exploits of the *yuga puruṣas*, and the heroes of the Mahābhārata and Rāmāyaṇa, suited the purpose of the writers (Kulkarṇī 1970: 113–15). It is possible that in the Marāṭhā wars against the Deccan Sultanate and the Mughal rulers, there was perhaps a need to have a literature which the Mahārāṣṭrians of that age could relate to and which, in turn, could excite their regional pride. As soon as the Marāṭhās stabilized their rule in Mahārāṣṭra in the eighteenth century, there was a further need to legitimize the new rulers, to elevate them as exceptional heroes. Śivājī and the brāhmaṇa *peśvās* (prime ministers) are depicted as almost semi-divine beings needed to sustain *dharma* of their subjects (see Wagle and Kulkarni 1976: 61, 69). It is worth noting that most of the heroic literature in Mahārāṣṭra, the *caritra-bakhars* and the *povāḍās*, was composed in the seventeenth and eighteenth centuries.

The most detailed description of the role of the heroes, and their ideological construct, is to be found in *Paraśarāma Caritra*, a historical biography of the *peśvās* composed in 1773 (see ibid.: 2). Its author, Vallabha, subsumes the historical events connected with the family of the brāhmaṇa *peśvās* in a larger framework of struggle between forces of disruption and evil, and forces of justice and cohesion, which, according to the author, are at work in this Kaliyuga (the age of darkness) (ibid.: 148–57). The author has effectively used the motif of Kali, the evil Kaliyuga personified, and the *peśvā* heroes, the *aṃśa* (the essence) of Paraśarāma (the sixth *avatāra* of the god Viṣṇu), who tames the evil Kali (ibid.: 10–12).

All the events which are construed as antisocial are attributed to Kali. Kali, the *Paraśarāma Caritra* asserts, cannot see the people of Mahārāṣṭra leading a contended life. Therefore he invites the Mughal emperor Auraṅgzeb to that land. Kali enters Auraṅgzeb's body. Auraṅgzeb then imprisons and kills his father (Śāhājahān). Śivājī, the incarnation of the god Śiva checks his power in Mahārāṣṭra (ibid.: 59–65). The narration continues. After Saṃbhājī's (Śivājī's son) death there is chaos. At god Indra's behest, Paraśarāma lays down his *aṃśa* (essence) in the house of the brāhmaṇa *peśvās*. Paraśarāma "manifests himself in human form to trouble the *mlecchas* (Muslims) and the wicked."[4] The *aṃśāvatārī* (the essence holder) Bājīrāv *peśvā*, for instance, becomes: "foremost the supporter of *dharma* and protects the best and revered ones of merit. He counteracts the afflictions perpetrated by Kali and the pretensions of all those who practice *adharma*" (ibid.: 47, 76).

The anti-hero Kali acts as a counterweight to the goodness of the brāhmaṇa heroes. In one instance, during the reign of Peśvā Mādhavarāva (1762–72), "Kali contaminates the minds of all the wicked ones and they decide to burn Puṇe"... "It appeared as if Kali was about to exterminate the people. Mādhava, the *aṃśadhārī*, when he comes to know of Kali's intentions became furious with anger like the biting sun" (ibid.: 90). This reference relates to a historical event when the Nizām of Hyderābād, in a military manoeuvre had invaded the *peśvās* territory and burned Puṇe while Mādhavarāva was busy campaigning in the Nizām's territory. Eventually, Mādhavarāva defeated the Nizām in the famous battle of Rākṣasa Bhavan. The *caritra* states: "By the grace of God, they (Mādhava's army) returned from foreign *deśa* (territory), certainly accomplishing more than ever before. The majestic and the powerful sun destroyed the darkness Kali. After this event had taken place, the people began to praise Lord Mādhava (*prabhu Mādhavāte*)" (ibid.: 95). But Kali had his ways. The text observes: "In every respect, the excellence [of Mādhava] was total. Kali's power was ineffective in penetrating his tough exterior. But Kali, seeing an opening inside the body, possessed it. Mādhava's body began to fall apart. He contracted *kṣaya* (tuberculosis), and he became weak with a prolonged fever."[5]

Povāḍā

The ballads of the heroes in Mahārāṣṭra known as *povāḍās* came into prominence with the advent of the Marāṭhā rāj under Śivājī (1627–80). The *caritra-bakhar*, based on the purāṇic tradition, was regarded as proper, sacred and of a longer antiquity. It was a "universal history" (Warder 1971: 17–25) for the court elites of the Marāṭhā rāj. The *povāḍās* catered to the more popular taste and were composed and recited by professional bards (wandering minstrels) known in Marāṭhī as *śāhīrs*,[6] who mostly belonged to the Gondhaḷī community/caste of the minstrels.[7] The Gondhaḷī bards were richly rewarded for composing ballads of the local warrior heroes. For instance, a bard Tuḷaśīdās of Puṇe was commissioned by Śivājī to compose a *povāḍā* of Tānājī Mālusare, Śivājī's brave warrior who had died in his service. Bard Tuḷaśīdās was given gold ornaments worth a thousand rupees.[8] Bāyājī bard received 3 pounds ($1\frac{1}{4}$ *śer*) of gold ornaments to compose Bājī Pālaskar's *povāḍā* (Keḷkar 1928: 71). A horse and three pounds of gold were given to Ajñāndās for his Afzal Khān *povāḍā* (ibid.: 22).

The narrative style of *povāḍās* is forthright and this-worldly. There are references to the gods and goddesses, but these are generally not purāṇic, but of local origin who are regarded as *jāgṛta* (potent and effective). The theme of the *povāḍā* must always deal with the exploits and the glories of the heroes who survive, and those who perish, in the service of their masters. Tānājī's *povāḍā* of Tuḷaśīdās revolves round the central figure of Tānājī, Śivājī's brave commander.[9]

Śivājī is engaged in a game of dice with his mother Jijābāī, who wins the game. She wants Śivājī to give her as a winner's stake the prize of the fort Siṃhagaḍ, a Mughal fort commanded by Udebhān Rājput. Śivājī is shown as frightened with the prospect of this venture. His mother could have a present of any of the 27 forts which he possessed, but not the Siṃhagaḍ guarded by Udebhān. Jijābāī is determined to have her way. She says to Śivājī: "If you do not give me Siṃhagaḍ, I will curse and burn your whole kingdom."[10] Śivājī reluctantly entrusts the capture of Siṃhagaḍ to Tānājī who is busy making arrangements for his son's wedding. But the king's service must come first. Tānājī decides to postpone his son's wedding. His wise uncle Śelāramāmā (his mother's brother) tries to dissuade him from going to Siṃhagaḍ. "Do not even speak of Siṃhagaḍ", he warns Tānājī, "all who had ventured to capture it, have died; you too will be destroyed." Tānājī replies: "Do not speak in this manner, my uncle. We are the brave *kṣatriyas*. We fear not death."[11] When Tānājī was about to scale Siṃhagaḍ, Śelāramāmā says to Tānājī, "[Desist,] the future does not look good." Tānājī replies, "But I owe Siṃhagaḍ to Śivājī. If I fulfil my obligations to him, I will attain a high [heavenly] state after life."[12]

The only way Tānājī could surprise the enemy was to scale the walls of the fort, unnoticed, and in the dark. Tānājī removes Yaśvantā *ghorpaḍ* (a lizard) from the box, propitiates her, applying seven layers of *śendura*, and adorns her by placing exquisite jewel on top of her head. He ties a chain to her waist and then lets her climb the wall. Half way across the wall, she returns. She knows the impending death of Tānājī. Tānājī says in anger to her: "I have conquered 27 forts. Never have I seen you return. I am the son of a Marāṭhā. I fear not death.[13] With one stroke of a sword, I shall cut you into 18 pieces and eat you with a cold *bhākrī* (flat bread)."[14] Fearing for her life, she takes seven turns and sticks to the fort's wall. Tānājī and his soldiers scale the walls with the help of the rope tied to the body of the lizard.

Śelāramāmā urges Tānājī to complete the vow to the god Bhairobā by offering the sacrifice of 12 goats to please him [in order to bring about success in his venture], since "Bhairobā is particular about these matters." Tānājī replies: "To die for the Māhārājā is to be assured of gaining the ultimate release (*mokṣa*). I do not acknowledge the greatness of Bhairobā. Why, my Śivājī Mahārāj is so powerful that 350 gods fill his water tank."[15] However, Tānājī prays to the goddesses: Aṃbābāī of Kolhāpur, Bhavānī of Pratāpgaḍha, Manglāī of Sātārā, and Pārvatī of Puṇe for success in his venture. They give their assurance: "Do not be afraid, Tānājī. Your sword will yield success." Thereafter, Tānājī's strength multiplies. He gives up thinking about past and future. The blood rises in his eyes (he becomes spirited). "Listen Śelāramāmā", he says, "my own hands are equal in power to 50 hands."

Udebhān, the Mughal commander of the fort, eats one and half a cow, one and half a sheep and 20 pounds of rice at meal time. He has 18 wives with whom he beds daily. He takes hold of a piece of steel and wraps it round his wrist with his bare hands. By breaking the silver rupees of Cāndvaḍ variety into two, he makes [half-moon] necklaces out of them for his wives. He has trained a she elephant, Candrāvalī, who is capable of destroying the earth. Udebhān's minister is Siddī Hilāl who daily eats one lamb, half a cow and forty pounds of rice. He has nine wives with whom he beds daily. Udebhān has twelve sons stronger than him.

Tānājī's 50 soldiers kill 900 unsuspecting Paṭhāṇ warriors. The *Boṃbyā* (the messenger) goes to Udebhān to tell him about the disastrous happening. Udebhān, the *povāḍā* states, had consumed 18 cups of opium and had topped it with *bhāṅg* and opium. He becomes charged and energetic. He retires to the 18 beds of his wives and removing his dress, begins to have sex with them. The *Boṃbyā* interrupts his activities. He says: "My Udebhān Mughal, to hell with your pleasure.[16] Siṃhagaḍ fort is about to fall. 900 Paṭhāṇs have been cut to pieces. The night is dark. The enemy cannot be seen." Udebhān says: "I am busy with my women. I shall not give up my enjoyment. Go and deploy the war-elephant."

As the fight between Tānājī and the elephant ensues, the elephant driver says to Tānājī: "Why this conceit, you are the son of a peasant (*kuṇbī*). Go back to the forest, cut the wood and sell it to the merchant." Tānājī says: "You are the son of the weaver of sacks which are needed to fill the rice. Come to the house of the peasant. Get in return a rupees worthy [of grain]. Your bitch of a woman (*tujhyā raṃḍīne*) should husk it. You shall eat the scum and sell the rice to the merchant."[17] Tānājī then proceeds to kill the elephant and his driver.

The *Boṃbyā* goes back to Udebhān to tell him the news. Udebhān continues to be preoccupied with his sexual activities. He assigns the task to his assistant Siddī Hilāl, who, too, was in bed with his nine wives. He reads the message. He gets up and dresses [for the battle]. Wielding his swords in both hands [he is ambidextrous], he makes his nine wives stand up in line and cuts them all in 18 pieces [to preserve the honour of his wives lest they fall in enemy hands]. Siddī taunts Tānājī: "You, the son of a peasant (*kuṇbī*), dissemble your headgear and, covering your neck with it, surrender."[18] Tānājī retorts: "Take the grass in your mouth and placing your shoes on your head, surrender."[19] The sword fight ensues between the two. Uttering *khudā, khudā* (oh God, oh God), Siddī dies.

The *Boṃbyā* again informs Udebhān of the events who then deputes his twelve sons to fight Tānājī. Tānājī gets in a chivalrous mood and addresses them: "You are mere lads of the Mughal. Have the first go at me."[20] The twelve sons twice wield their swords. Tānājī evades the strikes. Tānājī prays to the goddess Aṃbābāī. "Fulfill my vow,"[21] he says. He then cuts the boys into 24 pieces.

The *Boṃbyā* conveys the news to Udebhān who becomes so griefstriken that he could not get up from his bed. Finally he recovers. He kills his 18 wives. He sacrifices a pregnant cow and burns 50 pounds of frankincense before the tomb of a *pir* (a sufi saint).[22]

Udebhān rushes forward with swords in his two hands. The dialogue between the two is polite; Udebhān trying to win over Tānājī to the Mughal side and Tānājī asserting his loyalty to

Śivājī. Before the fatal sword fight between the two, Tānājī prays to the goddess Aṃbābāī for help. Aṃbābāī comes, but seeing the flesh of the cow, withdraws.[23] Before he dies, Tānājī tells Śelāramāmā to carry his salutations to Śivājī. Udebhān kills Tānājī. Śelāramāmā, in turn, kills Udebhān and the Marāṭhās capture the fort. Tānājī's body is taken to Śivājī, and he is present at his last rites. Śivājī observes the *sūtak* (after death rites) for Tānājī for the customary twelve days.[24]

Tānājī's *povāḍā* is replete with heroic episodes; only a synoptic version above is presented in this article. There are many episodes in this *povāḍā* that cannot be corroborated by other historical evidence. For instance, there is no evidence to suggest that Śivājī was motivated by his mother's wishes to capture Siṃhagaḍ. Udebhān was a Rājput Hindu general, serving the Mughals; there is no proof that he was ever converted to Islam. However, his sacrifice of a cow and eating of a cow makes him a Muslim. However, as a Muslim he does not have to follow the warrior code of the Rājputs to save the honour of his wives by killing them before entering the battle field. The gods and goddesses which play a role in this *povāḍā* are the local deities of Mahārāṣṭra like the god Bhairobā and goddesses Aṃbābāī, Bhavānī and others. There are virtually no references to the great god Viṣṇu and his ten incarnations, neither is there any reference to the concept of *yuga puruṣa*.

In his stratagem to conquer the fortress, Tānājī secures the help of the Koḷī highlanders whom he wins over to his side by bribery (Keḷkar 1928: 47). No gods help him secure the fort. The adversaries of Tānājī are not portrayed as wicked beings. They are powerful, extraordinary eaters and full of sexual vigour, and pray to the Muslim saints. They could be only attacked at night, by surprise. The goddesses help Tānājī, but not totally. Aṃbābāī retreated from helping Tānājī in his final encounter. Tānājī is a human warrior and not endowed with godlike prowess, neither is he an incarnation of god. The ultimate heroic deed of Tānājī is to serve the interests of his Lord Śivājī. For Tānājī, his Master is more powerful than Bhairobā; 350 gods fill the latter's water tank. If he dies for his Master he will have reached the ultimate release after life. Only the dead person's agnatic kins are entitled to observe the *sūtak*. Śivājī observes the *sūtak* for Tānājī, thereby treating him as one of his lineage. A supreme honour.

Expressions of warrior-hero's gusto are reflected in the "dialogues" between Śelāramāmā and Tānājī; Yaśvantā (a large lizard) and Tānājī; the elephant driver and Tānājī; Siddī Hilāl and Tānājī; Udebhān and Tānājī. Tānājī's adversaries are formidable. They act like Rājputs and maintain the honour of their women by killing them before the combat with the enemies, lest the latter fall into their hands. Even Siddī, a Muslim, kills his 9 wives in a Rājput fashion.

Though not written on a grand scale, Yamājī's *povāḍā* of Bājī Pālaskar is another example of one of the oldest extant *povāḍās* belonging to Śivājī's period (Keḷkar 1928: 64–67). The *povāḍā* centres on the heroic deeds of a son of a tailor and a Māṅg attendant of Bājī Pālaskar, the Deśamukh of Karaṇḍu. This *povāḍā* is strictly "non-religious" in that the gods do not act as intervening agents for the heroes. There are no miraculous happenings attributed to the gods in this *povāḍā*. The object of the raid on the *wāḍā* (palace) of Bājī Pālaskar was to steal a valuable horse. The raiders are killed and the attack repealed (ibid.: 65).

Sonu Daḷvī takes a wager in Adilśāhā's court to steal the horse of Bājī who has a "foot-long moustache (*daṇḍā evaḍhī miśī*)". Bājī's protégé, an orphaned boy of a tailor, Ānantyā, is known for his might. He daily drinks the milk of three water buffaloes and does 600 push-ups. Accompanied by a force of 500 infantry men (*pāyade*), Sonu Daḷvī comes to the plains of Kurd. He hides in the thickets nearby. Cāṅgyā, the *dhobī* (washerman) enters the *wāḍā*, disguised as woman. He reports [to Sonu Daḷvī]: "Rāv Rāṇe and Rāv Kṛṣṇājī, the sons of Bājī had gone away to perform a religious duty. Yelyā Māṅg had gone to fetch his wife. Khaṇḍyā Māhār is dead drunk with liquor. Bājī is having his dinner with 14 warriors. The elder wife Āṃbāī and the younger wife Biṃbāī are busy serving dinner to the guests. Hundred and one servants are at the temple." [Hence it is a good opportunity to begin the assault of the *wāḍā*.]

As soon as Makratrāv, the son-in-law of Bājī enters the precinct of the *wāḍā*, the watchman from the tower gives a general alarm. Āṃbāī, the elder wife locks the door of the main gate and Biṃbāī runs to shut the back door. Āṃbāī and Biṃbāī start the commotion: "This son-in-law of ours wants to destroy our house. Thrice has he attacked the house." Biṃbāī said: "Rāv Rāṇe, our son is not at home. Our Yelyā Māṅg, a helper like a god, is far away. If Khaṇḍyā Māhār were here, he would have broken the siege of this Daḷvī. I would have then given his wife my gold jewelry."[25]

At that time, seeing the crevice in the door, a herd of deer enters the *wāḍā*; along came the raiders. "I shall hit you with my wooden club", says Ānantyā Śimpī to Makratrāv. Makratrāv roars with laughter and says mockingly: "You, the son of a tailor, had been purchased for the price of 12 pounds of horse-grain. I shall finish you off with my sword. Away with your boasting. You are a bastard. Dare you come near and face me." Ānantyā replies: "I shall fight with my bare shoulders and shall repay my worth of 12 pounds grain paid by Bājī." Furious, Ānantyā becomes ready to fight. He charges the door and gateway. He pushes the soldiers out of the door and kills 14 of them within the *wāḍā*. The son-in-law turns the horse unto Bājī Pālaskar and shouts, "Save yourself uncle". Bājī expertly averts the charge and with the sheath of his sword pushes him off his horse, and with his pointed shield pierces him to death.

Yelyā Māṅg's mother goes to fetch Yelyā. She says to him: "Why are you resting, Yelyā, your Kuruḍu is being ravaged."[26] In comes Yelyā [to help]. Seeing him Ānantyā says: "Good, my brother has come. Do not just look on, brother. I shall now hit the horse's legs with my club[27] since I do not have any weapon." Turning around, Daḷvī charges Yelyā with his horse. Skilfully, Yelyā saves himself from the charge. Using his back hand, he severes the head of Daḷvī. He places it on a cloth and shows it to Bājī.[28]

This late seventeenth century *povāḍā* has several heroes and heroines; the orphaned son of a tailor, Yelyā Māṅg, Yelyā's mother, the two wives of Bājī who run out to shut the doors and who are bold enough to shout abuses at the raiding party, and Bājī who kills his son-in-law. The *povāḍā* writer's approach and style is, as in Tānājī's case, straightforward. All the heroic people in this *povāḍā* serve the interest of Bājī Pālaskar, their Master. Compared to the Sīṃhagaḍ *povāḍā*, we do not find any gods and goddesses influencing the events. Neither are they invoked for their support. It is significant that lower caste members of Mahārāṣṭra such as Māṅg, Māhār and Śimpī emerge as heroes. Equally meaningful are the heroic role of the women so graphically illustrated. The household collectively manages to stave off the raiders. The *povāḍā* is a depiction of an extended family chronicle. The son of a tailor calls the Māṅg fighter his brother.

Ākhyāna

The *Bhūteśa Ākhyāna* is a biography of Mālojī, the founder of the lineage of the Yādav Deśamukhs of Māṇḍavgaṇ, presently situated in the Śrīgonde district of Ahamadnagar in Mahārāṣṭra.[29] The biography was composed in the eighteenth century, but it is set in the context of the sixteenth century kingdom of Nizāmśāhā of Ahamadnagar (*Bhūteśa Ākhyāna* 1926: Introduction, 1).

Mālojī's father worships Śiva-Bhuteśvara. He gives his two eyes to Śiva in order to secure two sons. Mālojī, his eldest son, becomes the worshipper of Vetāl in secret. Day and night Mālojī begins his physical training to make himself strong. Assuming the guise of man, Vetāl, the king of the *bhūts*, begins to wrestle with him. Once Mālojī pins Vetāl down to the ground and with his hands grabs his hair. Vetāl reveals himself and tells him that he has been the sole object of his worship. Mālojī asks a boon from Vetāl that he should have the ability to become invisible and that he should protect his lineage and its descendants (*karī vaṃśāce pāḷaṇa paraṃparā*). The *bhūt* Bhairava (as the Vetāl is addressed in the *ākhyāna*) takes out three amulets (*tāīt*); he places two in Mālojī's two arms, and the third he inserts in the latter's head.

In order to display his newly found strength, Mālojī uproots large trees in the forest. The people think that it is the work of the *avatāra* (incarnation) of Mārutī (Hanumān). Single handedly, he begins to defend the villages from raiders. He ransacks the wealth of the raiders and keeps it for himself.

Bahiri Nizāmśāhā (sixteenth century ruler of Ahamadnagar) is ruling the Deccan. His officers could not trace the person who had uprooted the trees. Neither were they receiving the tribute from the conquered enemies. They report to the Nizām that a powerful person, who is a wrestler (*jeṭhī*), is the son of Bhūteśvara, who refuses to acknowledge the Nizām's territorial jurisdiction. The Nizām becomes crest-fallen. He consults his *umrāvs* (his grandees) for a course of action to take. His Vazir (prime minister), Rustamkhān, says to the Nizām: "Be calm, I shall send four *mallas* (strongmen) to bring him to the court." The four go to Mālojī's house. Mālojī lifts their four horses and places them on the loft of the house. While the four were eating, he inserts their long cloaks quietly underneath the pillars by lifting the pillars with his toe thumb. The four *mallas* could not get up from where they were sitting. Mālojī lifts the pillars, brings their horses down on the ground and sends them away. The *mallas* tell the king that Mālojī's power knows no bounds and that he is capable of destroying the whole kingdom. Rustamkhān, the Vazir, sends 1,000 men to capture him. He lets them tie his hands first. Then with one jerk he stretches his hands and kills 1,000 men.

The Bādśāhā (Nizām) decides to make truce with him and invites him to join his service. Mālojī takes his father's permission before leaving. Taking his mother and his entourage, he sets himself on his way to the capital Ahamadnagar. Bādśāhā sends Rustumkhān to welcome him. But the treacherous minister, taking the entire king's army, begins a full scale military operation against Mālojī. The army carries cannons (*ulhāṭa yaṃtre*), pulled by the bullocks and pushed by the elephants using their heads. There are Portuguese (*phiraṅgī*) gunners (*golaṃdāja*). The king's army is made of people of foreign origins, including *yavanas* from across the sea with *capitāna hāpasān* (captains and officers). There are handsome and fair looking Mughals, assuming fierce postures. The troopers are seen charging their horses with drawn swords. The powerful leaders are seen riding on elephants.[30] This army attacks Mālojī. The cannons start their volley of bombardment. The whole sky reverberates with the roar of the cannons. The earth shakes. The towers of the building in the city begin to collapse and people get crushed underneath them at once. The smoke fills the air in all directions. The infantry men (*pāyaka*) recalling god's name attack him on all four sides. Mālojī stands his ground.[31] Remembering Lord Śiva, he uproots a huge tree and begins leveling the army. He swats away the elephants and horses. A huge battle ensues. The enemy flees in ten directions. Some die and some become wounded. Many pray to Mālojī to save their lives. Many surrender. The people say to him: "Why do you destroy us. Those who were combatants in the war with you have fled. Why do you want to kill the poor helpless people?"[32] He spares them.

The king mollifies Mālojī. He gives him a palace in the city, and Mālojī moves in there with his mother. The wicked minister Rustumkhān says to the king that there should be a wrestling bout between Māṇikamal and Mālojī. [The author of the text interjects at this point]. "Look how foolish are these Muslim kings. They have encountered his power. He has uprooted trees as tall as mountains. He has walloped the entire army. He has tossed about huge boulders and elephants. What is there to fight with a small fly? Yet the Muslims want to pit him against their wrestler."[33] Mālojī thinks that by agreeing to fight Māṇikamal can only add to his fame.

Māṇikamal at first refuses the king's invitation, since he does not take the challenge seriously. But the king commands him to appear before him. How did Māṇikamal get to be so strong? How did this happen? There was a Muslim *auliyā* (a Sufi saint) living in the hills. Māṇikamal's mother used to feed him daily for seven years. Once the mother had gone away on some errand. She had asked her daughter to prepare the *roṭ* (a bread) for the *fakir* (the holy man). The daughter made the *roṭ* in the shape of a python and covered it with a dish. The mother unaware of the shape of the *roṭ* offered it to the *fakir*. Seeing the *roṭ* shaped like a python, the *fakir* gave a boon to the mother, "God (*khudā*) will give you a son like a python in strength."

Swaggering like a small elephant, and strong like him, with his 60 pupils, Māṇikamal goes to the king and salutes him. He says: "Let him stand up who craves for his death." Mālojī faces him and says: "You are a fool. You have become conceited. You are talking nonsense. You may have killed many helpless ones. Show me your prowess." Māṇikamal, removing his clothes, strikes the ground with his fists, and removing some dust, rubs it on his body. Mālojī smashes a nearby stone with his fists, leveling it to a fine dust which he applies to his body. The king observes this act of shattering of a stone. He addresses Māṇikamal: "Are you out of your senses. Save your life. Withdraw from the bout." The fool of a Māṇikamal becomes angry at the king's words. He throws dust in Mālojī's eyes. As Mālojī is wiping his eyes, the *malla* gives a blow to his stomach and another one to his chest. Mālojī tolerates this attack as if he was being caressed by a blade of grass. "Protect yourself, strong man," Mālojī says. Then he lifts the *malla* with his feet and swings him round and round, and with a punch, breaks his head. With his eyes drooping, Māṇikamal dies instantly.

The wicked Vazir makes Mālojī fight a tiger. Opening the tiger's jaw, Mālojī enters the tiger's body. As the king, thinking that the tiger had eaten Mālojī as he could not see him, was lamenting the incidence, out comes Mālojī, tearing off the tiger's stomach. The Vazir says that, since Mālojī's body was full of [tiger's blood], he should take a bath in the nearby tank before accepting the robes of honour. The Vazir had placed a huge crocodile in that tank. Mālojī tears the crocodile's body in half and flings it away. An elephant is set loose on Mālojī. Mālojī catches hold of the elephant's tusk, he thrice pushes him. Turning around and facing the royal court, he says: "Shall I fling the elephant away in the sky or should I fling it right into the assembly?" The royal assembly becomes terrified. The king takes him on his lap, gives him robes of honour and makes him an officer in his kingdom with a special seal and the title of Bhūpatirāv.

The wicked (*duṣṭa*) Vazir's plots against Mālojī continue. Once when Mālojī was sleeping, he had him lifted out of his bed and thrown in the well. The water deities take Mālojī to the Pātāl (the world below) and Lord Śiva brings him back to earth. While the king and his officers are being fated with opium pills in a garden party, Mālojī is given the poisoned pills by the Vazir. The pills have no effect on him, for he digests the poison. But he feigns death. He is attacked in that state by edged weapons which do not penetrate his body and which become blunt. Getting up, and holding a tusk of an elephant in his hand, he is about to exterminate his enemies. But the king pacifies him.

Once the Bādśāhā (king) takes Mālojī in confidence and says: "I am going to ask you a question. But you must give me a promise that you would answer it." Mālojī gives the promise. The Bādśāhā says: "Mālojī you are of Yādav lineage. You have defeated my army. . . . My question is: are you immune from death? Which is that deity that gave you the boon [of immortality]?"[34] Mālojī thinks: "I have reached the end of my life-span as the gods had preordained. I should ask the Bādśāhā for a *vṛtti* (a tenured holding of an office) for the sustenance of my descendants."[35] He first asks for the *vṛtti* before he gives the answer. The Bādśāhā gives him the Deśamukhī *vatan* with 360 villages, attested by a royal charter. Mālojī hands it over to his mother. Using his hands he removes the two amulets (*tāīts* given to him by Vetāl) from his arms by slitting them open. Reciting the name of Lord Śiva, he cuts his throat with his own hands.[36] The bells begin ringing in the Kailāśa, Śiva's abode. The divine *vimāna* (vehicle) descends to the earth and takes his body to the Kailāśa.

The main intent of this *ākhyāna* was to authenticate Mālojī Bhūpatirāv's Deśamukhī *vatan*. The secondary purpose was to narrate the history of the founder of the lineage of Deśamukhs of

Māṇḍavgaṇ. Thus, the Marāṭhā historian of eighteenth century used the model of the *ākhyāna* to validate the lineage and its founder. The *ākhyāna* genre of literature enrapped in a religious setting is essentially biographical, and deals with a single issue, the exploits of Mālojī, the martyred warrior.

The battle between Mālojī and the king's army, with its mixed mercenary contingent, the foreign officers and the use of the cannons, all point to the description of warfare in the third quarter of the eighteenth century when the *ākhyāna* was most probably composed. Mālojī is obviously a Mahārāṣṭrian version of a super hero, impervious and immune to all missiles and edged weapons. He punishes his enemy and spares the innocent bystanders. But all his acts are ultimately directed towards winning the favour of his king in order to receive a Deśamukhī *vatan* (office) in perpetuity. All through the *ākhyāna*, Mālojī appears as defying the king's authority. He deprives him of his revenues by appropriating them for himself. He defeats the king's emissaries, his army and his champion and the wicked plots of his minister. Eventually the king wins him over by an offer of an employment in his service. Only after that event, Mālojī becomes loyal to the king. He would not commit suicide unless he receives a Deśamukhī *vatan* first. However, the suicide of Mālojī must be regarded as an epitome of obedience and loyalty to the king; he died serving his wishes. The king in this case was a Muslim. As a hero, Mālojī is entitled to a place in the heaven.

Conclusion

Summing up, the article indicates how the Marāṭhā "historians" (the *caritra-bakhar* writers, *śāhirs* and *ākhyānakāras*) of seventeenth and eighteenth centuries perceived their heroes. The *caritra-bakhars* continue the purāṇic model of "universal history" and subsume historical events within that framework. Their canvas is necessarily broad, because they are dealing with the founders of major dynasties of Mahārāṣṭra. The House of Śivājī and the House of the Bhaṭs (the *peśvās*) deserve the grand treatment to be found in the purāṇic models of *yuga puruṣas*, the *avatāras* and *aṃśadhārīs* (the essence holders). There is the notion of Kaliyuga, and the ongoing conflict between Kali, the spreader of *adharma* and the *yuga puruṣas* and *aṃśadhārīs*, the upholders of *dharma*.

Povāḍās are essentially ballads sung by the minstrels and concentrate on a theme of major importance in the local and regional settings. The *śāhirs* composed the *povāḍās* at the patron's bidding to commemorate important events. Although the exploits of Tānājī are of epic proportions, the analogies drawn to compare his heroic deals have a local colouring and there are very few overt references to purāṇic stories. The heroic ideal represented in the person of Tānājī is to die, come what may, for his Lord and Master, Śivājī. Tānājī's adversaries are not depicted as cruel and evil. On the contrary, they are powerful and larger-than-life figures. The anti-heroes must match the strength and ability of the heroes. The goddesses aid the heroes to achieve their goal, but they are not responsible for changing the outcome of event.

Bājī Pālaskar's *povāḍā* delineates a theme of local raid on an aristocratic household which was deterred by the bravery of the protégé and dependents of the household. The main characters are the wives, a mother, the dependents, an employee and head of the extended household. The extraordinary solidarity and the courage of the members to protect their *wāḍā* (palace) against heavy odds makes this *povāḍā* all the more compelling.

Mālojī's *ākhyāna* extols the virtues of an ancestor, the founder of the lineage, whose powers equalled those of supra-human beings. Yet the heroic exploits in the *ākhyāna* are limited and localized, since Mālojī was merely a Deśamukh who receives a *vatan* from the local king. Once he becomes the employee of his king, he must obey him. The heroic code demands it, even if in the process of fulfilling the king's wishes he has to revoke his powers and commit suicide.

NOTES

1 Warder 1971: 17–25; see the detailed discussions of the genre of *caritra* and *bakhar* in Wagle & Kulkarni (1976: 3–5).

2 See, for example, *Śrī Śivadigvijaya* (1885: 353).

3 *tujhyā vaṃśāta āpaṇa avatāra gheū deva brāhamaṇāce saṃrakṣana karūna mlecchāṃcā kṣaya karato*, in Kṛṣṇājī Ananta Sabhāsad (1950: 2).

4 Wagle & Kulkarni 1976: 76, 47, *pragaṭa nara tanu trāsile mleccha duṣṭā*.

5 Ibid.: 95, 96, *utkarṣa sarva viṣaī paripurṇa jālā//nirbheda bāhyā kalibodha parākramālā//aṃta śarīra kṣaya prāpti praveśa bhoge kṣīṇatva jarjara parājitaṃ dirgha roge.*

6 For an analysis of the *śāhīrs* (bards) and their clientele, see Keḷkar (1928: 51–57).

7 Ibid.: 42–48. The Gondhaḷis' services were also required during the festivals of the goddesses and gods. Even today in some parts of Mahārāṣṭra they are employed in temples to sing and dance in praise of the deity. Their performance may last the whole night. The Marāṭhī expression *gondhaḷ kelā/jhālā* means a state of confusion. During a *gondhaḷ* session, the goddess is known to possess the members of the party.

8 Keḷkar 1928: 63. It was a convention of the authors of the *povāḍās* to mention the awards they received from their patrons at the end of their *povāḍā* compositions.

9 For the historical documentary evidence concerning the storming of the fort and the death of Tānājī, the Subhedār, a high ranking officer in Śivājī's army, see Keḷkar (1928: 29–30).

10 Keḷkar 1928: 34, *nāhī siṃahagaḍ killā dilyā mī śāpa deīna rājyā jāḷūna ṭākīna ubhe.* Rather harsh words to say to her son Śivājī!

11 Ibid.: 36, *āṃhī sūra marda kṣatrī nāhī bhiṇāra maraṇālā.*

12 Ibid.: 39, *mohore bare nāhī hoṇāra, rājā śivājīce deṇe aḍhāḷpadī sone.*

13 Ibid.: 49, *āhe marāṭhyācā pora nāhī bhiṇāra maraṇālā.*

14 Ibid., *eka hāta ṭākīn, aṭharā khāṇḍoḷī pāḍīna, śiḷyā bhākarīsaṃe khāīna.*

15 Ibid.: 48, *bahirobā āhe oṃgaḷa. . . nāhī āṃhī bahirobā jāṇita sāḍetinśe deva pāṇī rāṃjaṇāta bharatāta, aisā śivājī mahārājā.*

16 Ibid.: 52, *āga lāvo tujhyā conyālā.*

17 Ibid.: 54, *kaṇī koṇḍā āpaṇa khāvā, tāṇḍūḷa baniyālā opāvā.*

18 Ibid.: 55, *pāgoṭyāca veḍhe ghāla gaḷyāmadhī śaraṇa yāve.*

19 Ibid., *ghyāve toṇḍāta tṛṇa ghyāvī ḍoīvara vahāṇa, śaraṇa yāve.*

20 Ibid.: 56, *pahilā hāta yeūde tumcā.*

21 Ibid., *dhāvā āṁbecā maṇḍalā Aṃbābāī tū pāvage mājhyā navasālā.*

22 Ibid.: 58, *gābhaṇī gāī jo kāṭalī gelā pirācyā daragyālā savāmaṇa uda jāḷilā.*

23 Ibid.: 58, *bāīne ghosa gāīcā pāhilā, devī māge jī saralī.*

24 Ibid.: 62, *bārā divasāce sutaka dharala, śivājī mahārājāṃnī subhedārāce.*

25 Ibid.: 69, *tyācyā bāyakolā detye gaḷyātīla bilgirī.*

26 Ibid.: 70, *kāya basalāsa yelyā tujhī kurḍū mārūna nelī.*

27 Ibid., *hāṃga ālā mājhā bhāī, kāya pāhatosa dādā hāṇato ghoḍyācyā re pāyī.*

28 Ibid.: 71, *māgalyāna hastake jyāce śīra uḍavile, rumālāṃāta ghālūna bājīlā dāvāyāsī nele.*

29 *Bhūteśa Ākhyāna* 1926, I have given below a synoptic translation of the *ākhyāna.*

30 Ibid.: 26, *ulhāṭa yaṃtre thora thora juṃpile vṛṣabha apāra loṭatī gaja deūnī śīrā golaṃdāja phiraṅgī samudra beṭīcyā vyāti yavana kapitāna hāpasāna nānā jātī arbuja jāṇa nṛpā saṃgrahī asatī he*

mogala goregājare disatī ugra bāvare moṭhe moṭhe dhabare... sipāī baisale khaḍag upasūna ghoḍe uḍavīta jātī gagana.

31 Ibid.: 28, *ulhāṭa yaṃtrācā māra ekadāṃca kelā bhaḍimāra teṇedaṇāṇle aṃbara medanī kaṃpa jāhalā dhāṃsaḷatī nagaracīṃ maṅdireṃ manuṣyeṃ daḍapatī ekasare... dhurmeṃ koṃdalyā dāhī diśā pāyaka smaratī jadīśā cahū, kaḍūna varṣāva karatī nareśā.*

32 Ibid.: 29, *āmucā ghāta kāsayā karisī jaiṇe yuddha karāvayā, āṇile tujasī te paḷāle daśadiśesī garība anāthā kāṃ mārī.*

33 Ibid.: 33, *pāhā āviṃdha rāje kaise veḍe pāhūna tyāce baḷāceṃ pavāḍe jeṇeṃ upaḍilī, parvtākāra jhāḍeṃ tyāsī manuṣya bhiḍavītī nirdāḷileṃ avadheṃ sainya kuñjara didhale bhirkāvūna pāṣāṇa ṭākile ucalūna tetheṃ maśaka koṇateṃ aiseṃ pāhona yavanajātī jeṭhī yāsī bhiḍavitī.*

34 Ibid.: 57, *tuja āhe kīṃ nāhīṃ maraṇa koṇa daivata tuja prasanna kīṃ aisā vara didhalā.*

35 Ibid., *deve āyuṣya maryādā sāṃgitalī hotī tī jālī samāpta vaṃśa udarapoṣaṇāsī vṛttī māgāvīrājayāsī.*

36 Ibid.: 58, *mukhī smarile niḷakaṃṭhā āpule haste chedile kaṃṭha.*

REFERENCES

Bhūteśa Ākhyāna. 1926. Govindrāv Baḷavantrāv Yādav (ed.). Bhārat Itihās Saṃśodhak Maṇḍaḷ, Puraskṛta Granthamālā, number 10. Puṇe.

Hervāḍkar, R.V. 1957. *Marāṭhī Bakhar.* Puṇe: Venus Prakāśan.

Keḷkar, Y.N. 1928. *Aitihāsik Povāḍe kiṃvā Marāṭhyāṃcā Kāvyamaya Itihās (Bhāg Pahilā).* Bhārat Itihās Saṃśodhak Maṇḍaḷ, Puraskṛta Granthamālā, number 8. Puṇe.

Keśavācārya. 1924. *Mahikāvaticī ūrf Māhimacī Bakhar.* Rājvāḍe, V.K. (ed.). Puṇe: Citraśāḷā Press.

Kṛṣṇājī Ananta Sabhāsad. 1950. *Chatrapatī Śrī Śivājī Rāje Yāṃcī Bakhar (Sabhāsadāṃcī Bakhar).* V.S. Vākaskar (ed.). Baroda.

Kulkarṇī, Śridhar. 1970. *Prācīna Marāṭhī Gadya, Preraṇā āṇī Paraṃparā.* Bombay: Sindhu Prakāśan.

Malhār Rāmrāv Ciṭṇīs. 1924. *Śakakarte Śrī Śiva Chatrapatī Mahārāj Yāṃce Saptaprakarṇātmaka Caritra.* K.N. Sāne (ed.). Kalyāṇ.

Rājvāḍe, V.K. 1929. *Aitihāsik Prastāvanā, Rājvāḍe Lekhasaṃgraha,* Part I. Puṇe: Citraśāḷā Press.

Śrī Śivadigvijaya. 1885. P.R. Nandurbārkar and L.K. Dāṇḍekar (eds.). Baroda: Phatesiṃha Chāpkhānā.

Wagle, N.K. and A.R. Kulkarni 1976. *Vallabha's Paraśarāma Caritra: an Eighteenth Century Marāṭhā History of the Peśvās.* Bombay: Popular Prakashan.

Warder, A.K. 1971. *Introduction to Indian Historiography.* Bombay: Popular Prakashan.

Himalayan Heroes

Claus Peter Zoller

Introduction

The Garhwal region in the Indian Himalayas is widely known for its heroic traditions, and there are many authors who have already written on this topic.[1] But I would like to raise right at the outset a question which seemingly has not been asked by any of those authors. Why was there a heroic tradition in Garhwal in the first place? I fear that behind the failure to ask this obvious question lay the assumption that the answer is self-evident. Most of the authors say the texts[2] originated in medieval feudalism, when heroism experienced its florescence. The texts are thus portrayed as mere reflexes of a bygone era. Many authors dealing with heroic literature in general speak here of a 'heroic age',[3] an etic term referring to bygone times which live on among peoples as memories in the form of heroic literature. It has been pointed out, however, that in Garhwal the presentation of heroic songs is not merely reminiscence of past deeds, but also 'revivication' of the past.[4] This is considerably more than imagined by de Vries, according to whom heroic literature in its late phase is reduced to "pure literature", after having supposedly had "an educative power in the lives of the warlike nobility" (1963: 191). Although being a hero is certainly no longer a realistic alternative for any Garhwali, much of its social and religious environment is still extant. This may be illustrated by the following remarks, made by Gairola and Barker almost eighty years ago, about heroic songs sung by Garhwali bards (1917: 160):

> Such is the warlike spirit of these songs that the young folk who hear them become hypnotised, as it were, and begin to dance and perform extraordinary feats – such as uprooting trees, carrying huge weights, rushing into the burning fire, eating nettles, earth, etc.

Heroes

I would now like to turn to the results of my own field work on the topic. In so doing, I will concentrate primarily on the regions Bangan (*bɔṅgāṇ*)[5] and Parbat (*pərbət*) in northwestern Garhwal around the valleys of Tons and Pabar.[6] Galey says (1992: 181) that the population of Garhwal is made up of 60 per cent Rajputs, 20 per cent Brahmans, and 20 per cent service groups. The heroic tradition of this region is especially associated with male Rajputs (I am not aware of a single heroine story from Bangan or Parbat), whom I primarily deal with. As a consequence, the following description will most certainly not do justice to all viewpoints. In addition, it is a major problem that things must be represented as explicit knowledge, as concrete facts, which they often simply are not.

As far as I know, it was Sax (1990: 505f.) who first pointed out the fundamental distinction between explicit and implicit knowledge among the Garhwalis. He writes:

> ... if we acknowledge intersubjectivity, if we recognize the fact that human beings do indeed manage to communicate, then "shared meaning" or "tacit knowledge" must exist at some level... [I]t is important to distinguish between the implicit and the explicit, between the interested and the disinterested. Where cultural assumptions and presuppositions remain implicit and do not "rise to consciousness," they cannot become objects of contention, and hence they change much more slowly than the kinds of ideas – generally explicit and "interested," if not always coherent or rational – for which people fight and die.

He refers to a similar conceptual distinction when he, in the same passage, separates "shared cultural assumptions" from "assumptions [which] are subject to variant interpretations", whereby the latter are "related to particular interests". In practice, however, it will often be difficult to distinguish the two levels from each other and to clearly delineate the concept of "tacit knowledge" at all. Nevertheless, Sax's distinction remains significant. Explicit knowledge leans toward reification and rigidity, toward systematicity and objectivity, toward the greatest possible freedom from contradiction and toward self-transparency. Implicit knowledge is more like the articulation of various overlapping and superposed forms of knowledge that are flexible, fuzzy, and incomplete. It cannot simply be called up upon questioning; rather, it manifests itself indirectly in certain actions and behaviors, in everyday discourse, and in poetic forms of speech. Explicit knowledge is associated more with observation and distance; implicit knowledge, more with participation and closeness.

I think that any attempt on my part to reproduce aspects of this continuum between implicit and explicit knowledge, whether it be with respect to heroic tradition or something else, in a scholarly context which also bears both implicit and explicit structures of knowledge, must evoke images and associations that sometimes seem unsystematic, fragmentary, contradictory, and unclear, because these structures are tied to entirely different contents. What follows on the coming pages is polyvocality; it is not the knowledge of a single person, nor is it the general knowledge of all. But first, let us hear the voices of other "peepers" like me on a topic of importance.

Love of the Soil

According to Nautiyal (1981: 210), a "love of one's land" is expressed in the heroic songs of Garhwal.[7] This is a questionable assessment, since this love has nothing to do with the bond with the homeland familiar to us or with national pride. Instead, it is a deep, transpersonal tie to the earth of the homeland which has a great deal to do with the heroic tradition. This striking love of the Garhwalis and Kumaonis to the soil has also been noticed by others. Thus, Traill writes as early as 1828 (1992: 38) that "...the petty landed proprietors entertain an overwhelming affection for their hereditary fields". This affection is an expression of the certainty that the character and power of humans and other living beings are influenced by the earth on which they live. Sax says (p. 496):

> ...the place where one is born [is] thought to determine one's nature to a significant degree. ...Normally in Garhwal, the wife comes to live in her husband's village and is contained within it. People do not speak of

marrying such-and-such a person or family, but rather of *places.*[8]

This attitude is also revealed in a series of incidents and stories. The following happened more than a thousand years ago in Chamba. Hutchinson and Vogel relate (1982: 26):

> There is hardly a state in the Western Hills in which traditions are not found of a ... conflict between the feudal Chiefs and their overlords - the Rajas.... Before the conquest of the Lower Ravi Valley by Raja Sahila-Varman (A.D. 920-40), the country around the present capital was in the possession of a Rana whose fort stood on Bannu Hill... From this Rana... tribute was demanded and persistently refused. On being summoned to the presence of the Raja, the Rana is said to have laid aside his insolent demeanour and to have meekly promised compliance, but on returning to the other side of the Sal stream, separating the town from Bannu Hill, he became as obdurate as ever. The conclusion was arrived at, in explanation of this conduct, that it was due to the influence of the soil. To test the truth of this, a lump of earth was procured from Bannu Hill and spread on the floor of the audience chamber, with a carpet over it, and the Rana was then called to an interview. On arrival he was invited to take his seat on the carpet as usual, but when the question of tribute was mooted, he sprang to his feet, drew his sword, demanding at the same time to know who had a right to ask tribute of him. The result doubtless was his subjection, or expulsion from the barony, and removal to some other place where the soil did not exert so baneful an influence. Traditions similar to this are also found in Kulu and other parts of the hills, and are significant of the tension which existed between the petty chiefs and their suzerains.

There actually exist other such traditions about the influence of the ground upon the character and about its causing political tensions between petty chiefs and suzerains. The above authors themselves report the story of a quite similar incident (pp. 451f.).[9]

The local mythology contains similar ideas, as well. For instance, Jettmar-Thakur (unpublished manuscript) recounts a story from the Kulu Valley about Kuntī, mother of the Pāṇḍavas, who as a widow is to be married off by her sons:

> Kuntī, it is said, refused to leave Jagatsukh Koti,[10] pleading that she was too old to cross the mountains. Soon, however, her sons discovered the true reason: Kuntī wanted to marry a man from the village. Shocked, they took her forcibly to Lahaul. During this journey, Bhīma cut the pass at Rohtang with his club. Far from the rejuvenating climate of Kulu, Kuntī no longer remembered her desire. Now Yudhiṣṭhira conducted an experiment, building a platform (chowka) and filling it with earth from Kulu; when Kuntī stepped on it, she again felt young and romantic...

B.R. Sharma describes another such story from a different part of Himachal (1993: 41),[11] and Atkinson shows the significance of the soil in Jaunsar-Bawar, which borders Bangan on the east, in another context, this time having to do with the important regional god Mahāsu (Bangani Māsu) (1973: III, I, p. 357):

> A custom ... was that in cases of disputed possession a party took a stone from the field or a portion of the mud from the walls of the house and offered them to Mahásu, with the result that no one could cultivate the field or occupy the house – a very convenient way of annoying one's enemy.

Independently of these sources, Galey reaches similar conclusions regarding the importance of ground and territory (p. 181):

> ...the importance still given to-day to titles, brotherhoods and local origins may be the sign of an original system where territorial and clanic dimensions – two features ordinarily left aside from the characterization of castes and kept for the description of tribal populations – had here direct incidence over the definition of legitimate power.

Two Kinds of Power and Authority

Shortly thereafter (p. 188) he describes two different types of power connected with such territories and represented at the village level by the terms *Pradhāna* 'headman' and *Sayānā* 'elder'. The principal distinction between the two types of authority consists in the fact that the *Pradhāna* stands at the head of a variety of different groups (castes) whereas the *Sayānā* is the "oldest representative of a local lineage (*Āl*)". In the first case he speaks of "lordship" (this type of authority is delegated from above, formerly by the king and now by the district administration) and in the second, of "chiefdom" or "chieftainship" (it "emanates from local origin" [p. 193] and is founded on kinship ties). This bipartite system can now be related to two kinds of religious power and authority. "Lordship" corresponds to the "royal gods", who still reign in many parts of Garhwal like medieval sovereigns. In contrast, the "chiefdoms" are associated with cults of which Galey says the following (p. 196):

> ... clan cults deal primarily with matters of sickness, witchcraft and feud, and never coalesce with others, and more elaborate forms of worship which require the complementary participation of different social units strictly identified by their status.

Thus, the so-called clan cults are also associated with feuds, a fact leading one to suspect that the Garhwali heroic tradition is – at least 'originally' – associated with clan cult and chiefdom rather than lordship. And indeed, this seems to be especially clear in Bangan, a peripheral region in which the heroic tradition lives on more vividly in the memory of the people and the influence of kings as representatives of lordship has probably always been quite marginal.

Heroes of Bangan

The Bangani word for 'hero, heroic man' is *mōṛ*.[12] *Mōṛ*s may be Rajputs or lowly *Koḷi*s. It always denotes an individual. Alongside it we find the term *Khūnd*, which emphasizes class membership, since *Khūnd* refers to a hero belonging to the *Khūnd* Rajputs. These represent the traditionally most bellicose segment of the

Rajput caste. Beside the loanword *rājpūt*, the more warlike sounding word *Khɔśia* is often used in the sense of 'hero'.[13] However, the words *mōr̤*, *Khūnd*, and *Khɔśia* can also be used synonymously. In addition one sometimes hears *śūrɔ* 'hero' and *bīr* 'hero', albeit with a somewhat different meaning. *Bīr* typically refers to lower divinities, which are often subordinate to a regionally dominant god, like the vassals or bodyguard of a feudal lord. *Śūrɔ* is applied to men who are strong and brave but not *Khūnds*. Male illegitimate children (*j̈ɔleṭɔ*) are also called *śūrɔ*, since they are thought to be robust and incapable of being killed. They are, however, unclean (*nikamɔ*). Nonetheless the Bangani thunder god *Gur̤ku* is also a *śūrɔ*.[14] A rarer word is *kurɔ* 'hero', which may be avoided because of its phonetic similarity to *kurɔ* 'cruel'.

To add to this collection, there are – especially in oral literature – epitheta ornans, such as *mor̤ɛ kɔ pathɔ̄r* 'rock among the heroes', *ċaḷdɛ-boṭhɛ kɔ athia* 'the elephant of (the gods) *Calda* and *Botha*',[15] and *māsu kɔ śūgur* 'the wild boar of (the god) *Mahāsu*'. Moreover, there can be found (negative) shortened comparisons like *kukur mōr̤* 'a dog hero' or synecdoches like *megɔ śīgɔ* 'a big horn'.[16] The heroes did not wear a special costume that would have distinguished them from the other Rajputs. They commonly wore gray woolen pants (*gūḍiɛ*) and jackets (*jur̤kɛ*), silver rings (*dagulɛ*) in their ears and on their limbs, and a black cap (*ṭopi*) on their heads. They often had a full beard and shoulder-length hair, which is said to have sometimes been combined with a shaved crown. How are *Khūnds* recognized at birth? "They already have teeth when they are born", have a great deal of hair, are seldom sick, and drink mother's milk unusually long.[17] It is also a sign that someone is meant to become a hero if a liverspot (*lakheṇ*) moves from his belly towards his breastbone.[18]

A *mōr̤*'s hair stands up on end during a fight. For this reason, boys sometimes twist tufts of hair, saying, "*ċorɔ ki mor̤ɔ*" (thievish or outstanding). If the tuft remains erect, the boy hopes to become a hero. If *mōr̤s* did not get along although they were supposed to, they were secretly given flour with a few hairs from the other's head. This made them become friends, I was told. But what makes a man a hero at all? A preliminary answer is given in a *ċhor̤a* song:

A *Khūnd* is either one who has teeth in his stomach

> or a *Khūnd* is one who carries off sheep
> or a *Khūnd* is one who fights and abducts women.[19]

A hero's life is dangerous, hence the saying "Both son and he-goat should be heroes. What does time mean to them?"[20] A hero is the "son" (*beṭa*) of a female "earthpower-center" called *j̈aga* (see below). Neither he nor the sacrificial animal knows the time of his violent death.[21] Another saying is "The death of a *mōṛ* goes or takes."[22] That is, a *mōṛ* can kill or be killed at any moment. It is also claimed that heroes can learn of their impending death in dreams: they see a brook of blood or a panther holding a bloody animal in its mouth; or they are thirsty and are given a bowl of blood by a woman. I also occasionally heard that *mōṛ*s can be reborn.

Heaven and Earth, Soul and Body

To reach a deeper understanding of heroism in Bangan, two large topics must now be outlined:

1. Notions regarding body and soul and the 'psycho-physical' processes associated with fighting.
2. Notions regarding the village sanctuaries, called *j̈aga*, which are closely connected with the heroic fights and, at the same time, with lineages, clans, chieftainships, and similar concepts.

Humans receive their souls from God, their bodies from the earth. The physical heart (*j̈iḍoḷi*) is inhabited by the soul (*j̈iu*). The relationship between God (*bɔguan*)[23] and soul (*j̈iu*) on the one hand and between earth (*maṭi*) and body (*ɔbduar*) on the other are conceived as 'shading image' or 'projection'. The corresponding native words are *ɔı̃ś* 'shading image' and *ɔı̃śaḷi* 'projection'. The soul is a 'shadowing' or 'projection' of God or heaven, and the body, a 'projection' of the earth. All humans, the animals, and plants are *ɔı̃śaḷi*s of these two basic beings. The term *ɔı̃śaḷi* on the one hand means an 'image' of the 'essence' and 'form' of God and earth; on the other hand, I also heard that the 'actual' human soul and 'actual' human body always remained in heaven and the earth, respectively. In addition, there are projections of projections, which then may be expressed as follows:[24]

1. *bɔguan/gɔiṇ* → *jïu* (*kaṇċhɔ sās* → *jeṭhɔ sās*) → *pur, ai, pāp*

2. *maṭi* → *ɔbduar* → *jïan* → *mīr*

3. ↘ *jaga* → *giria*

The obvious complementarity of heaven and earth is reflected on the grammatical level: God/heaven is masculine, and all of his 'projections' are of masculine gender (including grammatically). Conversely, the earth is feminine, as are all of her 'projections'.

First Projection Series

bɔguan/gɔiṇ → *jïu* (*kaṇċhɔ sās* → *jeṭhɔ sās*) → *pur, ai, pāp*

The soul (*jïu*) is a projection of God or of heaven and is, as long as it inhabits a person, bipartite: Banganis speak of *jeṭhɔ sās* 'old soul' and *kaṇċhɔ sās* 'young soul', whereby the young soul is considered the projection (*ɔĩśaḷi*) of the old soul. The different functions attributed to the two souls are illustrated by the following proverb: *kaṇċhɛ sasɛ rɔ kām dukti; jeṭhɛ sasɛ rɔ kām nɔrdei* 'the work of the young soul is the heartbeat; the work of the old soul is the person'. To translate this into concepts familiar to us, one could say – simplifying somewhat – that the young soul is responsible for the 'unconscious', and the old soul, for the 'conscious'.

Whereas *jïu* 'soul' can be traced etymologically to OIA *jīva-* 'living being, vital breath', *sās* is derived from OIA *śvāsa-* 'breath, breathing'. The subtle difference in meaning has been preserved in Bangani: *sās* means not only 'soul' but also 'breath'. It bears noting, however, that 'breath' is not conceived of as a mere physiological phenomenon, but as 'soul plus breath' or 'something animate(d)'. Consequently, it is also said that at death the soul (*jïu*) leaves the body in the manner of breath (*sās*). The other aspect of *sās* can be seen in the fact that in inhalation the soul is said to *eat* the (material) breath (*sās khāṇɔ*), and in exhalation it digests the breath (*sās gaṛṇɔ*). For this reason, the 'digested' breath is unclean (*juṭhɔ*) and always potentially dangerous.

Like many other expressions in the Bangani language, *sās* has a mental-material double meaning as 'soul' and as 'breath'. This is also true of the various projections, each of which can in its way be conceptualized as simultaneously material and mental. It likewise explains why *sās* can also function as soul plus breath, after the fashion of a carrier or medium through which other 'spiritual' or 'supernatural' forces can be actively drawn out of a person and directed at an object or another person. These forces are the *pur*, *ai*, *pāp*, and *mīr* of the above diagram. As I understand it, the first three of these energies – *pur*, *ai*, and *pāp* – are associated in the order given with the three castes of Rajputs, *Koḷis*, and Brahmans. A full discussion of these forces would go far beyond the scope of this article, so I will confine myself to a few brief notes: If someone is treated unjustly or violently by a person of another caste, in a way affecting his caste status, the victim can call upon a god, curse, or make a vow. Doing so causes the force pertinent to his caste to travel from the injured party via his *sās* to his malefactor and do him damage.[25] However, of all the forces mentioned, the most important for us here is *mīr*.[26] It is the force which gives the Bangani heroes their power in fighting. Unlike the forces just discussed, *mīr* is not caste- but lineage-related. Moreover, it exists only in the lineages of the *Khũnds* (called *Khũndāl*) and in those of the *Koḷis* connected with them. It originates in the villages' sanctuaries, called *j̈agas*. Before I turn to the sanctuaries, however, we would do well to look at the second projection series.

Second Projection Series

maṭi → *ɔbduar* → *j̈ian* → *mīr*

The body is called *ɔbduar*, or sometimes *dār*.[27] It is the projection of the earth (*maṭi*). A projection of this projection is, in turn, the *j̈ian*. The *j̈ian* is a sort of complement to the *j̈iu*. In men it is located at the back of the neck, and in women, in the abdomen.[28] Although both *j̈iu* and *j̈ian* are invisible (*ɔdiśɔ*), interestingly enough the *j̈iu* is said to possess an ethereal 'substantiality', while the *j̈ian* is said to be like a 'pebble' (*pathri*).[29] The *j̈ian* is sometimes also called *j̈ɔ̄ṛ* ('root'). Whereas *j̈iu* 'soul' etymologically goes back to OIA *jīva-*, *j̈ian* is derived from the closely related OIA word *jīvanta-* 'long-lived'. Now, it is interesting to note that the NIA descendants of *jīva-* frequently mean 'soul'[30] yet the modern reflexes of *jīvanta-* seem especially numerous in the northwest (that is, in the Dard and Nuristani languages), where they usually have the meaning 'body'.[31]

Starting at the *jïan* in a man's neck there runs a 'nerve' or 'vein' called *sīr* or *nɔs* through (or along) the spine, down to a point in the perineum called *mūḷ* or *jɔ̄ṛ* 'root'. This part of the 'vein' between the 'root' and the lower end of the spine is not protected by bone and therefore is considered easily harmed (injury to it may lead to impotence, among other things). This 'root' in the perineum is the endpoint for a multiplicity of invisible 'roots'[32] which extend through the legs and feet down into the earth. Moreover, two other *sirɛ* (veins) run from the *jïan* to the two *bukṛu* 'kidneys' or *buksɔ/buksɔ̃di* 'renal area'.[33] From the *bukṛu* or *buksɔ/buksɔ̃di* there are a number of *sirɛ* going to the lungs (*bɔ̃ś*) and heart, the seat of the soul. The renal area is thought of as connecting the *jïan* at the back of the man with the *sās* at the front.

Now, the 'psychophysical' processes that occur in the body during battle in many ways resemble the processes in a man's body during the sexual act. The lung (*bɔ̃ś*) is considered the center or seat of two forces: *tēj* 'aura' and *tāp* 'heat'. *Tēj* is of no importance for the processes to be discussed here. But *bɔ̃ś* 'lung' has the additional meaning 'fat of the lung'.[34] In this second meaning *bɔ̃ś* is equated with 'male seed',[35] which is also called *suɔ mɔɔ*, *lēṛ*, or *biriə*.[36]

During combat or sex, *tāp* develops, thereby 'melting' *suɔ mɔɔ* in the breast like fat. During sexual intercourse, the *suɔ mɔɔ* then flows downward. Simultaneously, the force *mīr* concentrated in the *jïan* descends the back *nɔs* to the *jɔ̄ṛ* (root). *Mīr* and *suɔ mɔɔ* enter the biologically intended canals in the body of the female partner. *Tāp* causes an intense pulsating of the *jïu* 'soul' in both partners, especially during their first intercourse. The 'melting' of the 'seed' of both partners[37] produces *rōś* 'anger'. *Rōś* is the 'mental-emotional' side of *suɔ mɔɔ*. This constitutes the Banganis' explanation of why sexual intercourse among them contains an unmistakably aggressive component, in the man toward the woman, particularly the first time. In the opinion of the male Rajputs, women at this moment easily become unconscious, since they cannot direct their *rōś* outward as well as men can. This, in turn, is supposed to have to do with the location of their *jïan*, which after all occurs in the abdomen. Thus, in sexual intercourse 'anger' arises and liquefied 'fount honey' in the form of ejaculate 'shoots' (*uċhṛɛ*) the *mīr* from the man into the woman.

The 'psychosomatic' processes that take place in combat are quite similar. However, with heroes the heat does not lead to pulsating but to an 'expansion' of the *jiu* and to a reddening of the ears. This reddening is also taken as a sign of the development of *rōś*. The 'anger' emanates from the body of the hero 'like the wind' (*bagur baśi*), whereby some say it departs only through the nose and others say, through the ears, mouth, and eyes as well. Although the *suɔ mɔɔ* also melts during a fight, it is not discharged as ejaculate, and the force *mīr* does not flow down to the 'root'.

Yet it is not, as one might imagine, the *rōś* that the hero directs in an aggressive impulse at his opponent; rather, it is the *mīr*. *Rōś*, like *tāp*, is conceived by the Banganis as a condition that does not necessarily imply goal-oriented destruction. The aggressive goal-orientedness directed at the opponent is an expression of the *mīr*, which occurs in heroes in especially high concentrations. Like the other forces named above, the *mīr* has its specific effects: it makes the hero fearless (*niḍɔrɔ*) and, when it 'wakens' in him (*uċhṛɛ*),[38] causes a battle intoxication, called *jā̃j* or *gerɔ*. The *mīr* of the hero does not flow down to the 'root' *jɔ̃ṛ* in battle, but instead travels via two 'veins' (*sirɛ*) to the kidneys (*bukṛu*) or renal area (*buksɔ/buksɔ̃di*). From there it makes its way through a number of *sirɛ* to the heart. From the heart, the *mīr* is now borne out of the body and directed against the opponent. It leaves the hero through the eyes and mouth and levels itself at the antagonistic *mīr* that at the same instant is emitted by the enemy. In this context *sās* refers merely to the 'energy aspect' of the soul(s), for it is emphasized that neither the old nor the young soul leaves the body in combat (which in certain other situations may very well happen). The encounter of the antagonistic *mīr*s of the heroes is what determines the outcome of the battle – in theory, before their weapons have even touched. Pure muscle power, called *giṭṭi* does not count for much in this view. In quality, *giṭṭi* has nothing to do with the other forces mentioned, since these all possess a numinous dimension.

The special significance of the kidneys or renal cavities is also seen in various expressions. Among the Banganis, aggressive verbal threats are – if they are made in earnest – to my knowledge not directed at the sexual organs of the enemy but at his kidneys, which unite the two opposing powers of *sās* and *mīr*. I heard: *buksɔ̃di banu* 'I break your renal cavities' and *teri buksɔ̃di rɔ paṇi jaṛu* 'I brush down the water of your renal cavities'. The latter expression probably points to a Bangani interpretation (and an obvious one, at that) of the kidneys as being 'watery'. This would then give the following scheme:

> *jiu, sās* 'soul' = heavenly, ethereal
> *bukṛu, buksɔ, buksɔ̃di* 'kidneys, renal cavities' = watery, fluid
> *jian* 'life center' = earthy, solid

Thus, when in a fight the *mīr* shoots to the hero's exterior through the *sās*, a heavenly force is linked to an earthy one in a moment of supreme drama.[39] This kind of thing is called *śɔ̃g bɔg kɔṭhi raḷṇɔ* 'to mix together something low with something high'. What such a suspension of antithesis means to the Banganis is shown by the following saying: *jiu jiani rɔ mēl, ḍaki ḍumu rɔ khel* 'the mixture of *jiu* and *jian*, the game of musicians and low castes' (word-by-word translation). In other words, the fusion of these two opposing forces is like a suspension of the antitheses between the castes, thus between high and low. This is thought extremely dangerous and occurs only during special, short intervals of time: in fights between heroes, at 'carnevalistic' festivals of the lower castes and agonistic celebrations of the Rajputs, and during sex between man and woman. In all these situations human lives are viewed as more or less seriously threatened, and simultaneously, these are situations of exceptional life power: heroic battles end in death, but this outcome may give rise to new lineages, as I will show below; in sexual intercourse one fears death, although the act may beget new life; and the carnevalistic and agonistic celebrations, which sometimes become very bloody (also to be described below), are thought to promote all growing and flourishing. The paradoxical nature of the martial activities of central Himalayan heroes – involving simultaneous destruction and creation of life – will become more comprehensible after my explanation of the third projection:

Third Projection Series

maṭi → *jaga* → *giria*

One can find *j̈aga* sanctuaries in very many Bangani villages, especially older ones. The following information will serve as a brief description of the physical characteristics of a *j̈aga*: it consists of four stone walls, about four meters long and one half to two meters high, arranged in the shape of a square.[40] The tops of the walls are covered with wooden beams, called *nās*. Thus the whole construction ideally has a parallelepiped form, sometimes almost resembling a big cube. In the middle is a hole, called *mũ* 'mouth' or *gutu*, about half a meter deep and covered by an erect stone. In the past, the heads of slain hostile warriors were placed in the hole. It is said that every *j̈aga* has an invisible connection with a spring, and that strong *j̈aga*s are even connected with several springs.[41]

In this parallelepiped structure called *j̈aga* resides the *j̈aga*, a female numinous being.[42] The Banganis, however, do not regard her as a goddess (*debi*). They argue that, unlike the latter, she cannot live in more than one village. Every village has its own *j̈aga*. During the weeks and days before a fight she charges her warriors with the ferocious energy *mīr*, which stirs them into a frenzy. The energy is hers, not the warriors'. The *mīr* lies latent in every warrior and overwhelms him before and during a fight. It is this which induces within him the frenzy or battle intoxication called, as already stated, *gerɔ* or *j̈ãj̈*.

A *j̈aga* is a sort of 'tutelary spirit' pertaining to a Rajput lineage and its village, and to the area belonging to the village and lineage. In other words, she is the divine complement or realization of the Rajput chieftainship. She forms the center of the Bangani villages. She is a projection or, as the Banganis also say, a daughter (*beṭi*) of the earth (*maṭi*). In this aspect she is an 'individualized', territorially restricted and defined mode of existence of the boundless earth; she is the expression of an unlimited power projected onto a limited area. This is why she is named *j̈aga* 'place, locality' and why she is not a goddess. To be sure, every place is part of the same earth, yet regions and landscapes – and *j̈aga*s – vary. Every *j̈aga* is named after her village, for example, *kɔrɔḷi ri j̈aga* 'the *j̈aga* of Kiroli'. On the other hand, when talk is not of *j̈aga* but of her energy *mīr* (we could also say, of her as energy), the important thing is not her connection to the territory but to the lineage of the *Khūnd*s (*khūdāl*). I was told by *Khūnd*s that the *mīr* of her martial aspect abides only within them and 'their' *Koḷis*. Thus, an expression like *ṭholiaike ri mīr* 'the *mīr* of the Tholiaikes' would mean the 'earth power' connected with the *Khūnd* lineage of the Tholiaikes (whose ancestors are said to be the founders of the village Kiroli just mentioned).

The *mīr* of a *j̈aga* or a *j̈aga* simultaneously as *mīr* and as concrete sanctuary 'accompanies' a Rajput lineage through time. Her territory encompasses the village, the associated fields, and the forest utilized for economic purposes by the village. Such an area is called *ṭhɔ̄ṛi*.[43] It approximately corresponds to the 'inner zone' for the women of the village, within whose bounds they are protected.[44] All plants, animals, and humans belonging to a *ṭhɔ̄ṛi* are also filled with a specific *mīr*. In addition to its martial side, every *j̈aga* also has a protective function: she is responsible for the fertility and growth of all living beings in her territory. Up to now I have primarily spoken of an 'energy,' yet she may also appear before the local populace in anthropomorphic form from time to time. On such occasions she is said to look just like an ordinary Bangani woman. Perhaps the Banganis are referring to her aspect as a person when they call her *iṣṭēr*, a word which probably has nothing to do with OIA *iṣṭa-* 'sought, desired' but rather with the OIA root *īś-* 'to command, rule, reign'.

The mightiness of a *j̈aga* is reflected in the number of sacrificial animals. The Banganis distinguish five kinds of *j̈aga*: *cīn bɔḷi, pā̃ċ bɔḷi, ċhɔ bɔḷi, nɔ bɔḷi, bara bɔḷi* 'of three, of five, of six, of nine, of twelve sacrifices'. This refers to the *j̈agas* receiving three, five, six etc. sacrificial animals at more or less regular intervals. The *j̈agas* of three sacrifices are regarded as weak, those of twelve sacrifices as very strong, and the others as in between.[45] This is also true of their associated lineages, so that *j̈aga* and lineage are mutually validating. The *j̈aga-pūjā* is led by a Brahman (*deo puj̈ia*). It takes place during the night. At that time, the stone is removed from the 'mouth' of the *j̈aga*; weapons are placed next to the mouth; and then various animals, plants, and other things are sacrificed. The heads of the sacrificed animals are put in the mouth. 'Nine' and 'twelve-sacrifice *j̈agas*' formerly required a human sacrifice (the sacrifice of a girl *kumari-bɔḷi*).[46] The *j̈aga-pūjā* regularly leads to a meeting between the *j̈aga* and *deo puj̈ia* on the one hand and the *mɔśaṇ* 'lord of the cremation ground'[47] on the other hand (see below).

The unusual thing about a *j̈aga-pūjā* is that the *j̈aga* is not only strengthened and invigorated as in sacrifices to gods (with the result that she can be moved to do something). She is actually made young again; she turns into a baby. Thus within a couple of years she completes an entire life cycle and in the end becomes an old woman. This fact also demonstrates that she is not a goddess (*debi*). Rather, she is realized in all processes of birth, aging, and death in plants, animals, and humans in her *ṭhōṛi* as a diachronically operative 'earth power'. The 'nine' and 'twelve-sacrifice' *j̈aga*s are the strongest, for the sacrifice of a girl maintains their strength especially long. It is also said that the 'mood' and stage of development of a *j̈aga* have an influence on the character of a human at his/her birth.[48] The most important influences, of course, are, first, the character traits of the parents and, second, the time of day when one is born.[49]

And now a few words on *giria*. Many Bangani-Rajput houses have a *giria*, in the stalls directly below the kitchen.[50] The *giria* is thus a territory the size of a house belonging to a family.[51] In the center of the stable floor there is a hole covered over with a flat stone. Along the edges of the floor and ceiling are threads which are secured there by a Brahman when the *giria* is installed at the time the house is built. Perhaps this is meant to create a square sacred room in analogy to the construction of a *j̈aga*, which itself could be understood as an analogy to the earth, the latter being sometimes described in the oral literature as four-sided. This *giria* is considered a projection or daughter of the village *j̈aga*. She also receives occasional sacrifices. There are supposed to be about twelve different types of *giria*. Yet there can be no doubt that the *j̈aga* is viewed as much more important than the *giria*. People commonly know less about *giria*s than about *j̈aga*s. It is not clear whether they also go through life cycles like *j̈aga*s, and presumably they function only to protect the family and promote fertility. For it is unquestionably the *j̈aga*s, being associated with the lineages, that control the heroic activities of the *mōṛ*s, and not the *giria*s, which are associated with the individual families.

To recapitulate: A *j̈aga* in Bangan is connected with the 'earth power' of a territory and with the *Khūnd* lineages inhabiting it. She lives by consuming *mīr* and *sās*, which she receives through sacrifices and from the heads of slain enemies. She represents 'chieftainship', physically expressed in the design of the parallelepiped sanctuaries. 'Lordship', on the other hand, is represented by the gods and goddesses of Garhwal. In Bangan almost no goddesses are worshipped (a point which I will take up again below), and the dominating divine power is *Mahāsu* (Bangani *Māsu*). He comprises four brothers who rule their dominion in the manner of a feudal king, delegate offices, and administer justice. *Mahāsu* as well as the other gods is sustained by the consumption of the *sās* of sacrificial animals and by the drinking of the smell of their blood.[52] Physical expressions of the gods' power and presence are temples (*dām*),[53] busts (*mora*),[54] and symbols of kingship, such as the palanquins (*rəth*)[55] with the thrones (*siṅgāsən*),[56] or the sword (*kɔtari*).[57] About the sword, which here also functions as a representative of *Mahāsu*, Galey says (p. 216): "... in Garhwal, the emblem of royal power is not the traditional stick (*daṇḍa*)... but rather the sword (*talvār*)."

When I wanted to know about the relationship between *Mahāsu* and *j̈aga*, people always replied in the vaguest terms: their relationship is good. Apparently the two as a rule have little to do with each other. The complementarity of the two types of power that they respectively symbolize nonetheless finds its most striking expression in the villages *Jagṭa* and *Ciũa* (both in the Khaniaṭa Valley). There the temples to *Mahāsu* were built directly upon the *j̈agas*.[58]

Let me finish this section with an example showing that the polarity of 'chieftainship' and 'lordship' almost certainly already existed centuries ago not too far to the west in the Himalayas. This is an incident in the life of Madan-Sen, a king in the hill state of Suket, which took place in his capital, Pangna, in the thirteenth century. Hutchinson and Vogel write (p. 350):

> One night, while he was asleep in his palace, the *devi*, or goddess of the place, it is said, appeared to him in a dream and told him that the spot on which he lay was her ancient *asthan* or place, and that he must leave it or evil would befall him. On awaking in the morning, with the dream still in his mind and looking around, he found an image with a throne, and a sword lying beside it. He therefore erected a temple on the spot, which is still extant. He then decided to abandon Pangna....

Here an earthly king encounters a supernatural being which represents both 'chieftainship' (she is goddess of the place [*asthan*]) and 'lordship' (sword and throne). By leaving the place and building her a temple, he demonstrates his submission to both types of power. In Bangan, where to my knowledge there were no earthly kings, and where the influence of other kings was always marginal, 'lordship' is represented by the functionaries of *Mahāsu*: his priests, viziers, treasurers, temple servants, parasol bearers, drummers, and so forth. The exponents of the principle of 'chieftainship', in contrast, are the heroes.[59]

Easily Excitable Spirits

Whereas the *mīr* in the average member of a *Khūnd* family appears to be only latently present and is felt only in fighting, it appears to be constantly felt by the *mōṛ*s. A hero through whom the *mīr* frequently manifests itself is called *mirguḷia*. In contrast to the other members of *Khūnd* families, the hero seems to enjoy a relationship to his *j̈aga* like that between individuals. Some people say that when he sees her or dreams of her, she invariably appears to him in youthful beauty regardless of her current stage of development. This close relationship, however, does not commence until the *mōṛ* has "brought her blood",[60] that is, when he has placed the head of an enemy defeated by him in the 'mouth' of his *j̈aga*. From then on he is a hero.

So the strength to perform this deed comes from his *j̈aga*: her *mīr* has flowed into him via invisible 'roots' (*j̈ɔṛ*) and is stored in the *j̈ian* in his neck until it is discharged in combat. The route of discharge has been described above. It supposedly may take anywhere from a few minutes to several weeks for the *mīr* to 'awaken' for the battle. The reason for the slow building up of strength over several weeks is the fact that battles between heroes used to be carried out at agonistic festivals, which even today sometimes become bloody. Thus, showdowns were often known of far in advance. I was continually told that fights were provoked by various goading speeches;[61] however, the oral literature also describes ambushes.

The pugnacity of the *Khūnd*s in specific contexts, many examples of which were given to me, is considered by the Banganis to be linked to *mīr*. The flimsiness of many causes for dispute shows that heroes did not fight *because of* something, but that the provocations merely served as a trigger for encounters that had to take place anyway.[62]

Death and the Fields of Life

The *ṭhɔ̄ṛi*, the territory of a *ǰaga*, is also a realm of life. I said above that at the *ǰaga-pūǰā* a *mɔśaṇ* 'lord of the cremation ground' invariably turns up. The Banganis say that at this moment the dividing line between the power domains of the *ǰaga* and life on the one hand and *mɔśaṇ* and death on the other hand is called into question. So here as well we have a highly dramatic moment where life touches death. The *mɔśaṇ* attempts to fortify his domain of power, and I was told that the borderline between the two territories used to be flexible. It was reset at every *ǰaga-pūǰā* by the positioning of a stone. Today, after the *ǰaga-pūǰā* one goes toward the burning place (*tīth*) up to this boundary. There a wooden frame is erected, which probably is meant to represent a door. Next to it are set a millstone and a rice mortar, and a winnowing bowl and a wooden pot for flour go on the lintel. A ram is then sacrificed at the frame. Some of the objects mentioned, which here mark a boundary, are also used in other rituals intended to keep hostile forces away from the local *ṭhɔṛi*.[63]

The *mɔśaṇs* in western Garhwal live at burning places and in prehistoric stone circles with a single stone in the middle. Such formations are themselves called *mɔśaṇ*.[64] If a *mɔśaṇ* appears to a person, the latter is doomed to death. The *mɔśaṇs* are considered even more terrible than the god of the dead (*jɔ̄ra*), although the Banganis do not seem to have as detailed conceptions of them as the people of other regions. Oakley writes of such an embodiment of death (1991: 220): "[he lives] at places where dead bodies are burnt.... He is the chief or head of the other ghosts.... The belief is that wicked people ... and all who die a violent or wilful death ... become ghosts for a time. When the term of a thousand such ghosts expires ... the souls of the thousand are concentrated and transformed into one body, and the being thus formed is called Masan." Thus, the *mɔśaṇs* reign over the world of the dead, a world of violence, in which one can be either demonized or deified. However, it is not a world that the Himalayan heroes are associated with. They do not become deified. This is seen most clearly in Bangan: the *mōṛ*s are connected with the *jaga*s and *ṭhɔ̄ṛi*s, that is, with the fields of life![65]

Going from one *ṭhɔ̄ṛi*, a cultivated and inhabited 'island', to another is always accompanied by risks. Outside of a *ṭhɔ̄ṛi*, death in the form of a *mɔśaṇ* can easily cross one's path. This is also shown by a story recorded by Gaborieau[66] about Prince Ganga from west Nepal, who wants to become an ascetic. He sets off and wants to leave his kingdom Doti to go to Kumaon. As he attempts to cross the river Kali, which forms the border between Doti and Kumaon, with his horse, he encounters a "*māsan*", in the middle of the water, with whom he must fight the entire night before he reaches the opposite shore.

There is a Bangani saying *jagi khi mōṛ kadi nɛ mɔrdɔ* 'for his *jaga* a *mōṛ* never dies'. This means that the two remain linked even after the hero's death. In Bangan there is no traditional belief in reincarnation (other than recent importations); nonetheless, *mōṛ*s are supposed to be able to be 'reborn'. Now, if the *mōṛ*s are not associated with the realm of the *mɔśaṇ*, but especially closely associated with their *jaga*, then they cannot be subject to death in the same way as normal mortals. The latter go after death to *jɔmpri*,[67] the subterranean world of the god of the dead, *jɔ̃ra*.[68] Of a different nature is the world of the *mɔśaṇ*, which, like a sort of purgatory, does not seem quite so otherworldly as the realm of the god of the dead. It appears to represent less an underworld than a wilderness between the *ṭhɔ̄ṛi* 'islands'; the stone circles are located here, after all. There is yet another 'other world', one with which the Bangani heroes are quite likely associated. For when I inquired of Banganis where the other world is to be found, I often received the surprising response, "The other world is here." By that they meant that after death certain persons may remain present in the here and now in the form of an invisible force. Now, I do not think that the Banganis divide the other world into three parts ranging from maximal immanence in this world to maximal transcendence; rather, it seems to be a continuum. This world and the other world grade into each other like low and high, like visible and invisible – in short, like earth and heaven. A highland pasture is thus considered already somewhat more otherworldly than a deep river valley; likewise perceived as somewhat otherworldly are fairies and divinities, as well as the sun, moon, and other heavenly bodies. Of course, the three pairs of concepts (low/high, visible/invisible, earth/heaven) are not strictly correlated with one another, but rather overlap each other as well: thus, there is a dark, subterranean underworld (*jɔmpri*), while in the dark, subterranean parts of this world are found such things as the above-mentioned invisible springs associated with the *jagas*. In this multidimensional universe all things and beings have their specific location. Significantly, the Banganis here do not speak of *lok* 'world', but of *thāc* 'place, location';[69] they do not refer to the world of the gods (*devalok*), but instead say that God or the gods inhabit a *thāc*. Semantically, the word is related to *ṭhɔ̄ṛi* and *jaga*, and etymologically to the former as well; and the location of a hero in the universe is at his *jaga*, the place of the earth force of his lineage and the residence of his lineage.

Heroes and Lineages

Elsewhere[70] I have already described in some detail the mechanisms and structures that determined the head-hunting practices of the heroes in the upper Tons Valley. Therefore, I will only summarize a few relevant points. The heroes' actions are crucially based on their connection with a specific lineage and a specific territory. Lineage and territory are themselves closely related.

Krengel has shown for Kumaon that lineage and village are often equivalent there (1988: 57): "Schätzungsweise 50% aller Orte werden jeweils fast ausschließlich von einer bestimmten Ṭhākur-lineage bewohnt." [Approximately 50% of all villages are inhabited almost exclusively by one specific Thakur lineage.] The situation is surely the same for large parts of Garhwal.[71] Thus, Majumdar (1963: 86) stresses the intimate connection between lineage (*āl*) and territory in Jaunsar, a region bordering on Bangan: As a rule, the ancestor of a lineage is simultaneously the founder of the village (ibid.). Often a village is inhabited by several collateral *āls*, descended from a common ancestor and organized into brotherhoods (*dai chara*) (ibid.). Village and lineage exogamy prevail. *Āls* function moreover not only as local groups but also as kin groups: all families belonging to a lineage consider themselves members of one big family (p. 91). Regarding conflicts, Majumdar writes (ibid.): "Whenever a dispute arises between two individuals or families belonging to different *āls*, it may soon reach the *āl* level."

In Bangan, it is almost a prerequisite for a *Khũnd* lineage (*khũdāl*) (but not for the other lineages) that the founding ancestor has been beheaded. This fate made him the starting point of a new lineage and enabled his sons to name themselves after him. The sons of the fallen *Ṭholi* called themselves *Ṭholiaṇ* or *Ṭholiaikɛ* from their father's death on. The continued existence of a *khũdāl* then depended upon there being active *mõṛ*s in every succeeding generation. Thus, head-hunting caused a multiplication of lineages. Thus lineages, originally consanguinically related came to regard themselves as unrelated.

In a sense, some Bangani marriage rules have the opposite effect. For instance, it is common for a girl, let us say from the *Khũnd* lineage of the *Ṭholiaṇ*, to be addressed by her affines as *Ṭholiaṇṭi* even after her marriage.[72] This is related to the fact that she brings her affinal family a sort of 'dowry' in the form of the invisible *mīr* energies of the *ǰaga*s of her natal village and that of her mother. When, in turn, the daughters of the *Ṭholiaṇṭi* marry, the whole is displaced one step: they carry with them the *mīr*-energies of their own natal village and of that of their mother. So in addition to an alliance between *āl*s, a marriage constitutes an alliance between their *ǰaga*s. The power of a *ǰaga* is not restricted to her own *ṭhɔ̃ṛi*, but extends for two villages beyond. This suggests that an *āl* takes women from and gives them to only a few other *āl*s, in order to maintain as nearly as possible a closed system of '*mīr* fluxes'. This practice of limitation appears all the more important if one considers that the *ǰaga* consumes the *mīr*s stored in the heads of slain enemies. I was therefore always told that marriages were not possible between lineages standing in a relationship of perpetual enmity. Inimical relations are called *rɔgaĩtɛ-rośaĩtɛ*. *Rɔgaĩtɛ* are permanent enemies,[73] and one cannot marry them. In contrast, the discord between *rośaĩtɛ*[74] enemies is temporally limited and does not necessarily exclude marriage.[75]

Even though marriage customs have changed drastically in the recent past, it is still generally known that in former days a *khũdāl* maintained marriage alliances with only a few other *khũdāl*s. I heard that in Bangan exchange was often with but two other lineages; in the neighboring region Deogar, it was said to have usually been three. The rules for how many generations later intermarriages were again allowed were probably flexible. All of this suggests that under the *khũdāl*s matrilateral cross-cousin marriages were common in the region. This was not only confirmed by the Banganis I talked to; there are also indications in the literature. For example, B.R. Sharma claims of Himachal Pradesh (p. 45): "Some communities had the practice of matriarchal system under which marriage with the daughter of maternal uncle was possible."[76] A similar picture is painted of Jaunsar Bawar. Thus, Bhandari writes (1963: 19): "Among the Rajputs there is no preferential marriage ... but one can marry one's classificatory mother's brother's daughter." Majumdar, however, adds the qualification that this marriage form occurs but seldom, and Haas makes a comparable remark (1965: 371): "Kreuzvetter-Ehen sind erlaubt. Obschon solche Ehen eher selten [sind]." [Cross-cousin marriages are allowed. Although ... such marriages [are] rather rare.] These and similar marriage forms which once were widespread offered an excellent means of keeping the *mīr* forces of the *ǰaga*s together.

Beside the possibility of strengthening one's own *ǰaga* and weakening that of the enemy by head-hunting, woman stealing (*bɔgaṇɔ*), and theft of livestock, there were other opportunities and methods of weakening and damaging the *ǰaga*s of *rɔgaı̃tɛ* people. First, there are the agonistic games at festivals, which in Bangan consist of *iṇḍuaṛa* (a ball game in January during the festival days of the month *māgh*) and *ṭhoḍa* (a bow-and-arrow contest in April during the *biśu* festival).[77] Second, one might physically destroy the hostile *ǰaga*. It is said that not even recontruction and many sacrifices could restore a destroyed *ǰaga* to her original vitality. If it was not possible to destroy the *ǰaga*, one tried to steal earth from her sacred precinct and bring it to one's own *ǰaga*. Or one stole the stone with which her 'mouth' was closed and added it to the outer wall of one's own *ǰaga* at the point where the villagers enter the sanctuary. This is called *ǰaga biṭaḷṇɔ* 'contaminating the *ǰaga*'. These practices all had the same goal: to bring one's own *ǰaga* alien *mīr*, which she then took over. The most dramatic way of effecting this appropriation of alien *mīr* was, of course, by head-hunting: the captured head was placed in the mouth of the *ǰaga* for a time, then removed and buried at a secret spot in the forest under a large rock so that the enemy could not retrieve it. Moreover, to prevent a head still filled with *mīr* from falling into the hands of the enemy, there were various ways of making it 'worthless': by passing one's foot around it three times or by laying a battle-axe, a coin, or some earth from one's own *ǰaga* upon the head.

The associations and homologies between severed head and captured woman (the latter sometimes being called *muṇḍ* 'head') and the correlation between the acquisition of *mīr* and an increase in prestige have already been thoroughly described by me elsewhere.[78] The fact that a married woman retained the lineage name of her original family, as well as the fact that she brought as a 'dowry' the presence of the *mīr*s of the *ǰaga*s of both her own natal village and that of her mother, suggests the concept of some type of bilateral descendancy. And indeed, we find the term *ɓi-lūṅg*,[79] whereby *lūṅg* refers to the 'first' woman given in marriage by a lineage, and *ɓi*, to her female descendancy. Now, it is interesting to observe that heads taken from *khū̃dāl*s to which there existed a distant *ɓi-lūṅg* connection (i.e. a matrilateral relation) brought more prestige than heads without any such connection. This not only underscores the link between marriage and head-hunting, but also seems to imply that with such a severed head some thing of one's own is recovered.[80] To be sure, the direct extension of a *ǰaga* was only two generations or two villages long, but by virtue of the *ɓi-lūṅg* she is indirectly intertwined with a series of other *ǰaga*s. It is also said that *āl* is a 'blood lineage' (*lō*) and *ɓi-lūṅg* is a 'milk lineage' (*dūd*). The *āl* is principally associated with a male ancestor, whereas when people speak of their *ɓi-lūṅg*, they mean the youngest female descendants of previously outmarried women of their own lineage. The male ancestors are divided from lineage members by temporal distance, and one's female *ɓi-lūṅg* descendants are separated from one's village by spatial distance. The complementarity expressed here is reminiscent of the complementarity of heaven (*gɔiṇ*) and earth (*maṭi*) described above. And the particularly close connection of *khū̃dāl*s and *mōṛ*s with *mīr* and with the 'fields of life' suggests as well that these heroes, when they are slain, do not disappear into a transcendent other world like other people, but somehow maintain this connection. Statements to the effect that *mōṛ*s can be reborn, or that at that moment of combat when the *Khūnd* is fully in the grip of his *mīr* all the fallen ancestors of his lineage are present in or with him, can perhaps be best understood in this context.

There are no *ǰaga*s associated with any myths or other stories. At most it may happen that a woman claims that her *ǰaga* has appeared to her. One thus gains the impression that every *ǰaga* lives out her myth in the history of the lineages and heroes connected with her. This then means that there is no opposition or division between holy myth lived out by a divinity and profane history, emulating the divine, lived out by humans. So the two are not related (as often is the case elsewhere) by the myth of the divinity being cyclically reenacted during festivals. Nor, then, is the relation of hero and *j̈aga* an opposition of deity and human being after the pattern of creator and creation, master and servant, adored and adorer, and so forth. Instead, the *j̈aga* represents a 'vital force' or 'earth goddess' living out a 'vegetal' existence and development through her lineages, her village, her animals and plants, and especially her heroes. One need only think of the continually repeated plant images and symbols: the invisible 'roots' (*j̈ɔ̄ṛ*) that extend from the legs of humans and animals into the earth and the matrilateral *ɓi-lūṅg*, a 'creeper' that connects the female descendants of a woman.

Heroes and Territories

It can be observed that the territories of hostile lineages have a tendency to be geographically structured, as well. Thus, the antagonists tend to be divided by such topographical features as mountain ridges and rivers (for example, the 'hot' side *vs.* the 'cold' side of a valley). However, when feuds are acted out in antagonistic games, then the two sides more or less clearly take on the external form of moieties. This is seen quite plainly in the case of the *iṇḍuaṛa* ball game in the Khaniaṭa Valley, where traditionally one team is made up of villagers from the left side of the valley and the other, of men from the right side. But even today there exists in western Garhwal and eastern Himachal Pradesh a conceptual geographic division into two parts, called *śaṭi bīl* and *pā̃śi bīl*, which at the same time reflect moieties. This area in the Himalayas is one of the parts of India with a very prominent regional *Mahābhārata* tradition (in the form of epics, songs, festivals, temples, and so on). Now, it is said there that the *śaṭi bīl* is associated with the Kauravas (and sometimes, that the inhabitants of a *śaṭi bīl* are descended from the Kauravas), whereas the *pā̃śi bīl* is related in a corresponding manner to the Pāṇḍavas.[81] The basic functioning of such moieties is described by Lalit in the following words (p. 69):

> The Shāthi and Pānshi divisions were formerly bitterly hostile to each other and instances of *hār* and *dhār*, forcible abduction of married women and snatching of livestock, respectively, used to embitter their relations furthermore, which would culminate in the barbaric acts of *badla*, headhunting. Heads thus slain were buried underneath the Thāri temple and a count of the same kept, so that any shortfall of killings could be avenged on either side.... The enmity or *boir* between the Shāthis and the Pānshis was generally confined to specific Khondāi.[82] The Shāthis of a Khondāi would not inter-marry with the Pānshis of such Khondāi with which they entertained direct enmity....[83]

The opposition *śaṭi* and *pā̃śi* sometimes corresponds to the areas to the left and right of a river. This is the case in the Tons Valley, for example.[84] Now, it is noteworthy that in this region the fathers of the Pāṇḍavas and Kauravas are not brothers as in the classical Sanskrit *Mahābhārata*; instead, their mothers are sisters. The mythological battle between the Pāṇḍavas and Kauravas is consequently paradigmatic in the following sense, as well: for a Bangani *Khūnd*, as we have seen, a captured head brings especially much prestige if it comes from a *Khūnd* who is related to him through a distant *ɔi-lūṅg*. And this means nothing other than that the two antagonistic *Khūnds* perceive themselves as distant parallel cousins. It then can be said that their combat in a certain sense represents a contest between a Pāṇḍava and a Kaurava. But just this is the converse of a matrilateral cross-cousin marriage: the latter is the union of the son and daughter of brother and sister, respectively (both generations thus including a male and a female representative) whereas the former is a fight between the sons of two sisters:[85]

	Marriage		Combat	
B	Z	*vs.*	Z	Z
S	D	*vs.*	S	S

Lalit's above description shows that the links between marriage and head-hunting in Himachal Pradesh were very similar to those of Bangan. The kidnapping of women, the theft of livestock, and head-hunting were in his opinion "frequent" happenings (p. 70). Furthermore, there are other similarities. Regarding the "Thāri" mentioned in the quote, Lalit writes (ibid.):

> The cluster of villages inhabited by Khashas of one *dāicharā*[86] or fraternity is known as their Khondāi. Every Khondāi has a separate *kuldevi*, known as *thāri*, *jaga*, *thoir* or *kāli*. They unite in the name of the *thāri* and are always ready to lay down their lives for her prestige if challenged by any outsider. Their *thari*, their lord and their territory are sacred for them and any invader must perish or finish them.

Aside from *kāli*, the various names for the lineage goddess (*kuldevi*) all mean approximately the same as *jaga* (Bangani *j̈aga*), namely, '(a firm) place, territory'.[87] The *kāli* mentioned here probably has nothing in common with the Hindu Kālī. Thus, there is in all of Bangan not a single temple to a *devī*, but only the *j̈agas* and small *kāli* shrines beside some temples to *Mahāsu*. These shrines and their 'goddess' are not involved in any myths. The *kāli* has the task of accompanying *Mahāsu* on his travels. Presumably she is, in keeping with the 'lordship' paradigm of *Mahāsu*, a projection of the 'chieftainship' of the 'goddess of the place'.[88] The relationship between *Mahāsu* and *kāli* would then be the reverse of the relationship, common in other parts of Garhwal, between the king of a country and the 'regal' goddess, who is often called *rājarājeśvarī*, which can be translated 'lady of the supreme king'.[89]

The Head

The severed heads,[90] the captured women, and the balls of the agonistic ball games are linked in a reciprocal relationship of denotation and connotation. For instance, the ball may stand for the severed head and vice versa. In the Bangani version of the *Mahābhārata*, Draupadī, whom the Pāṇḍavas liberated from a demon by the use of force, is called *baḷi muṇḍi* lit. 'woman-head'. According to heroic songs, the Bangani hero Dalu Jaṛiaṇ plays soccer with the severed heads of his enemies;[91] in the ritual soccer game *iṇḍuaṛa*, the kicks of the opposing teams fill the ball with *mīr*, which then benefits the winning team and their *ṭhɔ̄ṛi.* All three 'objects of exchange' symbolize prestige (*ijət*), which, in accordance with Bangani mentality as we have come to know it, corresponds to a concrete equivalent in form of the *mīr* power. Consequently, all three share the characteristic of being a 'container' of *mīr*, which exists to be captured; and by capturing *mīr*, one increases the power of one's *jäga* and the prestige of one's lineage.

The custom of burying the severed heads of one's enemies on one's own estate is also known from other parts of Garhwal, where the heads, it seems to me, are buried to get control over some of the enemy's power: The hero Gauria buries the head of his enemy in the courtyard of his fortress (Oakley and Gairola, pp. 68f.); the Airwals bury the heads of their enemies in a drain of their house (ibid., p. 162). In a number of cases these heads are reconquered. The same reciprocal relation of denotation and connotation seems to have obtained here as well: the balls captured by the winning team at the agonistic games were borne home in a procession, honored with a *pūjā* at their own village, and then buried in the square before the village temple.[92]

All the connections described by me here fit into a larger geographical context, which one could title "worship of severed heads" following Postel et al. (1985: 182):

> ...it is likely that local tribes worshipped severed heads of enemies or sacrificial victims (kings, heroes, children) and in certain cases linked this to a fertility cult.... Moreover, both Saiva and Tantric Buddhist iconography is rich in wrathful deities bearing garlands of severed heads, and the pyramidal arrangements of *mohras* on *rathas* is evocative of the piles of heads of sacrificial victims.

The authors probably are not mistaken, if we consider that in Himachal *mohra* busts, which often represent the head of a divinity, may also refer to memorial stones.[93] Second, the layers of heads of the deities on the *rath* (litter) described by them resembles the old custom of Garhwali heroes of constructing a *cabūtarā* 'a platform; base (as of a temple)' out of the heads of slain enemies.[94] Therefore, one may speculate whether the *jägas* of the northwestern Garhwal Himalayas did not originally develop out of parallelepiped shrines built of heads in this fashion. Aside from that, there are reports of a real worship of heads in Himachal. The daughter of King Sur Purkash from Sirmur, over whose cut off head a temple was erected is worshipped as Devi Kudin.[95] Another example is the Yaksha Kamru Nag in the Mandi district, who according to a legend[96] lets himself be beheaded by Krishna. His head is then put on the top of a tall tree, which since has been replaced on the same spot by the temple to Kamru Nag.

Conclusion

It is well known that (self-)beheading has a place in many Indian traditions as an effective means of reaching worldly or spiritual goals. There is even evidence of the playful treatment of severed heads both in regional traditions and in some Puranas.

However, it strikes me as questionable whether (1) a clear tie was made between the earth force of a particular territory and the head of a hero in other Indian traditions, and (2) whether there were other areas and traditions where life-destroying martial acts did not serve primarily to protect one's own group and land from external dangers and to fortify them against enemies and strangers, but rather functioned more to stabilize a sociocultural internal structure. Naturally, the region I have described was also integrated into larger geographic-political structures. But these do not explain the peculiarities and idiosyncrasies of the heroic tradition there, which much more constitute the expression of a relatively high degree of sociocultural autonomy.

The martial act of the hero, head-hunting, was thus an act of self-affirmation with integrative consequences. For by his deed the hero transcended himself, causing a connection between heaven and earth within himself, by integrating *mīr* from a territory with which there were no marriage alliances into his *ǰaga*, and by creating the conditions for further bloody acts of revenge and further exchange of *mīr*. I have already pointed out the plant metaphors of the Banganis and, for the purpose of illumination, would now like to introduce two expressions that come from biology, yet here are not to be understood in terms of the usual meanings but rather quite of specialized ones. These are arborization (tree-like growth) and reticulation (network building). An example of arborization is the starting of new *khũdals* after a hero has been beheaded, and an example of reticulation is the capturing of a head. There were and are, however, other types of arborization (e.g. by migration, divorce, or legal separation of families) and of reticulation (e.g. by marriage, woman stealing, livestock theft), whereas in the agonistic festivals the two aspects are combined. The arborization of the *ǰagas*, who after all are 'daughters' of *one* earth, goes hand in hand with the reticulation produced by the exchange of *mīr* effected by the deeds of the heroes (who are also called 'sons' of the *ǰagas*, as I showed above). This spatial network correlates with a temporal one in the form of reproduction: the *ǰiān* 'life center' in the neck or abdomen of the human being, which stores *mīr* from the *ǰaga*, is passed on from both parents to their children. Corresponding to the idea of growth and maturation (which is, after all, closely bound with the earth), it is said that the *ǰiān* – unlike the *ǰiu* – matures over time and disappears at death. The Banganis say that the *ǰiān* is *riṇ* 'a debt, loan', which is handed down through the generations. Thus, arborization is here realized by the passing down of *ǰiān*s. Reticulation, in contrast, is effected by the flow of the fluid 'seed' (*suɔ mɔɔ*) of sexual intercourse and by the exchange of polluted food (*juṭhɔ*) between spouses and their families.

Thus, in Bangan we have an entire universe of different functional subsystems or subroutines with relatively autonomous patterns, which together lead to cultural structures of presumably great duration. Among the most important bearers of iconic significance are the *ǰagas*, which perhaps developed from cubic deposits of skulls. Whereas the (male) divinities associated with 'lordship', with their busts, litters, thrones, and wooden temples, with their hierarchies of priests, viziers, and so forth organized around the criteria for purity and the delegation of power, have surprisingly little to do with heroism, it is the *ǰagas* with their geometrically simple shapes and their few, streamlined forms of worship that gave the heroes in western Garhwal and eastern Himachal Pradesh pragmatic guidelines for behaviour. The heroes were not their representatives, but rather media through which they acted. Likewise, singers of heroic songs did not merely have the office of keeping alive memories of heroic deeds of old and in this way of creating tradition. They, too, were media through which action could be performed; they themselves became tradition. Their songs resulted in a network of bygone deeds and contemporary practice, a network in which text and action could not be separated.

NOTES

1 See references.

2 Texts dealing with heroism.

3 See, for instance, Chadwick and Chadwick I, 1932: 74ff.; Hiltebeitel, 1976: 48ff.; de Vries, 1963: 208.

4 Even though the entire Indian Himalayan area has been caught up in a broad range of modernizing trends, one still meets everywhere with clear evidence of an ancient hero culture. The situation here closely resembles the residual structures left behind by the old Himalayan kingdoms, which Galey thus describes for the Garhwal Himalayas (1992: 180): "Strong contemporary evidence and a massive number of facts illustrate to-day the presence of a kingship despite its disappearance from the political scene." Just as the ancient kingdom of Garhwal continues to influence the culture of this region although the kings are long gone, so too do the images and memories of long-since fallen heroes, which persist in many areas, influence the attitudes and actions of the living. But it is not only memories which we may study; it is also various concepts, institutions, edifices, etc., that were closely tied to Himalayan heroism and which even today – sometimes with altered significance and function – help to shape and influence the lives of the people.

5 All transcriptions in this article follow the Turner system (see Turner 1966).

6 I have worked there for some time now, but especially between 1985 and 1990 I had the opportunity to make frequent trips to the area from Delhi. In the following I use the relevant material from my tape recordings of songs, ballads, epics, tales, etc. Likewise songs, sayings, riddles, and so forth that were dictated to me. To these are added voluminous field notes made following numerous conversations, discussions, and other communicative processes in which I directly participated or which I observed.

7 *Des-prem in gītõ kī viśeṣtā hai.*

8 Galey describes this as follows (p. 196): "... the name of the clan and that of the founding village are usually the same and it is not possible to say which derives from which. It... points out the importance clanic identity attaches to its local origin...."

9 Bahadur Singh, Raja of Kulu state, subjugated a number of Ranas and Thakurs in the sixteenth century. But one Thakur who resided in Basa in Kothi Kot-kandhi refused to meet the king and therefore was captured. After he promised submission, he received a *jāgīr*. Then, according to the authors, the following happened: "But when he returned home he changed his mind, and sent word that he would neither serve nor obey the Raja. Having been captured a second time, some one suggested that his obstinacy was the effect of standing on his native soil. To test this some earth was brought from Basa and spread on the ground, and after being seated he was again asked

if he was now willing to submit. He replied: 'I will neither obey your commands nor serve you.' Thereupon the Raja is said to have remarked, that it was not the Thakur's fault, but that of the soil, for he was disobedient because he stood on his own ground. The Thakur was therefore imprisoned, and the earth of Basa was dug up and dispersed to the other villages, presumably to destroy its malign influence."

10 An ancient capital between Nagar and Manali.

11 "Mother Kunti has been depicted as a lady having command over her sons and in some cases, in places where they went during the course of their exile, she is referred to as desirous of getting married again. The wise Pandavas, in such cases would collect some clay from such places and spread it on reaching the next station to test its notorious elements. There are impressions that such places are not worth living and the inhabitants of such places, if found involved in unfair activities, should not be blamed as this is due to the bad environmental effect of a particular place."

12 The word is also used in Himachali, but apparently not in Garhwali, Kumaoni, and Nepali. It is perhaps of Iranian origin (Avestan *marəta-* 'mortal, man') with derivations in various Iranian languages that resemble the Bangani word, and which usually mean 'hero, manly man'.

13 The word is derived from OIA *khaśa* – 'name of a people in north India'.

14 In one tale in the *Pāḍuaṇ*, the regional Bangani version of the *Mahābhārata*, he is described as the son of the Pāṇḍava Bhīma and the giantess *Hirma Sitia*, who transforms herself into a stroke of lightning, and whom he, *Guṛku*, then marries.

15 There are rock inscriptions from Mandi state, probably from the fifth century, which mention a king "Maharaja Chandeshvara Hasti, the son of Isvara Hasti" (Hutchinson and Vogel, p. 63). It is doubtful, however, that the "cognomen Hasti (Elephant)" (ibid.) is historically connected with the Bangani expression. The epithet "elephant" for heroes is also well known from Sanskrit texts like the *Mahābhārata*.

16 That heroes are visualized as 'horned' is demonstrated by the following lines from a *ċhoṛa* song about the hero *Jitu Jaṛiaṇ*:

boiri duśmɔṇu tu ḍɔriai na
mastiɛ le, moṛu kɛ jāṛīṇɛ, ē bai, śĩ̄g
'Don't be afraid of enemies,
the horns of the heroes are knocked down.'

17 "Unusually long" can mean until they are adult men. The very ambivalent motif of grown-up men who like to drink mother's milk is widely known in this area of the Himalayas. It is not only Pāṇḍava *Bhīma*, the strongest of the five brothers, for whom a hundred streams of milk flow in the breast of his mother when she sees him. Of Thakurs who formerly lived in the Kulu Valley Hutchinson and Vogel write (p. 37): "Piti Thakur ... drank women's milk.... Under Piti Thakur were the Dirot and Bhararu Thakurs, who not only milked women but performed human sacrifice." (The same account is repeated by the authors on p. 447.) In a song I recorded about the demonic god *Pokhu*, who lives in the upper Tons Valley, it is said that he killed

the *dud pia raǰa*, a giant called "milk-drinking king", who lived on a mountain and regularly drank mother's milk.

18 A woman to whom this happens is destined to become a witch (*kuṭiṇ*).

19 *ki khũda, hãi le, seu ɔ̃dɔ ǰebɔ rɛ peṭe di dā̃d*
ki khũda, masta le, khai āṇɛ beṛuḷia
e bɔguan, ki khũda piṭi āṇɛ bā̃d.

20 *beṭa ki bakrɔ, duiã ċaĩ kurɛ. iũ khi ka lagɛ ber?*

21 The saying is also known in Garhwal: "... heroes and he-goats were born to die an early death" (Oakley and Gairola, p. 70).

22 *moṛe ri mɔ̄t ḍɛ ki giṇɛ.*

23 In oral literature, the word for 'God' is often replaced by that for 'heaven' (*gɔiṇ*).

24 In this way, chains are formed in which the element to the left of the arrow is represented by that to the right: thus 'x → y' means 'x projects to y'. The notions in italics introduced without translation will be explained later.

25 The gods also have an energy of their own, which they send out by means of their *sās* when an offense has been committed against them or one of their commandments or orders has been violated. This energy is called *dōś* (from OIA *doṣa-* 'fault'). But at least in the case of *pāp*, the situation is considerably more complicated, since this force also shows effects in totally different contexts, which I would rather not go into here.

26 In oral literature it is also called *ɔiś*.

27 *Dār* also means 'living thing' or 'door'.

28 Animals also have a *ǰian*. It is located in different places in the different species.

29 To be more precise, the domain of God, Heaven, is *diśɔ* 'visible', while the world of *maṭi* 'Earth', here including the earth's interior, is *ɔdiśɔ* 'invisible'. The world inhabited by humans lies in a 'twilight' between the two. For this reason, one can only sometimes see souls, divinities, fairies, and so forth, whereas this is much more likely to happen in the high mountains than in the valleys.

30 See Turner 5239.

31 See Turner 5244. Incidentally, this is one of several indications that Bangani has especially close ties to the northwestern NIA languages.

32 Because only the roots of plants are visible.

33 *Buksɔ̃di* is a feminine diminutive of the masculine *buksɔ*. However, there are some who say that both words refer to the heart.

34 Nobody could tell me (so far) whether this refers to fat deposits on the lung or to the pleura, which is lubricated with liquid.

35 The etymon of *bɔ̃ś* is OIA **bhāṣma-* 'lung' (Turner 9423a). In Turner's *Addenda and Corrigenda* (p. 76), it is suggested that the etymon may be connected with **bāṣma-* (*BĀṢPa-*, **BHĀṢPA-*) 'vapour'. OIA *bāṣpa-* actually means 'tear, tears, steam, vapour'. These are meanings that can easily be related to 'sperm' or 'seed'.

36 *Biriə* is, of course, *tatsama* of OIA *vīrya-* 'semen virile'. The basic meaning of *suɔ mɔɔ* is probably 'fount honey' and thus would derive from OIA *sruta-* 'streaming' and *madhu-* 'honey'.

37 Women also possess *biriə* or *suɔ mɔɔ*.

38 The same word as 'shoots', above.
39 There may be a distant connection with the Hindi idiom *zamīn-āsmān ek karnā* 'to leave no stone unturned'.
40 On flat ground these *jaga* walls are all high; on an incline they decrease in height on the upslope side.
41 A picture of a *jaga* can be found in Zoller 1993 (plate vi).
42 Thus, this word as well represents a double notion, comprising both a spiritual and a material meaning.
43 The word *ṭhɔ̄ṛi*, which is derived from the OIA root *sthā-* 'stand', is sometimes translated 'village' by the Banganis, which illuminates their specific conception of it.
44 Mountain pastures (and of course other villages) are thus not included in this zone.
45 It is now the case – and perhaps it was not much different before – that these sacrifices are offered at very irregular intervals.
46 Compare what Francke writes about a temple in the old hill state Bashahr (p. 8): "There is also an ancient Kali temple connected with the palace [of the Raja] which is not accessible to Europeans. It is said to contain a deep pit. There are rumours that human sacrifices were offered here every tenth year, and that they are still continued secretly. The victim is thrown into the pit."
47 The word derives from OIA *śmaśāna-* 'cremation ground'.
48 Her 'mood' may depend, for instance, on the receipt of due offerings, or on the state of safety of her village.
49 This influence is not caused by the stars; rather, there is a specific quality imputed to every time of night and day, which influences the newborn child.
50 The typical house in Bangan has two stories. The first floor contains the stable, and the second floor constitutes the family's living quarters.
51 Even today, the homes of poor Banganis may consist of but one room (with a stall beneath it). The word *giria* is probably related to OIA **ghir-* 'go round' (Turner 4474). Compare the West Pahari *ghero* 'courtyard' in Turner's *Addenda and Corrigenda.*
52 One of the brothers, however, has meanwhile become a vegetarian.
53 A *tatsama* of OIA *dhāman-* 'seat of the gods'.
54 From OIA *mukhara-* 'leader' (Turner 10167).
55 A *tatsama* of OIA *ratha-* 'chariot'.
56 A *tatsama* of OIA *siṃhāsana-* 'throne'.
57 From OIA **karttāra-* 'knife' (Turner 2860).
58 In other villages they are often situated relatively far apart. The *jagas* are mostly found more or less in the middle of their village, whereas smaller temples to *Mahāsu* sometimes stand at the edge of the village. In *Hanōl* on the Tons, where the main temple to *Mahāsu* is located, the *jaga* is integrated into the outer wall of the temple compound.
59 It is to be assumed that the centuries-long discord between Ranas and Thakurs in the Punjab hill states described by Hutchinson and Vogel (pp. 1ff.), examples of which were introduced above, was also a conflict between different *types* of political-religious power.
60 The expression is *lō lāṇɔ* 'to bring blood'.
61 Typical were provocative questions and insulting gestures, but woman

stealing and cattle thievery also took place (see the *ċhoṛa* lines above, p. 243).

62 Oakley and Gairola describe (p. 55) a vendetta that arises because a lump of earth from a field falls into the field of a neighbor. Handa writes (1988: 60) that, in the Middle Ages, in the area of modern Himachal Pradesh the smallest reason sufficed to induce a fight. The above quote from Oakley and Barker on pp. 237f. shows how the performance of heroic songs could affect such excitable spirits. My own participatory observation can only support the authors' conclusion.

63 Similar items, which likewise mark a boundary to hostile surroundings, are mentioned by Oakley and Gairola in a story about the hero Kunji Pal: "[Kunji Pal's] horse flew up in the clouds and then dropped down on the borders of the Doon, where the enemy had placed, by way of challenge, a heavy drum and a club weighing a hundred maunds." (1977: 109f.)

64 This represents another case of a word having both spiritual and material connotations. The circles are especially found on ridges in the forests. "Prehistoric" here has a purely local meaning and does not suggest that these sites are of very great antiquity. The people do not know the original purpose of these sites. My guess is that they are old graves.

65 For a more comprehensive discussion of questions of death and deification see the introduction of Schoembucher & Zoller 1999.

66 In the introduction to Oakley and Gairola (p. xxi).

67 A *tatsama* to OIA *yamapura-* 'the city or abode of Yama'.

68 From OIA *yamarāja-* 'King Yama'.

69 The word goes back to Vedic *sthātra-* 'station, place' (Turner 13752a). In West Pahari it often appears as part of topographical names; its basic meaning is probably 'highland pasture' or 'glade or clearing used as pasturage'.

70 Zoller 1993.

71 See, for instance, Bahuguna, 1932: 305.

72 However, her children are named after their father's *āl*.

73 The word is a derivation from Bangani *rāg* – 'enemy'.

74 A derivation from Bangani *rōś* – 'anger'.

75 As an aside, it is worth mentioning that in addition to these two basic social categories – 'positive' affinal and consanguineal relations as opposed to 'negative' ones (e.g. head-hunting, woman stealing, and theft of livestock) – there is a third, namely, that of avoidance and exclusion. On this, see Majumdar (p. 91) for the Jaunsar region.

76 In Sirmur in the southeast of Himachal there is even supposed to be patrilateral cross-cousin marriage (Negi, 1969: 115).

77 For details, see Zoller 1993, and Lalit.

78 Zoller 1993.

79 Literally, *ɔi* means 'creeper' and *lūṅg* means something like 'a prime cultivated plant'.

80 Fights with members of other castes were considered reprehensible. But for a *Khūnd*, even fighting with a non-*Khūnd* Rajput was thought cowardly. I myself looked on as *Khūnds* let some people of a lower caste slap them without defending themselves.

81 *Bīl* means 'side, direction'. The meaning of *śaṭi* and *pāśi* is not entirely clear; however, some say that *śaṭi* refers to 'sixty' (there supposedly having been 60 Kauravas, rather than 100) and *pāśi* to 'five' (in allusion to the five Pāṇḍavas). On these mythological lineages and their polarization into moieties, see also Lalit (p. 68) and Nanda (1993: 50).

82 "Khondāi" means a group of allied *Khūnd* lineages and the area inhabited by them.

83 See also a similar report by Handa, who writes (p. 60) that the *śāṭhā* and *pāṭhā Khūnds* in Sirmaur and Shimla carried on dreadful wars which lasted for generations, in imitation of the Pāṇḍava-Kaurava War.

84 Nevertheless, this correspondence does not appear to obtain everywhere. Lalit tells (p. 77) of a fight between two *Khūnds* who were both *pāśis*, but who lived on opposite sides of the river. Perhaps the geographic polarization has a different historical origin from the mythological polarization.

85 In the following informal diagram, the perspective is from the upper row.

86 The same word as Majumdar's above-quoted *dai chara*, and with a similar meaning.

87 See Turner (13765) **sthāra-* 'firm, firmness'.

88 In southernmost Bangan there is a shrine to a 'goddess' called *thɔnpɔti*. Even here, the transparent etymology points to a very similar meaning: *thɔn* comes from OIA **sthānya-*, which is related to *sthāna-* 'firm stance' (Turner 13753).

89 On this relationship, see Galey, pp. 206ff.

90 See the great number of examples in Himalayan folklore (Oakley and Gairola).

91 For a discussion of the story of this hero and his wife see Zoller 1997.

92 Zoller 1993, p. 204.

93 See Bindra, 1982: 175.

94 Compare the following line from a heroic song cited by Catak (1956: 248): *taun muṇḍu kā caura lagaun mardo* 'they made a rectangular formation out of (the) heads (of their enemies)'. And Upadhyay (1979: 201) reports how a 'warrior yogi' does the same with the heads of his enemies: *muṇḍõ se cabūtare banne lage* 'from the heads (of the enemies) were made rectangular formations'.

95 Rose 1986, 204f.

96 Justa, 1993: 61f. This legend is also known in Tamil Nadu (see Hiltebeitel 1999).

REFERENCES

Atkinson, Edwin T. 1973 (1882). *The Himalayan Gazetteer*. Vol. II, Part II and Vol. III, Part I. Delhi.

Bahuguna, S.D. 1932. Marriage and Marital Life amongst the Rawaltas. *Man in India* XII. Ranchi.

Baumann, Richard and Charles L. Briggs 1990. Poetics and Performance as Critical Perspectives on Language and Social Life. *Annu. Rev. Anthropol.* 19: 59-88.

Berg, Eberhard and Martin Fuchs (eds.) 1993. Kultur, soziale Praxis, Text. Die Krise der ethnographischen Repräsentation. Frankfurt.

Bhandari, J.S. 1963. Kinship Structure among the Rajputs of Baila – a Polyandrous Village of Jaunsar Bawar. *Bulletin of the Anthropological Survey of India* 72.

Blackburn, Stuart H. 1985. Death and Deification: Folk Cults in Hinduism. *History of Religions*, 24, 3: 255-74.

Bindra, P. 1982. Memorial Stones in Himachal. In: Settar and Sontheimer.

Brückner, Heidrun et al. 1993. *Flags of Fame: Studies in South Asian Folk Culture*. Delhi.

Catak, Govind. 1956. *Gaṛhvālī Lok Gīt*. Dehrādūn.

———. 1958. *Gaṛhvālī Lok Gāthāẽ*. Dehrādūn.

———. 1973. *Gaṛhvālī Lokgīt: ek sāṃskṛtik adhyayan*. Dillī.

Chadwick, H.M. and N.K. Chadwick 1932, 1936, 1940. *The Growth of Literature*, 3 vols. Cambridge University Press.

Chaudhury, C. Roy. 1981. *Temples and Legends of Himachal Pradesh*. Bombay.

Clifford, James and George E. Marcus (eds.). 1986. *Writing Culture. The Poetics and Politics of Ethnography*. Berkeley.

Francke, A.H. n.y. *Antiquities of Indian Tibet*. Part I: *Personal Narrative*. Delhi.

Gairola, Tara Dutt and D.A. Barker 1917. Games and Festivals of Garhwal. *The Journal of the United Provinces Historical Society* 1,1. Lukhnow.

Galey, Jean-Claude. 1992. Hindu Kingship in its Ritual Realm: The Garhwali Configuration. In: Joshi, Maheshwar P. et al.

Grünwedel, Albert. 1914. *Tāranāthas Edelsteinmine, das Buch von den Vermittlern der Sieben Inspirationen*. Aus dem Tibetischen übersetzt von Albert Grünwedel. Petrograd.

Haas, Susanne. 1965. Die "Polyandrie" der Jaunsari. *Anthropos* 60: 369–86.

Handa, Omcand. 1988. *Paścimī Himālay kī Lok Kalāẽ*. Dillī.

Hiltebeitel, Alf. 1976. *The Ritual of Battle. Krishna in the Mahābhārata*. Cornell University Press.

Hutchinson, J. and J.Ph. Vogel 1982 (1933). *History of the Panjab Hill States*. Vols. I and II. Simla.

Joshi, Maheshwar P. et al. (eds.) 1992. *Himalaya: Past and Present*, Vol. II (1991-92). Almora.

Justa, H.R. 1993. Temples and Village Gods associated with Heroes of Mahābhārata in Himachal Pradesh. In: K.S. Singh.

Krengel, Monika. 1988. *Sozialstrukturen im Kumaon. Bergbauern im Himalaya*. Wiesbaden.

Lalit, C.R.B. 1993. Thodā: A Martial Game of the Khasha People of Himachal Pradesh. In: K.S. Singh.

Majumdar, D.N. 1963 (1962). *Himalayan Polyandry. Structure, Functioning and Culture Change. A Field-Study of Jaunsar-Bawar*. Bombay.

Nanda, Neeru. 1993. The Mahābhārata in Himalayan Folklore. In: K.S. Singh.

Nautiyal, Shivanand. 1974. *Gaṛhvāl ke loknṛtya*. Gāziyābād.

———. 1981. *Gaṛhvāl ke loknṛtya-gīt*. Prayāg.

Negi, Thakur Sen (ed.). 1969. *Himachal Pradesh District Gazetteers; Sirmur*. Aligarh.

Oakley, E. Sherman. 1991 (reprint). *Holy Himalaya. The Religion, Traditions, and Scenery of a Himalayan Province (Kumaon and Garhwāl)*. Gurgaon.

Oakley, E. Sherman and Tara Dutt Gairola 1977. *Himalayan Folklore. Kumaon and West Nepal*. With an introduction to the 1977 edition by Marc Gaborieau. Kathmandu.

Postel, M., A. Neven and K. Mankodi 1985. *Antiquities of Himachal*. Bombay.

Raturi, Harikrishna. 1980 (1928). *Gaṛhvāl kā itihās*. Dehrādūn.

Rawat, Ajay S. 1989. *History of Garhwal 1358-1947*. Delhi.

Rose, H.A. 1986. *Hindu Gods and Goddesses*. Delhi.

Sax, William S. 1990. Village Daughter, Village Goddess: Residence, Gender, and Politics in a Himalayan Pilgrimage. *American Ethnologist* 17, 3.

Seethalakshmi, K.A. 1971. *Folktales of Himachal Pradesh*. Delhi.

Settar, S. and Günther-D. Sontheimer. 1982. *Memorial Stones. A Study of their Origin, Significance and Variety*. Dharwad & Heidelberg.

Sharma, B.R. 1993. Impact of the Mahābhārata on Folk and Tribal Culture of Himachal Pradesh. In: K.S. Singh.

Sharma (*Vyathit*), Gautam. 1991 (1984). *Folklore of Himachal Pradesh*. Delhi.

Singh, K.S. (ed.). 1993. *Mahābhārata in the Tribal and Folk Traditions of India*. Shimla.

Traill, George William. 1828. Statistical Sketch of Kamaon. In: Maheshwar P. Joshi, et al. 1992 (originally published in the Asiatic Researches, Vol. 16: 137-234).

Turner, R.L. 1966. *A Comparative Dictionary of the Indo-Aryan Languages*. London.

Upadhyay, Urbadatt. 1979. *Kumaū̃ kī lok gāthāõ kā sāhityik aur sāṃskṛtik adhyayan*. Barelī.

Vaishnav Ashok, Yamunadatt. 1979. *Saṃskṛti Saṃgam Uttrarāṃcal [Kumaū̃-Gaṛhvāl kī lok saṃskṛti aur partvatīya bhāṣā ke udbhav aur vikās kā itihās]*. Āgrā.

de Vries, Jan. 1963. *Heroic Song and Heroic Legend*. London.

Zoller, Claus Peter. 1993. On Himalayan Ball Games, Headhunting, and Related Matters. In: Brückner et al., 201–37.

———. 1997. Heroic Ballads and the Biography of a Woman: on Coping with Conflicts in the Western Garhwal Himalaya. In: *Perspectives on history and change in the Karakorum, Hindukush, and Himalaya*. Ed. Irmtraud Stellrecht and Mathias Winiger (Culture Area Karakorum, Vol. 3). Köln, 473-497.

———. and E. Schömbucher (ed.) 1999. *Ways of Dying: Death and its Meanings in South Asia*. Delhi.

Contributors

W.B. BOLLÉE (b. 1927) taught Vedic, Pāli, Sanskrit, Ardha-Māgadhi, and the older Indian religions in the South Asia Institute of Heidelberg University. Among his books are the *Kuṇālajātaka* (1970), *Studien zum Sūyagaḍa* (1977 and 1988), *Materials for an Edition and Study of Piṇḍa- and Oha-Nijjuttis of the Śvetāmbara Jain Tradition* (1991 and 1994), *The Nijjutis of the Seniors of the Śvetāmbara Siddhānta* (1995) and the *Bṛhat-kalpa-niryukti* and *Bṛhat-kalpa-bhāṣya* I–III (1998). A larger paper deals with traditional Indian notions about feet in literature and art (*Traditionell-indische Vorstellungen über die Füße in Literatur und Kunst*, 1984).

HEIDRUN BRÜCKNER (b. 1949) is Professor of Indology and South Asian Studies at the University of Würzburg, Germany. She is the author of a monograph on texts and rituals of Tulu folk religion (*Fürstliche Feste*, Wiesbaden 1995) and co-editor of Günther-Dietz Sontheimer's *Essays on Khandoba* (1997), his *Essays on Religion, Literature and Law* (2004), and a volume of essays in his memory *In the Company of Gods* (2005). She also works on Sanskrit drama and on the history of Indian Studies (co-editor of *A Dictionary with a Mission* (1998) and *Indienforschung im Zeitenwandel* (2003).

M. CHRISTOPHER BYRSKI (b. 1937) studied Indology in Warsaw (1955–60) and Benares (BHU), where, in 1966, he was awarded a Ph.D. degree in Ancient Indian History, Culture and Archaeology for a thesis entitled *Concept of Ancient Indian Theatre* (1974). He widely travelled the Indian subcontinent and was deeply impressed by the continuity of Indian tradition. From 1966 onward he taught Sanskrit and Hindi at the Oriental Institute of Warsaw University, interrupted by another stay in India, and in 1978 obtained the degree of D.Litt. for a thesis entitled *Methodology of the Analysis of Sanskrit Drama* (1997). In 1980–81 he became actively involved in the Solidarity Trade Union Movement, temporarily working underground. When Solidarity took over the government in 1990, he joined the Embassy of Poland in India as a Chancellor. In 1993 he became the first Polish Ambassador to India of the fully sovereign Republic of Poland and was nominated Professor in the same year. In 1996, he rejoined the University of Warsaw and was elected Director of the Institute of Oriental Studies. He is presently engaged in developing programmes of studies in intercultural relations. Byrski has more than 100 publications in Polish, English and Hindi. He is a member of several distinguished scholarly societies and has received prestigious awards in India and elsewhere.

IAN DUNCAN (b. 1940): BA (New Zealand), MA (Cantab), Ph.D. (Poona), did social-anthropological field work in Sagar district, Madhya Pradesh, in 1966–67, leading to a Ph.D. from the University of Poona. The dissertation was a village-based study of caste, kinship, marriage and religious rituals. Subsequently he carried out field work in Maharashtra in 1980–81, 1992 and 1994, collecting information on the history and practice of the Nāth Sampradāy in Maharashtra. From 1975 to 1992 he was a Lecturer in the Department of Social Anthropology, Massey University, Palmerston North, New Zealand. He is now living in Castel Gandolfo, Italy. Together with Hugh van Skyhawk he recently published "Holding Together the World: Lokasaṃgraha in the Cult of a Hindu/Muslim Saint and Folk Deity of the Deccan." In: *Zeitschrift der Deutschen Morgenländischen Gesellschaft*. Vol. 147, 2 (1997) pp. 405–24.

GABRIELLA EICHINGER FERRO-LUZZI, born in 1931 in Germany, Ph.D. in Geography, thesis in Anthropology (*Interdetti alimentari in Afrika orientale*) at the University of Rome (1968), is Associate Professor of Tamil language and literature at the Instituto Universitario Orientale, Naples. Her major research interests are Tamil culture reflected in modern Tamil literature and folktales, Tamil humour, Hindu mythology and ritual, and Indian food habits. Her publications include *The 'Incomprehensible' Writer: Tamil Culture in Ramamirtham's Work and Worldview* (1995), *The Smell of the Earth. Rajanarayanan's Literary Description of Tamil Village Life* (1996).

MARGOT GATZLAFF (b. 1934) studied Indology at the Universities of St. Petersburg and Moscow and Hindi at University of Delhi. She obtained her Ph.D. degree at Leipzig University in 1967 with a thesis on participles in Hindi, followed by a Dr. Sc. Phil. degree in 1978 with a thesis on functional development in Hindi in independent India. She has been Reader in Hindi at the University of Leipzig until her retirement in 1999 and has published widely on modern Indo-Aryan languages and sociolinguistics of South Asia. Her German-Hindi grammar and German-Hindi dictionary have become standard reference works. For her many translations of Hindi literature into German she obtained the Rabindranath Tagore Literature Award of the German-Indian-Association in 1996. In 1998, the Gisela Bonn Award of the Indian Council for Cultural Relations was confered on her.

ROLAND JANSEN (b. 1959) joined the South Asia Institute of Heidelberg University in 1982 as a student of Indology and Ethnology. He spent altogether three years studying (at the CASS, University of Pune) and researching in India, mostly in Maharashtra. Fieldwork focussed on the study of several folk cults in the area and was guided by the late Prof. G.-Dietz Sontheimer. He obtained his Ph.D. degree from Heidelberg University with a thesis on the religious history of the Maharashtrian Goddess Bhavānī of Tuḷjāpūr (*Die Bhavānī von Tuḷjāpūr. Religionsgeschichtliche Studie des Kultes einer Göttin der indischen Volksreligion.* Beiträge zur Südasienforschung, Band 168, Südasien-Institut der Universität Heidelberg. 1995). Since 1994 the author conducts study tours to various areas in India, Pakistan, Nepal, Tibet, Bhutan, China and Uzbekistan.

CHRISTINA OESTERHELD (b. 1952) studied Indology at the Humboldt University, Berlin, where she worked as a research assistant after finishing her studies. She did her Ph.D. on the contemporary Urdu novelist Qurratulain Hyder. Since 1990 she has been teaching Urdu and Hindi at the South Asia Institute of Heidelberg University. She has done research on modern Urdu literature and translated Urdu short stories and poetry into German.

PETER D. SAKHAROV (b. 1957) graduated from the Institute of Theatre, Moscow (history and theory of theatre). He did his postgraduate studies on Oriental literature at the Institute of Oriental Studies, Moscow, where he obtained a Ph.D. degree in 1987 with a thesis on the Purāṇas. From 1979 to 1989 he was research scholar at the Museum of Oriental Art. From 1989 to 1992 he headed the South Asia Department of the same museum. His publications include a book on the Purāṇas (*Mifologićeskoje povestvovanije v sanskritskich puranach* 1991) and several articles on the problems of literature, religion, mythology, iconography, and fine art of South Asia, as well as on some problems of comparative mythology and ritual. Since 1992 his main area of activity has been Christian education and journalism. He presently is the editor-in-chief of the Catholic radio in Moscow and also does some research on comparative liturgy.

T.N. SHANKARANARAYANA is Professor of Kannaḍa and Ex-Director of the Institute of Kannaḍa Studies, KUVEMPU University, Karnataka, India. He has been awarded Ph.D. for his dissertation on the Kāḍugollas, a seminomadic pastoral group in Karnataka. He has been teaching Kannaḍa language, literature and folklore for the past three decades and published extensively in Kannaḍa in the fields of folk customs, folk beliefs, folk epics, folktales, folklore theory and methodology. His English publications include the book *Epic of Junjappa: Text and Performance* (1994). He is ex-Secretary of the Folklore Society of South Indian Languages; Associate, Folklore Fellows, Finland, and Associate, Indian Institute of Advanced Study, Shimla.

CHRISTOPHER SHELKE, SJ, born 1944 at Sangamner in India, studied Philosophy in Munich, Literature in Darwar and Theology in Jnanadeepa Vidyapeetha, Pune. He finished his Ph.D. in 'Comparative mysticism' at the University of Pune and did post-doctoral research on "Christianity Interpreted in Marathi Literature". His publications include *Don Sakshtakari: St. Ignatius of Loyola and Sant Ramadas, Sacrifice and Priesthood* in Marathi. *Cokhamela: Lobpreis des Göttlichen Namens* in German. He has translated *De Visione Dei* and *De Pace Fidei* of Nicholas of Cusa into Marathi. He has been teaching Bhakti, Mysticism and Comparative Religions in Jnanadeepa Vidyapeetha, Pune and also at the University of Munich and was involved in the interreligious dialogue with Hindus and Muslims. At present, he is teaching "Comparative Religions" and "Theology of Religions" in Pontificia Università Gregoriana, Rome. He considers himself as a *sadhak* of Inculturation and Theology of Religions.

HUGH VAN SKYHAWK is Associate Professor (Privatdozent) of Indology and History of South Asian Religions at the Institute of Indology of the Johannes Gutenberg University Mainz. He has published widely on devotional religion (bhakti) and the cults of Hindu-Muslim saints of the Deccan. Since 1990 he has worked on the languages, cultures and religions of the ethnic groups of the Karakoram, publishing a monograph on the Gesar epic in the Burushaski of Nager in 1996 and a more comprehensive monograph on the archaic alpine culture of the people of Hispar (Nager) in 2003. From 1978 to 1992 he was a member (student, research assistant, research associate) of the late Professor Günther-Dietz Sontheimer's Department of the History of Religion and Philosophy of South Asia at the South Asia Institute of Heidelberg University. Together with Anne Feldhaus he co-edited a volume from Günther Sontheimer's literary legacy: *Folk Culture, Folk Religion and Oral Traditions as a Component in Maharashtrian Culture* (1995).

ROMILA THAPAR taught Ancient Indian History at University of Delhi and was later appointed to the Chair at Jawaharlal Nehru University where she is now Emeritus Professor. She is an Honorary Fellow of Lady Margaret Hall, Oxford and of the School of Oriental and African Studies, University of London. She has been a Distinguished Visiting Professor at Cornell and at the University of Pennsylvania and has lectured at the Collège de France, Paris. She was the General President of the Indian History Congress in 1983. The British Academy recently elected her a Corresponding Fellow. Among her publications are a study of the Emperor Aśoka in *Aśoka and the Decline of the Mauryas* (rev. edn. 1997); vol. 1 of *A History of India* (1969); a collection of papers – *Ancient Indian Social History: Some Interpretations* (1978); a collection of monographs published in an omnibus edition entitled *History and Beyond* (1997); an essay in literature and history – *Śakuntalā: Texts, Readings, Histories* (1999); and a children's book, *Indian Tales.*

N.K. WAGLE is Professor of History and Director, Centre for South Asian Studies, University of Toronto, Canada. Besides several papers on Maharashtra, among his edited books on Maharashtra are: *Images of Maharashtra: A Regional Profile of India* (1980); *Religion and Society in Maharashtra* (with M. Israel, 1987); *Writers, Editors and Reformers: Social and Political Transformations of Maharashtra* (1999) and *Region, Religion and Nationality in Maharashtra* (with A.R. Kulkarni, 1999). Currently he is engaged in writing a pre-British legal history of eighteenth century Maharashtra.

CLAUS PETER ZOLLER (b. 1952) is Associate Professor for Hindi at the University of Oslo. He studied Classical and Modern Indology, and Germanic philology. He did his Ph.D. in 1980 on the grammar of a Bhotia language of the Garhwal Himalaya. Subsequently he obtained fellowships for the study of Pahari languages and Himalayan folk traditions. Between 1985 and 1994 he was representative of the South Asia Institute, Heidelberg in New Delhi and Assistant Professor in Frankfurt and Heidelberg. His postdoctoral qualification (habilitation) comprised a thesis on the grammar and poetic style of an oral version of the *Mahābhārata* from the Garhwal Himalaya. Since 1997 he has been working in a Pakistan-German research project on the dialects and oral folk traditions of Indus-Kohistan. He has co-edited *Of Clowns and Gods, Brahmans and Babus: Humour in South Asian Literatures* (with Christina Oesterheld), and *Ways of Dying: Death and its Meanings in South Asia* (with Elisabeth Schömbucher), both 1999. Since 2004 he is Coordinator of the Heidelberg based Hindi Text Database Project.

Index